MENTAL MODELS IN REASONING

VARIA

Juan Antonio García-Madruga
Nuria Carriedo
María José González-Labra

(Editors)

MENTAL MODELS IN REASONING

UNIVERSIDAD NACIONAL DE EDUCACIÓN A DISTANCIA

VARIA (37220PB01)
MENTAL MODELS IN REASONING

© UNIVERSIDAD NACIONAL
DE EDUCACIÓN A DISTANCIA - Madrid, 2000

Juan Antonio García-Madruga
Nuria Carriedo
María José González-Labra

© Salvador Dalí, Fundación Gala-Salvador Dalí,
VEGAP, Madrid, 2000

Diseño de cubierta:
Francisco Gutiérrez y equipo de diseño gráfico de la UNED

ISBN: 84-362-4034-0
Depósito legal: M. 38.490-2000

Primera edición: octubre de 2000

Impreso en España - Printed in Spain
Fotocomposición: Safekat, S. L.
Belmonte de Tajo, 55. 28019 Madrid
Imprime: Fernández Ciudad, S. L.
Catalina Suárez, 19. Madrid 28007

INDEX

PART III
PROPOSITIONAL AND CONDITIONAL REASONING

PART IV
COUNTERFACTUAL REASONING

LIST OF CONTRIBUTORS

Bruno Bara. Università di Torino. Italy
Mónica Bucciarelli. Università di Torino. Italy
Ruth M.J. Byrne. Trinity College, Dublin. Ireland
Antonio Caño. Universidad de Málaga. Spain
Manuel Carreiras. Universidad de la Laguna. Spain
Nuria Carriedo. UNED. Spain
Jean-Paul Caverni. CREPCO. Aix en Provence. France
Pedro L. Cobos. Universidad de Málaga. Spain
Antonio Corral. UNED. Spain
Gino De Vooght. University of Ghent. Belgium
Vicky Dierckx. University of Ghent. Belgium
Orlando Espino. Universidad de La Laguna. Spain
Jonathan Evans. Plymouth University. UK
Pablo Fernández-Berrocal. Universidad de Málaga. Spain
M.ª José Ferraces. Universidad de Santiago. Spain
Juan García-Madruga. UNED. Spain
M.ª José González-Labra. UNED. Spain
Vittorio Girotto. CREPCO. Aix en Provence. France
David Green. University College, London. UK
Francisco Gutiérrez. UNED. Spain
Philip Jonhson-Laird. Princeton University. USA
Paolo Legrenzi. Universitá di Milano. Italy
Vincenzo Lombardo. Università del Piemonte Orientale. Italy
Francisco J. López. Universidad de Málaga. Spain
Montserrat Martín. Universidad de Santiago. Spain
Alice McEleney. Trinity College, Dublin. Ireland
Enrique Meseguer. Universidad de la Laguna. Spain
Sergio Moreno. Universidad de Granada. Spain
Marco Palmonari. Università di Siena. Italy
Jean-Luc Péris. CREPCO. Aix en Provence. France

ANA CRISTINA QUELHAS. Universidad de Lisboa. Portugal
ANTONIO RIZZO. Università di Siena. Italy
SANDRINE ROSSI. CREPCO. Aix en Provence. France
CARLOS SANTAMARÍA. Universidad de La Laguna. Spain
WALTER SCHAEKEN. University of Leuven. Belgium
WALTER SCHROYENS. University of Leuven. Belgium
SUSANA SEGURA. Universidad de Málaga. Spain
GLORIA SEOANE. Universidad de Santiago. Spain
MARÍA SONINO. Università di Padova. Italy
DOLORES VALIÑA. Universidad de Santiago. Spain
ANDRÉ VANDIERENDONK. University of Ghent. Belgium

PREFACE

In the last thirty years, the study of human reasoning has captured the attention of many researchers. This upsurge in interest has allowed us to have a clearer and more precise idea as to the mechanisms which underlie human inferential processes. Thus, we now know more about the possibilities and limits of human mind in coping with a variety of inferential tasks. In an important part, this improvement in our knowledge is due to the conceptual contribution of Phil Johnson-Laird's mental model theory. This book is a collection of the papers presented at the «Symposium on Mental Models in Reasoning», which took place in Madrid in November of 1998. This occasion enabled the Spanish experts in reasoning to meet with some of their European colleagues with the common aim to celebrate the award by the Universidad Nacional de Educación a Distancia (UNED) of an «honoris causa» doctorate degree to Phil Johnson-Laird.

The contributions in the present book have been grouped together in four different parts. The first part, dedicated to theoretical issues, begins with a chapter in which Phil Johnson-Laird reviews the current state of the theory, presents some recent developments, and considers the three main criticisms of the theory. In chapter 2 Jonathan Evans examines one of the central issues in the current study of reasoning: the role of prior beliefs. In chapter 3 David Green presents an extension of the model theory that incorporates the notion of a model of an argument and that analyses how arguments affect opinions. In chapter 4 Bruno Bara, Monica Bucciarelli and Vincenzo Lombardo explore how the empirical evidence fits their computer program implementing an unified and model-based account of deductive reasoning. The next chapters address three theoretical issues: Vittorio Girotto, Phil Johnson-Laird, Paolo Legrenzi, and María Sonino (chapter 5) examine how people resolve logical inconsistencies; Antonio Rizzo and Marco Palmonari (chapter 6), following Vygotsky, examine the mediating role of artifacts in syllogistic reasoning, and describe an empirical study on this topic; and Sergio Moreno and Juan García-Madruga (chapter 7) present a new experimental procedure that is based in the methodology of priming, and that allows them to test how people build mental models.

The second part of the book covers hypotheses testing, and probabilistic and relational reasoning. In chapter 8 Jean-Paul Caverni, Sandrine Rossi and Jean-Luc Peris present two new paradigms to investigate hypothesis-testing strategies in Wason's classical 2-4-6 problem. The next two chapters deal with probabilistic reasoning: María José González Labra (chapter 9) shows that prior knowledge can increase the use of base rates in inferring probabilities; Pedro Cobos, Antonio Caño y Francisco López (chapter 10) argue that some biases in probabilistic reasoning are cognitive illusions produced by associative learning, and hence can be accounted by a neural network. In chapter 11 Orlando Espino, Carlos Santamaría, Enrique Messeguer and Manuel Carreiras examine eye-movements during the process of solving categorical syllogisms, and confirm some of the model theory's predictions. In chapter 12 André Vandierendonck, Gino de Voogt and Vicky Diercx compare participant's performance in spatial and temporal linear syllogisms, analysing the role of working memory.

The third part of the book is dedicated to the important domain of propositional and conditional reasoning. In chapter 13 Carlos Santamaría and Orlando Espino report an empirical test of a model-based procedure, the negation heuristic, used by people when they reason about what is false. In chapter 14 Juan A. García-Madruga, Sergio Moreno, Nuria Carriedo and Francisco Gutiérrez analyse reasoners performance in some problems studied by Lance Rips, focusing mainly on time measures. Rips argued that his results contravened the model theory, but their new experiments in fact corroborate model theory. The next three chapters deal with the Wason's famous selection task. Monica Bucciarelli and Phil Johnson-Laird (chapter 15) investigate how young children understand and reason with factual and deontic assertions. Their results show that the children did not differ in their ability to test factual beliefs or deontic obligations and so there may not be an innate module to process deontic assertions. Antonio Corral (chapter 16) reports two experiments on the effects of attention and the clarification of the rule on performance in the abstract selection task. Dolores Valiña, Gloria Seoane, Mª José Ferraces and Montserrat Martín (chapter 17) examine individual differences measured by means of psychometric tests, and the influence of instructions and problem content on performance. They analyse their results in terms of the model theory and Evans´ dual process theory. In Chapter 18 Walter Schaeken and Walter Schroyens report two experiments examining the role of negation and its contrast class in conditional reasoning. The results confirm that a simple manipulation of the size of the constrast class may in deed affects performance with both explicit and implicit negation. In chapter 19 Francisco Gutiérrez, Juan A. García-Madruga, Nuria Carriedo and Sergio Moreno present some results concerning reasoners' performance with multiple conditionals. These findings appear to disconfirm rules theories, but they elucidate the process of constructing and integrating mental models.

Finally, part four of the book presents three contributions about the new and increasingly studied domain of counterfactual reasoning. Alice McEleney and Ruth Byrne (chapter 20) analyse the relation between counterfactual thinking and causal reasoning. Their empirical evidence allows them to conclude that counterfactual thinking mainly concerns the prevention of undesired outcomes whereas causal thinking mainly concerns to the prediction of future events. Ana Cristina Quelhas and Ruth Byrne (chapter 21) use latencies of responses to compare performance with factual and counterfactual conditionals. As the model theory predicts, reasoners were faster to draw inferences from factual conditionals than from counterfactual conditionals. In chapter 22 Susana Segura, Pablo Fernandez-Berrocal and Ruth Byrne report some results showing that temporal and causal order affects counterfactual reasoning in ways predicted by the model theory.

This book springs from a Spanish research context and it is addressed to Spanish and English readers alike. But, in order to make the chapters more accesible to Spanish readers, each of them is preceded by a summary in Spanish.

We thank various institutions for their help during our work in this project. In particular, the Symposium and this book was made possible with the financial support provided by Spanish Ministry of Education and Culture, the «Comunidad de Madrid», and our own university (UNED).

We dedicate this book to Phil Johnson-Laird.

Madrid and Princeton, November 1999

Juan A. García-Madruga
Nuria Carriedo
M.ª José González-Labra

PART I

THEORETICAL ISSUES

1

THE CURRENT STATE OF THE MENTAL MODEL THEORY

Philip N. Johnson-Laird

Este capítulo revisa el estado actual de la teoría de los modelos mentales. En su origen, esta teoría fue formulada para dar cuenta de cómo los seres humanos entienden y representan el discurso verbal. La teoría ofrece también una explicación de cómo razonan. Para ello, construyen modelos mentales que corresponden a las situaciones descritas en la información que es su punto de partida, la mayoría de los casos premisas o enunciados verbales. Cada modelo corresponde a una posibilidad, y de esta manera una conclusión debe ser verdadera si se mantiene en todos los modelos de las premisas, mientras que puede ser verdadera si se mantiene en al menos un modelo de las premisas. Existen otras teorías sobre el razonamiento deductivo que están basadas en la aplicación de reglas formales de inferencia. El capítulo revisa varios signos relevantes del uso de modelos y en contra del uso de reglas formales como las defendidas por las actuales teorías de este tipo:

1. *Sujetos sin formación específica utilizan contraejemplos para refutar conclusiones inválidas.*
2. *Las inferencias basadas en modelos múltiples son más difíciles que las que están basadas en un único modelo; es decir, las inferencias de modelos múltiples tienden a ser más susceptibles al error y a exigir más tiempo para su realización.*
3. *Los errores sistemáticos se corresponden frecuentemente con alguno de los modelos posibles y, a menudo, los sujetos yerran al considerar sólo un único modelo de las premisas.*
4. *Las creeencias de los sujetos afectan al proceso real de razonamiento. En las conclusiones absurdas tienden a buscar contraejemplos de forma más exhaustiva.*
5. *El razonamiento se ve afectado por diversas «inferencias ilusorias» que, como la teoría de los modelos mentales predice, los sujetos tenderán a extraer aunque sean inválidas. Estas in-*

*ferencias surgen del hecho de que los modelos mentales tienden
a no representar lo que es falso. Veamos un ejemplo:*
    *Una de las siguientes afirmaciones acerca de una mano de
cartas es verdad, y la otra es falsa:*
En la mano hay un rey o hay un as, o ambos.
En la mano hay una reina y un as.
¿Es posible que haya en la mano una reina y un as?
*Casi todo el mundo responde «sí», pero esta respuesta es una
ilusión. Si hay una reina y un as en una mano, entonces ambas afirmaciones serían verdad, lo que está en contra de la con-
signa de que una de ellas es verdadera y la otra falsa.*
    *El capítulo describe también tres extensiones recientes de la teoría
de los modelos. Así, la teoría ha sido aplicada con éxito al razonamiento
causal, a un enrevesado rompecabezas diseñado por Peter Wason lla-
mado THOG, y al significado de los enunciados condicionales (si entonces) y las inferencias basadas en ellos.*
    *Finalmente, el capítulo considera las tres principales críticas a la teo-
ría. Primero, se ha alegado que en principio la teoría de modelos no di-
fiere de las teorías basadas en reglas formales de inferencia. Segundo,
algunos escépticos argumentan que las teorías psicológicas no pueden
basarse en prinicipios semánticos (como hace la teoría de modelos), sino
que únicamente pueden ser sintácticas. Tercero, los críticos sostienen
que la teoría es vaga e incomprobable, una crítica planteada en diver-
sos grados de intensidad. El capítulo rebate las tres críticas y señala
que ninguna teoría de, por ejemplo, el razonamiento basado en conectivas proposicionales como «si», puede ser tratable computacional-
mente.*

INTRODUCTION

The idea that the mind constructs internal models of the external world was
first proposed by the Scottish psychologist, Kenneth Craik, in an
extraordinarily prescient book (Craik, 1943). This idea has led in turn to a
variety of different accounts of mental models (see e.g. Gentner & Stevens,
1983; Polk & Newell, 1995). My concern, however, is with just one version of
the theory, which postulates models as the end result of perception and
comprehension and as the starting point of reasoning. When people perceive
the world, understand a description, or imagine a scene, according to this
theory, they construct models of the corresponding situations. And when
they reason, they reason on the basis of such models, which they may have
just constructed or recalled from memory. This version of the theory of mental
models was formulated some time ago (Johnson-Laird, 1983), and it has
inspired research in both psycholinguistics and the study of thinking (see
Garnham & Oakhill, 1994, 1996; Oakhill & Garnham, 1996). The present
paper aims, not to review the literature, but to consider the current state of
the theory. It begins with the rudiments of the theory as it applies to deductive

reasoning. It outlines some recent developments extending the theory to causal reasoning, to Wason's (1977) THOG problem, and to the meaning of conditionals. Finally, it considers the major criticisms and gaps in the current theory.

THE THEORY OF MENTAL MODELS AND DEDUCTIVE REASONING

Thinking is governed by constraints. They include the thinker's goals, if any, the information in the starting point, and relevant general knowledge. The theory of mental models postulates that the principal representations used in thinking are models of the world. Each model corresponds to a possibility. The model's structure and content capture what is common to the different ways in which the possibility can be realized, where these different ways are irrelevant to the task. This claim raises some tricky issues, but we pass over them for the moment. Granted that each model represents a possibility, however, then a conclusion is *possible* —it may be the case— if it holds in at least one model of the starting information. It is *necessary* —it must be the case— if it holds in all the models of the starting information. And it is *impossible* —it cannot be the case— if it holds in none of the models of the starting information. If the models represent a set of equiprobable possibilities, then the *probability* of an event depends on the proportion of the models in which it holds. Because thinking is governed by constraints, there is not just a single path that it must follow. As computer scientists say, the process is «non-deterministic», that is, our theories do not postulate a single fixed sequence of mental operations as soon as the process gets under way.

A major component of the model theory is:

The principle of *truth*: mental models represent what is true, but not what is false, in order to reduce the processing load on working memory.

As an illustration of the principle, consider the following exclusive disjunction:

There is *not* a triangle on the board or else there is a circle on the board.

The disjunction is compatible with two possibilities, and its representation consists of mental models of these two possibilities:

¬ Δ

o

Each row depicts a mental model, and «¬» denotes negation. Following the principle of truth, the first model represents the truth of the proposition, *there is not a triangle*, but it does not represent explicitly that it is false in this possibility that *there is a circle*. Likewise, the model in the second row represents the truth of the proposition, *there is a circle*, but it does not represent explicitly that it is false in this possibility that *there is not a triangle*. Individuals represent this information about what is false in «mental footnotes», and the theory assumes that these footnotes are ephemeral. There is a special notation for footnotes (Johnson-Laird & Byrne, 1991), but it can be ignored in the present paper. The point for readers to bear in mind is that these footnotes can be used to construct *fully explicit* models, such as:

$$
\begin{array}{cc}
\neg \Delta & \neg \mathrm{o} \\
\Delta & \mathrm{o}
\end{array}
$$

for the preceding exclusive disjunction, where a true negation is used to represent a false affirmative proposition, and a true affirmative is used to represent a false negative proposition. Evidence suggests, as we shall see, that reasoners tend to forget mental footnotes rapidly.

A conditional assertion, such as:

If there is a triangle then there is a circle

has two mental models. One model represents the salient possibility in which both the antecedent (there is a triangle) and the consequent (there is a circle) are true. The other model is wholly implicit. It has no explicit content, but allows for the possibilities in which the antecedent of the conditional is false. The two models are:

$$
\begin{array}{cc}
\Delta & \mathrm{o} \\
& \cdots
\end{array}
$$

The ellipsis denotes the implicit model, and there is a mental footnote indicating the falsity of the antecedent in the possibilities that the model represents. A biconditional such as:

If, and only if, there is a triangle then there is a circle

has exactly the same mental models, but a footnote indicating that both the antecedent and the consequent are false in the possibilities that the implicit model represents. It is the implicit model that distinguishes the models of a conditional from the model of a conjunction. The fully explicit models of the conditional can be constructed from the mental models provided that the footnote on the implicit model is retained. They are as follows:

$$
\begin{array}{cc}
\Delta & \mathrm{o} \\
\neg \Delta & \mathrm{o} \\
\neg \Delta & \neg \mathrm{o}
\end{array}
$$

Likewise, the fully explicit models of the biconditional are:

$$
\begin{array}{cc}
\Delta & \mathrm{o} \\
\neg \Delta & \neg \mathrm{o}
\end{array}
$$

TABLE 1.1

Models for the sentential connectives: the central column shows the mental models postulated for human reasoners, and the right-hand column shows fully explicit models, which represent the false components of the true cases by using negations that are true: '¬' denotes negation and '...' denotes a wholly implicit model. Each line represents a model of a possibility

Connective	Mental models		Fully explicit models	
A and B:	A	B	A	B
A or else B:	A		A	¬B
		B	¬A	B
A or B, or both:	A		A	¬B
		B	¬A	B
	A	B	A	B
If A then B:	A	B	A	B
	...			¬A
B				
			¬A	¬B
If and only if A then B:	A	B	A	B
	...		¬A	¬B

Table 1.1 presents the mental models and the fully explicit models of propositions formed from the main sentential connectives that are truth-functional, i.e. that can be used to form compound propositions with truth values that depend only on the truth values of their constituent propositions. These connectives play a major part in the deductive inferences of daily life. We will return to the semantics of conditional assertions later in the paper, because they are notoriously controversial.

A conditional such as, «If there is a triangle then there is a circle», is closely related in meaning to the *quantified* assertion:

All the triangles are with triangles

The quantified assertion has a single mental model representing the different pairs of entities in the situation:

    Δ   o
        ...

This diagram, unlike those for connectives, denotes one model of a single situation. Its first row shows that in this situation there are triangles with circles, and a mental footnote indicates that the triangles are exhaustively represented in the explicit pair, i.e. all the triangles are with circles. The number of such tokens is arbitrary, but the model assumes a minimal number. The ellipsis represents other possibilities in the situation, which unlike the explicit pair in the model may or may not exist. The footnote can be used to flesh out the model in various ways by making the other possible pairs explicit, e.g.:

```
      Δ        o
   ¬ Δ         o
   ¬ Δ      ¬ o
```

The quantified assertion:

Some of the triangles are with circles

has the single mental model:

```
      Δ        o
         ...
```

in which the explicit pair exists in the situation. Neither triangles nor circles are exhaustively represented in the model, and so it can be fleshed out explicitly to represent the possibility of any other sort of pair, e.g.:

```
      Δ        o
      Δ      ¬ o
   ¬ Δ      ¬ o
```

The assertion is false in case:

None of the triangles are with circles

which has the mental model:

```
      Δ

            o
         ...
```

in which both circles and triangles are exhaustively represented, and so the model can be fleshed out explicitly to represent the following situation, for example:

```
      Δ      ¬ o
   ¬ Δ         o
```

We emphasize that each row in the models of these quantified assertions represents a different pair in the same situation, whereas each row in the models based on the connectives represents an *alternative* possibility.

Here is a simple example to illustrate deductive reasoning according to the model theory. Suppose you know the following facts:

Either there is *not* a triangle on the board or else there is a circle on the board.

There is *not* a circle on the board.

You can envisage the two possibilities consistent with the disjunctive premise:

```
   ¬ Δ
            o
```

The second, categorical, premise rules out the second of these two possibilities, and so you can infer:

There is not a triangle on the board.

This conclusion is valid, that is, it is necessarily true given the truth of the premises, because it holds all the models —in this case, the single model— consistent with the premises. The principles by which models are combined are summarized in Table 1.2. These principles apply both to the combination of sets of models, as in the preceding disjunctive inference, and to the combination of possible individuals in models of quantified assertions.

TABLE 1.2

The procedures for forming a conjunction of two sets of possibilities. The procedures apply either to individual models (based on sentential connectives) or to individual possibilities (based on quantified assertions). Each procedure is presented with an accompanying example. In principle, each procedure should take into account mental footnotes, but reasoners soon forget them

1. For a pair of explicit items, the result conjoins their elements, and drops any duplicates:
   a   b   and   b   c   yield   a   b   c

2. For a pair of items that contain an element and its contradiction, the result is null (akin to the empty set):
   a   b   and ¬ b   c   yield   null

3. For null combined with any item, the result is null:
   null   and   a   b   yield   null

4. For a pair of implicit items, the result is implicit:
   ...   and ... yield ...

5. For an implicit item combined with an explicit one, the result by default is null:
   ...   and   b   c   yield   null

But, if the explicit item contains no element in common with anything in the same set from which the implicit item is drawn, then the result is the explicit item:
   ...   and   b   c   yield   b   c

Mental models are not the only way in which individual could reason. Many psychologists have supposed instead that reasoning depends on following formal rules inference akin to those of a logical calculus (see e.g. Rips, 1994; Braine and O'Brien, 1998). People could make the disjunctive inference above, for instance, by mapping its premises onto those of the following rule of inference:

A or B
Not B
A

How can we test whether people rely on rules or models? The answer is that there are at least five «tell-tale» signs of the use of mental models in reasoning.

A first sign is that if reasoners make inferences based on models, then they can use counterexamples to refute invalid inferences. Readers are invited to solve the following problem:

More than half the people in the room speak English.
More than half the people in the room speak Spanish.

Does it follow that more than half the people in the room speak English and Spanish?

When people are given this problem (and pen and paper), as Hansjoerg Neth and the present author have recently shown in an unpublished study, they tend to respond correctly, «no», and they base their response on the construction of a counterexample. For example, they draw a diagram of ten people in the room, and represent six as speaking English and six as speaking Spanish, but with a minimal overlap (of two) between them. In other words, they construct an external model that satisfies the premises but that refutes the putative conclusion. Logically-untrained individuals are competent to construct such counterexamples (see also Bucciarelli & Johnson-Laird, 1999), and they also construct counterexamples in spatial reasoning (Roberts, 1999). There are formal methods in logic that emulate the process, but current psychological theories based on formal rules do not use this method to refute invalid conclusions. Instead, they establish invalidity by a search of the «space» of all possible derivations, and a check that none of these derivations leads from the premises to the conclusion. One drawback of this procedure is that it is time-consuming. Another drawback is that reasoners can never know for sure that an inference is invalid, because the search may have overlooked a particular derivation (Barwise, 1993). Indeed, the quantifier «more than half of», which we used in the example above, cannot be captured in the standard first-order predicate calculus. It calls for either a purpose-built extension of this logical calculus or else a higher-order calculus for which it is impossible to frame formal rules that allow the proof of all and only the valid deductions. Hence, the failure to find a derivation in this calculus does not justify the evaluation of inference as invalid. It may be valid but unprovable within the calculus. Of course, there is no guarantee that you will find a counterexample. But, where you do succeed, you *know* that the inference is invalid.

A second sign of the use of models is that inferences that call for multiple models are harder than those that call only for a single model. Reasoners take longer to make multiple-model deductions and they are more likely to err. There are demonstrations of this phenomenon in many different domains of reasoning. It has been established, for example, in reasoning about both spatial and temporal relations (Byrne & Johnson-Laird, 1989; Schaeken, Johnson-Laird, & d'Ydewalle, 1996), so that even critics of the model theory concede that people may rely on models in these domains (see e.g. Braine, 1990). An illustration of the phenomenon is a key interaction that occurs in *modal* reasoning, i.e. reasoning about what is possible and what is necessary. It is easier to infer that a situation is possible (one model of the premises suffices as an example) than that it is impossible (all the models of the premises must be checked for a counterexample); whereas it is easier to infer that a situation is not necessary (one counterexample suffices) than that it is necessary (all the models of the premises must be checked as examples). In a study of problems about one-on-one basketball games, Bell and the present author established this interaction both in the percentages of correct conclusion and their latencies (see Bell and Johnson-Laird, 1998).

A third sign of models is that systematic errors correspond to a subset of the mental models, often just a single mental model. This pattern has been observed in reasoning both from verbal premises and from diagrams (Bauer & Johnson-Laird, 1993). It is also common in syllogistic reasoning (Bara, Bucciarelli, & Johnson-Laird, 1995). Given premises of the form, for example:

All the A are B.
Some of the B are C.

Reasoners often conclude erroneously:

Some of the A are C.

The conclusion is consistent with the premises, that is, it corresponds to one model of them:

a   b   c
a   b

But, there are other models of the premises that are counterexamples:

a   b
      b   c

The explanation based on models gives an alternative account to the traditional «atmosphere» hypothesis (Shaw & Johnson-Laird, 1998). The model theory postulates a genuine attempt to reason; the atmosphere effect does not, and it is forced to propose several *ad hoc* principles. Ormerod and his colleagues have proposed a «minimal completion» hypothesis according to which reasoners construct only what is minimally necessary (see Ormerod, Manktelow, & Jones, 1993). Similarly, Sloutsky and Goldvarg (1999) propose a process of «minimalization» in which reasoners tend to construct only single models of premises, thereby in effect reducing them to conjunctions. Jonathan Evans (personal communication) has independently formulated a similar hypothesis.

A fourth sign of the use of models is that knowledge and beliefs affect the *process* of reasoning. Both the model theory and rule theories allow that beliefs can bias the interpretation of premises. Only the model theory, however, allows that reasoners who reach an uncongenial conclusion are likely to search harder for a counterexample than those who reach a congenial conclusion. Given the following premises, which are equivalent in form to those in the preceding example:

All the Frenchmen are wine-drinkers.
Some of the wine-drinkers are Spanish.

few reasoners are content with the conclusion:

Some of the Frenchmen are Spanish.

They envisage a model of the premises in which there are wine-drinkers of both nationalities (Oakhill, Garnham, & Johnson-Laird, 1990). This account explains the principal effect of beliefs on reasoning: they influence invalid inferences far more than valid inferences, because people refrain from drawing an unbelievable invalid conclusion (Evans, 1989; Newstead & Evans, 1993).

A fifth sign of mental models is the occurrence of what we refer to as *illusory* inferences (Johnson-Laird & Savary, 1998). They were predicted by a computer program implementing the model theory. And they arise from the principle of truth, i.e., the failure of reasoners to represent what is false. The illusions occur in a variety of domains. Indeed, they are perhaps the best sign of mental models, because they are outside the explanatory scope of any other current theory, including theories based on formal rules of inference or on pragmatic reasoning schemas. A simple illusion is illustrated in the next example (from Goldvarg & Johnson-Laird, 1999a):

One of the following assertions is true about a particular hand of cards and one of them is false:

There is a king in the hand or an ace, or both.
There is a queen and an ace in the hand.
Is it possible that there is a queen and an ace in the hand?

Nearly everyone responds «yes», but the response is an illusion. If there were a queen and an ace in the hand then both of the assertions would be true, contrary to the rubric that one of them is true and one of them is false. The model theory predicts the illusion, because when reasoners consider the truth of the second premise and its model:

Queen   Ace

they overlook the falsity of the first premise, i.e. there is neither a king *nor an ace* in the hand. Yang and the author have demonstrated the occurrence of illusions based on quantified premises, such as:

Only one of the following assertions is true:
At least some of the plastic beads are not red.
None of the plastic beads are red.
Is it possible that none of the red beads are plastic?

Reasoners tend to respond «yes» (Yang & Johnson-Laird, 1998). The falsity of the first premise, however, establishes that all the plastic beads are red and hence that some of the red beads are plastic. Likewise, the falsity of the second premise establishes that some of the plastic beads are red and hence that some of the red beads are plastic. The correct response is accordingly «no», it is impossible that none of the red beads are plastic.

In sum, the signs are that reasoning depends on mental models. The theory is accordingly growing rapidly. It is under development to account for reasoners' *strategies*, i.e. the different ways in which they organize their thoughts in coping with several premises (see Johnson-Laird, Savary, & Bucciarelli, 1999; and unpublished research carried out by Yingrui Yang & by Jean-Baptiste van der Henst). It is being extended to deal with deontic reasoning (Monica Bucciarelli at Turin University), semantic information (Schaeken & Schroyens, this volume), probabilistic reasoning (Girotto & Gonzalez, 1999), non-monotonic reasoning (Legrenzi and Girotto, this volume), and informal reasoning daily life (Green, 1996; Shaw, 1996). Model theories have been formulated for both sentential reasoning and reasoning with quantifiers, and Bara, Bucciarelli, Johnson-Laird, & Lombardo (1994) have proposed a unified account of the two domains. In what follows, the present paper describes three other recent developments.

MENTAL MODELS AND CAUSAL RELATIONS

Goldvarg & Johnson-Laird (1999b) propose that causal relations, such as *A causes B*, *A allows B*, and *A prevents B*, have meanings that concern only possibilities and a temporal constraint that B cannot precede A. In particular, they postulate that *A causes B* has the following mental model:

>   a   b
>   ...

in which A is exhaustively represented in the row representing the possibility of A with B. Hence, the model can be fleshed out explicitly to represent the following possibilities:

>   a   b
>   ¬ a   b
>   ¬ a   ¬ b

A allows B has the same mental model:

>   a   b
>   ...

and strictly speaking neither A nor B is exhaustively represented. There is, however, an implicature (see Grice, 1975) that without A, B is impossible, and so the fully explicit model can be:

>   a   b
>   a   ¬ b
>   ¬ a   ¬ b

There are four main causal relations, and Table 1.3 presents both their mental models and their fully explicit models. Unlike the models based on sentential connectives (see Table 1.1), the rows in these models represent alternative possibilities that can co-occur in the same situation.

TABLE 1.3
**The models for four general causal relations. The central column shows the
mental model normally used by human reasoners, and the right-hand column
shows the fully explicit model, which represents the false components of the
true cases using negations that are true: «¬» denotes negation and «…»
denotes a wholly implicit state**

Connective	Mental models		Fully explicit models	
1. A causes B:	A	B	A	B
	…		¬A	B
			¬A	¬B
2. A prevents B:	A	¬B	A	¬B
	…		¬A	B
			¬A	¬B
3. A allows B:	A	B	A	B
	…		A	¬B
			¬A	¬B
4. A allows not-B:	A	¬B	A	¬B
	…		A	B
			¬A	B

When participants had to list true instances and false instances of causal
relations, which were stated with a sensible everyday content, they almost always
started with cases corresponding to the mental models of the relations (Goldvarg
& Johnson-Laird, 1999b). But, they usually went on to list the fully explicit cases
of *A causes B* and *A allows B*, except that in the latter case many participants listed
all four possible contingencies as true instances, i.e. they grasped that what
falsifies the relation is, not the presence of any particular contingency, but the
absence of one in which A occurs with B. And they ignored the implicature
referred to earlier. One surprising result was that the participants tended to treat
A prevents B as a strong relation consistent with only two possibilities:

     a   ¬ b
   ¬ a   b

Philosophers and psychologists often argue that there is no logical
distinction between the meaning of causes and allows, that is, between a cause
and an enabling condition. What then does distinguish them? Many possible
answers are in the literature: enabling conditions occur early but causes
immediately precipitate the effect (Mill,1843); enabling conditions are common
but causes are rare (Hart & Honoré, 1985); enabling conditions are the norm
but causes violate the norm (see e.g. Kahneman & Tversky, 1982; Einhorn &
Hogarth, 1986); enabling conditions are constant but causes are inconstant
(Cheng, 1997); enabling conditions are irrelevant to explanations but causes
are relevant (e.g. Mackie, 1980; Hilton & Erb, 1996). And there are still other
views (see Hesslow, 1988, for a review).

All of these claims could be true, but, as our experiment showed, people do draw a semantic distinction between enabling conditions and causes. The two relations *are* logically distinct. Goldvarg & Johnson-Laird (1999b) propose:

> The principle of *circumstantial interpretation:* the causal interpretation of a situation depends on its *circumstances*, that is, the set of mental models representing the possibilities - real, hypothetical, or counterfactual - within which the event occurs.

Consider, for example, the following scenario:

> Given that there is good sunlight, if a certain new fertilizer is used on poor flowers, then they grow remarkably well. However, if there is not good sunlight, poor flowers do not grow well even if the fertilizer is used on them.

The circumstances described here are consistent with the following fully explicit possibilities:

Sunlight	Fertilizer	Grow-well
Sunlight	¬ Fertilizer	Grow-well
Sunlight	¬ Fertilizer	¬ Grow-well
¬ Sunlight	Fertilizer	¬ Grow-well
¬ Sunlight	¬ Fertilizer	¬ Grow-well

In these circumstances, sunlight is an enabling condition. It is a necessary condition for the flowers to grow well:

Sunlight	Grow-well
Sunlight	¬ Grow-well
¬ Sunlight	¬ Grow-well

All four possible contingencies occur interrelating the fertilizer and the growth of the flowers. The presence of the sunlight, however, enables the fertilizer to cause the flowers to grow well. The causal relation is a weak one, in that the presence of the sunlight can enable other causes for the growth of the flowers.

In contrast, consider the following scenario:

> Given the use of a certain new fertilizer on poor flowers, if there is good sunlight then the flowers grow remarkably well. However, if the new fertilizer is not used on poor flowers, they do not grow well even if there is good sunlight.

These circumstances are compatible with the following possibilities:

Sunlight	Fertilizer	Grow-well
¬ Sunlight	Fertilizer	Grow-well
¬ Sunlight	Fertilizer	¬ Grow-well
Sunlight	¬ Fertilizer	¬ Grow-well
¬ Sunlight	¬ Fertilizer	¬ Grow-well

The respective causal roles have been swapped around. The fertilizer is now the enabling condition for sunlight to cause the flowers to grow well. Once again, the cause and the enabling conditions have a distinct logic, and neither is constant in the situation. A further experiment showed that students were readily able to distinguish between the causes and the enabling conditions in a set of passages akin to the two examples above (see Goldvarg & Johnson-Laird, 1999b). It follows that causes and enabling conditions have different meanings, that neither of them need be constant in the circumstances (*pace* Cheng, 1997), and that naïve individuals are sensitive to this difference in meaning.

A MENTAL MODEL THEORY OF THOG

The THOG problem is a tricky deductive problem invented by Peter Wason (1977). You are shown a white diamond, a black diamond, a white circle, and a black circle. The experimenter tells you:

> There is a particular shape and a particular color, such that any one of these four designs that has *one*, and only *one*, of these features is called a THOG.

The experimenter then states:

> The black diamond is a THOG.

Your task is to state which of the remaining shapes are THOGs, which are not THOGs, and which are impossible to classify. If you have not encountered this problem, try it before you read on.

Most people classify the white circle as not a THOG, and the white diamond and black circle as impossible to classify, i.e., they may or may not be THOGs. They are wrong. The correct response is that the white circle *is* a THOG, and the white diamond and black circle are *not* THOGs. This response is usually the second most frequent one. Other miscellaneous errors occur, but less often than the correct response.

Why do people err in the THOG task? Various hypotheses have been advanced, but Mark Johns (a former undergraduate at Princeton University) has recently proposed an account of the task, which is based on mental models. According to this theory, reasoners envisage the two features that the experimenter wrote down. Given the initial information that the black diamond is a THOG, and following the principle of truth, they construct mental models representing the two possible features:

> black
>> diamond

They then infer that the white diamond *may* be a THOG because it has one of these features, but they cannot be certain because the other feature (black) could be the critical one. They likewise infer that the black circle *may* be a THOG because it also has one of these features. But they infer that the white circle cannot be a THOG because it has neither of these two features.

The correct response depends on fleshing out the initial models above in order to make explicit what is *false* in the two cases:

black	¬ diamond
¬ black	diamond

Granted that there are only two possible shapes and only two possible colors, the false cases in these two models can be replaced by their corresponding positive features:

black	circle
white	diamond

A design is a THOG if it has one feature in each of these models. It is not a THOG if it has both features in either of these models. And it is indeterminate —it may or may not be a THOG— if it has a feature in only one of these models. It follows that the white circle is a THOG because it has one feature of the first possibility and one feature of the second possibility. In contrast, neither the black circle nor the white diamond is a THOG because one has both features of the first possibility and the other has both features of the second possibility.

Johns wrote a computer program that implemented this account and that allowed him to explore a large space of problems similar to the original THOG problem. The program led him to a novel prediction that he was able to test experimentally in what he calls the «super-THOG» task. Super-THOG is carried out in two stages. First, the participants carry out the standard THOG task, which is described above. Second, they are told that everything that they learned in the first stage is still true, but now they have to classify two extra shapes: a grey diamond and a grey circle. The model theory predicts that they should classify the grey diamond as indeterminate because diamond is one feature in the mental models (shown above), but they should classify the grey circle as not a THOG because it has neither of the two features in the mental models. In contrast, the correct response, which is revealed by the fully explicit models, is that both the grey diamond and the grey circle are indeterminate because they each have one feature in one of the fully explicit models, i.e. they may be THOGs, but one cannot be certain. In Johns's experiment, the most frequent error was the one predicted by the model theory, which was made by 13 participants in comparison with the 7 participants who made the correct response. Johns argues that the model theory accordingly goes beyond the original THOG experiment to make a correct prediction about a new variant of the task.

MENTAL MODELS OF CONDITIONAL ASSERTIONS

What do conditionals mean? No-one knows for sure, which is odd because we readily understand them in daily life. One analysis treats them as having a «defective» truth table in which they have no truth value when their antecedents are false (see e.g. Wason & Johnson-Laird, 1972, p. 90). Thus, a conditional about a specific hand of cards, such as:

If there was a king in the hand then there was an ace

would be true given that there was a king and ace in the hand, false given that there was a king but not an ace in the hand, but it would have no truth value when it is false that there was a king in the hand. This analysis, however, leads to insoluble problems with biconditionals, such as:

If, and only if, there was a king in the hand, then there was an ace.

This assertion is true given two possibilities: there was a king and an ace in the hand, or else there was not a king and not an ace in the hand. It is false given two possibilities: there was a king but not an ace in the hand, or there was an ace but not a king in the hand. In other words, the biconditional has a complete truth table, not a defective one. Yet, it can be paraphrased by a conjunction of two conditionals, such as:

If there was a king in the hand then there was an ace; and if there was an ace in the hand then there was a king.

How can a definite truth table for the biconditional be equivalent to two conditionals with defective truth tables? The answer is: it is impossible. Suppose that there wasn't a king in the hand and that there wasn't an ace. It follows that neither conditional in the preceding conjunction has a truth value. Yet, the biconditional is true. The notion that a conjunction of two assertions that have no truth value should somehow lead to a true conjunction is a recipe for nonsense.

The model theory is therefore based, not on a defective truth table, but on an idea that captures a similar intuition. A conditional, such as:

If there was a king in the hand then there was an ace

has only one explicit mental model, which represents the possibility in which its antecedent and consequent are both true. Individuals do not immediately appreciate the relevance of cases where the antecedent is false. Hence, they defer a detailed representation of these possibilities, which they represent in a wholly implicit model denoted here by an ellipsis:

King   Ace
        ...

Again, reasoners need to make a mental footnote about what is false in the wholly implicit model, namely, it is false that there is a king. The representation of a biconditional:

If, and only if, there was a king in the hand then there was an ace

has exactly the same mental models, but now reasoners need to make a footnote that both the king and the ace are false in the implicit model. Our evidence suggests that reasoners soon lose access to mental footnotes, especially in the case of slightly more complex assertions.

Over & Evans (1997, p. 268) have pointed out an apparent problem with this account of conditionals. They assert that the model theory takes conditionals of the form, *If A then B*, to be material conditionals and accordingly equivalent to disjunctions of the form, *not-A or B, or both*. There are, however, notorious difficulties for treating conditionals as equivalent to material conditionals. One such problem, which Over & Evans cite, is that a material conditional makes valid the following sort of inference, which is known as «strengthening the antecedent»:

If A then C
If A and B then C.

In real life, however, there are many inferences of this sort that no-one would accept as valid, e.g.:

If you strike a match then it will light.
If you strike a match and it is wet then it will light.

The solution to these problems is to bear in mind that the antecedent of a conditional sets up a context for the interpretation of the consequent (see Johnson-Laird, 1986, for the following analysis). Indeed, if the context is common knowledge to both speaker and listener, there is no need to assert the antecedent. For example, a mother observing her child about to grab a forbidden cake can assert:

You'll get into trouble

where the force of the utterance is:

If you take the cake, then you'll get into trouble.

Granted that the antecedent of a conditional describes a context, then it must have the illocutionary force of an assertion. Unlike the consequent, it cannot ask a question or make a request. And one corollary is that the antecedent often fails to specify the context completely. For example, a conditional such as:

If you put sugar in your tea then it tastes sweet

has an antecedent that only partly describes the context. It has a *ceteris paribus* condition. This condition accommodates the following strengthened antecedent:

If you put sugar *and milk* in your tea then it tastes sweet,

It is violated, however, by strengthening the antecedent in the following way:

If you put sugar and diesel oil in your tea then it tastes sweet.

In fact, most sentences give only cues to the situations to which they refer and so they also have *ceteris paribus* conditions. Naive individuals balk at the preceding inference, so too they balk at certain valid inferences based on disjunctions, such as the following analogue of «strengthening the antecedent»:

You put milk or lemon in tea.
You put milk, lemon, or diesel oil, in tea.

If the premise is true, the conclusion must be true, and so the inference is valid.

In psychological studies, conditionals often have antecedents that describe the contexts as completely as necessary. Thus, the antecedent of the following conditional tells the participants all they need to know about the context:

If there was a king in the hand then there was an ace in the hand.

Such conditionals *are* akin to material conditionals. Hence, possibilities in which the antecedent is false are consistent with the conditional — they are true possibilities. But, logically-untrained individuals do not normally treat these cases as initially relevant. That is why they are represented by implicit models (represented by ellipses) that have no content. The model theory has more to say about conditionals and counterfactuals (see e.g. Byrne, 1997), but the present account should have shown that it offers at least a plausible account of their meaning.

CRITICISMS OF THE MODEL THEORY

The model theory has had many critics, and their criticisms fall into four main classes:

1. There is no difference between mental models and formal rules of inference.
2. Psychological theories, such as the model theory, cannot appeal to semantics, i.e. theories must be syntactic.
3. The model theory is vague and untestable, and there is no way to decide between it and theories of reasoning based on formal rules of inference.
4. The model theory is not computationally tractable.

In what follows, the paper will evaluate each of these criticisms, and then turn to some gaps in the theory.

Various authors have argued that no real difference exists between mental models and formal rules, because the model theory depends on formal rules (see e.g. Goldman, 1986; Rips, 1986; and Braine, 1990). One version of the argument goes like this:

The model theory has been implemented in computer programs.
Any computer program depends only on formal rules.
The model theory depends only on formal rules.

Another version of the argument is less a criticism than an important meta-logical claim: any inference that can be made using models can be made using formal rules (Stenning & Yule, 1997).

The rebuttal of the first version of the argument is simple. One should not confuse a computer simulation of a theory with the theory itself. The theory postulates that people can understand the meaning of discourse. Current computer programs cannot understand meaning, and they will be unable to do so until they have a much richer interrelation with the external world.

The second claim is correct. There are many logical domains in which formal rules and mental models yield the same set of inferences. But, the model theory is not restricted to postulating meanings for logical terms, such as quantifiers and connectives. No formal rule theory currently envisaged in psychology can make the following inference:

Ann is on the right of Beth.
Beth is on the right of Cath.
Ann is on the right of Cath.

Such theories have no access to the meaning of *on the right of*. They require an axiom (or «meaning postulate») specifying that the relation is transitive. Such an axiom is false, however. The description above may refer to individuals sitting at a round table, and so the inference would yield a false conclusion. In other words, the truth of the conclusion depends on the shape of the table and the arrangement of the seating. In certain contexts, the inference would be valid, taking into account the situation, and the model theory can account for this phenomenon (see Johnson-Laird, 1983).

In some of the domains to which the two sorts of theory do apply, they make contrasting predictions, e.g. spatial and temporal reasoning (Byrne & Johnson-Laird, 1989; Schaeken *et al.*, 1996), and reasoning with sentential connectives (García Madruga, Moreno, Carriedo, & Gutiérrez, this volume). The evidence corroborates the model theory's predictions. No systematic set of results from any domain for which the two theories have been compared supports rules rather than models. Hence, the final rebuttal of the claim that there is no difference between the two sorts of theories is that they do make different predictions. The late Martin Braine, for example, went so far as to claim that the model theory was false (see e.g. O'Brien, Braine, & Yang, 1994), though on grounds which were inadequate (see Johnson-Laird, Byrne, & Schaeken, 1994). Braine would not have made such a claim if he had thought that the model theory did not differ from rule theories.

The claim that theories cannot rely on semantics is encapsulated in the following remark: «... cognitive psychology has to do without semantic notions like truth and reference that depend on the relationship between mental representations and the world» (Rips, 1986). But, without truth and semantics, there is no notion of a valid inference, meta-logic disappears, and little of mental life is left (see e.g. Barwise & Etchemendy, 1989). Theories have to account for how people envisage and assess truth, and of how they make valid inferences. In short, there are no grounds for accepting Rips's claim.

The view that the model theory is vague comes in different strengths. A weak version of the criticism is that neither rule nor model theory is «fully and precisely defined» (Evans & Over, 1997, p. 27). A stronger criticism is that it is not clear what the model theory predicts (Dan Osherson, personal communication). And the strongest version of the criticism is that the model theory is untestable (Bonatti, 1994). The truth is that the model theory is not fully and precisely defined — indeed, no psychological theory meets this criterion. However, the model theory has been implemented in computer programs (see Johnson-Laird & Byrne, 1991; Bara, *et al.*, 1994), and it has been submitted to many tests, of which the most striking is the corroboration of illusory inferences. Hence, the criticism could be couched in a more plausible way by introducing quantifiers: there are *some* domains in which the model theory is untestable, because it makes no predictions about them. The range of the theory, however, is greater than that of its competitors. It makes specific predictions about deductive reasoning, and reasoning about possibilities, probabilities, and causal relations. Thus, the model theory attempts to specify the psychological «state space» for probabilities (Johnson-Laird, Legrenzi, Girotto, Legrenzi, & Caverni, 1999) and to account for reasoning that yields modal conclusions (Bell & Johnson-Laird, 1988).

In a series of papers, Chater & Oaksford (e.g. 1993) have made the following argument:

Everyday informal reasoning is rapid.
Neither mental models nor formal rules are computationally tractable.
Intractable systems are not rapid.
Everyday reasoning is based on neither mental models nor formal rules.

The sentential calculus is computationally *intractable*, that is, as problems are based on an increasing number of distinct atomic propositions, so the demands on memory and time grow at a rate that soon exceeds the capacity of any conceivable computational device (Cook, 1971). No method of reasoning can get round this constraint, and human performance does decline catastrophically as the number of premises increases. No-one, however, has formulated an account of *what* is computed in everyday informal reasoning. Hence, it is not yet possible to determine whether people are using a tractable or an intractable algorithm. We can contrast this case with, say, syntactic parsing. People can understand sentences in real time, and they do not fall behind in parsing as sentences increase in length. Hence, the human parser must use a tractable algorithm. Informal everyday reasoning, however, is an open question, because we have yet to discover what people are computing in such inferences. The considerations of tractability are important, but they do not impugn the model theory.

Readers may suppose from the preceding paragraphs that the present author regards the model theory as a paragon. Not so; the theory has many gaps and omissions. It recognizes that the pragmatics of communication plays an important part in how people interpret the premises of inferences, and in what conclusions they are likely to draw. The theory, however, offers no account of pragmatics (Evans & Over, 1997). It also offers no account of how general knowledge is mentally represented or of how it is triggered and used in the process of reasoning. The theory provides a semantics of standard connectives, temporal and spatial relations, and quantifiers, but these accounts have yet to be implemented in a single computational model (though cf. Bara, *et al.*, 1994). Likewise, a full compositional semantics has yet to be implemented for a significant fragment of natural language, such as Basic English, or for various quantifiers that are not standard in formal logic, such as «only», «most», and «more than half». A task of high priority is to implement such a semantics, because computer implementations of the theory have led in the past to significant discoveries, such as the phenomena of illusory inferences.

CONCLUSIONS

The psychology of reasoning is difficult, but not impossible. Hence, the theory of mental models is under active development. It is at present incomplete, with many radical gaps. Yet, it makes testable predictions in many domains, and it is distinguishable from other sorts of theory. Indeed, there are distinguishable variants of the model theory itself (see e.g. Ormerod, Manktelow, & Jones, 1993; Evans, 1993; Polk & Newell, 1995). The current theory is not fully and precisely defined. But, it is more likely to be refuted than to be made completely precise. If experiments establish systematic counterexamples to the model theory, then it will be overturned. Yet, it will have the ironic satisfaction of explaining its own demise. It recognizes the role of counterexamples in refutations.

ACKNOWLEDGMENTS

I am grateful for help from many colleagues. They include the participants at the workshop, and its organizers: Juan García-Madruga, Nuria Carriedo and María José González-Labra. I also thank my colleagues in Princeton and elsewhere for their helpful criticisms: Patricia Barres, Victoria Bell, Ruth Byrne, Yevgeniya Goldvarg, Vittorio Girotto, Paolo Legrenzi, Maria Sonino Legrenzi, Hansjoerg Neth, Mary Newsome, Cristina Quelhas, Sergio Moreno Ríos, Carlos Santamaría, Vladimir Sloutsky, Jean-Baptiste van der Henst, and Yingrui Yang.

REFERENCES

BARA, B., BUCCIARELLI, M., & JOHNSON-LAIRD, P. N. (1995): «The development of syllogistic reasoning», 108, 157-193.

BARA, B. G., BUCCIARELLI, M., JOHNSON-LAIRD, P. N., & LOMBARDO, V. (1994): «Mental models in propositional reasoning». *Proceedings of the Sixteenth Annual Conference of the Cognitive Science Society*. Hillsdale, NJ: Lawrence Erlbaum Associates, pp. 15-20.

BARWISE, J. (1993): «Everyday reasoning and logical inference». *Behavioral and Brain Sciences*, 16, 337-38.

BARWISE, J., & ETCHEMENDY, J. (1989): «Model-theoretic semantics». In Posner, M. (Ed.) *Foundations of Cognitive Science*. Cambridge, MA: Bradford Books MIT Press.

BAUER, M. I., & JOHNSON-LAIRD, P. N. (1993): «How diagrams can improve reasoning». *Psychological Science*, 4, 372-378, 1993.

BELL, V., & JOHNSON-LAIRD, P. N. (1998): «A model theory of modal reasoning». *Cognitive Science*, 22, 25-51.

BONATTI, L. (1994): «Propositional reasoning by model?» *Psychological Review*, 101, 725-33.

BRAINE, M. D. S. (1990): «The "natural logic" approach to reasoning». In Overton, W.
    F. (Ed.) *Reasoning, Necessity, and Logic: Developmental Perspectives*. Hillsdale, NJ:
    Lawrence Erlbaum Associates.
BRAINE, M. D. S., & O'BRIEN, D. P. (Eds.) (1998): *Mental Logic*. Mahwah, NJ: Lawrence
    Erlbaum Associates.
BUCCIARELLI, M., & JOHNSON-LAIRD, P. N. (1999): «Strategies in syllogistic reasoning».
    Cognitive Science, in press.
BYRNE, R. M. J. (1997): «Cognitive processes in counterfactual thinking about what might
    have been». In Medin, D. K. (Ed.) *The Psychology of Learning and Motivation,
    Advances in Research and Theory*, Vol. 37, pp. 105-54. San Diego, CA: Academic Press.
BYRNE, R. M. J., & JOHNSON-LAIRD, P. N. (1989): «Spatial reasoning». *Journal of Memory
    and Language*, 28, 564-575.
CHATER, N., & OAKSFORD M. (1993): «Logicism, mental models and everyday reasoning».
    Mind & Language, 8, 72-89.
CHENG, P. W. (1997): «From covariation to causation: A causal power theory».
    Psychological Review, 104, 367-405.
COOK, S. A. (1971): «The complexity of theorem proving procedures». *Proceedings of the
    Third Annual Association of Computing Machinery Symposium on the Theory of
    Computing*, 151-58.
CRAIK, K. (1943): «The Nature of Explanation. Cambridge: Cambridge University Press».
Einhorn, H. J., and Hogarth, R.M. (1986) Judging probable cause. *Psychological Bulletin*,
    99, 3-19.
EVANS, J. St. B. T. (1989): *Bias in Human Reasoning: Causes and Consequences*. Hillsdale,
    NJ: Erlbaum.
—   (1993): «The mental model theory of conditional reasoning: Critical appraisal and
    revision». *Cognition*, 48, 1-20.
EVANS, J. St. B. T., & OVER, D. E. (1997): «Rationality in reasoning: The problem of
    deductive competence». *Current Psychology of Cognition*, 16, 3-38.
GARNHAM, A., & OAKHILL, J. V. (1994): *Thinking and Reasoning*. Oxford: Basil Blackwell.
—   (1996): «The mental models theory of language comprehension». In Britton, B.K.,
    and Graesser, A.C. (Eds.) *Models of Understanding Text*, pp. 313-39. Hillsdale, NJ:
    Erlbaum.
GENTNER, D., & STEVENS, A. L. (Eds.) (1983): *Mental Models*. Hillsdale, NJ: Erlbaum.
GIROTTO, V., & GONZALEZ, M. (1999): «Solving probabilistic and statistical problems:
    A matter of information structure and question form». Under submission.
GOLDMAN, A. I. (1986): *Epistemology and Cognition*. Cambridge Mass., Harvard University
    Press.
GOLDVARG, Y., & JOHNSON-LAIRD, P. N. (1999a): «Illusions in modal reasoning». *Memory
    & Cognition*, in press.
—   (1999b): «Naive causality: a mental model theory of causal meaning and reasoning.
    Under submission».
GREEN, D. (1996): «Models, arguments and decisions». In Oakhill, J., and Garnham, A.,
    eds. *Mental Models in Cognitive Science*. Hove, East Sussex: Psychology Press.
GRICE, H. P. (1975): «Logic and conversation». In Cole, P., and Morgan, J. L. (Eds.)
    Syntax and Semantics, Vol. 3.: Speech Acts. New York: Academic Press.
HART, H. L. A., & HONORÉ, A. M. (1985): *Causation in the Law*. Second Edition. Oxford:
    Clarendon Press. (First edition published in 1959.)
HESSLOW, G. (1988): «The problem of causal selection». In Hilton, D. J. (Ed.):
    *Contemporary Science and Natural Explanation: Commonsense Conceptions of
    Causality*. pp. 11-32. Brighton, Sussex: Harvester Press.

HILTON, D. J., & ERB, H. P. (1996): «Mental models and causal explanation: Judgements of probable cause and explanatory relevance». *Thinking & Reasoning*, 2, 273-308.

JOHNSON-LAIRD, P. N. (1983): *Mental Models: Towards a Cognitive Science of Language, Inference and Consciousness*. Cambridge: Cambridge University Press; Cambridge, MA: Harvard University Press.

JOHNSON-LAIRD, P. N. (1986): «Conditionals and mental models». In Traugott, E.C., Meulen, A., Reilly, J.S., and Ferguson, C.A. (Eds.) *On Conditionals*. pp. 55 - 75. Cambridge: Cambridge University Press.

JOHNSON-LAIRD, P. N., & BYRNE, R. M. J. (1991): *Deduction*. Hillsdale, NJ: Lawrence Erlbaum Associates.

JOHNSON-LAIRD, P. N., BYRNE, R. M. J., & SCHAEKEN, W. (1994): «Why models rather than rules give a better account of propositional reasoning: a reply to Bonatti, and to O'Brien, Braine, and Yang». *Psychological Review*, 101, 734-739.

JOHNSON-LAIRD, P. N., LEGRENZI, P., GIROTTO, P., LEGRENZI, M. S., & CAVERNI, J-P. (1999): «Naive Probability: A mental model theory of extensional reasoning». *Psychological Review*, In press.

JOHNSON-LAIRD, P. N., & SAVARY, F. (1998): «Truth and illusion in deduction». *Cognition*, in press.

JOHNSON-LAIRD, P. N., SAVARY, F., & BUCCIARELLI, M. (1999): «Strategies and tactics in reasoning». In Schaeken, W.S., Vandierendonck, A., De Vooght, G., and d'Ydewalle, G. (Eds.) *Deductive Reasoning and Strategies*. Mahwah, NJ: Erlbaum, in press.

KAHNEMAN, D., & TVERSKY, A. (1982): «The simulation heuristic». In Kahneman, D., Slovic, P., and Tversky, A. (Eds.) *Judgment under Uncertainty: Heuristics and Biases*. Cambridge: Cambridge University Press.

MACKIE, J. L. (1980): *The Cement of the Universe: A Study in Causation*. Second edition. Oxford: Oxford University Press.

NEWSTEAD, S. E., & EVANS, J. St. B. T. (1993): «Mental models as an explanation of belief bias effects in syllogistic reasoning». *Cognition*, 46, 93-97.

OAKHILL, J., & GARNHAM, A. (Eds.) (1996): *Mental Models in Cognitive Science*. Hove, East Sussex: Psychology Press.

OAKHILL, J., GARNHAM, A., & JOHNSON-LAIRD, P. N. (1990): «Belief bias effects in syllogistic reasoning». In Gilhooly, K., Keane, M. T. G., Logie, R. H., and Erdos, G. (Eds.): *Lines of Thinking, Vol.1*, pp. 125-38. London: Wiley.

O'BRIEN, D. P., BRAINE, M. D. S., & YANG, Y. (1994): «Propositional reasoning by mental models? Simple to refute in principle and in practice». *Psychological Review*, 101, 711-724.

ORMEROD, T. C., MANKTELOW, K. I., & JONES, G. V. (1993): «Reasoning with three types of conditional: Biases and mental models». *Quarterly Journal of Experimental Psychology*, 46A, 653-678.

OVER, D. E., & EVANS, J. St. B. T. (1997): «Two cheers for deductive competence». *Current Psychology of Cognition*, 16, 255-278.

POLK, T. A., & NEWELL, A. (1995): «Deduction as verbal reasoning». *Psychological Review*, 102, 533-566.

RIPS, L. J. (1986): «Mental muddles». In Brand, M., and Harnish, R.M. (Eds.) *Problems in the Representation of Knowledge and Belief*. Tucson: University of Arizona Press.

— (1994): *The Psychology of Proof*. Cambridge, MA: MIT Press.

ROBERTS, M. J. (1999): «Strategies in relational inference». Under submission.

SCHAEKEN, W. S., JOHNSON-LAIRD, P. N., & D'YDEWALLE, G. (1996): «Mental models and temporal reasoning». *Cognition*, 60, 205-234.

SHAW, V. F. (1996): «The cognitive processes in informal reasoning». *Thinking & Reasoning*, 2, 51-80.

SHAW, V. F., & JOHNSON-LAIRD, P. N. (1998): «Dispelling the "atmosphere" effect on reasoning». *Analise Psicologia*, F, 169-199.

SLOUTSKY, V. M., & GOLDVARG, Y. (1999): «Representation and recall of determinate and indeterminate problems». Under submission.

STENNING, K., & YULE, P. (1997): «Image and language in human reasoning: A syllogistic illustration». *Cognitive Psychology*, 34,109-159.

WASON, P. C. (1977): «Self-contradictions». In Johnson-Laird, P.N., and Wason, P.C. (Eds.) *Thinking: Readings in Cognitive Science*. Cambridge: Cambridge University Press.

WASON, P. C., & JOHNSON-LAIRD, P. N. (1972): *Psychology of Reasoning: Structure and Content*. London: Batsford. Cambridge, MA: Harvard University Press.

YANG, Y., & JOHNSON-LAIRD, P. N. (1999): «Illusions in quantified reasoning: How to make the impossible seem possible, and *vice versa*». *Memory & Cognition*, in press.

2

THINKING AND BELIEVING

Jonathan St. B. T. Evans

En este capítulo se presenta una discusión de los medios por los que nuestras creencias influyen sobre nuestros pensamientos. En este sentido, se sostiene que al enfrentarse a problemas nuevos —incluso en el laboratorio—, las creencias asociadas relevantes se recuperan y aplican de forma automática. La influencia de las creencias se discute en relación a tres distintos campos de estudio psicológico: la tarea de selección con enunciados deónticos, el efecto del sesgo de creencia en el razonamiento silogístico y la seudodiagnosticidad en la comprobación de hipótesis. En cada uno de estos campos se sostiene que la influencia de las creencias permite el logro de una racionalidad personal en el sentido definido por Evans y Over (1996); es decir, las creencias previas ejercerían una influencia que sería normalmente adaptativa en la vida cotidiana. Sin embargo, la influencia de las creencias es en gran medida implícita y está fuera del control consciente. Si en las intrucciones experimentales se pide que las creencias previas no sean consideradas, la consecuencia es que las creencias puede parecer que sesgan a los participantes quienes fallan en lograr la racionalidad normativa en la tarea. Sin embargo, existe evidencia de que alguna gente —usualmente con puntuación alta en inteligencia general—, son capaces de suspender sus creencias y razonar correctamente dentro del marco establecido por las instrucciones experimentales.

How do beliefs influence thinking? In this chapter, I will argue that the influence of belief is highly pervasive and generally adaptive. However, I will also argue that beliefs influence us largely through pragmatic processes which are entirely implicit in nature. Hence, whilst the influence of beliefs may normally be effective in everyday life it may lead us to apparent error and bias in the psychological laboratory, when experimental instructions require that our prior beliefs be disregarded. In the terminology of Evans and Over (1996) beliefs exert influence which is rational1 but not necessarily rational2.The distinction between rationality1 and rationality2 was introduced originally by Evans (1993) to account for an apparent paradox. Why is it that on the one hand human beings are a species of proven high intelligence who can adapt the environment to their needs, but on the other hand their representatives exhibit countless errors and biases when participating in psychological experiments on reasoning and judgement? I suggested that we use the term rationality1 to refer to the kind of intelligence that results in achieving our everyday personal goals, and rationality2 to describe conformity with standard normative systems such as logic and probability theory (Anderson, 1990, discusses a similar distinction between adaptive and normative rationality).

There are many reasons why we are generally rational1 but frequently fail to be rational2. Evans and Over (1996) elucidate the distinction by developing a dual process theory of thinking in which separate implicit and explicit systems of thinking are proposed. Our proposals are related to and influenced by discussions of authors working in the implicit learning paradigm (see Berry & Dienes, 1993; Reber, 1993). The implicit system is regarded as evolutionarily primary and shared with other animals. It processes information in a rapid, parallel and preconscious manner and could be modelled by neural networks. The explicit system is by contrast uniquely human, related to language and reflective consciousness and relatively slow and limited in processing capacity loading as it does on working memory. Reber argues that the explicit system is related to general intelligence or g, but that the implicit system is not. Evans and Over (1996) argue that rationality1 can be achieved by the implicit system and essentially relies on actions that have proved successful in the past whether derived by evolution or by the individual's history of learning. Rationality2 on the other hand requires use of the explicit cognitive system in order to achieve hypothetical thinking about possible world states, or mental models.

Within this framework, the role of prior knowledge and belief is critical. In order to be rational1 it is essential that our inferences and actions are based upon all relevant beliefs. What is relevant will be cued both by the immediate features of the task present in the environment and the current goals which the individual is trying achieve. We have little understanding at present of the powerful pragmatic processes that allow us to retrieve and apply just those beliefs from our vast store of knowledge that are relevant to the problem at hand. However, we can show that people may err in experimental tasks because correct performance depends upon understanding some explicit and often quite artificial instruction. Because beliefs operate habitually and through implicit processes, their influence cannot easily be turned off, for example, by experimental instructions to base inferences only on the information presented.

In order to illustrate the effect of belief on thinking, I will discuss three separate areas of study in the psychology of thinking and reasoning. First, I consider the thematic facilitation effect in the Wason selection task. Here, the claim is that we can reason better with realistic materials, related to our everyday knowledge and belief. Second, I consider the belief bias effect in syllogistic reasoning where the claim —in apparent contrast— is that real world beliefs interfere with our reasoning. Finally, I will discuss some recent research in the study of pseudodiagnostic reasoning which sheds new light on the influence of belief.

THE THEMATIC FACILITATION EFFECT

The hypothesis that there is a thematic facilitation effect dates from the book published by Wason and Johnson-Laird (1972). The primary evidence for the effect is that a reasoning problem known as the Wason selection task (Wason, 1966) is known to be very difficult in its standard form using abstract problem content. However, certain versions of the same problem using thematic content can be quite easily solved by most participants (for detailed review of the relevant studies, see Evans, Newstead & Byrne, 1993, Chapter 4). A typical abstract selection task involves telling participants that a set of cards always have a letter on one side and a number on the other. They are then told that a rule applies to these four cards and may be true or false:

IF THE A CARD HAS A VOWEL ON ONE SIDE, THEN IT HAS AN EVEN NUMBER ON THE OTHER SIDE

Participants are then shown four cards whose exposed faces show the symbols E, T, 4 and 7. The question is to decide which cards need to be turned over in order to decide whether the rule is true or false. Most people choose E or E and 4. Normally, less than 10% choose what is generally regarded as the logically correct solution: E and 7. Logically, a rule of this kind cannot be proved true but it can be disproved by finding a card which has a vowel on one side and an odd number on the other. Only by turning the E and 7 cards could such a falsifying case be discovered. In logical notation, the rule is of the form «if p then q», and the correct choices are the p and not-q cards.

A typical example of a thematic version of the problem which people can solve, is the drinking age problem of Griggs and Cox (1982). Here participants are told to imagine that they are police officers observing people drinking in a bar. They have to ensure that people are conforming to a rule such as IF A PERSON IS DRINKING BEER THEN THAT PERSON MUST BE OVER 18 YEARS OF AGE.

The four cards represent individuals and have on one side the beverage they are drinking and on the other side their age. The exposed values are Beer (p), Coke (not-p), 20 years of age (q) and 16 years of age (not-q). Most people given this task turn over the card marked Beer and the card marked 16 years of age (p and not-q). These cards are the ones which could detect an underage drinker violating the rule, and so are generally regarded as the correct choices.

There are actually several differences between these versions. As Manktelow and Over (1991) were the first to notice, the abstract task is a problem in indicative logic, concerned with discovering what is true or false, whereas the thematic version is a problem in deontic logic, concerned with whether or not a rule is being followed. Most effective thematic versions of the selection task have this deontic form. However, this confound does not account in itself for the thematic facilitation effect. The results of a number of studies reviewed by Evans *et al.* (1993, pp. 104-107) can be summarised as follows. Giving an abstract version of the task a deontic form does not in itself facilitate correct choices. However, rephrasing the thematic version as an indicative problem does weaken or remove the effect. Hence, it appears that both deontic framing and thematic content are needed to produce the facilitation. In the case of the drinking age rule, it has also been shown that the brief scenario about the police officer role is required. If the rule and cards are presented without the scenario, performance drops to that of the abstract control group (Pollard & Evans, 1987).

What these experiments show is that performance on this problem is extraordinarily sensitive to pragmatic factors. Providing the appropriate cues are present to enable people to retrieve relevant prior belief about the content of the problem, this will profoundly influence the choices they make. Whether the thematic facilitation effect is correctly named, however, is moot. First, the term facilitation implies better reasoning. In fact, pragmatic cues do not necessarily produce the response pattern which is regarded as logically correct. Several studies have shown that patterns of choices in thematic selection tasks can be reversed according to the perspective cued to the participants. For example, Manktelow & Over (1991) used a problem in which a mother gives a son the following rule:

IF YOU TIDY YOUR ROOM THEN YOU MAY GO OUT TO PLAY

In this case the four cards are Tidied room (p), Did not tidy room (not-p), Went out to play (q), Did not to out to play (not-q). When given the child's perspective and asked to check if the rule is being followed, most people choose the p and not-q cards as in the thematic facilitation effect. Clearly, the child would feel cheated if he tidied his room and was not allowed out. However, given the mother's perspective, participants turn over not-p and q. From her point of view, the child is violating the rule is he goes out to play without tidying his room. These findings suggest that whatever is being facilitated, it is not a process of logical reasoning as such. One influential view is that people retrieve and apply pragmatic reasoning schemas which involve applying production rules to each card in turn (Cheng & Holyoak, 1985; Holyoak & Cheng, 1995). However, Evans & Clibbens (1995) have argued that this theory assumes more than is necessary to account for the data. It could simply be that beliefs serve to cues certain cards as relevant and that people choose on the basis of relevance rather than any process of reasoning as such (see Evans, 1995 and Sperber, Cara & Girotto, 1995 for alternative relevance theories of the selection task).

In support of this claim, Evans (1996) reported that when participants were asked to point with a mouse at cards they were thinking of selecting —leading to a record of card inspection times— it was found that they spent very little time thinking about cards that were not chosen. This finding was demonstrated on both abstract and thematic versions of the selection task, the latter including both facilitatory versions and ones which reverse choices due to perspective shifts. However, recent evidence has cast some doubts on the value of this method for investigation of relevance effects (see Roberts, 1998; Evans, 1998). However, other measures of attention, including those based on protocol analysis point to the same conclusions (see Evans, 1995). Also, some new evidence based on a quite different approach also supports the claim that thematic facilitation does not operate via a process of reasoning.

Stanovich and West (1998) investigated individual differences in performance on both abstract and thematic versions of the selection task and attempted to correlate these with measures of general intelligence or g. What they found was that on the abstract task, the minority of participants who are able to solve the task were significantly higher in g than non-solvers. Performance on the thematic versions, by contrast, was unrelated to g. Stanovich and West offered an interpretation of these results in terms of the Evans and Over dual process theory. Evans (e.g. 1989) has argued for many years that choices on the selection task are normally pragmatic or relevance based. On the abstract task, where no prior beliefs are available about the content of the problem, these influences are linguistic in origin and related to the normal use of terms such as 'if' and 'not'. When thematic content is introduced, however, the content introduces prior belief which often cues the logically correct cards as relevant. In Evans and Over's terms correct performance on the thematic task is rational1 rather than rational 2 reflecting only the helpful pragmatic processes of the implicit cognitive system. This would explain the lack of correlation with g. On the abstract task, Stanovich and West suggest, correct performance does indicate rationality2 because here participants need to suppress the pragmatic processes (which lead to bias on this version) and apply conscious deductive reasoning in order to solve the problem. The ability to reason in this way is, of course, related to g.

In summary, research on the 'thematic facilitation effect' shows us the extreme sensitivity of reasoning or decision making to pragmatic factors and that when prior beliefs are introduced they can radically affect choices. However, the effect is neither simply thematic (it depends upon other factors such as deontic framing and use of scenarios) and nor is it necessarily facilitatory in the sense of improving logical performance. What the evidence does clearly show, in my view, also shows that beliefs influence our thinking through the implicit cognitive system by cueing relevance rather than by facilitating any explicit process of logical reasoning. First, the choices cued need not coincide with a logical analysis as the perspective shift effect shows. Second, people attend to the relevant cards which they select and disregard the cards they do not select on both abstract and thematic versions. Finally, only performance on the abstract tasks is related to measures of intelligence. In summary, this area of research indicates a rational1 influence of belief, operating through the implicit system of thinking.

THE BELIEF BIAS EFFECT

The so-called 'belief bias' effect in syllogistic reasoning was first demonstrated by Wilkins (1928) and has been replicated many times since (see Evans *et al.*, 1993, Chapter 8 for review of relevant studies). In common with the thematic facilitation effect, the phenomenon is both inaccurately named and open to general misunderstanding. On close inspection, the influence that beliefs exert in this paradigm is seen actually to debias responses.

How could such a radical misinterpretation of the effect come about? Belief bias is normally described as a tendency to accept as logically valid conclusions which we believe to be true. Experiments within the standard paradigm do indeed appear to show this. A good example is found in the study of Evans, Barston and Pollard (1983) who presented syllogistic arguments in the conclusion evaluation paradigm. In the evaluation task, two premises are presented together with a conclusion and the participant is asked to decide whether or not the conclusion follows logically from the premises. Evans *et al.* used four types of problem, depending upon whether or not the conclusion was valid, and whether or not the conclusions was believable.

For example, an Invalid-Believable syllogism might be:

No addictive things are inexpresive
Some cigarettes are inexpensive
Therefore, some addictive things are not cigarettes

Across three experiments conducted by Evans et al (1983) acceptance rates were as follows:

Valid-Believable : 89%
Valid-Unbelievable: 56%
Invalid-Believable: 71%
Invalid-Unbelievable: 10%

Three significant effects are present here. First, people accept (in line with logic) more valid than invalid conclusions. Second (in line with belief bias) they accept more believable than unbelievable conclusions. Finally, there is an interaction - the effects of belief are more marked on invalid problems. To put it another way, people are much more likely to endorse fallacies if they believe the conclusion to be true. This result is easily replicated. The weaker effect of belief on valid arguments —present in the above data— is not always observed in replication studies. The reason that this apparent belief bias is misnamed is that it assumes that fallacies are being endorsed because they are believable. In fact, studies of syllogisms with abstract and neutral content show also very high rates of endorsement of fallacies. When neutral conclusions are introduced into belief bias studies (e.g. Evans & Pollard, 1990; Newstead, Pollard, Evans & Allen, 1992) it turns out that acceptance rates of believable and neutral conclusions are similarly high, but those for unbelievable conclusions are much lower. Since the bias operates mostly on invalid problems what this means is that fallacies which would normally be made are being suppressed by unbelievable conclusions. Hence, the influence of belief is a debiasing not a biasing one. The influence of beliefs is also negative (disbelief reducing acceptance) rather than positive (belief increasing acceptance) as is commonly believed.

The misunderstanding of the 'belief bias' effect is endemic in the literature. For example, the mental models account of the effect (Oakhill & Johnson-Laird, 1985; Oakhill, Johnson-Laird & Garnham, 1989) is as follows. According to mental model theory people reason by forming a mental model of the premises and deriving a putative conclusion from it. This conclusion is then tested for its logical validity by searching for counterexamples: i.e. trying to find a model in which the premises hold and the conclusions does not. Belief bias is explained on the grounds that when the conclusion is believable, people accept it uncritically - short-circuiting the search for counter-examples. There are two problems with this account. First, it implies that people would normally be searching for counter-examples and that the influence of belief is positive rather than negative. Second, it can offer no account of belief bias effects on valid syllogisms where no counter-examples can be found to refute an unbelievable conclusion. Oakhill *et al.* (1989) were forced to propose a very unsatisfactory post-reasoning conclusion filter to account for this kind of finding.

I propose here a new model based theory of belief bias, which I call the Selective Processing Model (see Figure 2.1). This theory applies to the evaluation task where a conclusion is presented. It assumes that if a conclusion is either believable or neutral people will try to find a model which supports it. If such a model is found then the conclusion will be accepted. People do not normally search for counter-examples and therefore will endorse a fallacy in either case. When the conclusion is unbelievable, however, people attempt to find a model which refutes the conclusion. For invalid problems, such a model exists and is often found, leading to the large suppression of fallacies with unbelievable conclusions. This accounts for the negative and debiasing effect of belief.

The rationale for the Selective Processing Model is as follows. We normally reason inductively rather than deductively and habitually try to represent states of the world which we believe to be true. Hence, when presented with a conclusion for evaluation, the default approach is to try and prove it by constructing a model of the premises which includes it. Unbelievable conclusions, however, are uncongenial and potentially threatening to our belief system. Hence, the most satisfactory outcome is to find a model of the premises which excludes such conclusions. If this fails, however, we may still not accept the conclusion on the basis that at least one premise must be unbelievable. This last assumption is additional to the model shown in Figure 2.1 but is well supported by recent evidence that people are reluctant to accept arguments based on false premises (George, 1995; Stevenson & Over, 1995; Thompson, 1996). It explains the presence of belief bias on valid problems, even very simple ones where it should be easy to see that no counter-example models exist (as shown by Oakhill *et al.*, 1989).

The selective processing model is well supported by recent evidence we have gathered in a large programme of experimentation on syllogistic reasoning

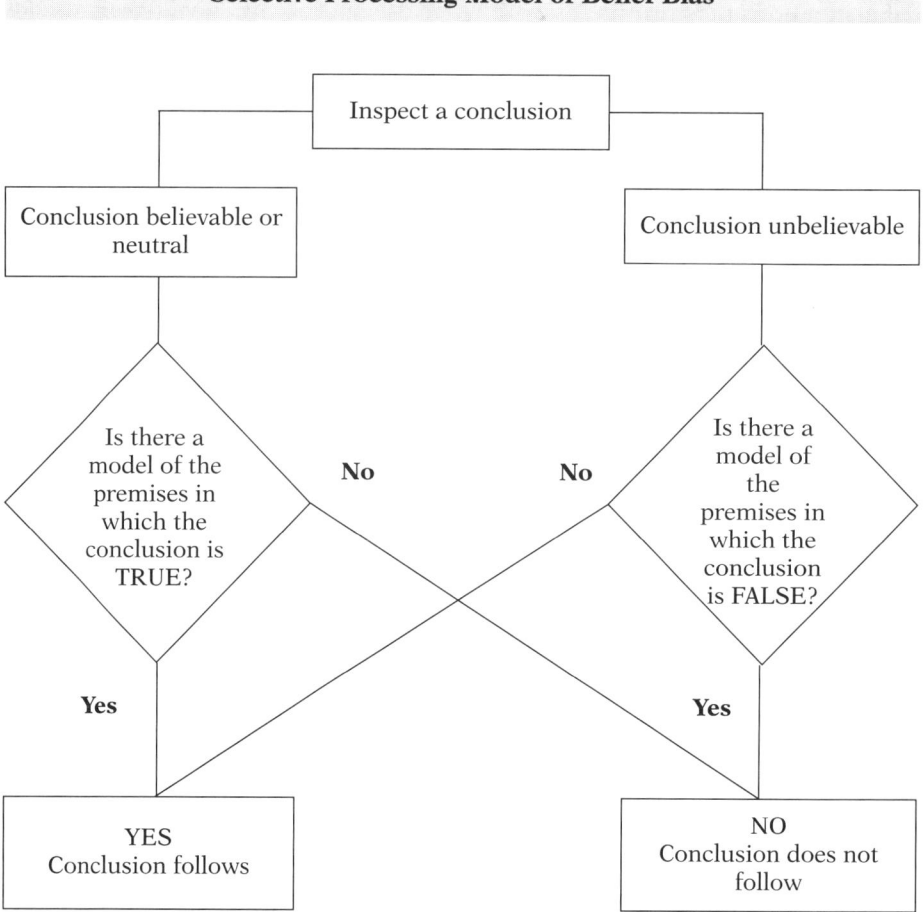

Figure 2.1. The Selective Processing Model of Belief Bias.

(Evans & Handley, 1996). Our earlier experiments studied abstract syllogisms only, but unusually required participants to consider every possible combination of premises and conclusions in a conclusion evaluation task. By this method, we discovered two distinct kinds of fallacies which we called Possible Strong and Possible Weak problems. In both cases, the conclusion present is possible (could be true) but not necessary (need not be true) given the premises. On Possible Strong problems, people very frequently endorse the conclusion, in fact as frequently as they endorse conclusion to valid syllogisms. On Possible Weak problems, however, endorsement rates are very low. We replicated these effects by presenting the same syllogisms in different experiments.

   Our interpretation here is that people are not searching for counterexamples. They accept a fallacious conclusion if the first model of the premises which comes to mind happens to support the conclusion (Possible Strong or PS) but not if the first model fails to support the conclusion (Possible Weak or PW). Johnson-Laird (personal communication) has found that his computational theory syllogistic reasoning fits this analysis. That is, the first model of the premises generated by the program supports the conclusion for PS but not PW problems in nearly all cases. Now, it turns out that the syllogisms used by Evans et al (1983) and in most other belief bias studies are of the type we call Possible Strong, i.e. ones where fallacies would normally be endorsed even if the conclusion was abstract or neutral.

In a later experiment Evans & Handley investigated belief bias on three kinds of problem: Necessary (valid), Possible Strong and Possible Weak. The results are shown in Figure 2.2. On Necessary problems we see equally high acceptance rates for Believable and Neutral Conclusions are predicted by the model and a small dip in acceptances Unbelievable Conclusions. On Possible Strong problems, there is again little difference in acceptance rates between Believable and Neutral problems but a substantial drop in acceptance of Unbelievable conclusions. This is exactly as the Selective Processing Model would predict. On this kind of problem a model supporting the conclusion comes to mind and will normally be accepted. However, when the conclusion is unbelievable people search for a model which refutes the conclusion which is there to be found.

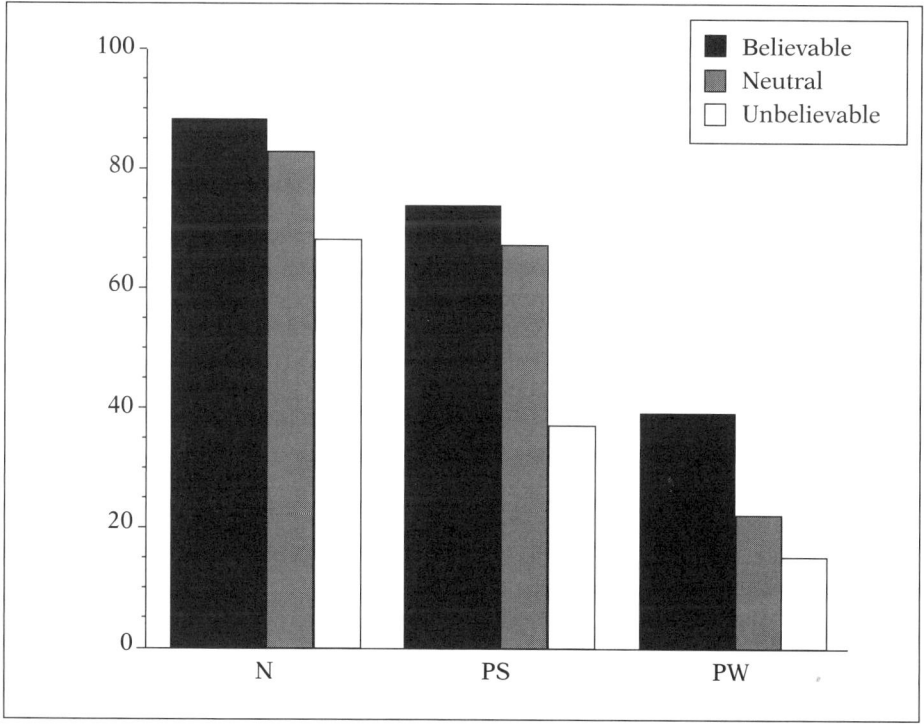

Figure 2.2. Study of belief bias by Evans & Handley (1996) using Necessary (N), Possible Strong (PS) and Possible Weak (PW) syllogisms.

To our knowledge, this is the first and only study to have investigated belief bias on Possible Weak syllogisms: recall that these are ones where although there is a model supporting the conclusion, it is not the one that usually comes to mind. For these syllogisms, we now find that the usual negative belief bias is absent: acceptance rates are equally low when the conclusion is neutral or unbelievable. This is because it is not normally easy to think of a model for such syllogisms which supports the conclusion: even though such a model exists. However, when the conclusion is believable, a small but significant positive belief bias is observed. Quite why this occurs is a matter for conjecture. It is one thing to accept a believable conclusion when it supported by the model that comes to mind without looking for a counter-examples (as on Possible Strong problems) but another to accept as valid a conclusion for which a counter-example has already been found. It may be, then, that for some participants the believable conclusion facilitates construction of the confirming model, so that this comes to mind first rather than the usual falsifying case.

What does the belief bias literature tell us about the influence of belief on thinking? These studies show effects that are irrational2 in that the instruction to decide the validity of an argument should not depend upon the believability of its conclusion and also because fallacies are frequently accepted even if the materials are neutral. However, we have seen that the effects of belief are generally facilitatory rather than biasing with regard to logic, in that the main finding is the suppression of fallacies with unbelievable conclusions. The Selective Processing Model is rational1 if we suppose that it is generally adaptive to combine the present information with relevant prior belief in order to model the most plausible or likely state of affairs.

Thus when focussing on a statement (conclusion) that we believe, we try to find evidence for it by constructing a mental model consistent with our beliefs in which it occurs. If the conclusion is unbelievable then we effectively try to construct a model which supports is negation. If the conclusion is fallacious we will thus reject it. If the conclusion is valid and unbelievable, we might also reject it because at least one premise will conflict with our prior belief. It is not rational1 to construct models which are inconsistent with our beliefs in either premises or conclusions.

PSEUDODIAGNOSTICITY

Suppose that we are trying to decide between two alternative hypothesis —H1 and H2— on the basis of some evidence or datum, D. According to Bayes' theorem, we should compute the posterior odds between the two hypotheses taking into account both the prior odds that the likelihood ratio provided by the evidence. Formally, this is expressed as

$$\frac{P\left(H_1/D\right)}{P\left(H_2/D\right)} = \frac{P\left(H_1\right)}{P\left(H_2\right)} \times \frac{P\left(D/H_1\right)}{P\left(D/H_2\right)}$$

The posterior odds reflect our relative belief in the two hypotheses after sampling the evidence. The prior odds reflect the base rates - our degree of belief in the hypotheses before we saw the evidence. The likelihood ratio reflects the degree to which the evidence is diagnostic, that is able to distinguish between the two hypotheses. Pseudodiagnostic reasoning occurs when we are impressed that a hypothesis H is supported by a datum because P(D/H) is high, without considering the value of P(D/.25H).

As an example, suppose that you switch on a television set in the UK and see an unfamiliar politician —say a newly elected MP— being interviewed. You try to decide whether he is a member of the Conservative or Labour parties. Suppose the man says he is against any policy to increase income tax. You might reason that he is probably a Conservative on the grounds that you know most Conservative MPs are opposed to increases in tax. However, this would be pseudodiagnostic because you would not be taking into account the fact that these days most Labour MPs oppose increases in income tax as well. Suppose instead you hear an assertion that the man is in favour of restoring the death penalty. You know that this is a view held by perhaps half of the Conservative MPs. Yet here you could confidently infer that the man is a Conservative because almost no Labour MPs share this view.

A paradigm for studying pseudodiagnostic reasoning has been proposed by Doherty, Mynatt, Tweney and Schiavo (1979). In a recent variant of this paradigm, Mynatt, Doherty and Dragan (1993) presented the following problem:

Your sister has a car she bought a couple of years ago. It's either a car X or a car Y but you can't remember which. You do remember that her car does over 25 mile per gallon and has not had any major mechanical problems in the two years she's owned it.

You have the following piece of information:

1. 65% of car Xs do over 25 miles per gallon.

Three additional pieces of information are also available:

2. The percentage of car Yx that do over 25 miles per gallon.
3. The percentage of car Xs that have had no major mechanical problems for the first two years of ownership.
4. The percentage of car Ys that have had no major mechanical problems for the first two years of ownership.

Participants must then choose to know just one of the pieces of information 2, 3 and 4. Mynatt *et al* argue that the correct choice is 2, because it provides a potentially diagnostic comparison between the two hypotheses whereas the typical choice of 1 is pseudodiagnostic, focussing on the hypothesis supported by the first piece of evidence.

I must take issue with this normative analysis because it does not take into account the background beliefs of the participants. In the earlier example, I argued that knowing an MP was in favour of capital punishment was diagnostic of him being Conservative, but this is based on background beliefs which provide the information that few politicians of other parties support this policy. In the sister's car problem above, both pieces of information are of a type we call common, i.e. both are quite likely events. Suppose we have a situation where one piece of information is common and the other rare. Imagine that we say that we remember that the car has a radio and a top speed of 160 mph. We are then told that car X has a radio.

According to the analysis of Mynatt *et al*, the correct choice of information is now to ask whether car Y has a radio. However, the expected diagnosticity of such information is actually low. Most cars have radios, so car Y will probably turn out to have a radio. Hence, we will be no further on in deciding between X and Y. However, few cars have a top speed of 160 mph. If we discover that X does, then we could feel that the car is likely to be an X, because are information is implicitly diagnostic. That is our background beliefs indicate that the chance of car Y also having such a top speed are low. Of course, if you add some further information such as - my sister always buys high performance sports cars - then the probabilities would change again. In fact, Aidan Feeney and I have shown in several unpublished experiments that when one feature is common and the other rare, most participants ask for information about the rare feature, whether or not this leads to the so-called diagnostic or pseudodiagnostic choices. A recent study by Feeney, Evans and Clibbens (1998) used a variation on the pseudodiagnostic paradigm in which people were presented with datum 1 in combination with either data 2 or 3. They did not have the opportunity to choose their own information, but instead were asked to rate their degree of belief in the hypotheses after viewing both the first and the second piece of information presented. In Experiment 1 participants were given pseudodiagnostic pairings concerning two features (F1 and F2) and the same hypothesis. Some evidence was strong: 95% of X's have F1 and some weak: 75% of X's have F1. For example, in the sister's car problem, they might be told first that 95% of X's do over 25 mpg and second that 75% of car X's are free of mechanical problems. This would be the order strong-weak. Other participants received the weak evidence before the strong. This manipulation resulted in a recency effect. That is, people were more impressed overall with the evidence if they received the stronger evidence second. Such recency (or primacy) effects are generally considered to be evidence of non-Bayesian reasoning as the order of evidence is irrelevant in Bayesian revision. The two features used were also either both common or both rare. Belief ratings were significantly higher when rare features were used, supporting our claim that people consider such evidence to be implicitly diagnostic by introduction of their background beliefs.

In a second experiment, Feeney *et al* provided two pieces of information which completed the likelihood ratio: that is P(F1/H1) and P(F1/H2). The belief rating task is of course exactly the same after the first piece of information and only differs when both have been presented. As was also the case in Experiment 1, people rated a stronger belief in the hypothesis in the first rating if the first information given was strong rather than weak, or based on a rare rather than a common feature. After the second piece of information was given, however, the results were quite different. The recency effect disappeared as did the effect of feature rarity. In other words, once the likelihood ratio is completed then people discard beliefs and order effects and base their final judgement on the diagnostic evidence which is explicitly available.

These experiments are particularly interesting with regard to the rationality1/rationality2 distinction. As with the interpretation of belief bias, I would argue that it is rational1 to base reasoning upon all relevant belief. Actually, in the experiments described in this section one could argue that it is also rational2 to introduce background beliefs, since there is no instruction to base judgements only on the information explicitly provided. The fact that the influence of feature rarity disappears in the second experiment of the Feeney, Evans and Clibbens study, but only after the likelihood ratio has been completed, is evidence that people do have some competence for rational2 reasoning in the Bayesian domain. The same conclusion is supported by some of our other work. For example, Girotto, Evans and Legrenzi (in preparation) found that if no anchor was given and people were asked simply to choose to learn two of the four possible pieces of information, they chose 'diagnostic' pairings on 71% of occasions as compared with just 25% in the anchored condition.

CONCLUSIONS

It is clear from the examples discussed here that prior beliefs associated with the problem materials used in our experiments exert strong influence on the experimental tasks, even if the instructions define the tasks in such a way that such beliefs are formally irrelevant. Such influences are rational1 in the terms of Evans and Over (1996) since they operate implicitly and habitually in such way as to be normally effective in achieving our goals. Specifically, we have seen (a) that prior beliefs assist people in make appropriate choices on deontic versions of the Wason selection task, (b) that people can avoid fallacious arguments when these lead to unbelievable conclusions and (c) that people are able to take appropriate account of background beliefs in assessing the value of statistical evidence.

We have also seen evidence that people can suspend their beliefs and engage in explicit reasoning in the context of experimental instructions. Some people —high in general intelligence— can solve indicative abstract versions of the selection task where prior beliefs are unable to assist. Strong emphasis on logical necessity can induce a more deductive mode of reasoning in syllogistic reasoning tasks in which (a) fallacies can be avoided with abstract materials and (b) the influence of belief is less marked when materials are thematic.

In the study of Feeney *et al*, described above, it was also shown that while background beliefs are taken into account in the assessment of evidence, these beliefs may be discarded when a completed likelihood ratio is avaliable, rendering such beliefs irrelevant. All of these facts point to the conclusion that people have a (limited) capacity to be rational2 as well as rational1.

ACKNOWLEDGEMENTS

This research was supported in part by a grant from the Economic and Social Research Council of the United Kingdom (R000222426).

REFERENCES

ANDERSON, J. R. (1990): *The Adaptive Character of Thought*. Hillsdale, N.J.: Erlbaum
BERRY, D. C. & DIENES, Z. (1993): *Implicit Learning*. Hove: Erlbaum.
CHENG, P. W. & HOLYOAK, K. J. (1985): «Pragmatic reasoning schemas». *Cognitive Psychology*, 17, 391-416.
DOHERTY, M. E., MYNATT, C. R., TWENEY, R. D. & SCHIAVO, M. D. (1979): «Pseudodiagnosticity». *Acta Psychologica*, 43, 11-21.
EVANS, J. St. B. T. (1998): «Inspection times, relevance and reasoning: A reply to Roberts». *Quarterly Journal of Experimental Psychology*, 51A, 815-818.
— (1993): «Bias and rationality». In K.I. Manktelow & D.E. Over (Eds). *Rationality*. London:Routledge.
— (1995): «Relevance and reasoning». In S.E. Newstead & J.St.B.T. Evans (Ed.). *Perspectives on Thinking and Reasoning*. Hove: Erlbaum. pp 147-172.
— (1996): «Deciding before you think: Relevance and reasoning in the selection task». *British Journal of Psychology*, 87, 223-240.
EVANS, J. St. B. T. & CLIBBENS, J. (1995): «Perspective shifts in the selection task: Reasoning or relevance?» *Thinking & Reasoning 1*, 315-323.
EVANS, J. St. B. T. & OVER, D. E. (1996): *Rationality and Reasoning*. Hove: Psychology Press.
EVANS, J. St. B. T. & POLLARD, P. (1990): «Belief bias and problem complexity in deductive reasoning». In J. P. Caverni, J. M. Fabre & M. Gonzales (Eds.). *Cognitive Biases*. Amsterdam: North-Holland.
EVANS, J. St. B. T., BARSTON, J. L., & POLLARD, P. (1983): «On the conflict between logic and belief in syllogistic reasoning». *Memory and Cognition*, 11, 295-306.
EVANS, J. St. B. T., NEWSTEAD, S. E., & BYRNE, R. M. J. (1993): *Human Reasoning: The Psychology of Deduction*. Hove & London: Erlbaum.
FEENEY, A., EVANS, J. St. B. T., & CLIBBENS, J. (1998): «Interpreting information when thinking about alternatives: Do background beliefs about evidence play a role?» Manuscript submitted for publication.
GEORGE, C. (1995): «The endorsement of the premises: assumption based or belief-based reasoning». *British Journal of Psychology*, 86, 93-113.
HOLYOAK, K. & CHENG, P. (1995): «Pragmatic reasoning with a point of view». *Thinking & Reasoning*, 1, 289-400.
MANKETELOW, K. I., & OVER, D. (1991): «Social roles and utilities in reasoning with deontic conditionals». *Cognition*, 39, 85-105.
MYNATT, C. R., DOHERTY, M. E., & DRAGAN, W. (1993): «Information relevance, working memory and the consideration of alternatives». *Quarterly Journal of Experimental Psychology*, 46A, 759-778.
NEWSTEAD, S. E., POLLARD, P., EVANS, J. St. B. T., & ALLEN, J. (1992): «The source of belief bias in syllogistic reasoning». *Cognition* 45, 257-284.
OAKHILL, J. & JOHNSON-LAIRD, P. N. (1985): «The effect of belief on the spontaneous production of syllogistic conclusions». *Quarterly Journal of Experimental Psychology*, 37A, 553-570.

OAKHILL, J., JOHNSON-LAIRD, P. N., & GARNHAM, A. (1989): «Believability and syllogistic reasoning». *Cognition*, 31, 117-140.

POLLARD, P. & EVANS, J. St. B. T. (1987): «On the relationship between content and context effects in reasoning». *American Journal of Psychology*, 100, 41-60.

REBER, A. S. (1993): *Implicit Learning and Tacit Knowledge*. Oxford: Oxford University Press.

ROBERTS, M. J. (1998): «Inspection times and the selection task: Are they relevant?» *Quarterly Journal of Experimental Psychology*, 51A, 781-810.

SPERBER, D., CARA, F., & GIROTTO, V. (1995): «Relevance theory explains the selection task». *Cognition*, 57, 31-95.

STANOVICH, K. E. & WEST, R. F. (1998): «Cognitive ability and variation in selection task performance». *Thinking & Reasoning*, 4, 193-230.

STEVENSON, R. & OVER, D. E. (1995): «Deduction from uncertain premises». *Quarterly Journal of Experimental Psychology*, 48A, 613-643.

THOMPSON, V. (1996): «Reasoning form false premises: The role of soundness in making logical deductions». *Canadian Journal of Experimental Psychology*, 50, 315-319.

WILKINS, M. C. (1928): «The effect of changed material on the ability to do formal syllogistic reasoning». *Archives of Psychology*, New York, No.102.

3

ARGUMENT AND OPINION

David W. Green

Los individuos y los grupos de individuos alcanzan decisiones y logran opiniones a través del habla. Necesitamos, por tanto, una teoría que abarque tanto la cognición individual, como la distribuida. Este capítulo propone y analiza una extensión de la teoría de los modelos mentales adaptada a tal tarea, en la que que se incorpora la noción de argumento (en forma sucinta, una declaración y una razón; por ejemplo: «el Reino Unido debería entrar en la Unión Económica y Monetaria ya que mejorará el comercio y la economía»). Desde esta perspectiva, las decisiones y las opiniones dependen de las acciones argumentativas que los individuos llevan a cabo (por ejemplo, si consideran o no los argumentos en contra un determinado curso de acción). Existe la necesidad de comprender la naturaleza de estas acciones dentro de los individuos, así como de considerar cómo las acciones argumentativas operan en la toma de decisiones en los grupos (el caso de la cognición distribuida). Este capítulo aborda las relaciones entre los argumentos y las opiniones expresadas en el caso individual, utilizando la noción de modelo de argumento. La opinión sobre asuntos prácticos debería depender de la fuerza de los argumentos a favor y en contra de determinada acción. Se describen dos nuevos estudios que examinaron las opiniones de los individuos sobre la entrada o no del Reino Unido en la Unión Económica y Monetaria (EMU). Los análisis de regresión multiple de los datos realizados en el primer estudio mostraron que la fuerza de los argumentos a favor era un predictor significativo de la opinión. En un segundo estudio se utilizó un método de diagramas que proporciona a los individuos un sistema natural de representación de las interconexiones entre los diferentes factores implicados en un asunto como la EMU (por ejemplo, la moneda común y la independencia política). Los individuos dibujaron sendas o caminos en los diagramas que representaban las conexiones tal y como las veían. Cada senda corresponde a un argumento; es decir, una declaración con una fuerza determinada y una razón implícita. Un factor puede ofrecer un argumento directo a favor de entrar en la EMU y uno indirecto en contra. El estudio confirmó que como mejor se predecía la opinión era mediante la fuerza relativa de los argumentos entrelazados a favor y en contra de la EMU, más que por la fuerza de los argumentos directos solos o por el número relativo de argumentos a favor y en contra. Se propone que la opinión es el resultado de un proceso de integración que implica la fuerza de los argumentos en un modelo de argumento. Se consideran, asimismo, brevemente algunas extensiones de esta explicación al caso de la cognición distribuida.

INTRODUCTION

Individuals think and reach decisions. Human beings are also social agents and reach decisions as a consequence of social interaction. We need a theory of both individual and collective rationality: of individual and distributed cognition. The aim of this paper is to contribute to the construction of such a theory. The route involves extending the theory of mental models by incorporating a specific level of representation to do with arguments. Here we define an argument as comprising a claim and a reason (e.g., Voss & Means, 1991) and allow for arguments to be interconnected in various ways.

Why extend the theory of mental models? Surely, it is general enough in some senses. Tokens and relations in the model correspond to entities and their relations in either actual or hypothetical states of affairs. Moreover, mental models can be derived from both perception and discourse (Johnson-Laird, 1983) and so allow the construction of shared representations. But in group discussion (e.g., where to eat) individuals adduce arguments for some course of action or decision; that is they make a claim and provide a reason for it. Moreover these arguments can be referenced and considered. We need to be able to represent them explicitly. Consider other examples of distributed cognition: the construction of a scientific model - such a model is a product of arguments contributed by different groups of individuals. Likewise the decision to invest by a multi-national firm is product of argument involving different individuals (or groups) within an organization (cf. Mason & Mitroff, 1981).

The notion that arguments are a separate level of representation can also be made in the context of individual thinking. For instance. in the abstract selection task, Green (1995) proposed that individuals seek reasons for their selections: the selection of a given card (e.g.,A) can be based on different reasons (e.g., because A is mentioned in the rule or because a 7 on the other side would prove the rule false). Decision and actions are argument-based (see also Lipshitz, 1995). Indeed, consistent with this idea, Moshman and Geil (1998) has shown how individuals reasoning together can outperform individuals working alone on the abstract selection task. In such a context individuals can hear and listen to arguments about different courses of action and assess their merits.

In informal reasoning, a reason for some action/decision or opinion might either be cognitive or affective and it might appeal to the way some system works (i.e. to the output of a mental model of the system). Likewise an argument might either support or undercut some other argument. This implies that individuals must not only be able to represent these arguments, they must also possess procedures for reaching decisions in the light of reasons either for or against some option. In informal reasoning, a decision or opinion may be based on relative benefit over cost -where such benefits and costs are not restricted to a purely fiscal calculation. In short, there must be operations other than model construction and validation in informal reasoning. There are trade-offs to be made.

In developing an account of individual and distributed cognition there are two requirements: a requirement to understand more about the relationship between arguments and decisions/opinions in individual thinking and a requirement to construct the theoretical apparatus so that it can apply to model distributed cognition. The present paper is directed at the first issue: to what extent do argumentative actions affect decisions or opinions?

Shafir, Simonson and Tversky (1993) proposed that in the absence of a compelling reason to do so individuals may be unable to reach a decision: their data were consistent with such a claim but reasons were not explored. We have shown (Green, McClelland, Muckli, & Simmons, 1999) that deontic decisions (e.g., amount of fine a restaurant should pay in the event of a case of food poisoning) do reflect the reason generated or endorsed and that where more than one reason is presented for consideration that decisions reflect whether the unendorsed reason is explicitly rebutted or not. In other words, argumentative actions change the decisions that individuals reach. We also confirmed that individuals adjust their decisions in the light of additional arguments that are explicitly presented.

However, to what extent do individuals spontaneously consider different reasons when reaching an opinion about some issue? and how do these reasons relate to their opinions? Baron (1995; see also Perkins,1989) demonstrated that individuals show a myside bias: when asked to list arguments on an emotive issue (e.g., abortion) they produced arguments related only to their own opinion. It is conceivable that such a bias is the norm. Kuhn (1991), for example, in an in-depth study of argumentation skills, reports a frequent failure to consider counter-arguments. But such a failure is not ubiquitous. In a study of juror reasoning, Kuhn, Weinstock and Flaton (1994) distinguished individuals who constructed a single narrative of the events (see Pennington & Hastie, 1993) and ignored conflicting evidence, with those who constructed multiple stories to handle the conflicting evidence. The former chose more extreme verdict categories than the latter. Individual differences appear to exist in the handling of conflicting information - indeed Baron (1995) has suggested that individuals may differ in their beliefs on what counts as a good argument.

In everyday reasoning (about less emotive topics than abortion or rape) individuals might well draw up a kind of balance sheet of the factors pro or con some opinion or course of action. In such a balance sheet, the relative strength of pro and con arguments might be more important than the sheer number of arguments pro or con some action. In order to check this prediction, we asked individuals in the first study to imagine that they were going to take part in an audience discussion programme on whether or not the UK should join the Economic Monetary Union (EMU).

STUDY 1

Method

Participants: 60 unpaid adult volunteers run individually and debriefed after the study.

Design: The experiment involved a number of different phases that were completed in sequence with the exception that the order with which individuals rated their opinion on the UK joining EMU and the listing of points or arguments about EMU was counterbalanced over participants. There was no effect of this manipulation and so it will not be considered further. The descriptions of the end points of the opinion scale and strength scales were swopped round over participants.

Procedure: Individuals were presented with individual booklets. They first rated their knowledge on the issue of UK joining EMU (together three other controversial issues) and then either expressed their opinion on these issues before listing their points about EMU or listed their points about EMU first. Individuals rated their opinion by ringing one number on a series of seven-point scales (e.g., Definitely for 1 2 3 4 5 6 7 Definitely against).

After listing their points, individuals were asked to state whether or not each point or argument was either for or against the UK joining EMU and then to assess the strength of each one by writing ONE number next to each argument or point using the following scale:

Very weak 0 1 2 3 4 5 6 7 8 9 10 Very strong.

Results and Discussion

Opinion on whether or not the UK should join EMU averaged 4.00 [on the seven point scale running from Very definitely against (1) to very definitely for (7)] and unlike the data reported by Baron (1995) on abortion, nearly two-thirds of individuals provided arguments on both sides of the issue. Table 3.1 illustrates some of the arguments pro and con EMU which mostly divided into economic or political arguments. Predictably, the sheer number of arguments mentioned increased with the degree of self-rated knowedge on the issue.

TABLE 3.1
Examples of arguments in Study 1

Type of argument	Example
Economic	
pro	A common currency increase trade and boosts the economy
con	There will be a loss of economic control
Political	
pro	EMU will strengthen European integration and so prevent wars
con	The UK will lose its political independence

The primary interest of the study was the relationship between the number and strength of pro and con arguments and opinion. We used the strength and number of pro and con arguments in a multiple regression analysis rather than the differences in their strength and number because the Pearson correlations of these four variables with opinion showed a marked disparity. In this regression analysis, the multiple R was highly significant (R=0.65) but only the strength of pro arguments was a significant predictor. In contrast to prediction then, opinion was primarily correlated with the strength of arguments for EMU rather the relative strength of pro and con arguments.

Although the study provides evidence for the importance of the strength of argument, listing does not reveal the possible interrelationship of arguments. Yet it seems likely that individuals can appreciate that a factor such as a single currency throughout Europe can be both an argument for joining EMU because it makes trade easier and eliminates the cost of converting currency. It can also be an indirect argument against joining because it undercuts political independence which itself is an argument against joining. We need also to examine individual's perception of the interrelationship of factors and establish how the entire pattern of pro and con arguments correlates with opinion. This was the aim of the second study.

STUDY 2

We used a diagram method (see Green & McManus, 1995; Green, McManus & Derrick, 1998) in which individuals draw lines representing the interconnections between various issues as they see them. Requiring individuals to construct verbal arguments in the form of an essay or discourse may underestimate the extent to which they appreciate the interconnectedness factors because of the verbal sequential demands of discourse.

In Green and McManus (1995) individuals were required to diagram the factors (such as smoking, eating fatty foods, exercise, high blood pressure) affecting the risk of coronary heart disease. In such diagrams a factor might be linked directly to CHD and indirectly via some other factor (e.g., individuals perceived exercise to exert a direct effect on the risk of CHD and an indirect effect on the risk of CHD via a reduction in blood pressure). Individuals also rated the strength of each path in their diagram. Green and McManus computed the total path strength of each factor (the sum of strength of direct and indirect paths). Having completed their diagrams, individuals rated the effectiveness of actions based on these factors to reduce the risk of CHD. The total path strength of the factors was highly correlated with these ratings (see also Green, McManus & Derrick, 1998 where similar findings obtained in the domain of employment).

The basic idea in the present study was to use the diagram method to assess the extent to which the relative strength of argument (i.e., the strengths of direct **and** indirect paths in the diagrams) predicted opinion on whether or not the UK should join EMU. Individuals were asked about their views on Economic Monetary Union (EMU) using economic and political factors derived from Study 1.

Method

Participants: 40 unpaid adult volunteers recruited from the same source as Experiment 1 and run individually.

Materials and procedure: Participants were instructed as follows:

> The diagram below presents some issues relating to EMU. You may feel some are reasons for joining and some are reasons against joining. For example, if you feel that a single currency throughout Europe is a positive reason for joining EMU then you would draw a line **from** single currency **to** the EMU box (single currency => EMU) and place a plus sign (**+**) on that line. Alternatively, if you feel it is a reason against joining EMU then you would put a negative sign on the line.
>
> You might also feel that there are some connections between the issues. For instance, you may feel that an issue (single currency, say) will have a positive impact on European unity. In this example, you would draw a line **from** single currency **to** European unity : with the arrowhead facing towards European unity (=>) and put a plus sign on it. If, on the other hand, you feel that the single currency will have a negative impact on European unity, you would draw a line **from** single currency **to** European unity : with the arrowhead facing towards European unity (=>) and put a negative sign on it.
>
> Immediately below six issues (single currency throughout Europe, UK control of own economy, Economic growth in the UK, Europe as a major economic power, European unity, UK political independence) were printed clockwise around the acronym EMU.

Having drawn their diagrams, individuals were asked to rate the strength of the connections on a scale from 0 (very weak) to 10 (very strong). On the following page they were asked their current opinion on whether or not the UK should join the Economic Monetary Union by ringing one number on the scale: Very definitely against 0 1 2 3 4 5 6 7 8 9 10 Very definitely for. The end points of the scale were swopped round over participants.

Results and discussion

Overall opinion on the UK joining EMU was again equivocal [M = 4.90 - on a scale running from very definitely against (0) through to very definitely for (10)]. Figure 3.1 provides a composite representation of the paths (arguments) included by at least 10% of the sample of 40 participants. It also depicts their mean strengths.

All but seven participants provided both direct and indirect arguments. As expected, a factor such as a single currency throughout Europe was seen in both positive and negative terms. Of those including an indirect argument (n = 33), sixteen saw a single currency as a direct reason for joining EMU and an indirect reason for not joining (e.g., because it reduced the ability of the UK to control its own economy). Four others saw it as a direct reason against joining but an indirect reason for joining (e.g., because it promoted European unity which was itself considered a positive reason for joining).

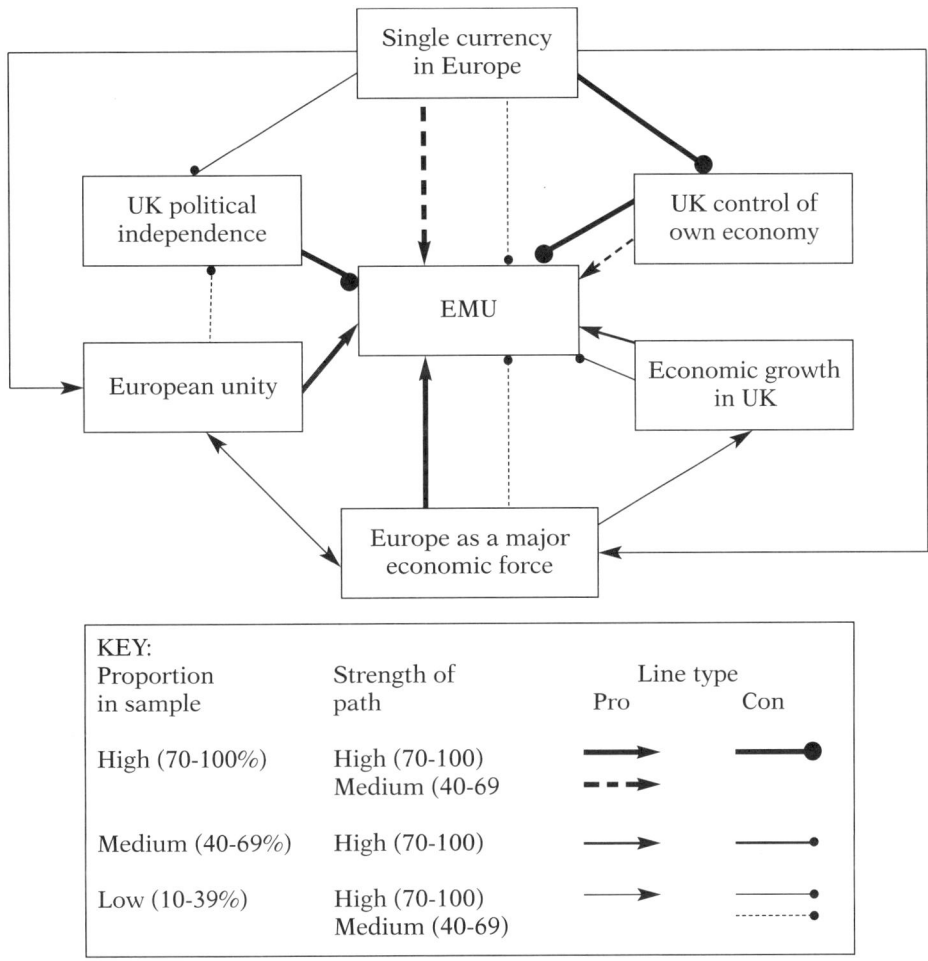

Figure 3.1. Composite diagram of arguments on Economic Monetary Union.

In order to examine the relationship between perception of the factors and opinion on joining EMU we computed the number of pro and con arguments (direct and indirect) for each factor as well as the strength of their pro and con arguments. In making these calculations, we treated an indirect argument as an argument for joining if it supported a direct argument for joining or undercut a direct argument against joining. Likewise, an indirect argument was an argument against joining when it either supported a direct argument against joining or undercut a positive argument. We computed the strength of an indirect argument in the following way: suppose individuals rated the strength of the argument connecting a common currency to European unity as 0.6 and the strength of the argument for EMU from European unity as 0.4 then the strength of the indirect argument from a common currency to EMU is $0.6 \times 0.4 = 0.24$. Given that the strength of the direct argument from a common currency to EMU is 0.5, the total strength of the argument from a common currency is 0.74 (0.5 + 0.24).

The correlations for the number of pro and the number of con arguments with opinion were equally strong - likewise the strength of pro and con arguments correlated equally strongly with opinion. We therefore contrasted the power of the relative strength of argument (the difference in the strength of pro and con arguments - direct and indirect) and the relative number of arguments in predicting opinion. Regressing both variables onto opinion yielded R= 0.76: relative strength was highly significant whereas relative number was marginal (p = 0.10).

In a further multiple regression analysis, we contrasted, as predictors of opinion, relative strength (which includes the contribution of indirect arguments) with the strength of the direct arguments alone. For those 33 participants who included an indirect argument, R = 0.80 but only relative argument strength was significant. In short, opinion is significantly predicted by the interrelationship of factors and specifically by their relative strength. Neither the number of arguments nor the strengths of direct arguments alone predicts opinion when relative strength is included in the regression analyses.

In summary, individuals diagrammed their views on EMU: each diagram encodes an individual's perceptions of the arguments about EMU though the reasons for the specific claims are not directly expressed. The study confirmed that a given issue (e.g., a single currency throughout Europe) can be perceived as both a direct argument for some action (here joining EMU) and as an indirect argument against it. It can also interconnect both economic and political factors. Further, the study supported the prediction that the relative strength of arguments (the sum of both direct and indirect paths) is a better predictor of opinion than either the relative strength of direct arguments alone or the relative number of pro versus con arguments.

GENERAL DISCUSSION

The aim of this paper was to explore the relationship between argument and opinion. In particular to examine the prediction that it is the relative strength of argument that is the key determinant of expressed opinion. Study 1 required individuals to list arguments to do with the UK joining EMU. In this situation, the strength of pro arguments rather than the relative strength was the major predictor of opinion. However, the process of listing arguments fails to allow individuals to express any interconnections amongst them. Study 2 confirmed that when individuals are allowed to express such interconnections then it is indeed the relative strength of argument that is critical. The strength of direct arguments alone (whether for or against) are inadequate predictors: the relative strength both direct and indirect arguments is the best predictor.

But are these correlations merely a product of the methodology? How do individuals reach their opinions? In the first study reported it is conceivable that they considered their opinion on the matter and judged the strength of the listed arguments or points with respect to it. In order to correlate with opinion individuals must keep track of their ratings of strength. But why should they do this? There was no task requirement to do so. The second study poses a further challenge for this view. Here individuals must also keep a tally of their strength ratings but in this case they must also compute the indirect connections between arguments.

It seems more plausible to suppose that expressed opinion reflects an implicit argument structure. In this case, opinion can reflect the integration of arguments with no explicit tally. We may think of this representation as an argument model - it can be expressed as separate verbal points or fleshed out as an exposition or be represented diagrammatically. The diagrams drawn in Study 2 make explicit certain claims (e.g., UK political independence is a reason to vote against EMU with strength 6/10) but leave implicit the reason (e.g., «because the UK will no longer be able to set its own policy»).

A number of questions may be asked of this representation. How is it constructed and changed? It may not preexist the study but be generated either in providing an opinion or in the course of producing points (Study 1)or considering connections between factors (Study 2). Other kinds of representations must be connected to it: e.g., the opinions of significant others, particular facts, mental models of the domain in question. For instance, in thinking about a particular issue: is it beneficial for the UK to join EMU economically? some individuals might simulate various possible worlds: how well is the economy likely to do if the UK does not join? what are the costs of not joining? The mental simulation of possibilities may therefore precede the representation of an argument: it provides a reason for the claim. Other individuals may simply retrieve the views of someone they trust or something they have heard. As Sperber (1996) argued the form and distribution of ideas in human groups derives from causal chains in which mental representations give rise to public representations (articles in the press, advertisements) which in turn elicit further mental representations and so forth.

On the present view, arguments play a causative role in the determination of opinion, decision or action (see also Green *et al.*, 1999). If so, opinion may change by the introduction of new distinct arguments or by a change in the strength of existing arguments (e.g., through undercutting or supporting them). New arguments can derive from other people and so the demonstration that opinion is sensitive to the relative strength of arguments provides a way in which group discussion can influence opinion.

There are likely to be various moderating factors. One factor which may be relevant to any change in opinion in the light of further arguments is the extent to which the arguments conflict with basic values (see Tetlock, 1986; Liberman & Chaiken, 1991). More complex argument models may be developed by individuals for whom basic values are in conflict. They have to trade-off one value against another. In other cases, additional arguments about an issue may lead to an articulation of a position rather than to any change in opinion as such (cf. Kuhn & Lao, 1996). However, such a change itself carries implication for distributed cognition because it allows explicit consideration of arguments.

An important aspect of an argument model (such as that depicted in composite form in Figure 1) is that it expresses not only explicit claims (the paths) but can also impound tacit information through the ratings of path or argument strength. The notion of an argument model therefore provides a way to interrelate explicit and implicit knowledge (Green, 1998). Accordingly, both types of knowledge can guide opinion and action.

ACKNOWLEDGEMENTS

I thank Rosita Shure for collecting the data and for contributing to the coding.

REFERENCES

BARON, J. (1995): «Myside bias in thinking about abortion». *Thinking and reasoning, 1*, 221-235.
GREEN, D. W. (1995): «The abstract selection task: thesis, antithesis and synthesis». In S. Newstead & J.St. B. T. Evans (Eds.), *Perspectives on thinking and reasoning*. Hove and London: Lawrence Erlbaum Associates.
— (1996): «Models, arguments and decisions». In J. Oakhill & A. Garnham (Eds.), *Mental Models in Cognitive Science: A Festschrift for Philip Johnson-Laird*. pp. 119-137. Hove: Psychology Press.
— (1998): «Cognition in context: an argument model approach to public representations». *Analise Psicologica* (Special Isssue), pp. 271-291.
GREEN, D. W., & MCCLELLAND, A., MUCKLI, L., & SIMMONS, C. (in press): «Arguments and deontic decision». *Acta Psychologica*.
GREEN, D. W. & MCMANUS, I. C. (1995): «Cognitive Structural Models: perception of risk and prevention in coronary heart disease». *British Journal of Psychology, 86*, 321-336.
GREEN, D. W., MCMANUS, I. C., & DERRICK, B. (1998): «Cognitive structural models of unemployment and employment». *British Journal of Social Psychology*, in press.
JOHNSON-LAIRD, P. N. (1983): *Mental models: Towards a Cognitive Science of Language, Inference and Consciousness*. Cambridge, MA: Harvard University Press.
KUHN, D. (1991): *The Skills of Argument*. Cambridge, England: Cambridge University Press.
KUHN, D., & LAO, J. (1996): «Effects of evidence on attitudes: Is polarization the norm?» *Psychological Science, 7*, 115-120.
KUHN, D., WEINSTOCK, M., & FLATON, R. (1994): «How well do jurors reason? Competence dimensions of individual variation in a juror reasoning task». *Psychological Science, 5*, 289-296.
LIBERMAN, A., & CHAIKEN, S. (1991): «Value conflict and thought-induced attitude change». *Journal of Experimental Social Psychology, 27*, 203-216.
LIPSHITZ, R. (1993): «Decision-making as argument-driven action». In G. A. Klein, J. Orasanu, & R. Calderwood, *Decision-making in action: models and methods*. Norwood, N.J.: Ablex Publishing Corp.
MASON, R. O., & MITROFF, I. I. (1981): *Challenging strategic planning assumptions: theory, cases and techniques*. New York: John Wiley & Sons.

MOSHMAN, D., & GEIL, M. (1998): «Collaborative reasoning: evidence for collective rationality». *Thinking and Reasoning, 4*, 231-248.

PENNINGTON, N., & HASTIE, R. (1993): «Reasoning in explanation-based decision-making». *Cognition, 49*, 123-163.

PERKINS, D. N. (1989): «Reasoning as it is and could be: an empirical perspective». In D. M. Topping, D. C. Crowell, & V. N. Kobayashi (Eds.), *Thinking across cultures: the third international conference on thinking*. Hillsdale, NJ: Lawrence Erlbaum Associates, cited in Baron (1995).

SHAFIR, E., SIMONSON, I., & TVERSKY, A. (1993): «Reason-based choice». *Cognition, 49*, 11- 36.

SPERBER, D. (1996): *Explaining Culture*. Oxford: Blackwell.

TETLOCK, P. E. (1986): «A value pluralism model of ideological reasoning». *Journal of Personality and Social Psychology, 45*, 118-126.

VOSS, J. F., & MEANS, M. L. (1991): «Learning to reason via instruction in argumentation». *Learning and Instruction, 1*, 337-350.

4

IN FAVOUR OF A UNIFIED MODEL
OF DEDUCTIVE REASONING

Bruno G. Bara
Monica Bucciarelli
Vincenzo Lombardo

Entre los diferentes tipos de razonamiento deductivo están el razonamiento silogístico, el relacional y el proposicional; éstos implican, respectivamente, razonar a partir de enunciados cuantificados, de premisas que contienen relaciones y de proposiciones que incluyen conectivas. La teoría de los modelos mentales (MMT; Johnson-Laird, 1983; Johnson-Laird & Byrne, 1991) explica y predice la actuación humana en estos tres campos del razonamiento. En Bara, Bucciarelli and Lombardo (1999), hemos propuesto un modelo computacional unificado del razonamiento deductivo mediante modelos mentales, que abarca los campos arriba mencionados del razonamiento silogístico, relacional y proposicional (UNICORE: UNIfied COmputer REasoner).

El modelo supone que cualquier tipo de razonamiento consta de cinco procesos principales: construcción de modelos mentales de las premisas, integración de modelos, formulación de conclusiones consistentes con los modelos integrados, falsificación de conclusiones y producción de respuestas. Para lograr esto, UNICORE supone que existe un conjunto de procedimientos que es común a cualquier tipo de deducción, y que forma parte de la competencia del sistema humano. La validez del modelo en los diferentes campos del razonamiento, proviene del hecho de que las predicciones de las respuestas de los sujetos se basan en un único mecanismo básico, cuyo funcionamiento puede verse afectado por una serie de restricciones cognitivas.

En este capítulo presentamos un experimento cuyo propósito es analizar las habilidades básicas implicadas en las diferentes fases de la deducción. En UNICORE algunas de las fases son dependientes de la tarea, mientras que otras son independientes. Los resultados del experimento apoyan la existencia de la serie de habilidades básicas supuestas por el modelo UNICORE de la deducción, contribuyendo así a reforzar su plausibilidad psicológica.

INTRODUCTION

The contribution of the different psychological theories to the understanding of deduction can be evaluated according to three criteria (see Bara *et al.*, 1999). First, the theory ought to scale up to explain multiple domains of reasoning: a global and parsimonious theory has to be preferred to a theory restricted to a single domain. Second, the theory ought to account for the differences in competence and performance. In particular, a theory should not only predict the correct responses, but also predict and explain, by means of its basic tenets, systematic errors. Third, the theory ought to explain developmental trends in deductive performance. This would ensure that the theory is better grounded than steady-state theories (Bara, 1995).

As for the first criterion, two relevant attempts for unified theories of deduction are those by Polk and Newell (1995) and Rips (1994). Polk and Newell (1995) propose, within the Soar unified architecture (Newell, 1990), the Verbal Reasoning Model. They argue that there are no specific mental processes devoted to reasoning: language comprehension and generation can give an account of the entire range of deductive phenomena. In particular, they analyze syllogistic reasoning and claim that it relies on the encoding and decoding of the verbal information given in the premises. Their proposal is an alternative theory within the model-based paradigm, but it states that the search for counter-examples plays little or no role in syllogistic reasoning. However, recent studies show that the search for counter-examples is a fundamental step of syllogistic reasoning (Bucciarelli & Johnson-Laird, 1999), and though SOAR might be extended in principle to incorporate developmental aspects of syllogistic reasoning (second and third requirements), current it does cover only the syllogistic domain.

Rips (1994) makes an attempt of unified theory of deduction inside the mental logic paradigm, and claims the existence of a central deductive mechanism devoted to formal reasoning. He reproduces the mental processes through a system named PSYCOP which, when presented with premise-conclusion pairs, uses a set of formal rules to construct the lines of a proof. Among the models based on formal rules of inference, this is the best account of both syllogistic and propositional reasoning. However, it has the major limitation of not accounting for consistent patterns of erroneous inferences (see Johnson-Laird, 1997), and developmental issues and relational inferences have not been considered.

Besides these relevant attempts for unified theories of deduction, there exist many microtheories developed to account for single domains. In particular, microtheories for syllogistic reasoning (e.g. Guyote & Sternberg, 1981, and Stenning & Oberlander, 1995), relational reasoning (e.g. Bar-Hillel, 1967, and Clark, 1969) and propositional reasoning (e.g. Braine, 1978, 1990, 1998; Braine & Rumain, 1983; Inhelder & Piaget, 1958; Piaget, 1953; Rips, 1990). Other microtheories have been formulated to account for a single phenomenon inside a single domain, as in the case of conditional reasoning (e.g. Cheng & Holyoak, 1985; Cosmides & Tooby, 1994; Gigerenzer & Hug, 1992; Griggs & Cox, 1982; Platt & Griggs, 1993; Pollard, 1981). A common property of all such microtheories is their limited scope: they lack a unified view of the deductive process. Also within mental model theory, the present state of the art does not offer a synthetic theory able to realize the paradigmatic claim of the mental model approach. Thus, one finds a constellation of microtheories, each devoted to analyze a specific sector of reasoning. Unfortunately, model microtheories are dishomogeneous among them, because they differ even in the crucial choices, like the primitive concepts and the basic abilities assumed as their foundations.

The debate whether the deductive capability is a unique machinery or a collection of micro-mechanisms needs further psychological evidence to be solved in either way. In this paper we present an experiment where results support the view of a unified machinery for deduction. In a previous work we have stressed the importance of unified models of deduction (Bara *et al.*, 1999), and we have presented UNICORE, a unified model of deductive reasoning which follows the basic tenets of MMT. The model is fully consistent with the microtheories developed within the mental model framework, and it does satisfy the three dimensions which assess the acceptability of a theory of deductive reasoning. The core of the system relies on a series of abilities that require some empirical evidence, which we are going to search in this paper.

THE REASONING PROCESS IN UNICORE

We assume that the reasoning process consists of the five phases illustrated in Figure 4.1.

The *Construction phase* takes as input the linguistic or perceptual premises of the task at hand and returns as output their model representations. In UNICORE, this phase is considered as a black box that translates the premises into their propositional representations, and then the latter into the mental models that are passed to the reasoning mechanism. As a consequence, UNICORE does not take into account possible incomplete representations of the input, due to the lack of general or linguistic knowledge.

Integration phase takes as input the models of the premises and returns as output an integrated model. This integrated model, which is the first result of the exploration in the space of the integrated models, is then passed to Conclusion, in order to extract the relevant information for a specific deductive task (e.g., syllogistic inferences, relational inferences, propositional inferences). If Integration fails to produce any integrated model, the reasoning process yields a failure, which interrupts the reasoning process.

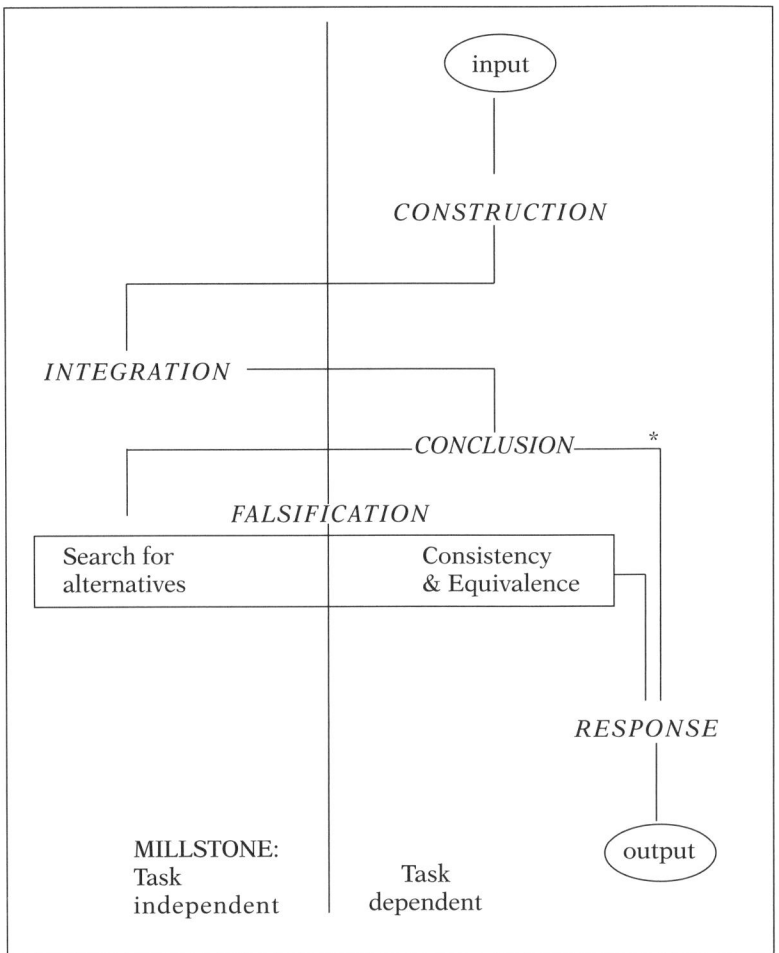

Figure 4.1. The reasoning process. * marks the erroneous control flow.

Conclusion phase takes as input an integrated model and produces a result model, which represents a first putative conclusion. For example, in the case of syllogistic reasoning, Conclusion marks the tokens and relations concerning the end terms. This result model becomes the (unique) current model in the working memory. In case there are no information relevant for the task, Conclusion exits with FAILURE.

The reasoning program maintains only one result model in the working memory, i.e. the current result model. The result model which is in the working memory after visiting the whole space of the integrated models will be passed to the Response phase.

After Conclusion, the control can flow in two directions: the correct one goes to Falsification; the erroneous one (which is marked by *) goes to Response, and shortens the reasoning process. This premature exit of the reasoning process, due either to the limited capacity of the working memory or to a poor degree of mastery of Falsification, can explain several data about subjects' erroneous conclusions.

The asterisk in the Figure (*) indicates that it is premature to exit at this point, because the conclusion which is based on the first integrated model may be falsified by a further integrated model of the premises. In case of failure, the control passes directly to the Response phase, which acts consequently (see below).

Falsification phase takes as input a putative conclusion (first result model), and gives as output a validated result model. It consists of *Search-for-alternatives* and *Consistency-&-Equivalence*. Each time it is invoked, Search-for-alternatives tries to produce a new integrated model (if any) of the premises. This integrated model is then passed to Consistency-&-Equivalence. Consistency-&-Equivalence first invokes Conclusion, which produces a new result model, and then detects the possible presence of contradictions between the current result model in the working memory and the new result model just yielded. If it does not detect any contradiction, but realizes that the new model supports the same conclusion as the current result model, Consistency-&-Equivalence leaves the working memory unaltered. Otherwise, if the new model does support a looser conclusion than the current result model, it replaces the current result model with the new result model. For instance, a model where 'Some A are C' supports a looser conclusion than a model where 'All A are C'. Finally, if it detects a contradiction, i.e. the two models support inconsistent conclusions, it generates INCONSISTENCY and passes it to the Response phase. When Search-for-alternatives exhausts the integrated models, the control goes to the Response phase.

In case of success of the previous phases, *Response phase* takes as input the current result model in the working memory and translates it into linguistic or motorial responses. Otherwise (either the flag FAILURE or INCONSISTENCY has been raised), it interprets the failure according to the task.

Detailed descriptions of the procedures which implement the five phases of the reasoning process are in Bara *et al.* (1999).

TASK DEPENDENT AND TASK INDEPENDENT PHASES OF THE REASONING PROCESS

Deduction occurs through some task dependent and some task independent procedures (see Figure 4.1).

The integration procedures and part of the falsification procedures (Search-for-alternatives) are task independent; they form a core system which we call *Millstone*. Construction, Conclusion, part of the falsification procedures (Consistency-&-Equivalence), and Response are task dependent.

The computational model UNICORE relies on the central role of the Millstone, which represents the core of the unified mechanisms for reasoning.

From an architectural point of view, however, deduction is conceived as the fruit of a continuous interaction between the Millstone and the task dependent procedures. As the latter behave in different ways depending on the task at hand, they link the core deductive processes and the context within which they operate. Moreover, the interface between the Millstone and the environment, represented by the task dependent phases, is sensible to the system's goals; in UNICORE the type of task counts as a pragmatic factor which influence the model manipulation process.

Thus, the context within which deduction occurs contributes to determine the sort of conclusion (either correct or erroneous) drawn by the reasoner. In particular, the experience of the subject in a specific reasoning domain will affect the reasoning process. We assume that the experience in a specific domain increases with increasing age.

In our view, the task independent phases of the reasoning process rely on some innate predispositions in the reasoner to make sense of the world; thus, the development of the ability to reason rely on the interaction between the mind and the environment. In particular, according to UNICORE, the innate pre-dispositions are the ability to integrate information in a single model, and the ability to search for alternative models of such information.

The ability to integrate information is involved in our ability to make sense of the world. An unpublished experiment by Johnson-Laird and Anderson (cited in Johnson-Laird, 1993) shows that subjects —when invited to consider two sentences randomly chosen by two different stories— are very good in making sense of them, by constructing plausible scenarios.

The ability to search for alternative models is also involved in our ability to comprehend and predict events of the world. As Bucciarelli and Johnson-Laird claim in this volume, the ability to conceive of alternative models of reality characterizes our abilities to attribute emotional states, perceptions, and mental states.

BASIC ABILITIES NECESSARY TO REASON

The architecture of UNICORE is based on a series of assumptions about the abilities the system must possess, in order to be capable to make deductions. The initial choices on which are the basic abilities have been made according to the findings of a pioneering experiment on the development of syllogistic reasoning (Bara, Bucciarelli & Johnson-Laird, 1995). The basic abilities involved in the task dependent phases should not be necessarily involved in any sort of deductive reasoning, whereas the basic abilities involved in the task independent phases should be involved in any sort of deductive reasoning.

Abilities involved in the task dependent phases

The *knowledge of the deductive terms* (e.g. *all*, *some*, *if-then*) should be clearly involved in the construction phase of the reasoning process, which is task dependent. Currently, UNICORE does not take into account possible incomplete representations of the input, but it can actually occur that reasoners construct incomplete representations of the premises. In particular, their lack of knowledge of quantifiers and connectives might affect their reasoning performance. Relational terms, instead, should be quite easy to understand also for very young subjects. Thus, we might expect a correlation between the ability to solve syllogistic and propositional problems and the knowledge of the deductive terms involved. Reasoners who have a poor knowledge of the deductive terms should perform poorly in the reasoning task where the terms are involved.

The ability to *use the middle term* of two premises in order to draw a conclusion concerning the end terms (in syllogistic and relational reasoning) might be involved in the Conclusion phase, which is also task dependent. Indeed, this ability allows to obtain information concerning the relation between the end terms once the models of the premises have been integrated. We hypothesize that reasoners deficient in this ability often err by drawing a conclusion involving the middle term.

Abilities involved in the task independent phases

The ability to *grasp* the importance of *falsification* might be crucial in deciding whether it is necessary to attempt a falsification once one has reached a putative conclusion. Thus, this ability should be involved in the Falsification phase, and in particular in its activation, which is task independent. We might expect that reasoners who do not grasp the importance to falsify will tend to produce erroneous responses for all the problems requiring the construction of more than one model. Thus, we could expect that this ability is not in relation with the ability to solve one model problems.

The ability to *search for alternative models* allows to produce alternative integrated models of the premises, and it is task independent. If reasoners are poor in producing alternative models, they will base their conclusion on a subset of the possible models of the premises and, as a consequence, they will draw an erroneous conclusion. Again, this ability should be involved in multiple-model problems.

Eventually, the five reasoning phases should be affected by the *working memory capacity* required by the task at hand. UNICORE incorporates constraints on the number of models retained in order to draw a conclusion. To compare the results of our experiment with the constraints already incorporated in the program would allow us to better calculate the increasing working memory capacity of reasoners of increasing age.

THE EXPERIMENT

In a previous experiment Bara *et al.* (1995) explored the relation between the ability to draw syllogistic inferences and possible basic abilities. In particular, they found out that the working memory capacity and the ability to perceive identities in pairs of configurations account for variance in the ability to solve syllogisms.

We have carried out an experiment which investigates the basic abilities hypothesized on the basis of the functioning of UNICORE, rather than on theoretical speculations. We have explored the basic abilities involved in relational and propositional reasoning along with those involved in syllogistic reasoning.

The participants were children (7-to-8 year olds), pre-adolescents (11-to-12 year olds), adolescents (15-to-16 year olds), and adults (over 21 year olds), with twenty in each groups. Children and adolescents attended four primary and high schools in Torino respectively, and adults were Psychology students at the University of Torino: none of them had a previous training in logic.

The experiment was in two sessions; each of them was carried out individually, in a quiet room. In the first session, participants dealt with the basic abilities tasks and, in the second session —which occurred one week later—, with the deductive tasks. The order of presentation of the basic abilities tasks and of the deductive tasks was counterbalanced.

The deductive performance of the participants was measured throughout syllogistic, propositional and relational problems. Syllogistic problems consisted of four syllogisms in each of the following categories: one model, multiple model and multiple model with no valid conclusion. Propositional problems were four, involving one of the following connectives: exclusive disjunction (two models), bi-conditional (two models) and conditional (three models). Relational problems were six one-model problems and six multiple model problems with no valid conclusion.

The participants' basic abilities were measured through a series of tasks.

In the *knowledge of deductive terms* task, participants were invited to select pictures consistent with some utterances involving either a *quantifier* (all, some, none, some not) or a *connective* (exclusive or, if, only if).

In the *middle term* task, participants were invited to form chains of figures by overlapping the elements which were identical in the figures. The aim was to connect two specific elements which were represented in different figures.

In the *grasp of falsification* task, participants were presented with utterances, and they were invited to make one critical question for each of them in order to discover whether the utterance was true or false with respect to an hidden state of affairs.

In the *search for alternative models* task participants were presented with 64 cards, each representing different elements (either star, square, triangle or circle) of different colors (either red, yellow, green or blue). The experimenter invited the participants to form as many 'families' as possible.

Finally, the *working memory capacity* was measured through the digit span. Participants were invited to repeat numerical series uttered by the experimenter.

The results concerning the deductive problems can be interpreted in terms of number of models they required (see Table 4.1).

TABLE 4.1
Percentages of correct responses in the deductive problems

Age groups (n=20)	Syllogistic (n=4x3)			Propositional (n=4x3)			Relational (n=6x2)	
	1-mod	m-mod	m-nvc	2-mod (bi-con)	2-mod (disj)	3 mod (cond)	1-mod	m-mod
7-8	23	13	34	64	66	40	40	39
11-12	44	16	29	80	78	60	54	56
15-16	59	30	30	88	95	65	78	70
>21	78	38	28	85	86	68	79	77
Global %	51	24	30	78	81	58	62	56

Model theory, in fact, predicts that the bigger is the number of models to construct, the harder is the reasoning problem. This prediction is confirmed for syllogisms: one model syllogisms were easier than multiple model syllogisms both valid (Wilcoxon test: z = –5.965, p <.0001) and invalid (Wilcoxon test: z = –3.42, p =.0006). Also, the prediction is confirmed for propositional problems: two-model problems, i.e. those involving bi-conditional and disjunction, were equally easy to deal with (Wilcoxon test: z=–0.676, p=.49). The three-model problems were more difficult: those involving the conditional connective were more difficult than those involving both the bi-conditional (Wilcoxon test: z=–7.113, p<.0001), and the disjunction (Wilcoxon test: z=–0.673, p<.0001). However, as regards relational problems, one-model and multiple-model problems with no valid conclusion did not significantly differ in difficulty (Wilcoxon test: z=–.903, p=.37). A possible explanation is the tendency of young subjects to conclude that 'no valid conclusion' follows from complex problems. As a consequence, they would draw the correct conclusion to the invalid problems, but for the wrong reason (see Johnson-Laird & Bara, 1984).

Further, mental model theory predicts that the ability to deal with multiple model problems increases with the increasing age. This prediction holds for all propositional problems (Jonckheere Trend test: z=2.14, p=.016) and for multiple model relational problems (Jonckheere Trend test: z = 4.81, p<.00003). Also, the performance of the different age groups with multiple model valid syllogisms increases with the age, although the improvement is not statistically significant (Jonckheere Trend test: z= 0.46, p=.32). However, the performance with multiple model invalid syllogisms does not increase with the age. Again, young subjects could perform well in invalid syllogisms for the wrong reason.

As regards the basic abilities, the results show that some of them increase with the age. In particular, the knowledge of connectives (Jonckheere Trend test: z= 3.25, p<.0005) —the knowledge of quantifiers did not improve with age—, the use of the middle term (Jonckheere Trend test: z= 4.62, p<.00001), the ability to search for alternative models (Jonckheere Trend test: z=2.95, p <.002), and the working memory capacity (Jonckheere Trend test: z=4.69, p =.00001).

Some of the basic abilities correlate (Fisher's correlation) with the ability to reason in a specific reasoning domain, others correlate with the ability to reason in all the three deductive domains we investigated (see Table 4.2). To stress the involvement of a specific ability in more than one sort of deductive reasoning, we present the correlation considering each ability separately.

TABLE 4.2
Significant correlations (Fisher's correlations) between the performance in the basic abilities tasks and the deductive problems

Abilities and deductive problems	Correlation	P - value
knowledge of disjunction - propositional probl.	.267	.016
knowledge of conditional - propositional probl.	.233	.037
grasp the importance to falsify - relational probl.	.226	.043
use the middle term		
— syllogistic 1model problems	−.44	<.0001
— syllogistic multiple model problems	−.267	.016
— syllogistic nvc problems	.327	.0029
— relational problems	−.473	<.0001
— propositional problems	−.306	.0055
search for alternative models		
— syllogistic problems	.364	.0008
— propositonal problems	.336	.002
— relational problems	.527	<.0001
working memory capacity		
— syllogistic	.278	.0122
— propositional	.255	.0224
— relational	.492	<.0001

The *knowledge of disjunction* and the *knowledge of conditional*, which are involved in a task dependent phase (Construction), correlate with the ability to solve propositional problems.

As regards the ability to *use the middle term*, which we considered as involved in a task dependent phase (Conclusion), we found a significant correlation with the general ability to solve syllogistic, propositional and relational problems. In the task devised to measure this ability, a high score corresponds to a poor performance, so the correlations are negative. Nevertheless, the correlation is positive for no valid conclusion syllogisms. This result is in line with our assumptions: when reasoners are poor in constructing the integrated models from complex problems, they tend to conclude that nothing follows from the premises. But, in fact, 'nothing follows' is the correct conclusion for invalid problems. Our hypothesis was that the ability to use the middle term is involved in a task dependent phase; the fact that it does correlate with the ability to deal with all sorts of deductive problems can be explained by the fact that it is also involved the Integration phase, which is task independent. In fact, it is through the overlapping of the identical tokens belonging to different models (i.e. middle terms) that Integration occurs. A significant improvement in using the middle term occurs around 11-12 years. Thus, we expect that children younger than 11 years may err by drawing conclusions involving the middle term. In fact, the 26% of errors in syllogistic reasoning and the 30% of errors in relational reasoning reflect this pattern. Such a pattern of errors is much more common in young children than in the other groups of participants. In propositional problems, where there is no middle term, this error is very rare.

The ability to *grasp the importance to falsify* correlates with the ability to solve relational problems. However, consistently with the fact that the ability to solve multiple model syllogisms does not significantly improve with the age, the grasping of the importance to falsify does not significantly improve with the age.

The ability to *search for alternative models* correlates with the general ability to solve syllogistic, propositional and relational problems. This ability improves with the age: as a matter of fact there is an improvement, with the increasing age, in the ability to solve multiple model problems.

The *working memory capacity* correlates with the ability to solve syllogistic, propositional and relational problems. The results concerning deductive problems show that a major improvement in the working memory capacity occurs around 11 years; such results are consistent with the mentioned correlation in that young children tend to base their responses on the first integrated model of the premises more often than the other participants.

CONCLUSIONS

In a preceding work, we substantiated the claim in favour of the existence of a unified mechanism for deduction, by devising a computer program able to reproduce the performance of human subjects in three different domains: syllogistic, propositional and relational reasoning. UNICORE is the proof that it is possible that such a mechanism does exist in the human mind.

Our approach differs from theories that are more concerned with the actual reasoning performances (see, e.g. Evans, 1989; Evans & Over, 1996); such theories, in fact, emphasize the understanding of performance constraints rather than reasoning competence. Also, our approach differs from theories claiming that deductive competence is part of the general thought processes (see e.g. Oaksford & Chater, 1994).

UNICORE is equivalent to a formal axiomatization of mental model theory; thus, it represents a computational evidence, but without a psychological validity. In the present paper we have tried to face a second question: does UNICORE possess a psychological plausibility? In other words, is our unified deductive mechanism not only theoretically possible, but also psychologically probable, in that people have something equivalent in their minds?

From the tenets of model theory, and from the architecture of UNICORE, we have devised some hypotheses on the basic abilities involved in deductive reasoning. The results of an experiment we carried out on subjects of different age confirm our predictions. In particular, we found that there exist basic abilities which are common to more than one sort of deductive reasoning, and some which are involved in a single reasoning domain. These results are in favour of the existence of a set of basic procedures involved in any kind of deductive reasoning, and the co-existence of contextualized abilities.

We regard our results as an important source of experimental evidence in favour of the plausibility of UNICORE. In fact, we have now an independent confirmation of the claim that humans possess in their brain/mind a unified mechanism for deductive reasoning. The weaknesses of UNICORE's predictions are many, and the next step of our research program is to incorporate into the computer model new constraints, in order to finesse its performance, especially in a developmental perspective.

ACKNOWLEDGEMENTS

This research was supported by the Ministero della Pubblica Istruzione of Italy (MPI ex-40%, 1999). The names of the authors are in alphabetic order.

REFERENCES

BARA, B. G. (1995): *Cognitive Science: A developmental approach to the simulation of the mind.* Hove, UK: Lawrence Erlbaum Associates.

BARA, B. G., BUCCIARELLI, M., & JOHNSON-LAIRD, P. N. (1995): «Development of syllogistic reasoning». *The American Journal of Psychology*, 108, 2, 157-193.

BARA, B. G., BUCCIARELLI, M. & LOMBARDO, V. (1999): «Model theory of deduction: A unified computational approach». *Cognitive Science*, in press.

BAR-HILLEL, Y. (1967): «Dictionaries and meaning rules». *Foundation of Language*, 3, 409-414.

BRAINE, M. D. S. (1978): «On the relation between the natural logic of reasoning and standard logic». *Psychological Review*, 85, 1-21.

BRAINE, M. (1990): «The "naturaral logic" approach to reasoning». In W. F. Overton (Ed.), *Reasoning, Necessity, and Logic* (pp. 133-157). Hove, UK: Lawrence Erlbaum Associates.

— (1998): «Steps towards a mental predicate logic». In M. D. S Braine. & D. P. O'Brien (Eds.), *Mental Logic*. Mahwah, NJ: Lawrence Erlbaum Associates.

BRAINE, M. D. S. & RUMAIN, B. (1983): «Logical reasoning». In J. H. Flavell & E. M. Markman (Eds.), *Carmichael's handbook of child psychology. Vol. III: Cognitive development* (4th Edn.). New York: Wiley.

BUCCIARELLI, M. & JOHNSON-LAIRD, P. N. (1999): «Strategies in syllogistic reasoning». *Cognitive Science*, in press.

CHENG, P. W. & HOLYOAK, K. J. (1985): «Pragmatic reasoning schemas». *Cognitive Psychology*, 17, 391-416.

CLARK, H. H. (1969): «Linguistic processes in deductive reasoning». *Psychological Review*, 76, 387-404.

COSMIDES, L. & TOOBY, J. (1994): «Evolutionary psychology and the generation of culture, Part II. Case study: A computational theory of social exchange». *Ethology and Sociobiology*, 10, 51-97.

EVANS, J. St. B.T. (1989): *Bias in human reasoning. Causes and consequences*. East Sussex, UK: Lawrence Erlbaum Associates.

EVANS, J. St. B. T. & OVER, D. E. (1996): *Rationality and reasoning*. Hove, UK: Psychology Press.

GIGERENZER, G. & HUG, K. (1992): «Domain-specific reasoning: Social contracts, cheating, and perspective change». *Cognition*, 43, 127-171.

GRIGGS, R. A. & COX, J. R. (1982): «The elusive thematic-materials effect in Wason's selection task». *Current Psychological Research & Review*, 3, 3-10.

GUYOTE, M. J. & STERNBERG, R. J. (1981): «A transitive-chain theory of syllogistic reasoning». *Cognitive Psychology*, 13, 461-525.

INHELDER, B. & PIAGET, J. (1958): *The growth of logical thinking from childhood to adolescence*. New York: Wiley.

JOHNSON-LAIRD, P. N. (1983): *Mental models*. Cambridge, UK: Cambridge University Press.

JOHNSON-LAIRD, P. N. (1993): *Human and machine thinking*. Hillsdale, NJ: Lawrence Erlbaum Associates,.

— (1997): «Rules and Illusions: A critical study of Rips's The Psychology of Proof». *Minds and Machines*, 387-407.

JOHNSON-LAIRD, P. N. & BARA, B. G. (1984): «Syllogistic inference». *Cognition*, 16, 1-61.

JOHNSON-LAIRD, P. N. & BYRNE, R. (1991): *Deduction*. Hillsdale, NJ: Lawrence Erlbaum Associates.

NEWELL, A. (1990): *Unified theories of cognition*. Cambridge, MA: Harvard University Press.

OAKSFORD, M. & CHATER, N. (1994): «A rational analysis of the Selection Task as optimal data selection». *Psychological Review*, 101, 608-631.

PIAGET, J. (1953): *Logic and psychology*. Manchester: Manchester University Press.

PLATT, R. D. & GRIGGS, R. A. (1993): «Darwinian algorithms and the Wason selection task: A factorial analysis of social contract selection task problems». *Cognition*, 48, 163-192.

POLK, T. A. & NEWELL, A. (1995): «Deduction as Verbal Reasoning». *Psychological Review*, 102, 3, 533-566.

POLLARD, P. (1981): «The effect of thematic content on the "Wason selection task"». *Current Psychological Research & Review*, 1, 21-29.

RIPS, L. J. (1990): «Reasoning». *Annual Review of Psychology*, 41, 321-353.

— (1994): *The psychology of proof: Deductive reasoning in human thinking*. Cambridge, MA: MIT Press.

STENNING, K. & OBERLANDER, J. (1995): «A cognitive theory of graphical and linguistic reasoning: Logic and implementation». *Cognitive Science*, 19, 1, 97-140.

5

REASONING TO CONSISTENCY: HOW PEOPLE RESOLVE LOGICAL INCONSISTENCIES

Vittorio Girotto
Philip N. Johnson-Laird
Paolo Legrenzi
Maria Sonino

¿Cómo razonan las personas desde la inconsecuencia hacia la consecuencia? Por ejemplo, dadas las premisas 'Si P y Q, entonces R', 'P y Q', las personas infieren 'R', pero cuando descubren que esta conclusión es incompatible con algún tipo de evidencia incontrovertible (i.e. 'no-R') tienen que resolver una inconsecuencia. En este capítulo se propone una explicación del razonamiento consecuente basada en la Teoría de los Modelos Mentales. El primer paso consiste en realizar una deducción válida a partir de las premisas que se consideran verdaderas. El segundo paso consiste en darse cuenta de que la conclusión es inconsecuente con algún tipo de evidencia incontrovertible. El tercer paso consiste en la comparación entre la evidencia categórica y los modelos explícitos de las premisas. Asumimos que este proceso se rige por un principio de desemparejamiento: los razonadores tienden a eliminar cualquier premisa que tenga un modelo explícito que entre en conflicto con el modelo de la evidencia (en el ejemplo anteriormente mencionado, la premisa 'Si P y Q, entonces R'). En caso de no existir dicha premisa, se tiende a rechazar cualquier premisa que no contenga un modelo que sea explícitamente consecuente con la evidencia. Se realizaron varios estudios para comprobar esta hipótesis. Los resultados mostraron que las personas razonan hacia la consecuencia por medio de la eliminación de cualquier premisa que no concuerde con la evidencia, independientemente de su condición lógica. Ésta puede ser una premisa categórica que afirme el caso en cuestión o una premisa compuesta que sea compatible con varias posibilidades. Nuestros resultados también mostraron que la eliminación de una premisa no depende de la facilidad que presente su falsación. Estos resultados se discuten dentro del marco de varias pers-

pectivas alternativas basadas en la teoría de los Modelos Mentales y de la lógica mental.

INTRODUCTION

An individual mind may contain conflicting preferences. People have desires that cannot be satisfied simultaneously. As Zerlina sings to Don Giovanni, who is wooing her on the day of her marriage to Masetto, «Vorrei e non vorrei...», i.e., «I would like to and I would not like to...». In contrast, the notion that an individual mind maintains conflicting *beliefs* appears to be a sign of irrationality. To be rational, it would seem, is at least to hold beliefs that are consistent. Indeed, logicians argue that a self-contradictory set of propositions logically implies any conclusion whatsoever. The price of consistency is high, however. As we will explain, it can be impossible to determine that a set of propositions is consistent.

Yet, there are occasions on which you appreciate that you are in danger of inconsistency. A vivid instance occurs when you draw a valid deduction from premises that you take to be true, and then you discover that the conclusion is incompatible with incontrovertible evidence. For example, you believe the following propositions:

If Paolo has gone to get the car, then he will be back here in five minutes.

and:

Paolo has gone to get the car.

You infer validly:

Therefore, Paolo will be back in five minutes.

Five minutes goes by, and then another five, with no sign of Paolo. Something has to *give*. You may decide that Paolo did not go to get the car, or else that your conditional assumption is false. The nature of your decision is no mere academic exercise: it is liable to determine what you do next.

In orthodox logic, the addition of a new premise never undermines the valid conclusions implied by previous premises. Logic is *monotonic*: as further premises are added further conclusions can be drawn, but no prior conclusion can be withdrawn. And, as we mentioned, when a new premise is inconsistent with the previous premises, then anything goes: any conclusion whatsoever can be proved from the premises. In other words, logic alone cannot tell you how to resolve an inconsistency. Hence we assume that the process of resolving an inconsistency is a special process of reasoning, akin to diagnosing a fault. It is not one that can be governed solely by logical considerations. And we refer to this special process as *reasoning to consistency*. Its starting point is a set of propositions that are known to the reasoner to be inconsistent, and its outcome is a modified set of propositions that are consistent.

One source of accounts of reasoning to consistency is artificial intelligence. In order to try to deal with inconsistency, researchers in the area have developed various systems of *nonmonotonic* logic, which allow for the withdrawal of previous conclusions in the light of new premises. None of these systems is without its problems (see e.g. Brewka, Dix, & Konolige, 1997), and no robust evidence implies that any of these systems is psychologically plausible. In fact, the psychological literature on how people reason from inconsistency to consistency is sparse. What does happen when individuals draw a valid conclusion from seemingly true premises only to discover that its conclusion conflicts with reality? Our aim in the present chapter is to begin to answer this question. We propose a model-based theory of reasoning to consistency, and we discuss the results of some empirical investigations designed to test it.

THE DETECTION OF INCONSISTENCY

The first step in reasoning to consistency is the detection of an inconsistency among a set of beliefs. It is tempting to think of inconsistency as a conflict between just two propositions, one of the form:

A

and the other of the form:

Not-A.

Unfortunately, inconsistency can arise among a set of N propositions, where any subset of N-1 of them is consistent. As a simple example, consider a set of the following form:

A or B, or both.
Not-B or C, or both.
Not-A and not-C.

Each pair of premises is consistent, but the three together are inconsistent. In general, the detection of inconsistency places bigger and bigger demands on time and as the size of the set of propositions increases. The task is computationally intractable: as the set increases in size, the demands on time and memory increase to the point that they exceed the power of any feasible computational system (see Cook, 1971). Strikingly, it is not even feasible to test the consistency of a set of 138 propositions:

> Suppose that each line of the truth table for the conjunctions of all beliefs could be checked in the time a light ray takes to traverse the diameter of a proton, and suppose that the computer was permitted to run for twenty

billion years, the estimated time from the «big-bang» dawn of the universe to the present. A belief system containing only 138 logically independent propositions would overwhelm the time resources of this supermachine (Cherniak, 1986, p. 93)

If testing 138 propositions entails such a vast combinatorial explosion, then a finite device such as the human mind cannot test the consistency of the enormous number of beliefs that it contains.

In some cases, individuals do not even detect an inconsistency among a small number of beliefs. It is no easy matter to determine that three propositions do not fit together if, say, they take the form of the example at the head of this section. Moreover, the mind may maintain separate *sets* of beliefs, which are insulated one from another (Klein, 1998). This hypothesis explains why some individuals accept both the scientific explanation of the world *and* unjustified belief systems, such as astrology (see Jahoda, 1969). It might also explain why individuals succumb to *self-deception*, holding simple contradictory beliefs, such as:

P and not-P

in situations that evoke emotionally disturbing thoughts (e.g. Elster, 1986; Mele, 1997). Self-deception is likely if the architecture of the mind allows emotions to be created by unconscious cognitions (see Oatley & Johnson-Laird, 1987).

Individuals may fail to detect inconsistency in situations that they have not represented correctly or completely. Consider, for instance, the following conversation:

First pilot «If the plane is on course, then the radar should show only water». Second pilot «The radar is showing a land mass».

According to Overton (1990), this dialogue occurred between the members of the crew of the ill-fated Korean Airlines Flight 007, before it was shot down by a Soviet weapon in September 1983. The two pilots had established the premises of a *modus tollens* inference, from which they could have derived a valid conclusion:

Therefore, the plane is not on course.

That is, the two premises are of the form:

If P, then Q.
not-Q.

which validly imply the conclusion:

Not-P.

Instead of drawing this conclusion, however, the crew changed the topic of conversation. They failed to detect an inconsistency between their correct premises and their tacit conclusion that they were on course.

Various factors are likely to have contributed to the crew's failure to detect the inconsistency. People in stressful situations often fail to pay proper attention to each other's statements. Similarly, it can be difficult to appreciate that the second premise:

The radar is showing a land mass

is inconsistent with the consequent of the conditional premise:

The radar should show only water.

Experiments show that it is harder to grasp such an implicit negation than an explicit negation (see Evans & Over, 1996, pp. 57-59):

The radar is *not* showing only water.

In sum, it can be hard to detect inconsistency. The set of inconsistent propositions may be too large for you to evaluate in a practicable time. The inconsistency may arise from elements in totally separate sets of your beliefs. You may be in a mental state that militates against a careful search. You may be confronted with propositions that do not wear their logic on their sleeves, such as an implicit negation between one proposition and another. The complexity of your relevant beliefs may be too great for you to lay out explicitly all their consequences.

In contrast, the following sort of problem should be simpler:

Imagine that you are an expert pilot who is flying with two crew members, Pat and Viv.
Pat says: «If the plane is on course, then the radar should show only water».
Viv says: «The radar is showing a land mass».
Now, you know for sure that you are on course. What would you infer about what Pat and Viv said?

In this problem, you have to consider just three propositions, which have to be reconciled within the same set of your beliefs. They should not trigger disturbing thoughts, and they should be easy to attend to and to understand. In sum, you should detect the inconsistency between your crew's assertions, which imply the valid conclusion:

We are not on course

and your knowledge:

We are on course.

Granted that individuals detect an inconsistency, how will they answer the question posed in the problem? How will they reason to consistency? And, in general, what processes of reasoning do they use to do so? In order to begin to answer these questions, we turn to current theories of naive deductive reasoning.

NAÏVE DEDUCTION AND REASONING TO CONSISTENCY

There are two main approaches to the psychology of naïve deduction. One is based on syntax, and the other is based on semantics. According to the syntactic view, naive reasoners are equipped with a set of formal rules of inference (inferential schema) similar to those of a logical calculus. They draw valid inferences by using these rules to construct proofs (see e.g. Braine & O'Brien, 1991; Rips, 1994). Given, say, the premises in the pilots' conversation, they first extract their logical form, and then try to use formal rules to derive a conclusion. Because these theories argue that there is no mental rule corresponding to *modus tollens*, the inference calls for a chain of deductions, and so it should be quite difficult.

According to the alternative semantic approach, naive reasoners draw inferences by constructing and manipulating representations of the meaning of the premises, i.e. *mental models* (see e.g. Johnson-Laird & Byrne, 1991; Polk & Newell, 1995). Hence, reasoners can draw the valid conclusion from the crew's premises only if they represent all the possibilities compatible with its first premise:

If the plane is on course, then the radar should show only water.

These possibilities are shown here, where each line represents a separate mental model (of a separate possibility):

C	W
¬ C	W
¬ C	¬ W

C denotes a model of «the plane is on course», W denotes a model of «the radar shows only water», and «¬» denotes negation. Thus, the third model represents the possibility that the plane is not on course and the radar does not show only water. A second premise that is an explicit negation:

The radar does not show only water

eliminates the first two models, which are directly inconsistent with it. Only the third model remains, from which it follows validly:

The plane is not on course.

A major source of inferential errors is the difficulty of representing all the models of the premises, that is, all the distinct possibilities with which they are compatible. Working memory has severe limitations on its processing capacity. Hence, the model theory postulates a principle of *truth*:

Reasoners tend to represent what is true, but not what is false.

For example, reasoners are likely to represent the conditional premise in the pilots' conversation as follows:

C	W
...	

in which the ellipsis denotes an implicit models, which is a place holder with no explicit content. It represents the possibilities corresponding to the *falsity* of the conditional's antecedent (the plane is on course). Reasoners often focus on the explicit model (Legrenzi, Girotto, & Johnson-Laird, 1993). Hence, when they interpret the second premise, they use it merely to eliminate the explicit model. All that remains is the implicit model, and so they conclude incorrectly that «nothing follows». This error is often observed in the psychological laboratory (Johnson-Laird, Byrne, & Schaeken, 1992), but, as the model theory predicts, it is reduced if the two premises are presented in the opposite order (Girotto, Mazzocco, & Tasso, 1997).

The advocates of formal rules have not produced a detailed theory of reasoning to consistency. But they have stressed the necessity of improving our knowledge of this domain, both normatively and psychologically. And they have suggested that naive individuals may reason about inconsistency by using rules:

> «For purposes of philosophy (and perhaps AI), we need normative rules about how to change our minds in the face of conflicting evidence... ; for purposes of psychology, we also need descriptive information on how people deal with the same sort of conflict... coming up with the rules, both normative and descriptive, is a core problem cognitive science.» (Rips, 1994, p. 299)

In previous studies, the model theory has been extended to reasoning about probabilities (Johnson-Laird, Legrenzi, Girotto, Legrenzi, & Caverni, 1999) and to causal reasoning (Goldvarg & Johnson-Laird, 1999). Such extensions depend on the core principles of the theory, but it is necessary to make additional assumptions to deal with the particular properties of the relevant domain. We adopt the same strategy here: reasoning to consistency calls for an additional assumption.

Mental models do not always represent the possibilities completely, and so we postulate that individuals tend to reason to consistency by eliminating whichever premise mismatches the incontrovertible evidence. We refer to this assumption as the *mismatch* principle:

«If there is an inconsistency between a valid inference from premises and incontrovertible evidence, then reasoners tend to eliminate the premise with an explicit model that is inconsistent with the evidence. If no premise mismatches with the evidence in this way, reasoners tend to eliminate the premise that has no models that explicitly include the evidence.»

The evidence too must be represented in models, but in the situations that concern us the evidence is categorical, i.e., it calls for only a single mental model. Hence, if the evidence is *inconsistent* with an explicit model of one of the premises, reasoners will be biased to eliminate such a premise, regardless of its logical status, i.e., whether it is a categorical assertion with one model, or a more complex premise with multiple models. And if the evidence does not falsify the explicit models of any of the premises, reasoners will reject the premise with models that do not represent explicitly the evidence. In other words, reasoning to consistency is controlled by the degree of apparent mismatch between the mental models of the evidence and the premises.

The nature of the mismatch principle should become clearer as we illustrate its use in deriving predictions. Consider a new sort of problem based on the premises of a *modus ponens* inference:

> Pat says: «If the plane is on course, then the radar should show only water».
> Viv says: «The plane is on course».
> Now, you know for sure that the radar does *not* show water. What would you infer about what Pat and Viv said?

The two premises have respectively the following mental models:

$$C \qquad W$$
$$...$$

and:

$$C$$

And the categorical evidence has the model:

$$\neg W$$

This model is inconsistent with an explicit element, W, in the models of the conditional premise. The mismatch principle accordingly predicts that reasoners should tend to achieve consistency by rejecting the conditional premise rather than the categorical premise.

Now, consider a problem in which the premises are those for a *modus tollens* inference:

> Pat says: «If the plane is on course, then the radar should show only water».
> Viv says: «The radar does not show water».
> Now, you know for sure that the plane is on course. What would you infer about what Pat and Viv said?

In this case, the premises have respectively the models:

$$C \qquad W$$
$$...$$

and:

$$\neg W$$

The model of the evidence in this case:

$$C$$

does *not* conflict with the explicit model of the conditional premise. Hence, the mismatch principle predicts that reasoners should be more likely to reject the categorical premise than to reject the conditional premise. Indeed, the models of the conditional contain an explicit representation of the evidence.

EXPERIMENTAL TESTS OF THE MISMATCH PRINCIPLE

In one of the few previous experimental studies of reasoning to consistency, Elio & Pelletier (1997) provided some support for the mismatch principle. In their Experiment 2, the most frequent revision for *modus ponens* problems was the elimination of the conditional premise (36% of participants). In contrast, with *modus tollens* problems, only few participants eliminated such a premise, and they tended to eliminate the categorical premise (26% of participants) or to consider both premises as uncertain (44% of participants). We have also carried out a series of unpublished tests of the model theory's account of reasoning to consistency (Johnson-Laird, Legrenzi, Girotto, & Sonino, 1999). Our experiments differed in several ways from those of Elio & Pelletier (1997). We used problems with a variety of sentential connectives, including both conditionals and disjunctions. We used materials that were close to the contents of inferences in daily life. And our participants were neither given the conclusion that they should derive from the premises nor told that such a conclusion conflicted with the evidence.

In our first experiment, we tested the hypothesis that reasoners tend to eliminate the mismatching premise, that is the premise which has a model conflicting with the model of the evidence. The participants had to solve two problems, one based on a conditional premise and one based on a disjunctive premise. We counterbalanced the order of the problems and the assignment of contents to the two problems, but for simplicity we will describe the two sorts of problem with the same content. In the experiment, each participant encountered a particular content only once.

The conditional problem was of the following sort:

Imagine the following conversation between two friends:
Pat says, «If the President owns a villa and a swimming pool, then he owns a plane».
Viv says, «The President owns a villa and a swimming pool».
But you happen to know that the President does not own a plane.

According to you, who asserted a false proposition:

Pat.
Viv.
None of them.
Both of them.

The disjunctive problem was of the following sort:

Imagine the following conversation between two friends:
Pat says, «The President owns a villa and a swimming pool, or else he owns a plane».
Viv says, «The President owns a villa and a swimming pool».
But you happen to know that the President owns a plane.

According to you, who asserted a false proposition:

Pat.
Viv.
None of them.
Both of them.

In the conditional problem, the first premise is a conditional statement that has the mental models:

V   S   P

   ...

in which V, S, and P denote models of «the President owns a villa», «the President owns a swimming pool», and «the President owns a plane», respectively. The second premise is a conjunction, which has the mental model:

V   S

Given these premises, the participants should infer that the President owns a plane:

P.

They know that the President does not own a plane:

¬P

and so they have to modify the set of premises. The mismatch principle predicts that they will reject the conditional premise, because the model of the evidence is inconsistent with its explicit model.

In the disjunctive problem, the first premise is a disjunction that has two mental models:

V   S

        P

The second premise is a conjunction, which has the model:

V   S

From these premises, reasoners should infer that the President does not own a plane:

¬P

They know that the President does own a plane:

P

and so they have to modify the set of premises. The mismatch principle makes a different prediction from the conditional problem. The model of the evidence is consistent with the second model of the disjunctive premise, and so the mismatch principle predicts that the participants will reject the conjunctive premise, because its model does not represent the evidence (the President owns a plane).

The results of the experiment corroborated the predictions: most reasoners rejected the mismatching premise. In the conditional problem, they tended to eliminate the conditional premise (83% of participants); and in the disjunctive problem, then tended to eliminate the conjunctive premise (43% of participants). In the disjunctive problem, however, 27% of participants chose not to reject either premise. This result indicates that it easier to detect the inconsistency in the conditional problem: conditional inferences are indeed easier than disjunctive inferences (Johnson-Laird *et al.*, 1992). In fact, the evidence explicitly falsifies a model of the conditional premise, whereas the evidence is consistent with the disjunctive premise.

As a control, the experiment also included a variant on the conditional problem in which the evidence was consistent with the premises. It was:

But you happen to know that the President owns a plane.

In this case, there is no inconsistency between the conclusion that follows from the premises and the evidence. Hence, the correct response is that both premises could be true. Indeed, most participants correctly responded that both friends were telling the truth, despite the fact that they were required to indicate which one asserted a false proposition. This result shows that individuals were reasoning, not guessing, in solving the problems.

MISMATCHING VS. ENVISAGING FALSITY

The results of the previous study are open to an alternative explanation: most reasoners eliminated the premise for which they needed to consider the smaller number of false cases. A conditional assertion, such as:

If the President owns a villa and a swimming pool, then he owns a plane

is false just in *one* case, that is, when the antecedent is true and the consequent is false:

V   S   ¬P

In contrast, the conjunctive premise:

The President owns a villa and a swimming pool

is false in *three* cases, that is, when one or both conjuncts are false:

V   ¬S
¬V   S
¬V   ¬S

Hence, the participants' tendency to reject the conditional premise may merely reflect the ease of working out the situations in which it would be false.

Likewise, in the case of the disjunctive problem, the problem which has the fewer false contingencies is the conjunctive premise (three cases). The disjunctive premise:

The President owns a villa and a swimming pool, or else he owns a plane is false in *four* cases:

```
V    S        P
V   ¬S       ¬P
¬V   S       ¬P
¬V  ¬S       ¬P
```

Hence, according to the explanation in terms of ease of falsification, reasoners in the first study merely eliminated whichever premise it was easier to envisage as false.

The mismatch principle and ease of falsification run in parallel in our first study, and so we carried out a second study in which we were able to pit them against each other. This study included both the conditional and disjunctive problems from the first study, but it also included a new sort of problem based on a conditional with a disjunctive consequent. Once again, we will state the problem using the same content as before.

Imagine the following conversation between two friends:

Pat says, «If the President owns a villa then he owns a swimming pool or else he owns a plane».
Viv says, «The President owns a villa and a swimming pool».
But you happen to know that the President owns a plane.

According to you, who asserted a false proposition:

Pat.
Viv.
None of them.
Both of them.

The conditional premise has the following mental models:

V   S

V   P

   ...

and the conjunctive premise has the model:

V   S

They yield the valid inference:

   ¬ P

But the evidence is:

   P

The matching principle predicts that reasoners will tend to reject the conjunctive premise, because the evidence is explicitly represented in a model of the conditional premise, but not in the model of the conjunctive premise. The ease of envisaging false cases makes the opposite prediction. The conditional premise is false in two cases:

$$
\begin{array}{ccc}
V & S & P \\
V & \neg S & \neg P
\end{array}
$$

and the conjunctive premise is false in three cases. Hence, if reasoners are guided by the ease of falsification, they should reject the conditional rather than the conjunction. But, if they are guided by the mismatch principle, then they should reject the conjunction rather than the conditional.

In the experiment proper, no participant encountered the same content more than once, and the contents were assigned to the problems in a counterbalanced way. Likewise, the problems were presented to the participants in a counterbalanced order. The results corroborated those of the first study, and they also corroborated the mismatch principle and eliminated ease of falsification. In the problem based on the conditional with a disjunctive consequent, most of the participants (58%) rejected the conjunctive premise.

CONCLUSIONS

How do people reason from inconsistency to consistency? In this chapter, we have proposed an account based on mental models. The first step is to make a valid deduction from premises taken to be true. The second step is to grasp that its conclusion is inconsistent with some incontrovertible evidence. This step can be difficult, if not impossible, but it was relatively easy in our experiments. The third step is to compare the categorical evidence with the explicit models of the premises. According to the mismatch principle, reasoners tend to reject whichever premise has an explicit model that is inconsistent with the evidence. And, if there is no such premise, they tend to reject whichever premise contains no model that is explicitly consistent with the evidence. What happens if there is no such premise, either? We do not know. The burden of our empirical studies, however, is that individuals prefer to reason to consistency by eliminating whichever premise mismatches the evidence, regardless of the logical status of the premise. It may be a categorical premise asserting what is definitely the case, or a compound premise compatible with several possibilities. Likewise, as our second study showed, the rejection of a premise does not depend on how easy it is to envisage its falsity.

Elio & Pelletier (1997) observed that reasoners tend to eliminate conditional premises to resolve an inconsistency. These authors proposed two psychological accounts of this non-monotonic phenomenon based on the two rival views of naive deductive reasoning. The mental logic account derives from Rips's (1994, pp. 58-62) assumption that the principles governing the revision of beliefs are «higher-level rules» that operate over the usual deductive rule system. One of these rules, according to Elio and Pelletier, leads reasoners to disbelieve conditional premises. Other theories also appear to place more weight on categorical information than on hypothetical information (cf. Harman, 1986; Thagard, 1989).

Elio and Pelletier's theory based on mental models is analogous to our own: the revision of beliefs depends on a comparison of models. Reasoners compare the model of the evidence to the models of the premises and conclusion. Consider a problem in the form of *modus ponens*:

If P then Q.
P
Therefore, Q.
But, the evidence shows that not Q.

The model of the evidence: ¬Q, eliminates the model of the valid conclusion, Q. It is silent about the model of the categorical premise, P. And it eliminates the models of the conditional premise: If P, then Q. In fact, Elio and Pelletier did not explain why a comparison with the evidence eliminates the conditional premise. The two propositions are, of course, consistent. Perhaps, they assumed that reasoners apply a version of the mismatch principle.

The results of our second study contravene both of the approaches formulated by Elio and Pelletier. Individuals do not always reason to consistency by abandoning a conditional premise. If the conditional premise has at least one model that is consistent with the evidence, then reasoners tend to reject the categorical premise rather than the conditional premise. Likewise, the following formulation is incompatible with our account:

> «By the same general reasoning, the mental-models approach would find itself predicting a preponderance of conditional denials for modus tollens problems». (Elio and Pelletier, 1997, p. 441).

In fact, the mismatch principle leads to differing predictions for reasoning to consistency from *modus ponens* and from *modus tollens*. It predicts that reasoners will tend to abandon the conditional premise in the case of evidence that is inconsistent with a *modus ponens* inference, whereas they will tend to abandon the categorical premise in the case of evidence that is inconsistent with a *modus tollens* inference. Our results, as well as those reported by Elio & Pelletier, corroborated these predictions.

There are many problems to be resolved in explaining how people reason from inconsistent information to arrive at consistency. The present account is only the beginnings of such an explanation, and it calls for further empirical study. Yet, even in its present nascent state, it shows that the model theory can be successfully applied to an important and puzzling domain of human thinking.

REFERENCES

BREWKA, G., DIX, J., & KONOLIGE, K. (1997): *Nonmonotonic Reasoning: An Overview*. Stanford, CA: CLSI Publications, Stanford University.

CHERNIAK, C. (1981): *Minimal Rationality*. Cambridge, MA: MIT Press.

COOK, S. A. (1971): «The complexity of theorem proving procedures». *Proceeding of the Third Annual Association of Computing Machinery Symposium on the Theory of Computing*, 151-58.

ELIO, R., & PELLETIER, F. J. (1997): «Belief change as propositional update». *Cognitive Science, 21*, 419-460.

ELSTER, J. (1986): *The Multiple Self*. Cambridge: Cambridge University Press.

EVANS, J. ST. B. T., & OVER, D. (1996): *Rationality and Reasoning*. Hove, Sussex: Psychology Press.

GIROTTO, V., MAZZOCCO, A., & TASSO, A. (1997): «The effect of premise order on conditional reasoning: A test of the mental model theory», *Cognition, 63,* 1-28.

GOLDVARG, Y., & JOHNSON-LAIRD, P. N. (1999): «Naive causality: a mental model theory of causal meaning and reasoning». Manuscript submitted for publication.

HARMAN, G. (1986): *Change in View*. Cambridge, MA: MIT Press.

— (1995): «Rationality». In E. Smith & D. Osherson (Eds.). *An Invitation to Cognitive Science. Vol. 3*. Cambridge, MA: MIT Press.

JAHODA, G. (1969): *The Psychology of Superstition*. Harmondsworth, Middlesex: Penguin Books.

JOHNSON-LAIRD, P. N., & BYRNE, R. M. J. (1991): *Deduction*. Hillsdale, N.J.: Erlbaum.

JOHNSON-LAIRD, P. N., BYRNE, R. M. J., & SCHAEKEN, W. (1992): «Propositional reasoning by models». *Psychological Review, 99,* 418-439.

JOHNSON-LAIRD, P. N., LEGRENZI, P., GIROTTO, V., & SONINO, M. (1999): «A model theory of non-monotonic reasoning». Manuscript in preparation.

JOHNSON-LAIRD, P. N., LEGRENZI, P., GIROTTO, V., SONINO, M., & CAVERNI, J. P. (1999): «Naive Probability: A model theory of extensional reasoning». *Psychological Review*, 106, 62-88.

KLEIN, G. (1998): *Sources of Power. How People Make Decisions*. Cambridge, MA: MIT Press.

LEGRENZI, P., GIROTTO, V., & JOHNSON-LAIRD, P. N. (1993): «Focussing in reasoning and decision making». *Cognition, 49*, 37-66.

MELE, A. R. (1997): «Real self-deception». *Behavioral and Brain Sciences*, 20, 91-136.

OATLEY, K. J., & JOHNSON-LAIRD, P. N. (1987): «Towards a cognitive theory of emotions». *Emotion and Cognition, 1*, 29-50.

OVERTON, W. F. (1990): «Competence and procedures». In W.F. Overton (Ed.), *Reasoning, Necessity and Logic: Developmental Perspectives*. Hillsdale, NJ: Erlbaum.

POLK, T. A., & NEWELL, A. (1995): «Deduction as verbal reasoning». *Psychological Review, 102*, 533-566.

RIPS, L. J. (1994): *The Psychology of Proof*. Cambridge, MA: MIT Press.

THAGARD, P. (1989): «Explanatory coherence». *Behavioral and Brain Science, 12*, 435-502.

6

EXTERNAL REPRESENTATIONS AND DEDUCTIVE REASONING

Antonio Rizzo
Marco Palmonari

Los artefactos, es decir, los objetos o representaciones artificiales desempeñan un papel fundamental en la cognición humana dado que median en la interacción con el mundo. La propiedad crítica de todos los artefactos es que no sólo representan el mundo físico, sino que además moldean los procesos de pensamiento al restringir la forma en la que la información representada puede seguir procesándose para alcanzar una meta determinada. Una implicación importante de esta tesis es que no se puede investigar la cognición humana sin considerar cómo interactúan en una tarea determinada las representaciones externas con los primitivos funcionales de la mente.

En este trabajo se describe un experimento que fue diseñado con el fin de estudiar el papel mediador que desempeñan los artefactos en el razonamiento silogístico. El objetivo del experimento se centra en la comparación de una representación de las premisas diseñada de acuerdo con algunos de los supuestos de la Teoría de los Modelos Mentales desarrollada por Johnson-Laird y otras dos representaciones más clásicas (círculos de Euler y proposiciones) utilizadas en experimentos anteriores sobre razonamiento silogístico. El aspecto crítico de la representación según la Teoría de los Modelos Mentales es que se encuentra diseñada para apoyar a los sujetos en las tres etapas propuestas por esta teoría para el razonamiento silogístico, es decir, en el despliegue (fleshing-out) de las premisas, en la construcción de un modelo de las premisas y en la búsqueda de contraejemplos del modelo.

Los resultados ofrecen datos empíricos preliminares que apoyan la hipótesis del experimento. En concreto, las diferentes representaciones de las premisas no son equivalentes: la representación diseñada según los principios de la Teoría de los Modelos Mentales ofrece mejor apoyo a los sujetos en una tarea de razonamiento silogístico que las otras dos representaciones. Además, el rendimiento depende de la interacción entre la representación utilizada y el tipo de silogismos que se tiene que resolver. De hecho, este resultado es una consecuencia de un corolario del concepto de actividad humana mediada por artefacto: las propiedades de los artefactos no son absolutas, sino que se encuentran estrechamente relacionadas con la forma en que logran encajar la representación que evocan y el espacio representacional de un silogismo determinado. Por ejemplo, un silogismo que conlleve un solo modelo, como Todos los A son B- Todos los B son C, sería más fácil con las notaciones que no expresen modelos irrelevantes o implícitos. Por el contrario, aquellos silogismos que conlleven varios modelos serían más fáciles con las notaciones que sustentan la búsqueda de modelos alternativos.

ARTEFACTS AND HUMAN COGNITION

Recent developments within Cognitive Science (Zhang & Norman 1994; 1995; Norman 1991; 1993) have provided empirical support to the long lasting thesis that human cognition is mediated by artefacts (rules, tools, models, representations), which are both internal and external to the mind (cf. Cole, 1996). According to these findings, human activity cannot be investigated without taking into account the artefacts which mediate it because human activity and artefacts are the two inseparable sides of the same phenomenon, human cognition.

An artefact can be defined as an artificial device designed to maintain, display or operate upon information in order to serve a representational function (Norman, 1991). Cognitive artefacts mediate between human activity and the world in that they determine the actions required to get a task done and distribute these actions across time (pre-computation) and across people (distributed cognition).

The concept of the mediating role of artefacts was originally put forward by the cultural-historical approach developed by Vygotsky at the beginning of this century (Vygotsky, 1978). One of the central tenets of Vygotsky is that higher mental processes can be understood only if we understand the tools that mediate them. Indeed, on one hand, the mediating role of artefacts results in the modification of humans higher psychological processes: the ontogenetic psychological development is not just due to the biological maturation and the interaction with the «natural» world but it occurs thanks to the interaction with external informational structures embodied in the material tools and symbolic systems developed within a given culture (language, arithmetic, mental schemata). On the other hand, artefacts are the expression of cultural processes, the modification of the natural and cultural environment through the production of tools and symbolic structures.

Thus, artefacts can be conceived as representations as well as in terms of the activity they mediate and support; in fact, we claim that the representational and the processing aspects of artefacts are not separable because artefacts are created and modified over the time by human goal-directed activity, which means that representational properties of artefacts «embody» the activity of which they are the product. Within the cognitive science community, the general term 'external representation' is used to indicate all kinds of information which are external to the human mind; however, the way in which representation and processing are inter-linked is not the same for all artefacts. The three levels hierarchy put forward by Wartofsky (1973) is relevant here in that it allows one to better define the properties of different kinds of artefacts, namely the primary and the secondary ones [1].

According to Wartofsky, primary artefacts, such as a knife, a word or a telephone, are artefacts which directly mediate between humans and reality; the critical features of primary artefacts are that they always «stand for» an entity in the physical world (like a word), mediate the interaction among humans and the physical world itself (like a knife), or mediate human interaction (like a telephone).

Unlike primary artefacts, secondary artefacts do not mediate the interaction between humans and the physical world; instead, they represent primary artefacts and mediate the interaction of humans with them. Secondary artefacts (algorithms, rules, norms, procedures) are representations of modes of interaction with primary artefacts. A procedure, as a checklist, or a recipe, is a representation of a sequence of actions one should apply to reach a particular goal using a set of primary artefacts; as a secondary artefact, the procedure can be conceived of as a representation of the sequence of actions that one could perform using primary artefacts, that is a representation of objects in the world. Secondary artefacts are, thus, second-level representations, they represent modes of actions using first level representations of the real world. The crucial property of secondary artefacts as second level representations is that they can be easily transformed and worked upon. Again, similar to primary artefacts, it is impossible to clearly distinguish between representational properties and the manipulations they afford: nevertheless, the claim we make in the present paper is that the main characteristic of secondary artefacts (as external representations) does not lie simply on their representational properties; rather, the crucial property is that secondary artefacts afford the manipulation and recombination of their constituent elements. To put it in another way, secondary artefacts shape thinking processes not just because they represent only part of the elements of the represented world leaving aside other elements, but also because they strongly constrain the way in which the represented information can be further elaborated.

---

[1]   Originally Wartofsky proposed 3 levels of description of artefacts (primary, secondary and tertiary); the first two levels will be discussed in the present paper.

A compelling example of the role played by secondary artefacts in shaping human higher cognitive functions throughout history is the evolution of the notation scheme used to represent numbers.

A pebble can represent a cow, a sheep, or whatever else. And a set of pebbles can stand for a set of cows in a unique correspondence: so many pebbles, so many cows. According to this description, a pebble is a primary artefact in that it stands for an object of the world by «capturing» and representing some of its properties. But this is not the whole story: the characteristics of the pebble, as an artefact, depend also on the activity it mediates. The choice of a small and light pebble instead of a heavy stone is due to the human activity this representation is meant to support.

The Sumerians, an ancient people who established a nation of city-states in the current Middle-East in the fourth millennium BC, counted on their fingers and used objects such as pieces of wood and pebbles as counters (Campiglio & Eugeni, 1990) ; in addition, they used to record the results of their counting by means of tally marks. Indeed, until 3500 BC there is no record of any operation that goes beyond mere «counting by enumeration». Lack of any notation, even of numerals, made it impossible to refine the concept of number. The process of development of a secondary artefact for counting, that is a numerical notation supporting the activity of trading, took several hundreds years, from 3500 BC until 2800 BC.

During the first phase, around 3500 BC, administrators started using different sorts of small objects, namely sticks, marbles, disks and cones to represent different values, respectively one, ten, sixty and a hundred: the unique correspondence between objects in the world and artefacts is no longer present, as single artefact can now represent a group of elements. Those artefacts for counting and representing numerical values were instrumental to the activity of keeping track of commercial transactions; indeed, transactions were recorded by putting into a clay pot a number of artefacts corresponding to the entity of the transaction (say two marbles and five sticks to represent the number twenty-five) and by storing the pots in an archive. Despite this improvement, the artefacts, instrumental to the activity of recording commercial transactions, didn't support other activities related to trading; for instance, to retrieve the information concerning a past transaction, administrators had to break the corresponding pot. The shift toward a different representation of numerical values, supporting not just the storing but also the retrieving of information, took place around 3300 BC: the content of each sphere was represented, on the surface of the sphere itself, using different sorts of signs, namely a small tally mark for every stick, a small circle for every marble, a large circle for every disk and a large tally mark for every cone.

The crucial issue in the process described above is the relation between the notation (representation) and the manipulation: the features of the notation are increasingly related to the operations one can perform on the representation itself, and the notation maintains a less direct link with the object it represents. It is important to highlight that secondary artefacts (as a notation) are not an expression of the abstract features of the object they represent, but rather they are an expression of the human activities related to the use of the notation itself.

As illustrated by the example described above, secondary artefacts are socio-cultural products which originate in the manipulation of primary artefacts. In fact, secondary artefacts originate also in the manipulation of other secondary artefacts: the Arabic numeral notation (e.g. 1112), an example of a secondary artefact, both embodies and at the same time improves the capabilities of the Roman notation (e.g. MCXII), another secondary artefact that, however, does not support the operation of multiplication. This particular activity, the manipulation of numerical representation by iterative addiction of the same number, is on the contrary, well supported by Arabic notations. The latter directly embody the multiplication in the notation itself through the use of the positions occupied by the digits as indicators of the number of iterations (e.g., the «1» in the first position is worth 1000 times 1, whereas the «1» in the second position is worth 100 times 1; on the contrary, in the Roman notation every symbol has a defined value that does not vary according to position). It is important to note that to perfect the Arabic notation it was necessary to create an artefact, the zero, that was defined not in relation to any object of the physical world but instead in relation to the operations made possible by the Arabic notation itself. The same principle applies also to other artefacts in the domain of numbers, such as the logarithm.

To summarise, the critical property of all artefacts is that they do not just represent the physical world, they also mediate a particular activity, namely their manipulation; specifically, secondary artefacts differ from primary ones in that their main object of representation is centred on the modality of manipulation of the primary or secondary artefacts themselves. The representations used for secondary artefacts thus become much more independent of the physical reality, while becoming increasingly related to the goal-directed activity that they embody.

In this way the evolution of artefacts becomes part of the social history of human cognition. But, as stated before, they are not human cognition, they are but one aspect of cognition. The knowledge that they embody is not passively mapped onto internal representations, instead the internalisation process by which artefacts are able to accomplish their mediation role is a complex process that produces an internal activity that is not identical to the external activity, yet it is related (Wertsch, 1985).

If we accept the idea of cognitive artefacts as mediating tools, then by definition, they should mediate between some primitive properties of the mind and the external world. The concept of mediation has at least one important implication, i.e., different artefacts can mediate similar activity according to how they best fit the primitive properties of the human mind. That is, artefacts can dramatically change the content of our interaction with the world but they cannot modify the primitive processing of the human brain. But what are these primitives? Based on the development of Cognitive Science in the last 30 years we can distinguish between at least two levels of human information processing, sub-symbolic and symbolic. At the sub-symbolic level the evidence produced by the connectionist approach has shown how most of the empirically supported heuristics/biases of our brain identified and explored by cognitive psychology can be employed by a model in which knowledge is represented in an interconnected network of distributed and parallel processing units. For example, availability and representativeness can be conceived as two emergent properties of such connectionist systems (Levine, 1991). At the symbolic level, one of the few theories that is empirically well supported by results is Model Theory (Johnson-Laird & Byrne, 1991). The Model Theory has been applied to different paradigms of research concerning human reasoning (thinking), i.e. deduction, induction, decision making, narratives. In all of these domains Model Theory has been useful in guiding research on the basis of a few well stated principles, but the domain to which it has been more extensively applied is deductive reasoning. This is the domain where we will attempt to produce some empirical evidence concerning the mediating role of artefacts in human symbolic reasoning. Specifically, our aim is to investigate the design of external representations developed according to some of the assumptions of the Model Theory, and applied to a special kind of deductive reasoning, i.e. syllogisms.

ARTEFACTS AND REASONING

Syllogistic reasoning

According to Johnson-Laird (1983), deductive reasoning is the form of goal-oriented thinking that starts from a definite set of assumptions and ends with another set of assumptions (the conclusions) which are consistent with the premises, that is they are true if the premises are true.

Syllogistic reasoning is a particular kind of deductive reasoning; a syllogism is composed of two premises containing a single quantifier (all, none and some) and describing the relation among classes of elements (for instance «As» and «Bs» for the first premise and «Bs» and «Cs» for the second premise); those two premises have to be combined to obtain, when possible, a valid conclusion describing the relation among the «As» and the «Cs». A valid conclusion describes a state of the world that is true when the states of the world described by the premises are true.

What is relevant in syllogistic reasoning is that all theories posit that people construct internal representations of the premises and combine those representations to draw conclusions. Different kinds of internal representations have been proposed to account for the differences in difficulty of different syllogisms, the most relevant attempts being formal rules (Braine & Rumain, 1983), Euler circles (Erikson, 1974, Guyote & Sternberg, 1978) and mental models (Johnson-Laird, 1983, Johnson-Laird & Byrne, 1991).

Among these approaches, mental models theory is the one that has received most empirical support to date. The basic tenet of this theory is that syllogistic reasoning is a semantic (non syntactic) process based on a particular kind of mental representation, mental models, that is, models which are structurally isomorphic to the state of the world they describe. According to the theory, syllogistic deductions are the result of a three stage process: first, a model representing the relation among the «As» and the «Bs» in the first premise is built; second, the relation among the «Cs» and the «Bs» described in the second premise is then added to obtain a model representing the relations among the different elements mentioned in the two premises (the relations among the «As» and «Bs» and the relations among the «Bs» and «Cs»); at this point subjects are able to draw one or more conclusions about the relation among the «As» and the «Cs»; third, a procedure of revision of the particular model built is applied in order to look for different models which satisfy the premises and lead to different conclusions. The procedures of revision of the model guarantee the validity of the conclusion: if no counterexamples of the conclusions compatible with the premises are spotted, the conclusion is valid; otherwise, every time a different model of the premises is identified, new conclusions taking into account the different possible relations among «Bs» and «Cs» are formulated.

The theory allows one to formulate detailed predictions on subjects' performances and errors which have received strong empirical confirmation; for instance, it has been shown that the difficulty of a particular syllogism is a function of the number of different models of the premises the subject have to flesh out and take into account to formulate valid conclusions.

The range of mental models theory goes beyond the domain of syllogistic reasoning. Indeed, unlike the theories which postulate the existence of a particular sort of mental artefact such as logic of rules of inference, (Braine & Rumain, 1983; Rips, 1983), mental models theory provides a general explanation of rationality that accounts for human performance in a broad range of cognitive process such as reasoning (both deduction and induction) and language comprehension. According to the theory, the principle of rationality is embodied in the semantic process of construction of the models of reality and their recursive revision in search for counterexamples. Models Theory is thus viewed as an account of a basic functional primitive of the human mind (Johnson-Laird & Byrne, 1991).

The effect of different representations of premises

Although mental models theory assumes that there can be different sources of external information one could retrieve for building mental models, the experiments carried out so far on syllogistic reasoning have used only one kind of secondary artefact, namely propositions, to represent the premises of syllogisms (but see Bucciarelli & Johnson-Laird, 1998).

Propositions play a crucial role in this experimental setting in that they support the subjects in the process of search for counterexamples of the mental model of the premises; indeed, according to mental models theory, while the reasoning process relies on the elaboration of semantic representations, that is mental models, the search for alternative models needs, as input, an independent representation of the premises.

As outlined above, propositions, as artefacts, have properties that mediate the elaboration of the information they provide. What would be the impact of different representations of the premises on subjects' performance and errors? What would be the impact of a representation of the premises designed, according to mental models theory, to support the subjects' search for alternative models of the premises ?

The experiment described below has been designed to test the impact that different representations of the premises have on the subject performance and errors in syllogistic deduction.

EXPERIMENT

Mental models theory has focused on representations, that is mental models, and the procedures to build and to recursively revise the models in order to draw, when possible, valid conclusions. We believe that the theory, which seems to capture a basic process underlying human thinking namely the construction of a model and the revision of the model in search of counterexamples, has to some extent overlooked the role played by the specific kinds of representations subjects are provided with. Indeed, in syllogistic reasoning, different representations of the premises are not equivalent in that that have different impacts on the subjects' cognitive behaviour in solving syllogisms. In particular, according to the three stage model put forward by the mental models theory and the theory of artefacts outlined above, different representations have different impact on the ease with which subjects perform the following task:

- Flesh out the content of the premises;
- Combine the first and the second premises;
- Modify the model of the two premises to search for counterexamples.

Would subjects using a specially designed representation according to mental models theory, have better performance than subjects provided with different representations of premises, namely propositions and Euler circles ? This was the main hypothesis we wanted to test by means of three different kinds of representations of the premises.

First representation: Propositions

Propositions, that is strings of symbols close to natural language, are the «standard» way to represent premises. In spite of this, propositions are just one of the possible representations which can be used; in particular, our hypothesis is that propositions are not well suited to support subjects in any of the three stages of the process. Indeed, unlike Euler circles and Valence representations (see below), propositions do not explicitly represent the possible states described by a premise and unlike Valence representation they do not support the combination of the elements of the premises in a model and its revision. Again, the properties of this representation depend on the kind of processing required to get the task done: previous studies on syllogistic reasoning (Johnson-Laird, 1983) have shown that subjects' performance varies according to the number (1, 2 or 3) of models which need to be built to draw a valid conclusion.

Second representation: Euler circles

Euler circles, a geometrical representation of the formal rules introduced by the mathematician Leonhard Euler, represent premises using a circle as a model of a set of elements; the advantage of this representation is that it explicitly represents all the possible relations between two entities contained in a single premise (see fig. 6.1). In spite of this, the representation doesn't support the combination of the premises in a single model because the representations of all the possible relations between the elements of a given premise are not «integrated» in a single configuration or model; instead, for every premise, a different set of models (from 1 up to 4) representing alternative models of the premise, is provided. It follows that for most syllogisms the number of alternatives one has to take into account to build a single model of the two premises is too high. In this case, the representation can even hamper the formulation of a correct model of the premises. As stated by Johnson-Laird, Euler circles are not a plausible way for subjects to represent premises. We argue that in most cases, Euler circles are not an appropriate secondary artefact for supporting syllogistic reasoning.

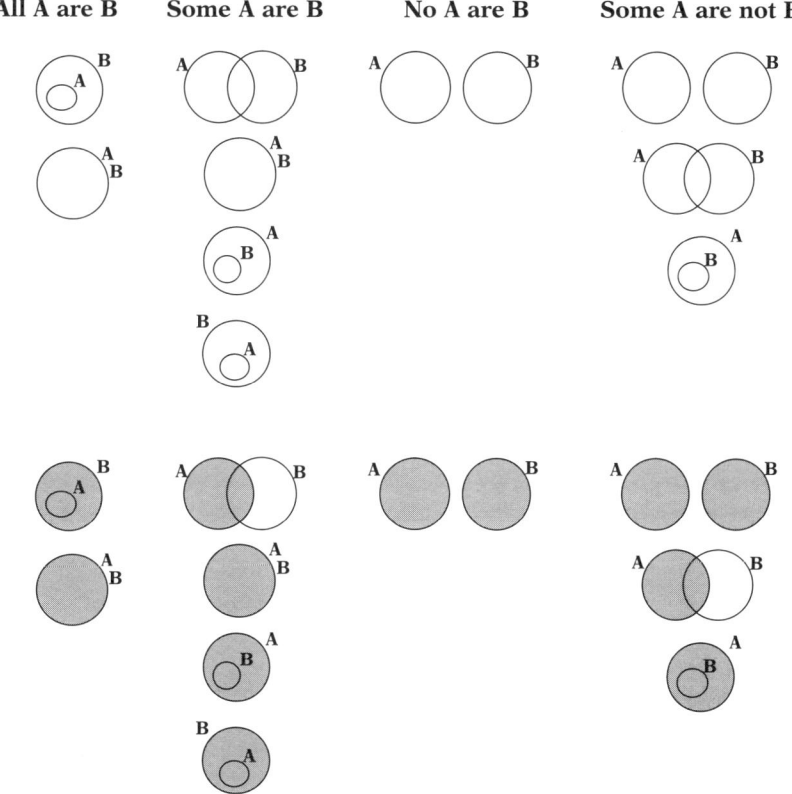

Figure 6.1. Representation of the four possible kinds of premises using Euler circles.

Third representation: Valence

The Valence representation, described below has been designed on the basis of the three steps process put forward by mental models theory. Here is a description of its representational properties for each of the three steps.

1) *Fleshing out the states of the world described by each premise*. Unlike propositions, which do not explicitly represent elements which can or cannot exist and like Euler circles, which represent all the possible states of the world described by the premise but using a different model, Valence representations explicitly represent (see fig. 6.2) in a single representation both the entities which exist (black colour) and the entities which might or might not exist (grey colour). This is a critical feature that should help subjects in taking account of all the possible models of a premise.

2) *Build up a model representing the content of the two premises using the magnetic metaphor*. The rationale underlying the representation is to support

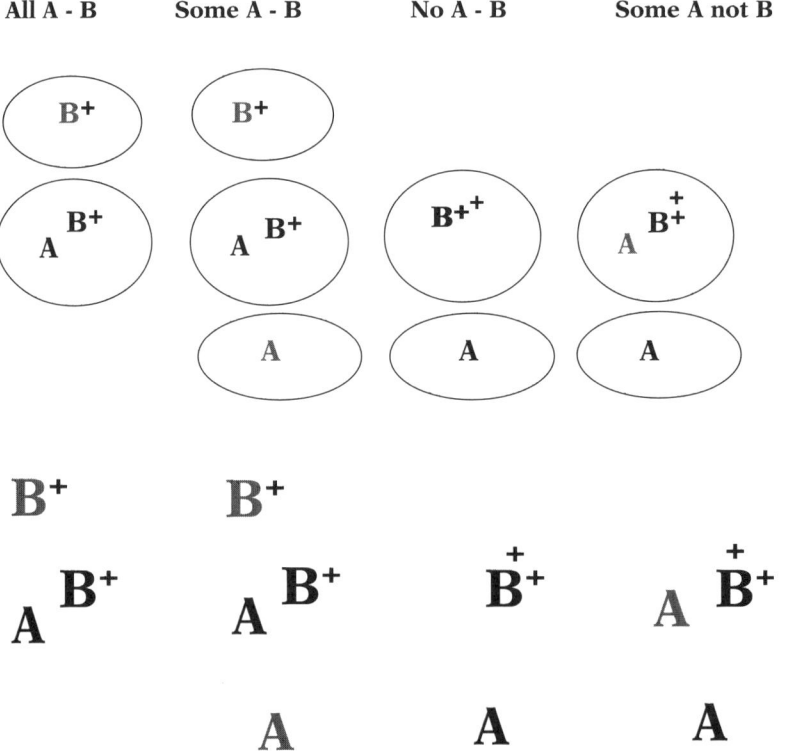

Figure 6.2. Representation of the 4 premises with valence. The elements of the premise are clustered in semicircles so to represent the relationships of association and separation. The premise «Some A are B» is represented by means of an A and a B that certainly exist and are associated (the bold ones), however there could be some other A and B which could exist separately (the grey ones). The fact that the B exists for sure and is associated with the A could not be the only one is stressed by the single valence.

reasoners in putting into relation the «As» in the first premise and the «Cs» in the second by means of the «Bs» which can be combined according to the magnetic metaphor: As depicted in fig. 6.3, the «Bs» in the first premise have positive valence, the «Bs» in the second have negative valence. According to the magnetic principle, different valences attract each other, equal valences repulse each other. When a black «B» has a double valence («+ +» or «- -»), it represents all the «Bs» that could exist in one of the premise. When a black «B» has just a single valence it means that in the premise there are others «Bs» (in grey) which might or might not exist. In this case, one cannot be certain that the black «B» represents all the «Bs» in the premise.

The possibility of building up a model of the two premises depends on the way «Bs» of the first and second premise combine: when (as shown in fig. 6.3) it is not possible to group the «Bs» in a stable configuration, there are no definite links between «As» and «Cs» because there isn't any definite identity between the «Bs» in the first and the «Bs» in the second premise. In this case, the answer to the syllogism is always «no conclusion».

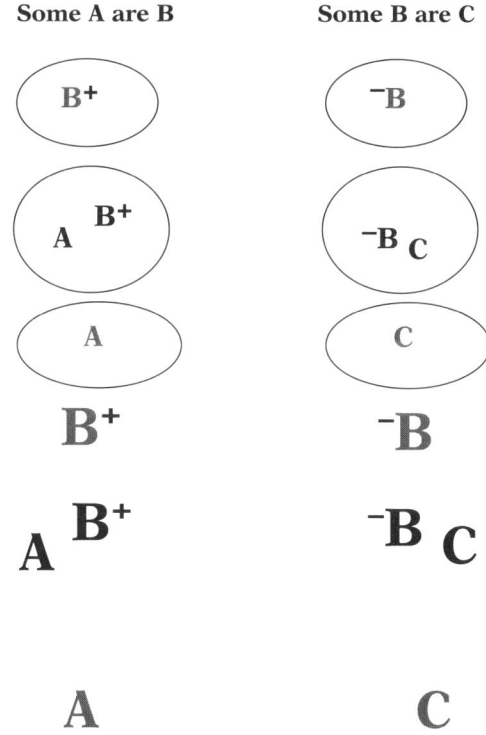

Figure 6.3. «Bs» do not form a single stable configuration; there are two «Bs» with a single valence «+» and two with a single valence «-». Thus there is no certain relationship between the As and the Cs: if the positive B connects with the upper negative B it could be that No A are B; if the positive B connects with the lower negative B it could be that All A are B. Further models are possible if we consider the grey As and Cs, but the two possible models No A are C and All A are C are enough to draw the deduction: No conclusion.

On the contrary, when «Bs», according to the magnetic metaphor, group in a single stable configuration, then it is possible to look at the relations among the «As» and «Cs» because the «Bs» mentioned in the first and second premises refer to a single set of «Bs» that can bridge between «As» and «Cs» (fig. 6.4). In this case, there is a certain identity between the «Bs» in the first and second premise.

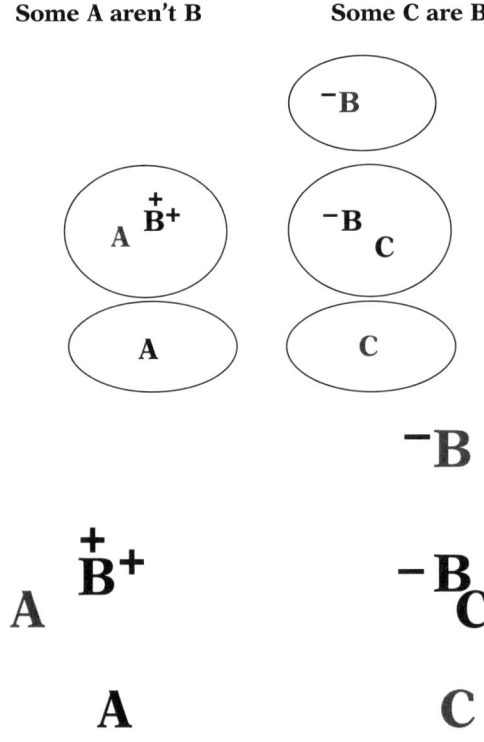

Figure 6.4. According to the magnetic metaphor, «Bs» can be grouped in a single stable configuration (there is a «B» with a double valence «++» and two «Bs» with a single valence «–»).

3) *Derivation of the conclusions and search for counterexamples*

As shown in fig. 6.5, 6.6 and 6.7, conclusions can be drawn by analysing the overall configuration resulting from the combination of the two premises. The black line indicates the disjunction between the elements placed above and below it, whereas the dashed line indicates a possible but not certain conjunction among the elements placed below the dark line.

According to the magnetic metaphor, «Bs» can combine in three different configurations; when, as depicted in fig. 6.5, they do not group in a single and stable configuration, they might be linked to different set of «Bs». In this case it is not possible to get any permanent state across configurations; the correct answer is «no conclusion». The attempt to combine the premises has already produced two conflicting models.

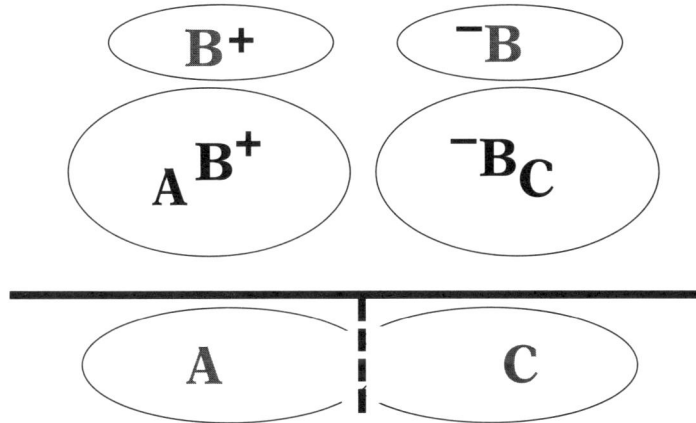

Figure 6.5. «Some A are B, Some C are B». Conclusion: «No conclusion».

In this representation, and in the following ones as well, the separation between As (or Cs) and Bs is stressed by a bold line. The relationship between the As and Cs certainly separated by the B is represented by a dashed line, which imply the uncertainty about their relationship; i.e. they could be completely separated as well as fully associated. This representation was used in the tests with the subjects.

When, as depicted in fig. 6.6, «Bs» combine in a single configuration, it is the relations among «As» and «Cs» that determine the conclusion. In this case, it is sometimes possible to draw valid conclusions about the black «As» and «Cs», that is the elements that certainly exist, by looking at their location in the representation. To figure out the relation among dark «As» and dark «Cs» participants can read the emergent configuration using the same syntax used to represent the premises. In particular, the meaning of the notation is the following:

- when they are separated by the line, there is disjunction among them;
- when both are below the dark line, their relation is not certain (they are separated by the dashed line).

The grey elements in the representation play a critical role in that, by explicitly representing entities which might or not exist, they can support subjects in figuring out alternative models of the premises. Again, we believe that this is a crucial property of the representation: if, according to Mental Models theory, the difficulty in solving syllogisms is related to the numbers of models representing the state of the world described by the premises, a representation which includes the entities which might or might not exist should support subjects in taking into account all the possible models of the premises. In fig. 6.6, for instance, the black «A» does not represent the whole set of «As» because of the grey «A» below the line, which stands for the possible existence of some other «As» which might or might not a relation of identity with the black «Cs». In this case the valid conclusion one can draw is «Some A are not C» instead of «All A are not C». It is important to note that the conclusion can be read according to the same notation as the statement of the premises.

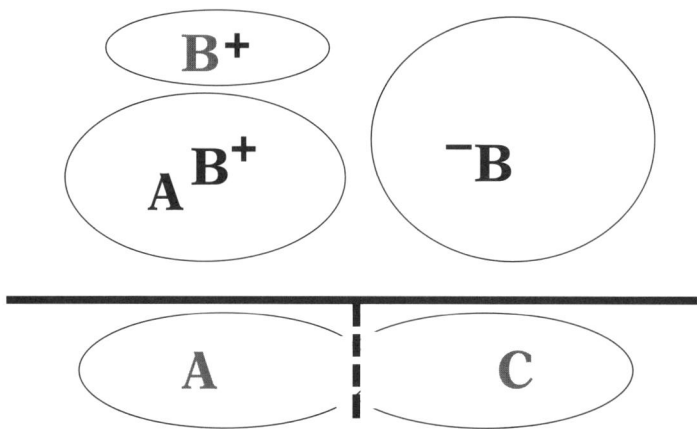

Figure 6.6. Some A - B, No C – B. Conclusion: «Some A not C».

When different models of the premises are in conflict, no valid conclusion can be drawn. In the case shown in fig. 6.7, the possible existence of a set of «As» and a set of «Cs» (the ones in grey) prevents one from drawing any conclusion: all form of premises can be read out.

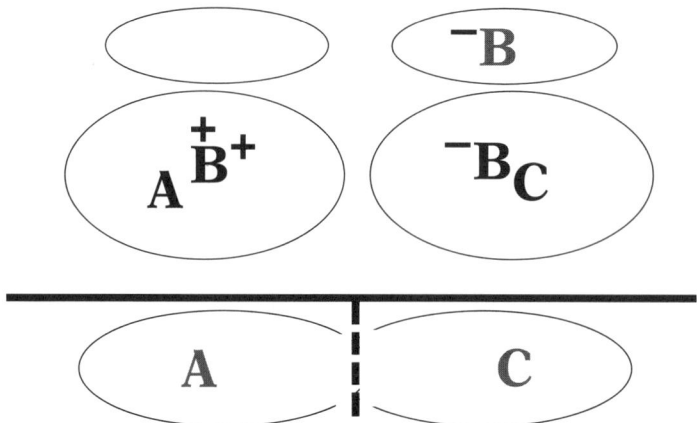

Figure 6.7. Some A not B, some B – C. Conclusion: «No conclusion».

TABLE 6.1
Differences among representations in supporting the three phases of syllogistic reasoning according to Mental Models theory

	Propositions	Euler circles	Valence
Fleshing out the properties of premises	No	Yes	Yes
Combination of the premises in a model	No	No	Yes
Search for counterexamples of the model	No	No	Yes

The hypothesis

We expected two main results:
- *A main effect due to the kind of representation.* Subjects provided with the Valence representation would show, on a 24 syllogisms trial, a better performance overall (in terms of both *accuracy* and *response time*) than subjects provided with Euler circles and propositions. This hypothesis is based on the assumption that artefacts have a dramatic impact on the subjects' cognitive behaviour; in terms of syllogistic reasoning it means that the different representations of the premises are not equivalent, that is that the representation specifically designed to support subjects in the process of construction and revision of the mental models of the premises should determine the best performance both in terms of *accuracy* and *response time*.
- *Interaction between representation and syllogism.* Subjects' performance depends on the interaction between the representation they are provided with and the kinds of syllogism they face. This hypothesis is, in fact, a corollary of the concept of *artefact mediation* of human activity: the properties of the artefacts are not absolute because they depend on a specific combination with the property of the primitive function of the mind, i.e. a mental model. Thus, for example, syllogisms that involve a single model, as All A are B – All B are C, should be made easy by notations that do not express irrelevant or implicit models. On the contrary, syllogisms that involves multiple models should be made easy by notations that support the search for alternative models.

Experimental design

Based on the hypothesis, three experimental conditions corresponding to the different external representations of syllogisms were set up. Thus, the experimental design was a *between subjects* design with three conditions (Proposition, Euler, Valence).

Participants

18 participants, all students in Communication Sciences at the University of Siena, participated in the experiment. Each subject was randomly assigned

to one of the three experimental conditions (6 subjects per condition). Each subject faced the same 24 syllogisms (see Appendix 1) which were randomly presented.

Training

Before the experimental session, each participant received a 30 minute session concerning syllogistic reasoning (an explanation of the semantic premises and their combination) and underwent a supervised trial on 6 syllogisms. The aim was to eliminate any differences between subjects due to prior different knowledge or expertise on syllogistic reasoning and to provide every subject with the basic knowledge needed to understand the syntax of the representation they would have to interact with.

Dependent measures

Participants' performance was evaluated by means of two dependent measures, the *accuracy* (the number of syllogisms properly solved) and the *speed* (the amount of time, in seconds, employed by each subject to solve the syllogisms). Accuracy was rated by assigning the value 1 for every syllogism solved and assigning the value 0 for every syllogism not solved (wrong conclusion). For syllogisms with two valid conclusions, the value 1 was assigned when both conclusions were provided; accordingly, the value .5 was assigned when just one out of two conclusion was provided.

Results

An analysis of variance for each dependent variable (*accuracy* and *time*) was performed.

A main effect due to *Condition* was found for the dependent variable *accuracy* ($F= 8.107$, $p<.01$): in particular (see table 6.2) the score in the Valence condition was significantly better than the score in the Euler condition ($p<.01$) and in the Proposition condition ($p<.025$). No significant difference was found between Proposition and Euler conditions.

TABLE 6.2
Summary of results for *accuracy*

	solved syllogisms (mean)	Std Deviation	Std Error
Valence	19.0	1.673	.683
Proposition	15.6	1.862	.760
Euler	13.8	2.994	1.222

A main effect for *Condition* was also found for the dependent variable *time* ($F= 4.424$, $p<.05$): as showed in table 6.3. The difference in *time* between the

Valence and Euler conditions is significant (p<. 025) as well as the difference between the Proposition and Euler conditions (p<.05).

TABLE 6.3
Summary of results for *time*

	Time needed to solve a syllogism (mean)	Std Deviation	Std Error
Valence	49.9 seconds	15.124	6.175
Proposition	58.3 seconds	11.078	4.523
Euler	84.0 seconds	30.487	12.446

In addition, an analysis of variance for the variable *Accuracy* was performed with the aim of analysing the interaction between *Condition and Type of Syllogism*.

As described in Table 6.4, subjects in the Valence condition showed a significantly better *Accuracy* than the subjects in the Proposition and Euler conditions for some syllogisms without any valid conclusion and for some syllogisms with valid conclusions. For instance, for the syllogism «Some A are not B»/ «All B are C» (without any conclusion) both the differences between Valence and Euler (p<.0001) and between Valence and Proposition (p<.0001) are significant.

Similarly, for the syllogism «Some A are B»/ «No C are B» (with conclusion «Some A are not C») subjects performance in Valence conditions are significantly better than the ones in the Proposition and Euler conditions (p<.05 and p<. 025, respectively).

Nevertheless, for some syllogisms (for instance, «All A are B» /»All B are C») subjects in the Proposition condition show higher (although not statistically significant) *accuracy* than subjects in the Valence and Euler conditions.

TABLE 6.4
Mean scores for *accuracy* in the three conditions for three syllogisms

	Some A are not B All B are C	Some A are B No C are B	All A are B All B are C
Valence	.83	.83	.67
Proposition	0	0	1
Euler	0	.33	.83

To summarise, the data provide empirical support to the hypothesis that representations mediate reasoning and that a representation designed according to the three steps proposed by the Mental Model theory supports subjects in solving syllogisms better than alternative representations, namely propositions and Euler circles. Nevertheless, external representations are not mental models, nor do they ever become mental models without further effort and transformation (cf. the internalisation process proposed by Vygotsky). Rather, external representations play a mediating role in syllogistic reasoning, that is their content or structure can support or hamper the construction of the appropriate mental models and the formulation of the appropriate conclusions.

Euler circles, for instance, support the fleshing out of premises but do not support the combination of the premises in a single model and revision of the model; moreover, sometimes this representation affords the construction of partial models of the premises which lead subjects to wrong conclusions. On the other hand, Valence representations, which support the construction of alternative models of premises, can support the formulation of partial or incomplete conclusions; for instance, subjects who face syllogisms which require the formulation of just one mental model (e. g. «All A are B» / «All B are C») give just one out of two possible conclusions, the less general (e. g. «Some C are A» instead the more general «All A are C»). Finally, propositions are the form of representation that put less constraints on the construction of mental models since they do not afford any kind of search for models. This feature accounts for the fact that, according to Johnson-Laird's previous findings, subjects using propositions easily solve syllogisms requiring the construction of just one model of the premises.

CONCLUSIONS

Scaife & Rogers (1996) in their analysis of the literature on external representations identify three central characteristics of external representations which can account for the role they play in human cognition:

i) *Computational off-loading.* External representations are informational resources which, by activating *perceptual processes*, can be picked-up and used without being explicitly internally re-presented and kept in working memory. This property relies on the fact that perceptual processes require less cognitive resources than memory processes (it is well acknowledged, for instance, that it is much easier reading a list of items than recalling it).

ii) *Re-representation.* The features of the external representations affect the likeliness that the properties of the elements and their relations are *perceived* by the task performer; indeed, every representation makes part of the features of the represented world salient (or available) to the subjects. This means that a good external representation is the one that captures and highlights properties of the represented world which are relevant for the particular task or goal at hand.

iii) *Graphical constraining.* This property refers to the way a static external representation both supports and constrains subject's «internal» manipulation and recombination of its elements. This property becomes crucial in problem solving settings (such as reasoning) where the information provided by the external representations needs to be further internally processed by the subjects.

Though all three characteristics are important in defining the properties of external representations, we claim that the crucial properties of secondary artefacts lie in their power to mediate human activity. Indeed, according to the theoretical approach presented in the first part of this paper, it is not possible to separate the three above mentioned features because representation and processing cannot be kept apart in investigating the role played by artefacts, in particular secondary ones. In addition, it is not possible to consider the role of external representations without taking into account how the features of external representations interplay with the functional primitives of the mind. The experiment presented provides preliminary empirical evidence supporting this thesis.

REFERENCES

BUCCIARELLI, M., & JOHNSON-LAIRD, P. N. (1998): «Syllogistic Reasoning». Under submission.

CAMPIGLIO, E., & EUGENI, V. (1990): *Dalle Dita al Calcolatore*. Milan: Gruppo Editoriale Fabbri.

COLE, M. (1996): *Cultural Psychology, a once and future discipline*. Cambridge, Massachusetts: the Belknap Press of Harvard University Press.

BRAINE, M. D. S., and RUMAIN, B. (1983): «Logical Reasoning». In J.H. Flavell and E.M. Markman (Eds.), *Carmichael's handdbook of child psychology*. Vol 3: Cognitive development (4th ed.) New York: Wiley.

ERIKSON, J. R. (1974): «A set analysis theory of behaviour in formal syllogistic reasoning tasks», in R. L. Solso (Ed.), *Loyola symposium on cognition*, vol.2, Hillsdale (NY): Erlbaum.

EVANS, J. St. B. T. (1982): *The Psychology of Deductive Reasoning*. London: Routlege and Kegan Paul.

GUYOTE, M. J., & STERNBERG, R. J. (1978): «A transitive chain theory of syllogistic reasoning», *Cognitive Psychology*, 13, 461-525.

HUTCHINS, E. (1995): *Cognition in the wild*. Cambridge: the MIT Press.

JOHNSON-LAIRD, P. N. (1983): *Mental Models. Towards a Cognitive Science of Language, Inference and Consciousness*. Cambridge: Cambridge University Press.

JOHNSON-LAIRD, P. N., & BYRNE, R. M. J. (1991): *Deduction*. Hove: Lawrence Erlbaum Associates, Publishers.

LEVINE, D. S. (1991): *Neural and Cognitive Modeling*. Hillsdale, NJ: Lawrence Erlbaum Associates, Publishers.

NARDI, B. (1996): *Context and Consciousness: The role of activity theory in human-computer interaction*. Boston: MIT Press.

NORMAN, D. A. (1993): *Things that make us smart*. New York: Addison-Wesley.

— (1991): «Cognitive artefacts». In J. M. Carroll (Ed.), *Designing interaction,*. Cambridge, MA: Cambridge University Press.

SCAIFE, M., & ROGERS, Y. (1996): «External cognition: how do graphical representations work?», *International Journal of Human-Computer Studies*, 45, 185-213.

VYGOTSKY, L. S. (1978): *Mind in society*. Cambridge, MA: Harvard University Press.

WARTFOSKY, M. (1973): *Models*. Dordrecht: D. Reidel.

WERTSCH, J. V. (1985): *Vygotsky and the social formation of the mind*. Cambridge (MA), Harvard University Press.

ZHANG, J., & NORMAN, D. A. (1994): «Representations in Distributed Cognitive Tasks». *Cognitive Science*, *18*, 87-122.

— (1995): «A representation analysis of numeration systems». *Cognition*, 57, 271-295.

APPENDIX

The six syllogisms used in the training session:

All A are B	No C are B
No A are B	Some B are C
Some B are A	Some B are C
Some A are B	Some C are not B
Some B are not A	Some C are B
Some A are not B	All C are B

The 24 syllogisms used in the experimental session

All A are B	All B are C
All A are B	All C are B
All A are B	No B are C
All A are B	Some B are not C
All A are B	Some C no B
All A are B	Some C are B
All B are A	All B are C
All B are A	No B are C
All B are A	Some B are C
No A are B	All B are C
No A are B	All C are B
No A are B	No B are C
No A are B	Some C no B
No A are B	Some C are B
Some A no B	All B are C
Some A are B	All B are C
Some A are B	All C are B
Some A are B	No C are B
Some A are B	Some B no C
Some A are B	Some B are C
Some B no A	All B are C
Some B no A	No B are C
Some B no A	Some B no C
Some B no A	Some B are C

7

PRIMING IN MENTAL MODELS[1]

Sergio Moreno
Juan A. García-Madruga

En este capítulo justificamos el uso de una tarea de tiempos de reacción que hace posible poner a prueba algunos supuestos de la teoría de los modelos mentales. Para ello, simplificamos las tareas deductivas tradicionales mediante el uso del análisis de los estadios de la deducción propuestos por la propia teoría. Los estadios de descripción y validación fueron simplificados mediante la aplicación de una tarea de evaluación de la suficiencia. El estadio de comprensión fue también facilitado mediante la presentación de premisas esquemáticas. En estas condiciones, el número de observaciones fue suficiente para obtener una medida del «efecto de priming». El priming es un fenómeno muy estudiado en la psicología cognitiva. Se ha interpretado como evidencia de la existencia de ciertas representaciones mentales. Con la utilización de esta nueva tarea hemos encontrado apoyo empírico a las principales predicciones de la teoría de los modelos mentales: la construcción de ciertos modelos mentales afecta al resultado de la deducción. Los problemas indeterminados, que son congruentes con más de una situación posible, fueron más difíciles que los problemas determinados, que son congruentes con una sola situación. Pero, el resultado más importante es que los modelos mentales, al igual que otras representaciones mentales, son susceptibles de ser primados. En este capítulo describimos un procedimiento utilizado en uno de nuestros experimentos. Con esta metodología pueden ser exploradas nuevas formas de estudiar los procesos mentales implicados en deducción. Por ejemplo, es posible comparar respuestas a condiciones muy similares que únicamente difieren en la participación de un proceso mental: un procedimiento utilizado con frecuencia en el estudio de la relaciones entre las operaciones mentales y las estructuras del cerebro. Por el momen-

---

[1] This paper describes a task that has been explored in our laboratory as the doctoral thesis of Sergio Moreno.

to, el procedimiento ha permitido mostrar que durante la deducción se activan modelos mentales.

The Mental Model theory aims to account for thinking on the basis of suppositions taken for granted in other areas of cognition. The main assumption is that people represent and manage mental models of the world. Comprehension and reasoning depend on this capacity. This concept is akin to the one used in David Marr's (1982) theory of vision that accounted for the derivation of perceptually-based models of the world. The perceptual mental model is one of the most direct ways of representing information. However, the mental model theory has usually been tested by studying another type of model, the conceptual model proposed by Johnson-Laird (1983). In this chapter we shall show how the predictions of the mental model theory can be tested with perceptual models using tasks different from the traditional ones. We expect the new tasks to require some of the same cognitive operations as the traditional deductive tasks.

One of the main virtues of the mental model theory is its capacity to predict results in fields different from that for which it was originally conceived. The mental model theory was first employed to explain syllogistic reasoning (Johnson-Laird, 1983), subsequently it has been applied to spatial reasoning (Byrne & Johnson-Laird, 1989), propositional reasoning (Johnson-Laird, Byrne & Schaeken, 1992) and recently, probabilistic reasoning (Johnson-Laird, Legrenzi, Girotto, Sonino & Caverni, 1999). We consider that the capacity of this theory to extend to new fields is due, first, to its very few assumptions, and second, to the fact that those assumptions concern very simple cognitive operations involved in many deductive tasks. Moreover, we think that the predictions of the mental model theory should be applied to any task that includes the mental operations proposed by the theory. This has an interesting implication: it is possible to test the cognitive mechanism proposed in very different tasks.

TESTING THE MENTAL MODEL THEORY

The predictions of the mental model theory are usually tested by manipulating factors, such as the linguistic structure of the premises, that affect the construction of particular mental models. The result of the deduction is compared with the predicted effect of the initial mental models constructed from the premises. For example, let us look at a determinate and an indeterminate problem about the possible arrangement of three balls («A», «B» and «C»):

Determinate problem:
B is on the right of A
C is on the left of A.
What is the correct arrangement of the three balls?

Indeterminate problem:
B is on the right of A
C is on the left of B.
What is the correct arrangement of the three balls?

The mental model theory predicts that people make deductions in a chain of three stages: (1) At the *comprehension* stage, they represent what is said in the premises. Thus, in the determinate problem people would represent the model «C A B», and in the indeterminate problem they could create «C A B» and «C B A». In fact, mental model theory assumes that representing two mental models is more difficult than just representing one. The construction of two models from the indeterminate premises depends on certain factors, such as the complexity of the problem, the load on working memory, and so on. Some participants may represent just one mental model. At the second stage (2), *description* of a tentative conclusion, people propose a conclusion - for example, «C is on the left of B» (C A B). In evaluation tasks, people do not need to make a description of a tentative conclusion because they are provided with one. At the last stage (3), *validation*, the conclusion is compared with other alternatives derived from the premises. If some of them are incompatible with the conclusion, then the conclusion is discarded and a new tentative conclusion considered. Again, in some tasks this stage is not needed - for example, in a sufficiency evaluation task.

One typical way of testing predictions of the mental model theory is to compare the difficulties between determinate and indeterminate problems. Even when people are asked after each problem «Is C on the left of A?», deciding correctly «yes» takes longer in the indeterminate problem than in the determinate one (Byrne & Johnson-Laird, 1989). The theory predicts that in indeterminate problems people try to construct two mental models from the indeterminacy, which takes longer and leads to increase the number of errors. However, the construction of multiple or simple mental models takes place at just one stage of the deduction. Thus, is it necessary to construct complex tasks that integrate the three stages to test this prediction? If not, why are the same kinds of tasks so frequently used for testing the predictions of mental models?

A NEW WAY OF TESTING THE MENTAL MODEL THEORY

There are two important common features in prediction testing using traditional tasks. The first is the use of propositional material, and the second is the preference for error rate as a measure of difficulty. A common way of testing the mental model theory is by comparing its predictions with other reasoning theories, mainly mental rules theories. Perhaps for this reason, the tasks used to test predictions have some limitations: for example, the linguistic component of these theories is essential, and premises are therefore usually expressed in a propositional format. However, mental models are not restricted to making predictions from propositional descriptions - it is also possible to do so from diagrammatic or perceptual materials. Moreover, perceptual material may offer a more homogeneous way of representing the mental models of different subjects. Some properties of the stimuli are better determined in a diagrammatic description than in a propositional description. For example, it is more likely that people represent a person in different ways when they read the expression «a person» than when they see the image of a specific person (e.g., a tall female). In addition to the content of the models, in some kinds of task it is easier to predict clearly the number of models derived from the premises than in others. As Carreiras and Santamaría (1995) stated, in relational reasoning the number of models representing a given problem is very easy to predict, and some of the criticisms about the method of counting mental models can be avoided (Rips, 1994; Bonatti, 1994). In relational problems, the number of models is the number of situations that could be consistent with the sentence expressed in the problem. In the previous example about three balls, the determinate and indeterminate problems were consistent with one and two arrangements, respectively. The number of models and their content can be well determine with diagrammatic premises in relational problems

A second common feature of traditional tasks is the preference for using error rates as the main dependent variable. This makes sense, since tasks with complex problems are difficult for the participants, so that they can solve only a few problems in an experimental session. However, some other measures have been used as a complement to error rates, such as reading time and global response latencies in the problems. Recently there have been many studies that include reaction time. Generally, however, the small number of observations in each condition makes it very difficult to obtain information from other sources other than errors rate, such as reaction time. In other fields of cognitive science (e.g., attention or memory), the study of mental processes has been possible through the application of some methodologies using reaction times (e.g., Donder's subtractive or Sternberg's additive factors methodologies). For example, the study of mental processes with Donder's subtractive methodology is carried out comparing two very similar conditions that differ in just one process. The subtraction of the reaction time of one condition from the reaction time of the control condition that differs only in the process studied provides information about the latency of that process. The same idea is applied in the study of the relationship between mental operations and brain structures. For example, the ERPs (event-related potentials) technique can experimentally evoked the activity of brain tissue when people carry out a task. As in the previous case, the task is composed of two kinds of conditions that differ in only one mental operation. The cortical areas (or structures of the brain) involved in a mental operation can be identified by observing the areas that are differentially activated in the two conditions - the areas that are activated only in a certain experimental condition but not in the control condition. The success of using these methodologies depends on two requirements: first, many recordings are necessary, and therefore, a procedure for simplifying the tasks (especially in reasoning) is required; second, the basic mental operations must be specified.

Recently, there have been some very interesting applications of new procedures in reasoning research: for example, the analysis of the components of working memory involved in deduction using concurrent tasks (e.g. Vandierendonck & De Vooght, 1996), or the study of the integration of premises in deduction through eye-movement records (Espino, Santamaria, Meseguer & Carreiras, this issue).

We consider that a very interesting measure for testing the mental models theory is also one based in reaction times: the priming effect. Priming is a well known phenomenon in cognitive psychology. Response to a target stimulus that has been shown previously is faster than when it has not been shown. The response is also more rapid even when the previously-shown stimulus was different but related to the new stimulus. For example, reading time for the target word «CAR» is faster when the related word «VEHICLE» (a prime) was previously displayed than when the non-related word «ANIMAL» was previously presented. The most accepted explanation for this effect refers to the activation of mental representations. When a stimulus is presented, its mental representation as well as all related representations are activated. When a representation is activated its access is facilitated and, therefore, its response takes less time. In this case, the previous stimulus primes the mental representation of the second stimulus. This effect, called «priming», has been taken as evidence for the existence of some particular representations (e.g. Baddeley, Logie, Bressi, Della Sala, & Spinnler, 1986). Thus, if mental models have the same nature as other mental representations studied in the field of memory they should show the property of being primed.

There are some additional issues in reasoning that could be clarified using priming measures. One is the construction of mental models. In particular, Evans (1995) proposes that the construction of mental models occurs in an automatic way during the «heuristic» stage. The Heuristic-Analytic theory of Evans (1989), assumes that reasoning proceeds in two stages: a heuristic stage in which preconscious heuristics (automatic processes) serve to select aspects of the problem information as «relevant», and an analytic stage in which deductions are made on the basis of the selected information. As Evans affirmed (1995, p.150) the mental model theory is an attractive candidate for the analytic reasoning mechanism of the heuristic-analytic theory. He also equated the concept of «relevance» with the notion of explicit representation in a mental model, connecting his theory with the mental model theory. The heuristic stage can explain which items of the information are explicitly represented in the models; that is, which items are relevant. However, it is difficult to study directly the automaticity of certain processes with traditional reasoning tasks. Evans (1996) developed a variant of the selection task (called inspection time paradigm) to study the relationship between relevance and response. Evans' results showed that the cards with longer inspection times (as a measure of relevance) are more likely to be finally selected. However, as Roberts (1998 a, b) showed, there is a strong relation between what is attended to and what is finally responded to. In Roberts' experiments inspection time reflected the attention given to some cards, even when they were non-relevant for the task. The concept of relevance could not clearly be disentangled from the concept of attention with this task: it was not clear whether what is attended to becomes relevant or whether what is relevant becomes attended to. What happens when people see information (attend to it), but know that the information is not relevant for the task? Attention and relevance (for the task) are disentangled. In this situation, then, do participants construct a mental model that affects the analytic phase?

The application of the priming procedure may allow us to obtain other convergent measures for studying these theoretical questions. For this reason we feel it is worthwhile to try and simplify reasoning problems in order to obtain as many observations as possible, without, obviously, excluding the reasoning operation we wish to test. We shall present two ways of representing a description of the position about three balls labeled «A», «B», and «C»:

C is on the left, B is in the middle, and C is on the right
C B A

The first description is similar to the first premise of the previous example, in a typical spatial reasoning task. The second description is a diagrammatic one.

If we wish to study mental operations involved in reasoning and we have a theory of mental operations (such as mental model theory), we can reduce the difficulty of some stages and eliminate others. As in the study of the construction of multiple versus simple models, we can compare two very simple situations in which description and evaluation will be excluded, and comprehension is very easy. Let us suppose that we know that there are three different balls: «A», «B» and «C», and that we have to test whether a given arrangement of the three balls is a possible one from the premises. There will be the same kinds of problems:

Determinate problem:
«ball C is in the middle and A is on the right»
Is the following possible?
A is on the right of C and B is on the left of C

Indeterminate problem:
«ball C is in the middle»
Is the following possible?
A is on the right of C and B is on the left of C

Now let us look at the same problem, but in a diagrammatic presentation where «-» means that no information is given about the ball located in that place:

Determinate problem:
- C A
Is B C A possible?

Indeterminate problem:
- C -
Is B C A possible?

If people simply matched the information of the conclusion against the premise in the diagrammatic problem, the determinate problem (which requires two matches) would be more difficult than the indeterminate one (which requires just one match). On the contrary, if people construct mental models from the premises, the determinate problem will be easier than the indeterminate problem, since in the first case only one model is required, whereas solving the indeterminate problem requires the construction of two models.

What are the predictions of mental model theory from the following diagrammatic information?:

B C -

In this case, only one possibility is compatible with this situation: «B C A». In contrast, from the following diagrammatic information:

- C -

two mental models are coherent with it, and four are contrary to it:

Possible	Non-possible
B C A	A B C
A C B	B A C
	C A B
	C B A

The mental model theory predicts that people represent the minimum amount of information as possible. If this affirmation is true, then people would try to represent the first set of models (assuming that the number of models is two and the load on working memory is very small). The same would happen if we were to display a negative premise indicating that the «C» ball is not located in the middle:

- C̶ -

Now it should be more plausible that people represent the information that is given, that is, the non-possible situations:

Possible	Non-possible
A B C	B C A
B A C	A C B
C A B	
C B A	

With this kind of material, and selecting some mental operations, the difficulty of the problems can be reduced in those stages that we do not wish to study. On the one hand, the use of evaluation instead of construction tasks may facilitate the description stage, and on the other, the evaluation of sufficiency instead of necessity may facilitate the validation stage. In diagrammatic materials the structure of configurations of stimuli is shown explicitly. Therefore, the diagrammatic premises do not require translation from propositional codes to mental models (see Bauer & Johnson-Laird,

1993). In this kind of problem diagrams should improve the possibility of creating multiple models. With indeterminate problems, participants should try to create the two mental models instead of creating four mental models (which could exceed the working memory load). The results confirmed this prediction (Moreno, 1999), showing that when the premise was possible (congruent with two possible models but incongruent with four non-possible models) it took longer to consider non-possible conclusions than possible conclusions. The opposite occurred when the premise was non-possible (congruent with two non-possible models but incongruent with four possible models) - the evaluation was faster for non-possible conclusions than for possible ones. Likewise, in two-model problems the global reaction time was the same, but longer than in one-model problems.

A PROCEDURE TO TEST PRIMING IN MENTAL MODELS

In the following section we will describe one of the procedures we have used in one of our experiments. At the beginning of each trial a red triplet (prime) was displayed, and participants were told they were to ignore this information. Participants were then given the diagrammatic premises and asked to decide whether a conclusion (target) was possible or not.

We shall first present an example of a complete trial to illustrate the whole task. This trial corresponds to the evaluation of possible-conclusion target in a prime congruent condition, in which participants had to respond by pressing the «Yes» button:

A C B (prime-in red)
C - (premise 1)
A C - (premise 2)

Is it possible A C B (target- conclusion) ?

If perception alone leads to the construction of a mental model, even when it is not relevant for the task, the evaluation of the triplets should be affected. Therefore, we wanted to test the following predictions:

1. An initial model (even when it is not relevant for the task) primes the evaluation of possibilities.
2. The previous display of an indeterminate premise, which could activate two mental models, facilitates the later evaluation of one of these models.
3. Thinking with two models takes longer than with one.

There were two premises providing information about the correct arrangement of a triplet of balls (labeled as «A», «B» and «C»). Participants had to evaluate a conclusion (target triplet), deciding whether it was possible from the information contained in the premises.

Tables 7.1 and 7.2 show an example of the kind of premises and primes used in the experiments.

TABLE 7.1
The three types of premise used in the experiments

Premise type	Premises	Possible triplets	Predicted activated models
Non-informative	- - -	All six possibilities	
Two-model premise (indeterminate)	- - C	Two possibilities	A B C B A C
One-model premise	- A C	One possibility	B A C

TABLE 7.2
The two types of primes with regard to premises

Primes	Prime congruent	Prime non-congruent
Prime	A C B	C A B
Premise 1	- C -	- C -
Premise 2	A C -	A C -

We predict that evaluation times will be shorter when a mental model, which is required to evaluate a conclusion, is formed early on, than when a model is formed later. Thus, the evaluation of one «possible» triplet will be facilitated by displaying:

1. A prime triplet congruent with the models of the premises, even when it is irrelevant for the task.
2. A two-model premise presented prior to a one-model premise (and congruent with it).

Method

All of the stimuli were displayed on a Macintosh computer in black, except the prime configuration, which was in red. Each stimulus consisted of three letters that indicated the linear position of three balls labeled with the letters A, B and C. The premises offered information about the arrangement of the balls, indicating their position or assigning them an «X» (incognito). For example, the premise A - - (A X X) indicates that the ball A is at the left extreme, and no other information is offered about the other balls and their location.

The instructions informed participants that the first arrangement (prime) presented in red for every trial should be ignored «because it has nothing to do with your task». Every trial began with the display of the prime centered on the screen for 1500 ms. The first premise was then presented on the top line for 1500 ms, and when it disappeared, the second premise was displayed two text lines below for 1500 ms. Below this, the conclusion was represented under the question «Is it possible?», and this remained on the screen until an answer was given by pressing the «Yes» or «No» keys. Participants began a new trial by pressing the space bar.

Participants were thirty-four 3rd-year Psychology students at the UNED. They carried out a block of 16 practice trials before beginning the 216 trials of the experimental block. Trials contained the same proportion of two-model, one-model control and one-model facilitated problems. In half of them the non-informative premise was presented first and in the other half it was shown in second place. All of the trials were distributed in equal numbers among the four conditions by crossing the factors *prime* (congruent and non-congruent) and *conclusion* (possible and non- possible).

Results

ANOVA analysis was applied to prime congruence (congruent or non-congruent) x condition (two-model, one-model or one-model facilitated) x possibility evaluation (affirmative or negative). Results are shown in Table 7.3.

As it was predicted the initial model (not relevant for the task) primed the evaluation of possibilities. Prime congruent evaluations were faster than prime non-congruent evaluations. The representation of the prime affected the processing of the premise information.

The information given by the problems were congruent with one (one-model problems) or with two (two-model problems) possible configurations, but they were incongruent with five and four non-possible configurations, respectively. If people represent this given information then their responses should be faster for possible (represented in the mind) than for impossible (not represented in the mind) configurations. Results confirmed this prediction. Possible configurations were evaluated more quickly than non-possible configurations.

A main prediction of the mental model theory was also confirmed: one-model problems were evaluated more quickly than two-model problems. The possible configurations were more easily evaluated when one model instead of two models was required to be constructed.

The evaluation of possible configurations was facilitated by displaying a two-model premise prior to a one-model premise. One-model facilitated evaluations were made marginally more quickly than one-model control evaluations. This difference was significant for prime non-congruent, but not for prime congruent.

Subsequent analysis showed that matching of prime and target configurations did not affect reaction time. Likewise, in two-model problems the position of the informative premises (in first place 1059 ms versus in second place 1070 ms) did not affect response time. However, response time speeded up when the prime was congruent and the informative premise was in second place (1062 ms versus 1009 ms).

TABLE 7.3
Evaluation time (in ms) for possible conclusions.
Prime congruence and condition factors

Prime	Two-model	One-model	
		Control	Facilitated
Congruent	997	941	935
Incongruent	1053	1017	976

CONCLUSIONS

In this experiment the number of observations was sufficient to analyze reaction time and priming effects. These analyses were possible because some stages of the mental model theory were simplified. In previous studies (Moreno, 1999) we replicated the main results found here, even with the evaluation of necessity instead of sufficiency. One of these results is that two-model problems always take longer to be solved than one-model problems. With this kind of methodology it is possible to study the construction of mental models, as well as the relationship between attention and relevance in the construction of the initial representation. As we have seen, the perception alone of a diagrammatic stimulus makes possible the construction of a mental model and, more importantly, it can prime the integration of the information contained in the premises, when this information is congruent with it, but is discarded in other cases. A similar mechanism has been proposed to explain the effect of the inversion of the premises (Girotto, Mazzoco & Tasso, 1997; Legrenzi, Girotto & Johnson-Laird, 1993). The mental model theory assumes that some conditional expressions, such as «only if», (Johnson-Laird, Byrne & Schaeken, 1992) or «unless» (García-Madruga, Carriedo, Schaeken & Moreno, 1997), and counterfactuals (Byrne & Tasso, 1994) are represented with two initial models. An indeterminate premise can also lead to the construction of two mental models, when the load in working memory is not too high. With the same procedure we have shown that the inclusion of indeterminate diagrammatic premises (which leads to a low load on working memory) allows the construction of two mental models. Once again these models show a priming effect: when one of the models is congruent with a new premise, the evaluation of the conclusion is made more quickly than when it is not congruent.

The procedure presented in this chapter is an example of how new tasks can be used to test the predictions of reasoning theories. In particular, the descriptions of simple constituents of the deductive process by the reasoning theories can help us to construct new tasks which, moreover, may allow us to isolate these cognitive components so that they can be more precisely studied.

REFERENCES

BADDELEY, A. D., LOGIE, R., BRESSI, S., DELLA SALA, S., & SPINNLER, H. (1986): «Dementia and working memory». *Quarterly Journal of Experimental Psychology*, 38A, 603-618.

BAUER, M. I., & JOHNSON-LAIRD, P. N. (1993): «How diagrams can improve reasoning». *Psychological Science*, 4, 372-378.

BONATTI, L. (1994): «Propositional reasoning by model?» *Psychological Review*, 101: 725-33

BYRNE, R. M. J. & JOHNSON-LAIRD, P. N. (1989): «Spatial reasoning». *Journal of Memory and Language*, 28, 564-575.

BYRNE, R. M. J. & TASSO, A. (1994): «Counterfactual Reasoning: Inferences from hypothetical conditionals». In Ram, A. & Eiselt, K. (Eds). *Proceedings of the 16th Annual Conference of the Cognitive Science Society*. Hillsdale: Erlbaum. pp.124-129.

CARREIRAS, M. & SANTAMARÍA, C. (1997): «Reasoning about relations: spatial and non-spatial problems». *Thinking and Reasoning*, 3, 191-208.

EVANS, J. St. B. T. (1989): «Bias in Human Reasoning: Causes and Consequences». Hillsdale, NJ: Erlbaum

— (1995): «Relevance and reasoning». In S.E. Newstead y J.St.B.T. Evans (Eds.). *Perspectives on thinking and reasoning.* pp 147-172. LEA.

— (1996): «Deciding before you think: Relevance and reasoning in the selection task». *British Journal of Psychology*, 87, 223-240.

GARCÍA-MADRUGA, J. A., CARRIEDO, N., SCHAEKEN, W. & MORENO, S. (1997): «Comparing conditional reasoning from different formulations: "if then", "if not then", "only if" and "unless"». Technical report. UNED.

GIROTTO, V., MAZZOCCO, A. & TASSO, A. (1997): «The effect of premise order in conditional reasoning: a test of the mental model theory». *Cognition*, 63, 1-28.

JOHNSON-LAIRD, P. N. (1983): *Mental Models*. Cambridge: Cambridge University Press.

JOHNSON-LAIRD, P. N. & BYRNE, R. (1991): *Deduction*. Hove, East Sussex: LEA.

JOHNSON-LAIRD, P. N., BYRNE, R. & SCHAEKEN, W. (1992): «Propositional reasoning by model». *Psychological Review*, 99, 418-439.

JOHNSON-LAIRD, P. N., LEGRENZI, P.; GIROTTO, V.; SONINO, M. S. & CAVERNI, J. P. (1999): «Naive Probability: A mental model theory of extensional reasoning». *Psychological Review*.

MARR, D. (1982): *Vision*. San Francisco, CA: W.H. Freeman.

MORENO RÍOS, S. (1999): «El efecto de las representaciones iniciales en el razonamiento deductivo. Evaluación de la teoría de los modelos mentales». Tesis doctoral. UNED.

RIPS, L. J. (1994): *The psychology of proof*. Cambridge, MA: Routledge.

ROBERTS, M. J. (1998a): «Inspection times and the selection task: Are they relevant?» *Quarterly Journal of Experimental psychology*, 51a, 781-810.

— (1998b): «How should relevance be defined? What does inspection time measure? A reply to Evans». *Quarterly Journal of Experimental psychology*, 51a, 815-817.

VANDIERENDOCK, A., & DE VOOGHT, G. (1996): «Evidence for Mental-model-based reasoning: a comparison of reasoning with time and space concepts». *Thinking and Reasoning*, 2 (4), 249-272.

Part II

HYPOTHESES TESTING AND PROBABILISTIC AND RELATIONAL REASONING

8

THE ALTERNATIVES TAKEN INTO ACCOUNT IN HYPOTHESIS TESTING: TWO NEW PARADIGMS FOR INVESTIGATING STRATEGIES

JEAN-PAUL CAVERNI
SANDRINE ROSSI
JEAN-LUC PÉRIS

Uno de los problemas principales en el estudio del razonamiento humano es la explicación de las dificultades con las que se encuentran las personas cuando tienen que considerar varias alternativas. En este capítulo hemos utilizado el conocido problema 2-4-6 para mostrar la insuficiencia del método clásico en la investigación de las estrategias utilizadas para la comprobación de hipótesis. Además de la estrategia clásica mediante la cual se propone un contraejemplo de la hipótesis bajo consideración, hemos demostrado que existen otras dos posibles estrategias.

En este estudio hemos utilizado los protocolos de 67 participantes para comparar cada una de las tríadas (o serie de tres números) con (1) su hipótesis (codificación en curso), por un lado, y (2) por otro, con la hipótesis formulada para la tríada que se ha considerado previamente (codificación previa). Se calcularon los porcentajes medios de la estrategia confirmatoria de estos dos métodos de codificación (codificación en curso vs. codificación previa) considerando, en primer lugar, toda la muestra de participantes y, luego, por separado aquellos que descubrieron la regla (n= 56) y aquellos que descubrieron la regla en su primera aproximación (n= 18/56). En todos los casos se encontró que la media de la codificación en curso con la hipótesis en curso era significativamente superior a la media de la codificación previa con la hipótesis previa.

El otro paradigma comprende la retroalimentación negativa. Si los participantes esperan recibir una retroalimentación positiva del experimentador, entonces tiene sentido que un ensayo con una hipótesis y una tríada para verificarla se denomine ensayo confirmatorio y que un ensayo con una hipótesis y una tríada para su falsación se denomine ensayo desconfirmatorio. Ahora bien, si los participantes esperan una retroalimentación negativa, entonces se daría todo lo contrario. Cuando se pidió a los participantes que expresaran la retroalimentación que esperaban recibir después de cada ensayo se encontró que la proporción de retroalimentación negativa esperada era aproximadamente el 47% del total de ensayos empleados para resolver el problema. Cuando se intenta falsar una hipótesis, el participante espera recibir una respuesta negativa en lugar de probar una tríada que viole su hipótesis.

Estas dos nuevas estrategias desafían los resultados clásicos, aunque no niegan la verosimilitud de que los participantes se ajusten a los supuestos de Wason. No obstante, estas estrategias muestran que los resultados clásicos suponen que se cumplen estos supuestos.

One of the main problems in the study of human reasoning is to explain the difficulties people have in considering alternatives. Numerous studies are concerned with the fact that people tend to focus on favoured hypotheses (e.g. Legrenzi, Girotto & Johnson-Laird, 1993). This phenomenon, studied in cognitive and social psychology, has been referred to as belief preservation and as the confirmation bias. The confirmation bias is defined as a tendency that people exhibit to seek confirmation rather than disconfirmation of their hypotheses (Wason, 1960, 1962, 1966, 1968). They fail to produce counterexamples and to consider alternative hypotheses. This definition is linked to Karl Popper's philosophy of science and to the refutation criterion (Popper, 1959).

Hypothesis testing is an essential component of mental activities. Nevertheless, there is no consensus about the cognitive processes involved. In this paper, we report studies which aim to examine a quite provocative question. Is the failure to consider alternatives a phenomenon that is genuinely related to the properties of cognitive processes or is it a result of an inefficiency in the classical paradigm of investigating cognitive processes? To answer this question, we used the well-known 2-4-6 problem (Wason, 1960).

THE WASON 2-4-6 PROBLEM: CLASSICAL RESULTS AND INTERPRETATIONS

Let us first remember the 2-4-6 problem. The experimenter tells the participant that s/he has a rule in mind regarding number triples (i.e. «all sequences of increasing numbers»). The triple 2-4-6 is then presented as satisfying this rule. The participant is instructed to attempt to discover the rule by proposing other triples.

For each proposed triple, the experimenter says to her/him whether or not it follows the rule (yes-no). The participant is provided with a sheet on which s/he writes down (1) the proposed triple, (2) the tested hypothesis, and (3) the experimenter's feedback. Whenever s/he thinks s/he has discovered the rule, s/he states it. Then, the experimenter says whether it is correct or not. If incorrect, the participant continues to propose triples until s/he finds the rule or gives up.

Conventionally, the strategies implemented by participants have been investigated by comparing the current triple the participant proposes with the current hypothesis s/he claims to test. Typically, participants tend to adopt hypotheses that are a subset of the rule, for example «increasing by two», and propose triples like «10-12-14» or «20-22-24». With the paradigm for investigating processes presented above, it is shown that in general participants propose triples that are positive examples of the hypotheses they claim to have tested. Even when participants discovered the rule, few of them discovered it on the first announcement.

The prevailing interpretation for quite some time was that participants are prone to a *confirmation bias*: they would rather verify (confirm) their hypotheses than falsify (disconfirm) them. Such a behaviour has been claimed to be ineffective. In fact, because the to-be-discovered rule is «all sequences of increasing numbers», when giving triples such as «10-12-14» or «20-22-24» participants are told that these triples satisfy the rule and receive an ambiguous verification of their (wrong) hypothesis (such as «increasing by two»). A good triple to receive a conclusive refutation would be a negative example (a counterexample) of the tested hypothesis, as for instance «10-20-30».

Two competitive interpretations have been proposed. For Evans (1983, 1989), if the phenomenon is really a result of a bias, it is not caused by participants' deliberate choice, but by a cognitive difficulty in processing negative information: «It is not that participants do not wish to falsify, it is simply that they cannot think of the way to do it» (Evans, 1989, p. 143). According to Evans, the confirmation bias is not a motivational bias but the result of a set of cognitive failures. The failures are caused by pre-conscious selective processing, that is, a bias towards thinking about positive rather than negative information. This *positivity bias*, in most cases, leads participants to propose positive examples rather than negative examples of their current hypotheses. For Klayman and Ha (1987, 1989), positive hypothesis testing is not necessarily a bias. They considered participants' behaviour as a manifestation of a *positive test strategy*. This strategy entails testing hypotheses by considering the cases in which the property is expected to occur or it is known to have occurred. This strategy is not incompatible with a deliberate search for falsification and is a very good heuristic in many situations. It is only because of the particular relationship between the participant's hypothesis (specific) and the rule (general) that such a strategy turns out to be ineffective in Wason's original task. That is, the 2-4-6 problem, by its very nature, focuses the participants' attention on the specific property of the triple and therefore draws her/his attention away from the more general property that might apply also (that is, simply a series of increasing numbers). A hypothesis consistent with the triple's specific property such as increasing by two, necessarily leads to positive feedback but does not allow the participant to discover the rule. All triples of numbers increasing by two also fit the experimenter's rule. In fact, as said before, in this particular situation, it is only by using a negative example (or test), such as «1-2-3», that the participant is in a position to falsify her/his hypothesis and thus eventually arrive at the solution. But let us suppose that the to-be-discovered rule was more specific than the hypothesis being tested, the latter could be rejected only by testing triples that verify it, but falsify the to-be-discovered rule. For instance, if the rule was «three consecutive even numbers» and the participant tested the hypothesis «three increasing even numbers» using the triple «4-8-10», then s/he would receive negative feedback from the experimenter which would disconfirm her/his hypothesis. Klayman and Ha suggest that people use the positive test strategy as a general default heuristic in which the consequences vary with the characteristics of the task. This strategy is one that people use in the absence of specific information that identifies some tests as more relevant than others, or when the cognitive demands of the task preclude a more carefully designed strategy.

THE FIRST PROBLEM WITH THE USUAL METHOD OF INVESTIGATING STRATEGIES

Is a negative example of the current hypothesis the one and only way to reject this hypothesis in the Wason's problem? Let us consider the following protocol excerpt (Table 8.1), in which the participant first tests a «even numbers» hypothesis by a «8-10-12» triple, and then a «odd numbers» hypothesis by a «3-5-7» triple.

TABLE 8.1
Excerpt of protocol

Proposed Triples	Tested Hypotheses
8-10-12	even numbers
3-5-7	odd numbers

As in both cases the participant tests her/his hypotheses by proposing examples rather than counterexamples, the usual explanation argued that s/he is exhibiting a confirmatory (or positive) strategy. But a competing explanation can be proposed. In particular, there is no theoretical reason to assume that people test their hypotheses (1) by considering only the current triple they give, and (2) by failing to take into consideration both the previous and present hypotheses. It can be argued that in the second step of the excerpt shown above, the participant's goal is to disconfirm the previous «even number» hypothesis. To this aim, s/he uses a positive example of the «odd number» alternative, which is a negative example (a counterexample) of the «even number» hypothesis.

    Given that the participant will be informed that both triples satisfy the rule, s/he will be able to reject both properties «even» and «odd» as belonging to the to-be-discovered rule. Thus, one might conclude that the participant exhibited not a confirming strategy but a disconfirming strategy.

Investigating such a strategy involves comparing the current triple, not with the current hypothesis (as has been the usual procedure), but with the previous hypothesis that the participant has proposed (i.e. the hypothesis s/he proposed on the preceding trial). Every time the current triple is a negative example of the previous hypothesis, it can be assumed that participants use a disconfirmative strategy, which can be done with either a positive or a negative test.

Is such a strategy used in solving the 2-4-6 problem? In order to answer this question, 67 participants were presented with the usual instructions of the 2-4-6 problem (Wason, 1960). Participants were undergraduate students (in various disciplines, excluding psychology) at the Faculty of Literature and Humanities at the University of Provence in Aix-en-Provence, France.

For each participant, we computed the proportion of confirmations of the total number of triples, by comparing each triple (1) on the one hand with its current hypothesis (current coding) (2) and on the other hand with the hypothesis held for the triple considered immediately prior (prior coding). Table 8.2 gives a sample of protocol coded with each coding paradigm.

TABLE 8.2
Excerpt of Participant's protocol coded with (1) current and (2) prior coding paradigms (Adapted from Caverni & Rossi, 1997)

Triples Proposed	Tested Hypotheses	Feedback	Current Coding (1)	Prior Coding (2)
4-6-8	Even numbers increasing by two	YES	C	/
6-8-10	Even numbers increasing by two	YES	C	C
10-14-18	Increasing even numbers	YES	C	D
14-18-10	Even numbers independent of order and interval	NO	C	D
120-122-128	Increasing even numbers	YES	C	D

rule proposed: Even increasing numbers independent of interval

18-14-10	Even numbers decreasing by four	NO	C	D
18-10-06	Decreasing even numbers	NO	C	D
18-16-14	Even numbers decreasing by two	NO	C	C
14-16-18	Even numbers increasing by two	YES	C	D
14-18-22	Even numbers increasing by four	YES	C	D
01-02-03	Increasing even and odd numbers	YES	C	D

rule proposed: Increasing numbers

(1)   Current coding takes into account the triple and the hypothesis at the same step (e.g. step n.° 2: 6-8-10; even numbers increasing by two: confirmation).

(2)   The prior coding takes into account the triple and the hypothesis at the previous step only (e.g. step n.°3: 10-14-18; even numbers increasing by two: disconfirmation).

C = Confirmation
D = Disconfirmation

We compared the mean percentages of confirmative strategy for these two coding methods (current coding vs. prior coding), considering first the whole sample of participants [89.46 vs. 48.76, $F(1,66) = 138.40$, $p < .0001$], and then separately those who found the to-be-discovered rule (n=56) [88.52 vs. 45.30, $F(1,55) = 154.13$, $p < .0001$], and those who found the rule at their first attempt (n=18/56) [89.17 vs. 33.78, $F(1,17) = 87.83$, $p < .0001$].

In all cases the mean for the current coding using the current hypothesis was significantly higher than the mean for the prior coding using the previous hypothesis. Let us point out that for the successful participants who found the rule at the first announcement this mean was 33.78%, so in other words 66.22% of their hypothesis tests were disconfirmative.

We ran a final analysis, in which we used both coding methods to compare successful participants who found the rule at their first attempt (n=18/56) with those who did not (n=38/56). Although the means were not significantly different when we used the current coding method [89.17 vs. 88.21, $F < 1$], when we used the prior coding method, participants who were correct on their first attempt used significantly less confirmative strategies than those who were correct only on later attempts [33.78 vs. 50.76, $F(1,54) = 6.51$, $p < .01$].

This first study showed that the positive test strategy is also effective in the 2-4-6 problem, that is it also led to the rejection of hypotheses. It seems that participants were able to test a hypothesis and its alternative. Whereas it would have been usual to expect them to do so with only a single step, they did so with two successive steps. We have seen that the most successful participants were the most disconfirmative. A possible interpretation is that this result demonstrates the manifestation of a deliberate strategy (Caverni & Rossi, 1997). However, a way to be sure of the alternative hypotheses' consideration is to take into account the participants' expected response to the experimenter's feedback. This leads us to present a second problem.

THE SECOND PROBLEM WITH THE USUAL METHOD OF INVESTIGATING STRATEGIES

Although we have just shown the contrary, let us postulate, as Wason did, that strategies can be investigated by comparing the current triple the participant proposes and the current hypothesis s/he claims to be testing. The simple fact that a participant tries a triple that follows the hypothesis s/he claims s/he is testing is not proof that s/he is using a confirmative (or positive) strategy.

As long as the participant expects positive feedback from the experimenter, then it makes sense to call a trial made with a hypothesis and a triple verifying it a *confirmatory* trial, and to call a trial made with a hypothesis and a triple falsifying it a *disconfirmative* trial. But if the participant expects negative feedback, then the opposite is true (Table 8.3): a trial made with a hypothesis and a triple verifying it must be called a *disconfirmative* trial, while a trial made with a hypothesis and a triple falsifying it must be called a *confirmatory* trial. So, our assumption is that to investigate the participant's strategies, her/his expected feedback must be taken into account.

TABLE 8.3
The four trial types when expected feedback is taken into account

Triple Proposed	Expected Feedback	Strategy
satisfying the hypothesis	yes	confirmation
falsifying the hypothesis	no	confirmation
satisfying the hypothesis	no	disconfirmation
falsifying the hypothesis	yes	disconfirmation

We ran an experiment in which forty-eight participants participated. They were undergraduate students (in various disciplines, excluding psychology) at the Faculty of Literature and Humanities at the University of Provence in Aix-en-Provence, France. Three between participants experimental conditions were compared which differed only in the instructions given. Participants were randomly assigned to one of three experimental conditions (n=16 per condition).

The conditions differed in whether or not participants were required to inform us about the feedback they expected to receive from the experimenter. They were asked to use a provided sheet of paper to write down: (1) in the «usual» condition, each proposed triple, the corresponding hypothesis, and the actual experimenter's feedback; (2) in the «feedback» condition, each proposed triple, the corresponding hypothesis, the feedback they were expecting from the experimenter, and the actual experimenter's feedback.

Additionally, we used a third set of instructions less directive than the last to make sure that the participants were not informing us about something that they did not genuinely think. In a «feedback if» condition, they were asked to write down each proposed triple, the corresponding hypothesis, the feedback they were expecting from the experimenter *if any*, and the actual experimenter's feedback.

First, we computed the proportion of negative feedback expected on the basis of the total number of steps taken to solve the problem. This rate is 47% in the condition «feedback» and 47.1% in the condition «feedback if» [$F < 1$].

Considering the percentages of positive hypothesis tests, the positive hypothesis rate is significantly greater in the «usual» condition than in the «feedback» condition [93.2 vs. 73.7, $F(2,45) = 6.83$, $p < .01$], and greater than the «feedback if» condition [93.2 vs. 76.7, $F(2,45) = 4.85$, $p < .03$]. However, the difference between the «feedback» condition and the «feedback if» condition is not significant [76.7 vs. 73.7, $F < 1$].

Finally, we computed the proportion of the four trial types when expected feedback is taken into account (Table 8.4). The most frequently employed type of hypothesis test is a positive hypothesis test associated with positive expected feedback [«feedback» condition, $F(1,60) = 51.58$, $p < .0001$; «feedback if» condition, $F(1,60) = 21.21$, $p < .0001$]. This type of trial refers to the classical confirmatory strategy that Wason has pointed out.

TABLE 8.4
Proportion (%) of the four trial types when expected feedback is taken into account

	«feedback if» Condition	«feedback» Condition
satisfying the hypothesis & «yes» expected	48.1	50.5
falsifying the hypothesis & «no» expected	18.4	23.9
Confirmative tests	*66.5*	*74.4*
satisfying the hypothesis & «no» expected	28.6	23.2
falsifying the hypothesis & «yes» expected	4.9	2.4
Disconfirmative tests	*33.5*	*25.6*

Negative hypothesis tests are less frequent but most are associated with a negative feedback [23.9 vs. 2.4, $F(1,60) = 13.73$, $p < .0005$, in the «feedback» condition; 18.4 vs. 4.9, $F(1,60) = 2.67$, $p < .10$, in the «feedback if» condition]. The most interesting finding is that negative hypothesis tests associated with a positive feedback – which refers to the classical disconfirmative strategy defined by Wason – are less employed whatever the condition [«feedback» condition, $F(1,60) = 33.43$, $p < .0001$; «feedback if» condition $F(1,60) = 15.96$, $p < .0002$]. In other words, when a participant does try to falsify his/her hypothesis, s/he does it by expecting a negative answer rather than by testing a triple that violates his/her hypothesis.

CONCLUSION

We have shown that the classical method of investigating hypothesis testing strategies is insufficient. In addition to the classical strategy that involves proposing a counterexample of the hypothesis that is conceived, we have shown that two other possible strategies exist.

One involves testing the hypothesis at the next step, by proposing an example of the former alternative hypothesis formulated at the previous step. This strategy allows participants to make only positive tests of their current hypothesis, by mobilising a disconfirmative strategy. To the extent that the task is unconstrained either by time or by the number of possible tests, this strategy is efficient. It has been shown that the protocols of participants who succeed at the first attempt exhibit a high rate of disconfirmation when they are coded with the «prior coding» method.

We have shown a second strategy that allows participants to falsify hypotheses by proposing a positive example of the hypothesis: this strategy involves expecting negative feedback. Bringing to the fore this strategy, which takes into account the participant's expected feedback from the experimenter, does not allow the confusion between positive test strategy and confirmation strategy on the one hand, or negative test strategy and disconfirmative strategy on the other hand. It allows us to distinguish confirmative and disconfirmative strategies, independently of positive and negative test strategies, and independently of the confirming or disconfirming test result made by the participant.

These two new possible strategies, which challenge the classic results, do not deny the plausibility that participants behave according to Wason's presuppositions. Nevertheless, they show that the classic results suppose that these presuppositions are satisfied. However, if Wason's assumption that participants expect positive feedback from the experimenter is not correct, then two aspects of the classical interpretation would have to be questioned: the inability to produce counterexamples (which we have shown to be consistent only with the current coding method) and the inability to deal with negation (we have shown that participants expect negative feedback half of the time). Our two new strategies confirm that the main strategy is indeed a positive test strategy, in the sense that participants propose an example of their current hypothesis. However, by using the prior coding method, we have shown that the current hypothesis is often an alternative of the previous hypothesis, and by taking into account expected feedback, we have shown that participants often propose an example of their current hypothesis while expecting negative feedback.

REFERENCES

CAVERNI, J. P., & ROSSI, S. (1997): «A nice bit of scandal: About a disconfirmation bias in the Wason's 2-4-6 problem». *Swiss Journal of Psychology, 56,* 239-242.

EVANS, J. St. B. T. (1983): «Selective processes in reasoning». In J. St B. T. (Ed.), *Thinking and Reasoning: Psychological Approaches.* London: Routledge & Kegan Paul.

— (1989): «Confirmation Bias». In *Bias in Human Reasoning. Causes and Consequences.* Hove, UK : Lawrence Erlbaum Associates.

LEGRENZI, P., GIROTTO, V., & JOHNSON-LAIRD, P. H. (1993): «Focussing in reasoning and decision-making», *Cognition, 49,* 37-66.

KLAYMAN, J., & HA, Y. W. (1987): «Confirmation, disconfirmation, and information in hypothesis testing». *Psychological Review, 94,* 211-228.

— (1989): «Hypothesis testing in rule discovery: Strategy, Structure and Content». *Journal of Experimental Psychology: Learning, Memory and Cognition, 15,* 596-604.

POPPER, K. R. (1959): *The logic of scientific discovery.* London: Hutchinson.

WASON, P. C. (1960): «On the failure to eliminate hypotheses in a conceptual task». *Quarterly Journal of Experimental Psychology, 12,* 129-140.

— (1962): «A reply to Wetherick». *Quarterly Journal of Experimental Psychology, 14,* 250.

— (1966): «Reasoning». In B. M. Foss (Ed.), *New Horizons in Psychology.* Harmondsworth: England Penguin.

— (1968): «On the failure to eliminate hypotheses-A second look». In P. C. Wason & P. N. Johnson-Laird. (Eds.), *Thinking and reasoning.* Harmondsworth, England : Penguin.

9

CONTENT PRESENTATION IN REASONING ABOUT BASE RATES

M.ª José González Labra

Al abordar el estudio del razonamiento probabilístico es habitual encontrar, en varias revisiones en este campo, que el razonamiento con valores estadísticos se encuentra sujeto a varios sesgos o ilusiones cognitivas. (Kahneman, Slovic y Tversky, 1982; Gilovich, 1992; Piatelli-Palmarini, 1994). Se piensa que esta limitación se debe a una capacidad de procesamiento o de cómputo limitada, a una comprensión deficiente de los conceptos probabilísticos o a la utilización de unos heurísticos de razonamiento semejantes a los propuestos por Tversky y Kahneman. Los dos experimentos que se presentan en este capítulo se centran en el estudio del razonamiento probabilístico, no tanto desde la perspectiva del cómputo según los axiomas del Teorema de Bayes, sino más bien desde el grado de atención que dirige el sujeto a determinada información estadística, en concreto las tasas base.

La precisión de los juicios probabilísticos se evalúa generalmente contrastándolos con los resultados predichos por el Teorema de Bayes. En los trabajos sobre problemas con tasas base es habitual presentar a los sujetos datos ajenos a su conocimiento y para los que no tienen probabilidades subjetivas y encontrar que los sujetos ignoran o subestiman los datos relevantes para resolver el problema (Kahneman y Tversky, 1972; 1973; Schwarz, Strack, Hilton y Naderer, 1991). Sin embargo, en trabajos, como los de Legrenzi y Girotto (1996), sobre el razonamiento condicional se ha logrado que los sujetos consideren hipótesis alternativas al presentar contextos o escenarios que invitaban a la representación de posibles estados alternativos. La relevancia pragmática que se otorgaba a la información hacía que los sujetos se centraran sobre una representación concreta de la situación. En otras palabras, los sujetos representaban la información explícita contenida en los problemas y cuando se daban indicios sobre hipótesis alternativas los sujetos las consideraban. El concepto de focusing utilizado por Legrenzi y Girotto se encuentra estrechamente relacionado con otros conceptos que hacen énfasis en la representación selectiva de la información, como los de relevancia de Evans (1995) y de Sperber, Cara y Girotto (1995), y el de focalización de Klar (1990). En esta línea, nuestro trabajo se centró en el planteamiento de problemas probabilísticos en un ámbito de conocimiento familiar con el fin de estudiar la medida en que pueden influir el nivel de experiencia y el formato de presentación sobre el tipo de información que atienden los sujetos.

En este trabajo se analiza el razonamiento probabilístico en función del grado de experiencia y del tipo de presentación de las tasas base en la formulación de los problemas. La falta de atención a la información que se presenta sobre las tasas base puede desaparecer o atenuarse según sean los objetivos y el conocimiento de los sujetos. En el primer estudio se trabajó con una muestra de alumnos de matemáticas que habían estudiado la teoría de la probabilidad según el programa curricular, otra muestra de alumnos novatos y una muestra de profesores de matemáticas como grupo con mayor conocimiento en este ámbito. La tarea de los sujetos consistía en seleccionar la alternativa que fuera más probable ante la presentación de problemas con tasas base semejantes a los del programa curricular habitual y problemas acompañados de información sobre aspectos de la vida cotidiana que eran irrelevantes para la tarea, aunque dicha información era representativa de la situación descrita en el problema. Los resultados pusieron de manifiesto que el grupo con conocimiento (alumnos y profesores) obtuvo mejores puntuaciones que el grupo novato en los problemas curriculares y solo el grupo de profesores logró mejores puntuaciones en los problemas acompañadas de información irrelevante. En el segundo estudio se planteó seguir explorando las condiciones que podrían fomentar la consideración de las tasas base. Para ello se diseñaron los problemas considerando las aportaciones de Gigerenzer (1991) y Cosmides y Tooby (1996) en las que se demuestra que el formato de presentación de las tasas base como frecuencias influye favorablemente sobre el rendimiento de los sujetos. Los problemas fueron iguales a los del primer estudio, pero se introdujo una versión de las tasas base presentadas como frecuencias. En este estudio sólo participó una muestra de estudiantes con conocimiento, dado que éste fue el grupo que en el primer experimento no logró diferenciarse del grupo con mayor conocimiento en los problemas con información irrelevante. Los resultados volvieron a mostrar que este grupo seguía obteniendo mejores resultados en los problemas curriculares que conocía, pero que la presentación de las tasas base como frecuencias no produjo los beneficios esperados para los problemas con información irrelevante. En general y de acuerdo con los resultados obtenidos, podríamos decir que existe una aproximación probabilística intuitiva mediante la cual los sujetos tenían en cuenta las tasas base según su nivel de experiencia en el ámbito en el que era habitual considerar esta información. En este sentido conviene distinguir las tasas base de las probabilidades a priori, ya que el modelo bayesiano admite la inclusión de probabilidades subjetivas como probabilidades a priori, de forma que el sujeto puede asignar una probabilidad basándose en sus observaciones, conocimientos previos o incluso opiniones y creencias.

INTRODUCTION

When faced with uncertainty individuals predict or assess the probability of an event by the subjective evaluation of this uncertainty. Probability Theory as a normative standard offers an objective way in which to quantify the uncertainty of many events. However, numerous experimental results show that human reasoning deviates from normative standards such as Bayes's theorem (Kahneman, Slovic & Tversky, 1982; Gilovich, 1992; Piattelli-Palmarini, 1994) and base rate neglect constitutes one of these empirical discrepancies. This effect shows that individuals do not pay attention nor use base rates specified in a problem when required to make probabilistic estimations.

A base rate is defined as the relative frequency with which an event occurs or an attribute is present in a given population. A typical base rate task presents a reasoning problem containing a statistic such as a percentage and participants are expected to attend and use this statistic even if there is additional information that supports another opposing hypothesis. Empirical research in general shows that people tend to ignore base rates when this information is presented with individual and non diagnostic descriptions. Even trained statisticians ignore information about base rates and their judgements seemed to be based on the similarity between information contained in the problems and the prototypical or representative categories under consideration. (Bar-Hillel, 1980; Christensen-Szalanski & Bushyhead, 1981; Kahneman & Tversky, 1973). However, there are certain conditions that seem to favor the use of base rates, such as task properties and previous experience with problem content. For example, in a previous research we found that experts' judgements were not influenced by nondiagnostic information when reasoning under their domain of knowledge (González-Labra, Artieta-Pinedo & Ceacero-Cubillo, 1995). In other words, the more experienced individuals paid attention to base rates and ignored the individuating information when problem content corresponded to their professional responsibility. Also, in this study we analyzed confidence judgments and our results showed that the more experienced subjects were the best calibrated, despite their natural tendency to overestimate their performance. Judgment under uncertainty involves working with an incomplete knowledge base and one important aspect of this process deals with the awareness of how much confidence is to be place in evaluations. It is very common to find that individuals show overconfidence when assessing their judgments on the relative frequencies of correct answers. However, the results showed that the richer the knowledge base from which subjects evaluate their confidence the lesser the degree of overconfidence.

The next two experiments intend to further explore the role of previous experience in probability trained individuals as a condition that promotes the use of base rates. The main interest of this study was to identify the variables that direct people's attention to problem representation in an effort to develop a more optimistic view of appropriate reasoning that takes into account individual's optimal representation of probability. The cognitive principle of relevance states that cognitive processes are aimed at processing the most relevant information in the most relevant way (Sperber, Cara & Girotto, 1995). It is presumed that experienced individuals should be able to base their judgments on all available relevant information and to appropriately discriminate irrelevant information. In Experiment 1 problems were designed to analyze content presentation and previous instruction on probability. It is expected that individuals trained on probability will attend base rates when reasoning on formal problems and to disattend base rates when problems are framed within non diagnostic information. In this case, formal problems represent individuals' knowledge domain and nondiagnostic problems are structurally similar to formal problems but introduce irrelevant information. Experiment 2 further analyzed content presentation and format as the information factors that mediate base rate neglect. It is argued that individuals have developed a frequentistic conception of probability and reasoning performance will be enhanced when problems contained frequencies rather than probabilities (Cosmides & Tooby, 1996; Gigerenzer, 1991). In this second study, formal and non diagnostic problems also varied format presentation in order to test frequency based predictions in relation to content presentation.

EXPERIMENT 1: CONTENT PRESENTATION

The objective in this study was to identify the degree of influence that experience has on the consideration of base rates when individuals are confronted with reasoning problems in their domain of knowledge. For this purpose the study included experienced math teachers and math students who were presented with base rates problems that contained non diagnostic descriptions. Also, confidence judgements were required expecting to find higher confidence and better calibrations in the more experienced groups.

Participants

Fifty students with no previous instruction on probability and thirty-six students with a semester instruction on probability participated in this experiment as the naive and student group, respectively. Twenty-five math teachers participated as the experienced group (10 or more years of teaching experience).

Design and material

The experimental task presented ten base rate problems, five problems framed within curricular content and the other five with non diagnostic content. The non diagnostic problems presented base rate information and then a description which contained non diagnostic representative information. The response suggested by the description was contrary to the response adequate to the base rate information contained in the problems. The following are an English example of each Spanish version of the problems:

Curricular Content

In a box there are 60% of red marbles and 40% of green marbles. Marbles have a positive or a negative sign. 30% of the red marbles and 15% of the green marbles have a negative sign. Blind-folded John picks a marble and it has a positive sign. Which of the following alternatives do you consider most probable?

a)   the marble is red.
b)   the marble is green.
c)   both alternatives are equally probable.

Non Diagnostic Content

In a class there are 60% of girls and 40% of boys. 30% of girls and 15% of boys wear glasses. Recently, Maria a student of this class won a composition contest. Maria is a very shy person and an excellent student, specially in mathematics. On her spare time she likes to read and listen to classical music. Which of the following alternatives do you consider most probable?

a)   Maria doesn't wear glasses
b)   Maria wears glasses
c)   both alternatives are equally probable.

After making a selection, participants were required to rate their response confidence on a 0-100 scale in which 0 was no confidence and 100 was full confidence.

Results and discussion

Data were subjected to a 3 x 2 ANOVA, with experience level (experienced, student and naive group) as a between-subject variable and content type (curricular and non diagnostic) as within-subject variable. There was a significant main effect of experience level [$F_{(2, 108)}= 59.47$, $p< 0.0*$] and problem type [$F_{(1, 108)}= 96.76$, $p<0+*$]. Also the interaction between these two variables was significant [$F_{(2, 108)}= 5.21$, $p<0+*$].

The results showed that there were significant differences in the proportion of base rate responses with curricular content between the naive and the experienced and student groups. In these problems, the more experienced groups obtained a higher proportion of base rate responses than novices. However, the differences between level of experience between students and math teachers were not significant.

The results on problems with non diagnostic content showed that there were no significant differences in the proportion of base rate responses between the naive and student group. Only the experienced group obtained a higher proportion of base rate responses in comparison to the other two groups.

Within group comparisons showed that there were no significant differences between the two types of content in the experienced group and that naive and student participants obtained a higher significant percentage of base rate responses in curricular content problems.

In relation to confidence we observed a similar pattern of results. The more experienced groups (students and math teachers) presented a similar mean confidence and both showed a higher mean confidence than novices on curricular content. However, mean confidence was similar for non diagnostic content in naive and students and their mean confidence was lower than the experienced mean confidence. Within group comparisons showed that mean confidence is similar for the two types of content in the experienced and naive groups, but students showed a decreased in mean confidence when responding to non diagnostic problems.

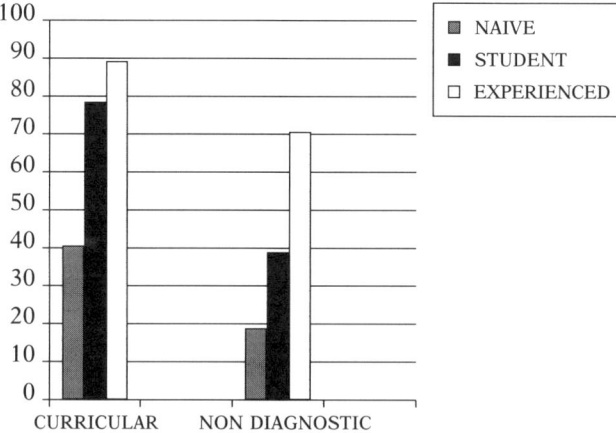

Figura 9.1. Percentage of base rate responses with different content presentations.

If we consider calibration as the difference between mean confidence and proportion of correct responses we observe that overall all groups showed an overconfidence effect. Novice overconfidence on non diagnostic problems was the highest. However, both the experienced and students groups were close to perfect calibration in curricular problems and the experienced group showed a slight underconfidence effect.

Overall, the results showed that base rates are attended when problems are presented with additional information not linked to a relevant reference class from the individual's perspective. When people can identify individuating information as non diagnostic of the problem presentation, their judgements are based on the base rates provided. Our results so far show that experience in the knowledge domain makes people attach more weight to base rates than to individuating non diagnostic information. In the next experiment we were interested in studying format presentation as another condition for promoting base rate consideration, specially in the student group which showed base rate neglect on problems with non diagnostic information and also a decreased in the mean confidence assigned to these problems.

EXPERIMENT 2: FORMAT PRESENTATION

Empirical support provided by Gigerenzer et cols. (Gigerenzer, 1991; Gigerenzer & Hoffrage, 1985) and Cosmides & Tooby (1996) have demonstrated along several experiments that frequentist versions of the problems positively affected base rate performance. The frequentist perspective holds that there is an innate inferential mechanism specially prepared for the computation of frequency data. Thus, when the task is presented in a frequency format rather than a single event probability individuals are explicitly informed of the sample space and the random selection procedure, and probabilistic reasoning is easier and more reliable. The objective of this second experiment was aimed to study the influence of the frequentist version on problems containing representative irrelevant information. According to the frequentist hypothesis base rates will be used if the task contains information about a well defined sample space or reference class.

Participants

Fifty-six students (mean age 15 years) with previous instruction on probability participated in this experiment.

Design and material

Problems with base rate information were similar to the first experiment but were adapted to a frequentist format. The experimental task presented ten base rate problems, five problems framed within curricular content and the other five with non diagnostic content. The following are an English example of each Spanish version of the problems:

Curricular Content

In a box there are 30 marbles, 18 are red marbles and 12 of green marbles. Marbles have a positive or a negative sign. 5 red marbles and 2 green marbles have a negative sign. Blind-folded John picks a marble and it has a positive sign.

Which of the following alternatives do you consider most probable?

a) the marble is red.
b) the marble is green.
c) both alternatives are equally probable.

Non Diagnostic Content

In a class there are 30 students, 18 are girls and 12 are boys. 5 girls and 2 boys wear glasses. Recently, Maria a student of this class won a composition context. Maria is a very shy person and an excellent student, specially in mathematics. On her spare time she likes to read and listen to classical music. Which of the following alternatives do you consider most probable?

a) Maria doesn't wear glasses
b) Maria wears glasses
c) both alternatives are equally probable.

Results and Discussion

Data were subjected to a 3 x 2 ANOVA, with presentation format (probabilistic and frequency) as a between-subject variable and content type (curricular and non diagnostic) as within-subject variable. There was a significant main effect of content type [$F(1, 54)= 39.15$, $p< 0.0*$]. Presentation format [$F(1, 54)= 1.13$, $p<0.29$] and the interaction between these two variables were not significant [$F(1, 54)= 1.79$, $p<0.19$].

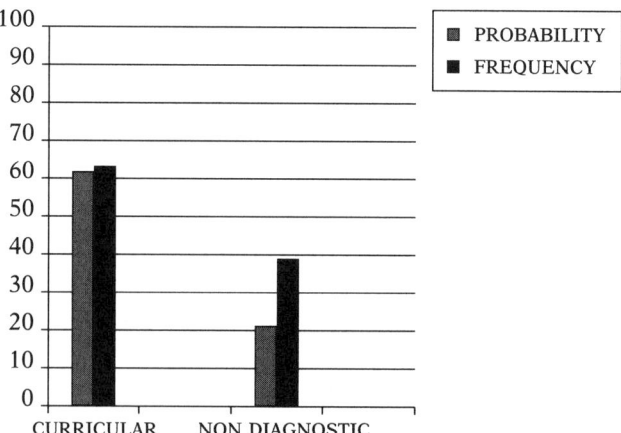

Figura 9.2. Percentage of base rate responses with different content and format presentations.

The results showed that there were no significant differences between performance on curricular and non diagnostic content when problems were framed in a probabilistic and frequentist format. Again, significant differences were found on problem content showing that student participants obtained a higher significant percentage of base rate responses in curricular content.

Whether base rates are considered relevant or not is dependent on content presentation and previous instruction helps to promote base rate consideration. Results presented by Cosmides and Tooby (1996) and Gigerenzer and Hoffrage (1995) showed that problems with a mixed format in which the information is presented in frequencies but the answer required is a single-event probability produce a decrease in the effects of the frequency format. Even if we consider that the problems posed to our participants were in a mixed format we still did not find a slight benefit in favor of the frequentist format. The results showed that people ignore base rates when problem content deviates attention to irrelevant representative information. However, format presentation, either as probability or frequency, by itself did not reduce base rate neglect. This result does not support Gigerenzer's (1991) argument that base rate neglect disappears when probabilities are presented as frequencies because this presentation format contains more information than single event probabilities in relation to sample size. The results showed that performance on the frequentist problem versions was not superior than the non-frequentist versions.

CONCLUSIONS

Overall, the results showed that experienced individuals pay attention to base rates and trained students use base rate in the absence of case date (formal problems). People understanding of probability rests on assumptions which are unstated and when reasoning with irrelevant content from the experimenter perspective, individuals might be induced to take in consideration this information specially if it is easily related to their everyday experience (Nickerson, 1996). A base rate is an objective probability that may or may not be the same as a prior probability or state of belief which are subjective. From this perspective, our results are in line with Koehler's review (1996) on the base rate fallacy which shows that base rates are not systematically ignored. When people can identify individuating information as non diagnostic of the problem presentation, their judgements are based on the base rates provided. However, if problems are presented with additional information that is linked to a relevant reference class from the individual's perspective then we should expect the representation of this information. The problem is that diagnostic and non diagnostic information is not being defined from the individuals' standpoint but from a normative aseptic model. The results so far show that experience in the knowledge domain make individuals attach more weight to base rate than to individuating information. If people are provided with base rates that are inconsistent with their experience, counterintuitive or base on sample information that is no considered relevant we should expect their neglect.

In general the conclusions point towards an optimistic view of people's understanding of statistical principles such as base rates. One of the main misunderstandings that characterizes base rate neglect research is the assumption that people hold prior beliefs that are equal to the base rates provided by the experimental task. Since Bayes' theorem considers prior probabilities (states of beliefs), base rates as an objective statistical standard does not guarantee meeting this assumption. Thus, it is not a matter of base rate neglect but rather of understanding how people represent the task and the assumptions they make. The results presented do not contradict a normative standard at least from the standpoint of understanding the concept of prior or subjective probabilities which includes the usage of all available information specially the one that is derived from experience and that will conform our states of beliefs. Performance is not a matter of right or wrong but rather of adequate or inadequate from individuals' standpoint. Individuals will use base rates only when they can be sure that the additional information is not valid. So, when confronted with base rate problems, people have to determine if diagnostic individuating information is relevant or not, and they do by experience in the knowledge domain.

The reported results show that base rates are attended when related to experience but the question on how people represent and compute probability is still open. The frequency hypothesis does not hold as the only or best cognitive mechanism that encodes frequency information automatically and the Bayesian model assumes that prior probabilities and likelihood ratios are independent and empirical research shows their dependency (Birnbaum, 1983). Also, likelihood ratios and posterior odds are commonly confused and there are different formulae to compute conditional probabilities. Reasoning heuristics can better accommodate problem content but as Kahneman and Tversky (1996) have indicated there is a general misunderstanding concerning the characterization of heuristics as independent of content, context and problem representation. Reasoning heuristics have been repeatedly criticized for their vague definitions, despite the emphasis given since their formulation to the relation between the properties that make problems easy or hard and the mental models or schemas that the problems evoke (Kahneman & Tversky, 1982). Reasoning conceived within the mental model theory seems to be a more appropriate starting point for studying problem representation given that this theory specifies the nature of mental representations. This theoretical framework and recent research on Mental Model Theory applied to probabilistic reasoning (Johnson-Laird, 1994; Johnson-Laird, Legrenzi, Girotto, Sonino & Caverni, 1999) is successfully approaching problem representation and computation by the construction of mental models with equiprobable possibilities or models with different numerical tags on the possibilities that represent different states of beliefs related to problem content. In this way, probabilities are not attached to events but to the mental description of these events. Individuals construct mental models for different true possibilities and the judged probability of an event will depend on the proportion of models that describe the event and on the probabilities attached to these models. Base rates will be attended when they are related to individual's experience or knowledge and they will be tagged to the mental models that represent the state of affairs described by the problems.

REFERENCES

BAR-HILLEL, M. (1980): «The base rate fallacy in probability judgments». *Acta Psychologica*, 44, 211-233.

BIRNBAUM, M. H. (1983): «Base rates in Bayesian inference: Signal detection analysis of the cab problem». *American Journal of Psychology*, 96, 85-93.

CHRISTENSEN-SZALANSKI, J. J., & BUSHYHEAD, J. B. (1981): «Physician's use of probabilistic information in a real clinical setting». *Journal of Experimental Psychology: Human Perception and Performance*, 7, 928-935.

COSMIDES, L., & TOOBY, J. (1996): «Are humans good intuitive statisticians after all? Rethinking some conclusions from the literature on judgment under uncertainty». *Cognition*, 58, 1-73.

EVANS, J. St. B. T. (1995): «Relevance and reasoning». En S. E. Newstead y J. St. B. T. Evans (Eds.), *Perspectives on thinking and reasoning* (pp. 147-171*)*. Hove: Erlbaum.

JOHNSON-LAIRD, P. N., LEGRENZI, P., GIROTTO, V., SONINO, M., & CAVERNI, J. P. (1999): «Naive probability: A mental model theory of extensional reasoning». *Psychological Review*, 106, 62-88.

JOHNSON-LAIRD, P. N. (1994): «Mental models and probabilistic reasoning». *Cognition*, 50, 189-209.

KAHNEMAN, D., SLOVIC, P., & TVERSKY, A. (Eds.) (1982): *Judgment under uncertainty: Heuristics and biases*. Cambridge, UK: Cambridge University Press.

KAHNEMAN, D., & TVERSKY, A. (1972): «Subjective probability: A judgment of representativeness». *Cognitive Psychology*, 3, 430-454.

— (1973): «On the psychology of prediction». *Psychological Review*, 80, 237-251.

— (1982): «On the study of statistical intuitions». *Cognition*, 11, 123-141.

— (1996): «On the reality of cognitive illusions». *Psychological Review*, 103, 582-591.

KOEHLER, J. (1996): «The base rate fallacy reconsidered: Descriptive, normative, and methodological challenges». *Behavioral and Brain Sciences*, 19, 1-17.

GIGERENZER, G., (1991): «How to make cognitive illusions disappear: beyond heuristics and biases». *European Review of Social Psychology*, 2, 83-115.

GIGERENZER, G. & HOFFRAGE, U. (1995): «How to improve Bayesian reasoning without instruction: Frequency formats». *Psychological Review*, 102 (4), 684-704.

GILOVICH, T. (1992): «Seeing the past in the present: The effect of association to familiar events on judgments and decisions». *Journal of Personality and Social Psychology*, 40, 5, 797-808.

GONZÁLEZ LABRA, M. J., ARTIETA PINEDO, I., & CEACERO CUBILLO, J. (1995): «Domain specificity of probabilistic reasoning and confidence judgments», *Paper presented at the 36th Annual Meeting of The Psychonomic Society,* Los Angeles, California, November.

KLAR, Y. (1990): «Linking structures and sensitivity to judgment-relevant information in statistical and logical reasoning tasks». *Journal of Personality and Social Psychology*, 59, 841-858.

LEGRENZI, P., & GIROTTO, V. (1996): «Mental models in reasoning and decision making processes». En J. Oakhill y A. Garnham (Eds.), *Mental Models in Cognitive Science. Essays in Honor of Phil Johnson-Laird* (pp. 95-118). Hove: Psychology Press.

NICKERSON, R. S. (1996): «Ambiguities and unstated assumptions in probabilistic reasoning». *Psychological Bulletin*, 120, 3, 410-433.

PIATTELLI-PALMARINI, M. (1994): *Inevitable illusions: How mistakes of reason rule our minds*. Princeton, N.J.: Princeton University Press.

SCHWARZ, N., STRACK, F., HILTON, D., & NADERER, G. (1991): «Base rates, representativeness, and the logic of conversation: The contextual relevance of "irrelevant information"». *Social Cognition*, 9, 67-83.

SPERBER, D., CARA, F., & WILSON, D. (1995): «Relevance theory explains the selection task». *Cognition*, 57, 31-95.

10

BIASES IN PROBABILISTIC REASONING MAY BE PRODUCED BY ASSOCIATIVE LEARNING MECHANISMS

PEDRO L. COBOS,
ANTONIO CAÑO
FRANCISCO J. LÓPEZ

En los primeros estudios sobre sesgos en tareas de categorización probabilística, Kahneman y Tversky (1973) pusieron en relación tales sesgos con el modo en que las categorías se aprenden, se representan en la memoria y se usan. Desde esta perspectiva, los procesos de categorización basados en la similitud entre un objeto y los prototipos de las posibles categorías eran los responsables de sesgos como el de la desestimación de frecuencias de categorías o el de la falacia de la conjunción. Como tales procesos se concebían como rápidos, poco costosos y disparados por las propiedades de los estímulos, se asimilaron como la base constituyente del razonamiento intuitivo, proceso opuesto al razonamiento extensional (Tversky y Kahneman, 1983). Una de las principales razones por las que el enfoque de los sesgos y heurísticos de Tversky y Kahneman ha terminado por desanimar a muchos investigadores descansa en el escaso compromiso con la formulación de su teoría en términos de modelos computacionales. Nuestra propuesta, en pocas palabras, es que los mecanismos de aprendizaje asociativo, que interesantemente son rápidos, poco costosos y disparados por las propiedades de los estímulos, resultan ideales para la formalización computacional del razonamiento intuitivo (en Hinton, 1990 y Sloman, 1996 se puede encontrar una caracterización del razonamiento intuitivo basada en procesos asociativos). Más concretamente, la desestimación de frecuencias de categorías y la falacia de la conjunción en tareas de categorización probabilística se pueden interpretar, en algunas circunstancias, como ilusiones cognitivas debidas a la intervención de procesos de aprendizaje asociativo que resultan disparados por los contenidos presentes en las tareas de categorización. Cuando las personas

*experimentan situaciones en las que algunos acontecimientos o
propiedades (claves) son seguidos por otros (resultado), se forman lazos
asociativos que permiten predecir los últimos a partir de la ocurrencia
de los primeros. Los lazos asociativos formados durante tal situación
de aprendizaje permiten la generación automática de un producto en
una situación posterior de enjuiciamiento probabilístico si los argumentos de los juicios incluyen contenidos iguales o similares a las
claves y resultados de la anterior situación de aprendizaje. Este producto, a su vez, sesga los juicios de las personas llegando a producir
resultados normativamente inadecuados como la desestimación de frecuencias de categorías o la falacia de la conjunción. En el presente
capítulo hemos revisado una serie de trabajos experimentales, especialmente los realizados en nuestro laboratorio, que apoyan nuestra propuesta. Asimismo, mostramos cómo una red neuronal asociativa puede
dar cuenta de los fenómenos originados en los diferentes experimentos.*

INTRODUCTION

In the first studies on biases in probabilistic categorisation tasks, Kahneman
and Tversky (1973) explained the biases on the basis of frequently used
heuristics, i. e., a sort of cognitive *shortcut* to solve daily life tasks. Some of these
heuristics were related to the way in which knowledge about categories is
acquired, represented in memory and used. Under this view, categorisation
processes based on the similarity between an object and each of the category
prototypes were responsible for biases as the base rate neglect and the
conjunction fallacy. As these processes were conceived as rapid, effortless and
feature-driven, they were taken as the basis for intuitive reasoning, as opposed
to extensional reasoning (Tversky & Kahneman, 1983).

Under this perspective, biases in probabilistic reasoning tasks were also
conceived as cognitive illusions. Two main reasons can be mentioned for this.
First, heuristics, though responsible for the errors, were thought to be
appropriate solutions for some current tasks out of the laboratory context.
Second, heuristic processes were supposed to be primed by some elements of
the laboratory task that are characteristic of those extra-laboratory contexts
where heuristics are appropriate. Thus, in some sense, people are induced to
take the experimental task as if it were another one (Cohen, 1981; López,
Cobos, Caño & Shanks, 1998).

Unfortunately, Tversky and Kahneman's heuristics and biases approach
has lacked of instantiation in terms of cognitive processing models. This, as
well as other related aspects, has led the research program to two undesirable
states (Dougherty, Gettys, & Ogden, 1999; Gigerenzer, 1996): a) heuristics have
been invoked to explain almost every thing, but the conditions that switches
on or off such heuristics remain obscure; b) there has been a tendency to base
the explanation and description of behaviour on the normative principles
violated. For example, the base rate neglect has served to refer to a violation
of the Bayesian theorem as well as an explanation of that violation. Thus,

though initially promising and stimulating, this theoretical view has disenchanted a good number of researchers who have verified how little advance has been produced after three decades of research on biases in probability judgement.

Our claim, in a few words, is that associative learning mechanisms are good candidates to be the processes underlying the rapid, effortless and feature-driven intuitive reasoning conceived by Tversky and Kahneman (see Hinton, 1990 and Sloman, 1996 for an associative-based characterisation of intuitive reasoning). Specifically, the base rate neglect and the conjunction fallacy in probabilistic categorisation tasks can be characterised, in some circumstances, as cognitive illusions due to the associative learning processes evoked by the contents of the categorisation task. When people are repeatedly exposed to situations in which some events or features (cues) are followed by others (outcomes), associations are formed allowing to predict the second from the first ones. The associative links formed during the learning situation can automatically generate an output in a later probability judgement situation if the same or similar cues and outcomes constitute the judgements' arguments. This output, in turn, biases people's judgements and yields some normatively inadequate responses as the base rate neglect and the conjunction fallacy.

Along this chapter, we report some empirical evidence that support our claim. We have focused on two experiments made in our laboratory, though other interesting results have been published which have inspired our proposal. As will be shown, there is a common research strategy in all the experiments we will cite. Such strategy includes the following aspects: a) participants are provided with an associative learning task followed by a judgement phase where they have to estimate the probability of some statements relating the cues and outcomes of the learning phase, b) the learning and the judgement phase are arranged so as to meet the conditions under which some biases are typically obtained. Briefly speaking, a cognitive illusion is experimentally induced by providing an associative learning context. We also report the result of a simulation run with an associative neural network to assess the adequacy of associative learning principles to account for participants' judgements. Before starting with the empirical evidence, however, it is important to envisage which task associative mechanisms are aimed at and how such task can be performed. After that, we will articulate an associative explanation of biases in probability judgement tasks.

Associative mechanisms and predictive learning

Associative theories of learning have benn mainly developed in the field of animal learning. A good amount of phenomena have led researchers to think of animal conditioning as reflecting the learning of predictive relationships between events. Animal learning in classical conditioning, for example, is said to be a mechanism to acquire a sort of knowledge which reflects the causal texture of the environment (Dickinson, 1980; Tolman & Brunswick, 1935). One important phenomenon on which this assertion is based is the effect of relative validity of cues (more commonly known as selective learning effects). It is largely known that for conditioning to occur it does not suffice it to provide individuals with a temporal contiguity relationship between a cue and an outcome. If the target cue always appears with another which, on its own, is a reliable predictor of the outcome, then the target cue will develop little or no conditioning at all. This is what happens in blocking experiments, for instance. In these experiments a given cue A is repeatedly paired with the outcome during a first stage. During the second stage, the target cue, B, and cue A are jointly paired with the outcome. At test, the target cue elicits little conditioned response compared with another condition including only AB trials (Kamin, 1968).

In these cases, the target cue is said to have a low relative validity. That is, when cue B is paired for the first time with the outcome, it is less valid as a predictor of the outcome than its accompanying cue. A similar way to think of B is as a redundant cue, for A is all what is needed to predict the outcome in AB trials. As a consequence, we cannot be sure of how reliable is B as a predictor of the outcome. But we can provide a more precise measure of unidirectional predictive relationships. Allan (1980) has proposed a contingency based measure, ΔP, which is the result of the probability of the outcome given the cue minus the probability of the outcome given the absence of the cue, holding constant everything else. A strict application of this contingency formula to the blocking design yields a value of 0 for the target cue B because the probabilities of the outcome given the presence and absence of such cue, holding constant the presence of the accompanying cue A, both equal 1. Interestingly, it has been shown that animals are impressively sensitive to variations of the DP measure of the relationship between cues and outcomes (Rescorla, 1966, 1968) as well as between responses and outcomes (Hammond & Paynter, 1983). Moreover, animals are said to be well-calibrated with respect to ΔP. Therefore, it is not unjustified to say that learning rely on a device well suited for the task of detecting predictive relationships between events.

Probably the most popular associative theory proposed to explain such phenomena is the Rescorla-Wagner theory (Rescorla & Wagner, 1972). This is a highly parsimonious theory which is able to account for an overwhelming number of data coming from animal as well as human learning experiments. The theory establishes a rule to calculate associative strength changes between the representations of the cues and the representations of the outcomes on the basis of the occurrences of such cues and outcomes. This rule, which is mathematically equivalent to the well known delta rule extensively applied in connectionist networks (Sutton & Barto, 1981), states that the change of the associative strength between a cue representation and an outcome representation is directly proportional to the surprise caused by the outcome (namely, the difference between what is expected to occur about the outcome from all the cues present and what actually occurs). It is mathematically formalised as follows:

$$\Delta V_{ij} = \alpha_i \beta_j (\lambda_j - \Sigma V)$$

where α_i and β_j refers to the salience of the cue and the outcome, respectively; λ_j is 1 when the outcome is present and 0 when it is absent; and ΣV is the sum of the associative strengths between all the cues present and the outcome (i.e., the expectation of the outcome). It has been shown that, under some conditions, this rule yields equivalent asymptotic results as the ΔP calculus (see Cheng & Holyoak, 1995, and Cheng, 1997 for a detailed computational analysis of the RW rule). Thus, the RW rule is an algorithm that effectively detects predictive relationships between cues and outcomes. Finally, it gives a good explanation of the relative validity effect. In fact, this model was conceived to account for this phenomenon.

Since the last few years, some researchers have been interested in determining how strongly human predictive learning parallels the findings found in the animal conditioning research (Allan, 1993; Dickinson, Shanks, & Evenden, 1984; Shanks, 1993, 1995; Wasserman, 1990). Experimental designs inspired in animal learning experiments have been used in causal, contingency, and category learning experiments. The results obtained greatly resemble those obtained in animal conditioning. Two frequent aims in these experiments have been to determine whether contingency, predictive and causal judgements are affected by the ΔP measure of contingency and to verify whether contingency, predictive, causal and probability judgements are affected by the relative validity of cues. There is convincing evidence that contingency, predictive and causal judgements are nicely sensitive to ΔP. Moreover, there are some data showing that contingency judgements accurately fit ΔP when trial-by-trial learning procedures are used (López, Almaraz, Fernández, & Shanks 1998; Wasserman, Elek, Chatlosh, & Baker, 1993). Actually, there is some controversy in non-contingent situations, for some experiments show that people tend to overestimate non-contingent relationships between cues and outcomes in high outcome-density conditions, i.e., when the outcome occurs very frequently. This result also parallels animal learning findings. However, there is evidence that such overestimation disappears if the number of trials is incremented and if participants are properly instructed (López, Almaraz, Fernández and Shanks, 1998; Matute, 1996). Interestingly, there is evidence that overestimation in animal learning also tends to disappear with extended training (Benedict & Ayres, 1972).

On the other hand, the relative validity effect has been repeatedly obtained in different situations. It has been found in predictive, contingency, and causal learning situations (Baker, Mercier, Vallee-Tourangeau, Frank, & Pan, 1993; Chapman & Robbins, 1990; Dickinson & Shanks, 1985; Shanks & López, 1996; Van Hamme & Wasserman, 1993). Relative validity effects have also been found in probabilistic categorisation tasks (Cobos, López, Rando, Fernández & Almaraz, 1993; Estes, Campbell, Hatsopoulos & Hurwitz, 1989; Gluck & Bower, 1988; Kruschke, 1996; Myers, Lohmeier & Well, 1994; Nosofsky, Kruschke & McKinley, 1992; Shanks, 1990). As we will see later, the later results are relevant here because they allow to establish a link between relative validity effects and some biases in probability judgements. Specifically, it is noteworthy that relative validity effects make people to deviate from empirical conditional probabilities.

The RW model has been successfully employed to account for the above mentioned results as well as others. As will be shown, in some cases, it has been even used to give a quantitative account for the observed judgements, obtaining an impressive good fit (Gluck & Bower, 1988; Estes *et al.*, 1989; Cobos *et al.* 1993). Of course, some assumptions have to be made, though minimal, to extend the RW theory to account for judgements because such theory is only concerned with connection strengths between representations of cues and outcomes. Normally, it is assumed a monotonically increasing function relating connection strengths and judgements. In categorisation tasks where people have to assign a series of stimuli to a set of mutually exclusive categories, a ratio rule is usually applied (Gluck & Bower, 1988; Estes *et al.*, 1989). That is, if we think of a given category representation as a given output node of a feedforward connectionist network, the probability of that category would be equal to the amount of activation of the corresponding output node divided by the summed amount of activation from all the output nodes:

$$P(i) = \frac{O_i}{\sum_j O_j}$$

Here, the amount of activation of a given output node is assumed to be equal to the summed connection strengths of the representations of the cues present [1].

Other more sophisticated connectionist models have been proposed in some predictive learning situations, such as ALCOVE (Kruschke, 1992), Pearce's configural model (Pearce, 1994), or ADIT (Kruschke, 1996). These models make different assumptions about how stimuli are represented or about attentional shifts as part of learning. However, it is noteworthy that a crucial feature of these models to account for the data is still the error driven learning rule on which they are based. Thus we will focus on the more simple RW model for several reasons: a) it instantiates the essential error-driven learning principle to account for the data, b) despite its simplicity, it can cope with a wide range of phenomena of animal and human learning, c) it contains very few free parameters, d) the other models do not improve the RW's fit to the data of the experiments we will describe.

In summary, there is consistent evidence that animal and human learning is intended to capture the predictive structure of the environment. On the other hand, there is nothing new in saying that associative and, more generally, connectionist mechanisms are ideal devices to learn predictive relationships. In fact, models belonging to this family accounts for most of the data coming from animal learning research and many human learning results.

An associationist-based explanation of biases in probability judgement

Though we will focus on the base rate neglect and the conjunction fallacy, the explanation offered here is not intended to be restricted to these fallacies. However, as our proposal is applied to these phenomena, let us start with a short description of each one.

---

[1]   As many other researchers, we will assume some equivalence between associative and connectionist models. So, we will interchangeably use connections and associations, associative strength and connection weight, cues representations and input nodes, and outcomes representations and output nodes.

The base rate neglect refers to a fallacy obtained in Bayesian problems. Generally, participants have to estimate the probability of an object or person belonging to a series of mutually exclusive categories. Participants are usually informed of the frequency of the different categories (the base rates) and of the probabilities of finding the features which define the object they have to categorise in each category (conditional probabilities). The Bayesian formula to calculate the probability of the object belonging to one of the categories (A) is as follows:

$$P(A|O) = \frac{P(O|A) \cdot P(A)}{P(O|A) \cdot P(A) + P(O|A) \cdot P(\overline{A})}$$

where O is the object to be classified; A and $\overline{A}$ are the target category and its complementary set, respectively; P(A|O) is the probability that object O belongs to category A; and P(O|A) and P(O|$\overline{A}$) are the probability of object O in category A and category $\overline{A}$, respectively.

The base rate neglect is obtained when participants' judgements are not affected, or are only slightly affected, by information about category frequency [P(A) and P($\overline{A}$)]. This phenomenon has been mainly studied in cases where there is some kind of conflict between the base rates and the conditional probabilities information. This happens when those features which define the object are more probable in a low-frequency category [that is, P(O|B)>P(O|A), and P(B)<P(A)] (see Figure 10.1). In such cases, participants' judgements can be better predicted from the conditional probability information rather than from the base rates.

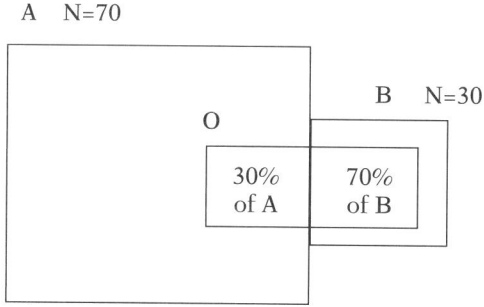

Figure 10.1. A Bayesian structure problem with a conflict between base rate information and conditional probability information.

The conjunction fallacy occurs when someone assigns a higher probability to a conjunction of events than to one of its constituents. This implies the violation of the conjunction theorem, which states that the probability of the conjunction of events is always lower or equal to the probability of any of the events that constitute the conjunction [that is, P(A∩B) ≤ P(A), and P(A∩B) ≤ P(B)]. In the Linda problem (Tversky & Kahneman, 1983), surely the most cited in this context, a character named Linda is described to participants as an activist woman. Later, they have to sort in a decreasing order a series of statements depending on their probability. The most relevant statements are: Linda is active in the feminist movement (A), Linda is a bank teller (B), Linda is a bank teller and is active in the feminist movement (A & B). As a result, many participants estimate that statement A & B is more likely than statement B (Agnoli & Krantz, 1989; Fiedler, 1988; Politzer & Noveck, 1991; Wolford & Taylor, 1990).

According to our proposal, biases in probability judgements are a consequence, in some cases, of a cognitive illusion due to the operation of an associative learning mechanism (ALM). This type of cognitive illusion occurs when the contents of the probability judgement task are involved in a previous predictive learning situation, that is, a situation where an individual has to learn from examples to predict some outcomes from some cues. As we said before, associative learning mechanisms are specially well suited to learn predictive relationships from examples. The repeated exposure to examples favours the creation of associations between representations of the cues and representations of the outcomes so that, when a given cue is detected, the associated outcome representation is automatically activated. The amount of activation of the outcome representation can be taken as a measure of to what extent the outcome is expected.

When participants in an experiment have to make a probability judgement on the relationship between, say, two contents that have played the role of cue and outcome in a predictive learning task, the ALM automatically generates, as an output, a certain amount of expectation about the outcome occurrence. This amount of expectation is interpreted as a measure of the relationship between both contents. So, in a way, participants have a direct and automatic access to knowledge about the relationship between the contents involved in the probability judgement task. The bias in probability judgements occurs if that knowledge is accepted when the requested probability judgement is made, provided that ALM's output violates some assumption of the experimenter's normative analysis of the probabilistic reasoning task. In short, the learning context favours a way of coding and storing certain information which efficiently solves the problem faced in such context, but which generates a cost in a subsequent task if it requires solving different problems with similar contents (see López, Cobos, Caño & Shanks, 1998 for further details; see also Ratcliff & McKoon, 1996, for a similar account of some biases in implicit memory tasks).

To simplify, we can summarise our associationist explanation of biases in probability judgements in the following four steps: 1) the contents of the probability judgement have played the role of cues and outcomes in a previous associative learning situation; 2) during the learning situation, directed associations from representations of cues to representations of outcomes are formed that allow for a direct and automatic access to knowledge about the relationship between cues and outcomes; 3) during the judgement task, the contents that are made explicit for participants activates ALM which, in turn, can produce a single-step output that violates the experimenter's normative analysis of the task; 4) ALM's output can bias individual's judgement if it is accepted as the basis for the response.

How can our proposal be applied to explain the base rate neglect? As we said before, the base rate neglect has been shown many times in probabilistic categorisation tasks in which the features that define the object to be categorise is more likely given the least frequent category. The task we have used in our experiments, which is based in Gluck & Bower (1988)'s, will serve as an example. In Gluck and Bower's task, participants had to learn to diagnose two fictitious diseases from four possible symptoms on a trial by trial basis. At test, participants had to rate the probability with which a series of hypothetical patients suffered from one or the other disease given each of the possible symptoms. 75% of the hypothetical patients suffered from a common disease (C), while the remaining 25% suffered from a rare one (R). Table 10.1 shows the conditional probabilities relating the diseases and the symptoms. One of the patients showed symptom S_1, which is more likely in disease R ($p=.6$) than in disease C ($p=.2$). Despite this, there are as many patients with S_1 who suffer from disease R as patients with S_1 who suffer from disease C. However, participants gave higher ratings to the probability of disease R given S_1 than to the probability of disease C given S_1.

To show how participants' judgements could be accounted for on the basis of the RW learning rule, Gluck and Bower run a simulation with a two layered neural network which updated its weights via the RW rule. The input layer contained four units (S_1, S_2, S_3, & S_4), one for each symptom, while the output layer consisted of two units, one for disease R (R) and another for disease C (C). Input units could take on values of 1 or 0 depending on whether the represented symptom was present or absent in a given patient, respectively. The output units were linear ones.

A key aspect for an associationist-based account of this sort of base rate neglect is that the difference between the probability of S_1 given R and the probability of S_1 given C correlates with a difference between the relative validity of S_1 as a predictor of R and as a predictor of C. That is, S_1 is the most valid symptom to predict disease R, while it is the least valid symptom to predict disease C (see Table 10.1). So, on the basis of the RW learning rule, unit S_1 will end up with a stronger association with unit R than with unit C. If we keep this in mind, the application of our four step account to this situation is straightforward. First, participants rated the probability of statements relating contents that had formed part of a previous predictive learning situation. Second, during the learning stage, associations between such contents (S_1-R and S_1-C) developed allowing to predict diseases from symptoms. Third, the explicit presence of S_1 in the judgement required automatically and rapidly triggered a sort of knowledge of the predictive value of S_1 for disease R and for disease C. Fourth, such knowledge was accepted as the basis for the probability judgement.

Now, it is clear why we said before that relative validity effects produce some deviations from empirical conditional probabilities. However, such deviations are unimportant if we take into account the overall set of training trials. Gluck and Bower's model produces a qualitatively significant deviation from empirical probabilities only in trials in which the patient presents symptom S_1 as the only symptom[2]. These trials are very unfrequent in the overall set of training trials, and at the same time, the associative weights responsible for this deviation are also responsible for a greater accuracy in the remaining training trials. On the other hand, as will be shown in the simulation's results, the neural network is very sensitive to category base rates. It could not be otherwise because neural networks that use error driven learning methods are trying to optimise predictions in the overall training set. Therefore, it could be claimed at the same time both that ALM is responsible for the above base rate neglect, and that this mechanism essentially produces Bayesian behaviour (McClelland, 1998). We think that this is an interesting point because it allows to conciliate two empirically based claims about probability judgement: a) on the one hand, probability judgements are plagued with irrationalities; b) on the other hand, humans are well calibrated in real life situations.

Finally, it is important to realise how crucial is the role of steps 3 and 4 in accounting for the above base rate neglect. According to such steps, the information that is made explicit in the judgement requirement makes ALM to generate an output which, in turn, strongly determines people's responses. This is also a key aspect because ALM cannot generate a response to the item $P(R|S_1)$ in a single step. Note that this item is not equivalent to test the neural network with the input vector 1000, which stands for the presence of symptom S_1 in isolation. S_1 in item $P(R|S_1)$ refers to the set of patients with symptom S_1, among which we can find patients who also present S_2 or S_2 & S_3 or S_3, etc. Thus, to obtain an adequate response from the neural network we should test it with many input patterns. Using mental models theory's terms (Johnson-Laird, 1983), this should involve creating a mental model for each possibility compatible with having S_1 to feed ALM and storing the result in working memory (see Shanks, 1990). Tversky and Kahneman (1983) refers to this as a decompositional strategy. But this is very hard when we have many possible mental models. Interestingly, according to the principle of cognitive economy of the mental models theory, the first mental model people create is determined to a large extent by the information that is made explicit in the premises and such mental model strongly influences people's responses (Johnson-Laird & Byrne, 1991; see also Johnson-Laird, Legrenzi, Girotto, Sonino Legrenzi & Caverni, 1999). Thus, steps 3 and 4 can be thought of as deriving from the mental models theory.

Regarding the conjunction fallacy, it has usually been found when an unfrequent event is joined with a frequent one. In these situations people tend to judge the conjunction of the two events as more likely than the unfrequent one. We can arrange a similar situation in Gluck and Bower's task. For example, suppose that people have to judge the probability of symptom S_4 in disease R patients and the probability of symptoms S_4 & S_1 in the same set of patients. As will be shown later, S_4 ends up with a negative associative weight with R and with a large positive weight with C, while S_1 ends up with a positive associative weight with R and a negative associative weight with C. As ALM is fed by the explicit information, the unfrequent constituent item would produce an output

---

[2] This is only true in Shanks (1990; Experiment 3). In Gluck and Bower (1988; Experiment 1), though the probability of R and of C were the same in patients with S_1, they were not in patients with S_1 as a unique symptom. In the later case, disease R was more likely than disease C. However, Shanks arranged training trials so that the probability of R and of C were also the same in patients with S_1 as a unique symptom. Despite Shanks' procedural modification, Gluck and Bower's neural network still predicts a bias toward disease R with an input vector consisting of 1000.

which is highly incompatible with being a disease R patient compared with the conjunction item. Thus, the conjunction item would be judged as more likely than the unfrequent constituent item. Of course, this would implicitly involve an inversion in the judgements direction. That is, while the items ask for the probability of symptoms given the diseases (D-S direction), ALM's outputs are based on S-D directed associations which allow to predict diseases from symptoms. But just because of ALM's functioning, knowledge about S-D directed relationships are readily accessible, while D-S directed relationships are not. In other words, because during the learning stage some stimuli are repeatedly processed so as to learn to predict diseases, people are biased to process those stimuli in the same way even if they have to judge D-S directed relationships in a later test stage.

We are not claiming, however, that conjunction fallacies in such cases are the byproduct of participants confounding the probability of symptoms given diseases with the probability of diseases given symptoms. We state, rather, that participants are biased to process the symptoms as the inputs of ALM, whose outputs exert an influence on probability judgements. The extent to which ALM's outputs determine probability judgements could depend, among other things, on participants' opportunities to detect normative violations of such outputs.

As we have tried to show, associative learning mechanisms could well be those rapid, effortless and feature-driven (content-addressable) processes envisaged by Tversky and Kahneman as responsible for biases in probability judgement. Furthermore, associative learning mechanisms can be conceived as an instantiation of some sort of representativeness heuristic. As knowledge from the different examples is superimposed to a large extent in the same weight matrix, associative networks develop a sort of abstracted prototype. Moreover, the outputs of this kind of networks are nothing more than the computation of the similarity between input patterns and the prototypes stored in the weights (Cobos & Almaraz, 1995)[3]. Finally, it could also be argued how these mechanisms provide a way of thinking of other heuristics such as accessibility and plausibility.

Evidence supporting the associative-based explanation of biases

If biases in probability judgement can be caused by cognitive illusions due to the use of contents that have taken part in a previous predictive learning situation, then these biases should be experimentally elicited by the use of a predictive learning task before the judgement stage. In fact, this is just what Gluck & Bower did. In their experiments, participants received information about the relationship between a series of events through a predictive learning task rather than through the usual verbal descriptions or numeric presentations in terms of likelihoods. Later on, participants were asked to judge the probability of a series of statements relating the same events. As mentioned before, participants judged the less frequent disease as more likely than the more

---

[3] Associative neural networks can, at the same time, store specific information of exemplars. Thus, learning from exemplars does not necessarily means abstracting a prototype at the cost of learning specific information of exemplars (McClelland & Rumelhart, 1985).

frequent one despite S_1 having been paired the same number of times with each disease. This is what happens in base rate neglect experiments, and this is why the phenomenon found by Gluck and Bower is called apparent base rate neglect. As far as we are concerned, Gluck and Bower's experiments were the first to establish a link between a very known fallacy in probability judgement and associative learning processes.

The apparent base rate neglect has been replicated in a good number of experiments using Gluck and Bower's task or similar procedures (Cobos *et al.*, 1993; Estes *et al.*, 1989; Kruschke, 1996; Myers *et al.*, 1994; Nosofsky *et al.*, 1992; Shanks, 1990). Among these works, there are three empirical evidences that strengthen the associationist explanation of this phenomenon. First, in all these experiments participants are well calibrated regarding empirical probabilities. Observed judgements seem to be quite sensitive to base rates. So there seems to be no room for an explanation based on ignoring base rates as suggested by Tversky and Kahneman's representativeness heuristic. The way in which Tversky and Kahneman conceive such heuristic is equivalent, in many cases, to applying the Bayesian formula without the base rates (Gigerenzer & Murray, 1987). As the simulation's results will show, sensitivity to base rates is just what should be expected from Gluck and Bower's neural network. This model fits reasonably well Bayesian probability calculus and predicts, at the same time, the apparent base rate neglect observed in participants' judgements in patients with S_1.

Second, the associative neural network has been used to obtain quantitative fits with impressive good results. Estes *et al.* (1989) obtained learning curves from participants' performance through the training stage. The learning task they used was the same as Gluck and Bower's except for some minimal procedural changes. All participants were trained with the same sequence of hypothetical patients. They also ran a simulation with Gluck and Bower's neural network using the same training sequence participants experienced to obtain learning curves from the neural network's performance. The simulation's results nicely fitted the observed curves. The fit provided by the neural network was even better than the fit provided by an exemplar-based memory model. Estes et al. also reported the results of a series of analysis showing that both participants and the neural network produced categorisation responses well calibrated with respect to Bayesian probabilities. We have also obtained quantitative fit results in our laboratory using the same task and the same model. Specifically, Cobos *et al.* (1993) recorded participants' probability judgements for every possible combination of symptoms at the test phase. The simulation's results were almost identical to those of Figure 3, where we can appreciate how closely the network approached the observed judgements.

Third, there is evidence supporting the explanatory status of relative validity regarding the apparent base rate neglect. For example, Gluck and Bower (1988; Experiment 2) altered the relative validity of S_1 and S_4 while holding the same programmed conditional probabilities of these symptoms. To achieve this, they changed the conditional probabilities of S_2 and S_3 so that the former became the best predictor of R and the latter became the best predictor of C. As a consequence, participants gave lower ratings for the probability of R given S_1 and for the probability of C given S_4 than participants in Experiment 1. Moreover, the apparent base rate neglect tended to disappear. Similar results have been obtained by Kruschke (1996) and Cobos (1996). Apart from these base rate neglect designs, there are other experiments showing relative validity effects in probability judgements (e.g. Price & Yates, 1995).

We will show in what follows some evidence regarding the adequacy of an associationist-based account of biases in probability judgement. These experiments constitute, to a large extent, a replication of Cobos *et al.* (1993)'s, experiments. We used Gluck and Bower's learning task with some changes. For example, there were 160 training trials rather than 240. In each trial participants received information about the symptoms present in a hypothetical patient and made a diagnostic decision. After the diagnostic response, participants were provided with corrective feedback. We used the same programmed probabilities as Gluck and Bower, which can be seen in Table 10.1. However, as Shanks (1990), we also arranged training trials so that the probability of R and of C were the same in patients with S_1 as a unique symptom. With such arrangement, any apparent base rate neglect result would be very difficult to explain from conventional exemplar-based memory models or multiple-trace ones as MINERVA2. Hypothetical patients with no symptoms were also included in the learning phase. To simulate the results we used a modified version of the network described above (see Figure 10.2), including a single node in the output layer (see also Gluck & Bower, 1988). Now, the target output for the single node is +1 for disease R and –1 for disease C. The logistic function was used to transform the output activation values in to probability judgements as indicated below:

$$P(R) = \frac{1}{1 + e^{-c \cdot net}}$$

where *net* is the net input to the output unit and c is a constant free parameter. The training consisted of several epochs of 160 trials as it was done for the training of participants. A small learning rate was used to obtain weight values near asymptote ($l = 5 \cdot 10^{-5}$).

TABLE 10.1
Programmed probabilities of each symptom given each disease and of each disease given each symptom in Experiment 1

	Symptoms			
	1	2	3	4
P(symptom|common)	0.2	0.3	0.4	0.6
P(symptom|rare)	0.6	0.4	0.3	0.2
P(common|symptom)	0.5	0.7	0.8	0.9
P(rare|symptom)	0.5	0.3	0.2	0.1

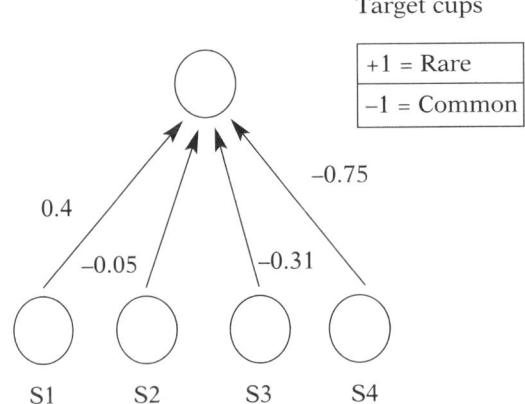

Figure 10.2. Asymptotic weight values obtained with the neural network used for the simulation.

In Experiment 1 we focused on four objectives: 1) to test whether the diagnostic learning task could induce the apparent base rate neglect bias in a later probability judgement phase; 2) to assess the extent to which category base rates affect participants' judgements; 3) to test whether the learning task situation could also induce the conjunction fallacy bias; 4) to assess the extent to which the neural network explains the whole set of data.

As explained above, we centered our attention on symptom S_1 to search for the apparent base rate neglect. We expected to replicate participants' bias toward indicating the presence of disease R in patients with S_1 found by other researchers. Figure 10.2 shows the asymptotic weights of the different connections. As can be seen, input node S_1 has a positive connection with the output node, meaning that symptom S_1 is more diagnostic of disease R than of disease C. As explained before, this result of the simulation is due to S_1 having more relative validity as a predictor of R than as a predictor of C. To test participants' sensitivity to category base rates, we recorded their ratings on the probabilities of R and of C given every possible symptom configuration so as to allow an analysis of category frequency on probability judgements. If we look at the weights in Figure 10.2, we can easily appreciate the network's sensitivity to base rates. Note that the sum of the absolute values of the negative weights is largely greater than the sum of the corresponding values of the positive weights. This means that, for the overall set of possible symptom configurations, the network will give much more disease C responses than disease R responses.

To search for evidence of conjunction fallacy biases, participants had also to judge the probability of some symptoms given each disease. Specifically, in patients suffering from R they had to judge the probability of the following items: S_4, S_4 & S_1, S_4 & S_2, and S_4 & S_3. Likewise, in patients suffering from C participants had to judge the probability of the following items: S_1, S_1 & S_2, S_1 & S_3, and S_1 & S_4. The conjunction fallacy would involve higher ratings for the conjunction items than for the critical items S_4 and S_1 in the context of R and of C, respectively. As we mentioned in point 2, our central claim is that ALM will automatically generate outputs whenever the same cues (symptoms) and outcomes (diseases) constitute the judgements' arguments. This would be the case even if participants have to judge the probability of symptoms given the diseases, which is in the opposite direction of the associative links. To the extent that such output influences probability judgements, some conjunction fallacies should be expected. A look at Figure 10.2 again reveals that some conjunction fallacies are clearly expected, while others should not occur. For example, the input pattern 1001, which stands for symptoms S_1 & S_4, would produce an output which is much more consistent with suffering from R than the input pattern 0001. So participants should judge the conjunction S_4 & S_1 as more likely than symptom S_4 in patients suffering from R. On the other hand, the input pattern 1001 produce an output which is much more consistent with suffering from C than the input pattern 1000. So participants should judge the conjunction S_1 & S_4 as more likely than symptom S_1 in patients suffering from C. Another conjunction fallacy that could be expected consists in judging the conjunction S_1 & S_3 as more likely than symptom S_1 in patients suffering from C, though this is not as greatly expected as the others.

We went to considerable length to prevent participants from confusing the probability of a disease given a symptom with the probability of a symptom given a disease, and to prevent them from confusing the explicit absence of a symptom with the absence of information about the presence or absence of a symptom. Otherwise, the biases could be interpreted as simple linguistic misinterpretations. This was achieved via instructions, visual cues during the task that helped to discriminate, and filler items that compelled participants to discriminate between those kinds of items.

The median rating for the probability of R given S_1 was 0.63, which was statistically higher than the empirical probability 0.49. Consequently, participants biased their judgements toward the rare disease, as it was expected.

Figure 10.3 shows the mean ratings for the probability of R given each of the possible configurations except for the no symptom case. In this figure the simulation data obtained with the neural network model is also displayed as well as the judgements that should be expected if participants were absolutely insensitive to category base rates.

As can be seen, contrary to the representativeness heuristic explanation, participants' judgements, as well as the neural network's estimations, were strongly influenced by category base rates, for both were far from what could be expected on the basis of simple base rate neglect.

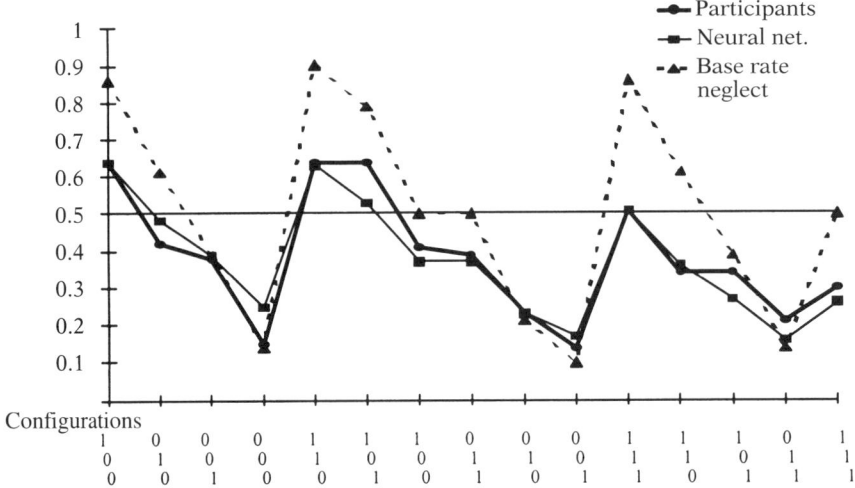

Figure 10.3. Participants' mean probability judgements, simulation data obtained from the neural network and judgements expected from neglecting category base rates in Experiment 1.

Finally, Table 10.2 shows the mean ratings regarding the test for the conjunction fallacies, as well as the net input for the output unit for each item.

TABLE 10.2
Mean ratings for the probability of the items concerning the test for the conjunction fallacy and the corresponding net inputs for the output unit in Experiment 1

Diseases					
R					
	Items	S_4	S_4 & S_1	S_4 & S_2	S_4 & S_3
	Judgements	0.26	0.45	0.26	0.32
	Net input	−0.75	−0.35	−0.80	−1.06
C					
	Items	S_1	S_1 & S_4	S_1 & S_3	S_1 & S_2
	Judgements	0.45	0.64	0.50	0.45
	Net input	0.40	−0.35	0.09	0.35

Regarding disease R patients, only the conjunction S_4 & S_1 received significantly higher ratings than the S_4 constituent. Regarding C, only the conjunction S_1 & S_4 received higher ratings than the S_1 constituent. Both conjunction fallacies were expected by the model. In the context of C, judgements for the conjunction S_1 & S_3 were not statistically different from judgements for the S_1 item. However, it is also the case that the network does not predict the latter conjunction fallacy to the same extent as in the former cases. Specially remarkable are the differences found between the empirical probabilities and participants' probability estimates in those conjunction items that were rated as more likely than their critical constituents (S_1 & S_4 in R patients, and S_1 & S_4 in C patients). For instance, only 14% of the patients suffering from R presented both S_1 and S_4 whereas the mean probability judgement was .45. In patients suffering from C, 10% of the patients presented S_1 and S_4, while participants' mean probability judgement was .64. According to the net activation values shown in Table 10.2, we can easily explain why these estimations reached such high values. Note that the output node activation value with input pattern 1001 is –0.35. This value, which is not very extreme, is highly consistent with being a disease C patient. This explains why participants' ratings are above .5 in the case of disease C patients. On the other hand, such value is not extremely inconsistent with being a disease R patient, so the ratings obtained in disease R patients were close to .5.

Accordingly, we could say that we have answered the four objectives of Experiment 1. It has been shown that: 1) the diagnostic learning task may induce the base rate neglect bias in a later probability judgement phase (what constitutes a replication of other researchers' findings); 2) overall, participants' judgements are strongly affected by category base rates; 3) the learning task may also induce the conjunction fallacy bias; 4) the neural network used provides a reasonably good account of the whole pattern of results.

To explain the conjunction fallacies found in Experiment 1 we assumed that probability judgements in the D-S direction [P(S|D)] are based on the outputs generated by the associative learning mechanism, where links are in the S-D direction. We have carried out Experiment 2 to obtain convergent evidence supporting this assumption. We wondered to what extent judgements in the D-S direction were determined by the same mechanism as judgements in the S-D direction. Thus, we manipulated three within-subjects factors: 1) judgement direction (S-D vs. D-S), 2) category base rate (.75 vs. .25), and 3) the probability of a symptom given each disease (.2, .3, .4 and .6).

As we showed before, the associative neural network, as well as participants' judgements in the S-D direction, were influenced by category base rates. On the one hand, if the associative learning mechanism determines judgements in the D-S direction to the same extent than judgements in the S-D direction, we should expect the main effect of the conditional probability of symptoms and the main effect of category base rate, but neither the main effect of judgement direction nor the interaction between category base rate and judgement direction. On the other hand, normatively, we have no reason to expect a category base rate effect in the D-S judgements. Consequently we should expect the main effect of the conditional probability of symptoms, the main effect of judgement direction, and the interaction between category base rate and judgement direction. This interaction should be the result of having a category base rate effect in the S-D direction but not in the D-S direction.

The same learning task, apparatus and stimuli used in Experiment 1 were also used in Experiment 2. Table 10.1 shows the programmed probabilities

TABLE 10.3
Mean ratings for the probability judgements in the different conditions
of Experiment 2

Disease C				
	Symptoms			
	S_1	S_2	S_3	S_4
D|S	0.30	0.57	0.58	0.91
S|D	0.33	0.62	0.58	0.92
Disease R				
	Symptoms			
	S_4	S_3	S_2	S_1
D|S	0.16	0.49	0.47	0.71
S|D	0.20	0.49	0.50	0.77

used in the present experiment. The design, as well as the results, are shown in Table 10.3.

According to the design, all participants had to judge the probability of 16 experimental items.

The statistical analysis revealed the reliable main effects of category base rate and of conditional probabilities of symptoms. Judgement direction was only marginally significant, and interestingly, the interaction between category base rate and judgement direction was far from statistical reliability. An important prediction from our proposal was that the category base rate should have an effect in the S-D and D-S levels. The analysis of simple effects confirmed our predictions. The simple effect of category base rate was significant in the S-D direction, as well as in the D-S direction. This is difficult to explain if we do not assume that the processes underlying the D-S judgements are strongly determined by a mechanism specialised in predicting diseases from symptoms. This is the case for the associative learning mechanism we have postulated, which is well suited for the predictive learning task in the S-D direction but not for the D-S judgements lately required. Therefore, these results support our claim that a predictive learning situation primes the ALM participation, which is an efficient algorithm at dealing with the predictive learning problem. But this happens at some cost because ALM is a content driven process and so can generate outputs by the contents of the predictive learning situation even in a new task where ALM is not an efficient process any more.

CONCLUSION

In Experiments 1 and 2 we have shown that predictive learning tasks can induce biases typically found with very different procedures (e.g. Kahneman and Tversky,

1973). This support our view that biases as the base rate neglect and the conjunction fallacy could, in some circumstances, be related to the way in which knowledge about categories and predictive relationships is acquired and represented in memory. We have also shown an interesting relationship between associative learning processes, which have been successfully employed to understand category and predictive learning, and biases in probabilistic categorisation tasks. Specifically, a simple neural network model has provided a good account of the whole pattern of results (see also Gluck & Bower, 1988 for similar results and theoretical interpretation). All this research shows relative validity effects and relates such effects with the phenomenon of the base rate neglect.

Finally, though our approach is indebted to Tversky & Kahneman's heuristics and biases approach, we would like to stress some differences to underline what our own contribution may be. The heuristics approach has been a general framework to account for a set of biases in probability judgements made by individuals in a wide range of situations. Within this framework, biases as the base rate neglect or the conjunction fallacy have been considered as the result of the operation of a series of intuitive and fast processes (heuristic) which enable the individual to solve efficiently and without effort certain tasks frequently found in everyday life. The presence of some features which are characteristic of these tasks in the probabilistic reasoning problems that participants must solve in the laboratory can activate such heuristics. This is a source of deviations from the standard normative theory that supports the experimenters' analysis of the reasoning task.

One of the main criticisms against this explanatory framework is its limitations regarding formal modelling and its lack of a detailed specification of the cognitive processes involved (Gigerenzer, 1996). A closely related issue is the dependency of the explanation and the description of the behaviour on the normative principles violated. This fact is manifested in different ways. For example, the characterisation of the base rate neglect and the conjunction fallacy from the heuristic approach has been mostly based on the lack of adjustment between participants' responses and the results obtained from the application of the normative theory by the experimenter. This has led the research program to a somehow paradoxical situation: to explain the non-normative behaviour we have nothing but the normative framework. Thus, though people neglect base rates, for instance, they are quasi-bayesian after all (Gigerenzer & Murray, 1987). Another example is the identification between the observed behaviour and the labels used to designate the violated principle. As a consequence, this fact has tended to conceal the diverse origins of the identified bias. The base rate neglect is a clear example of this situation (Koehler, 1996).

Unlike the heuristics approach, our explanation does not intend to cover all biases nor all the situations in which they occur. In fact, it is limited to a specific set of situations. In such situations, people make probability judgements about the relationship between a series of events that are similar or identical to those involved in a previous predictive learning situation. In this case, judgements can be affected by the intervention of an ALM. This mechanism solves efficiently the task of predicting relevant events from numerous cues that can occur at any time. However, the efficiency of these processes entails the production of inadequate responses when different decisions have to be made about similar or identical contents.

On the other hand, our explanation shows a degree of precision and formal modelling which can neither be found in the heuristic approach nor in many other explanations of biases in probabilistic reasoning. Although this attempt to reach precision and formal modelling in our explanation of probabilistic judgements means sacrificing the range of those phenomena which can be explained, it also involves a deeper understanding of the origins of biases in probabilistic reasoning. First, because it enables us to specify more precisely the conditions in which biases are obtained in probability estimates. One of the criticisms launched by Gigerenzer against the heuristics and biases approach is the lack of precision in the specification of the conditions in which biases are obtained. Secondly, because the experimental data are much more informative to the extent that they can be interpreted in the light of theories specified as information-processing models.

Finally, another crucial difference between the heuristics and biases approach and our own lies in the underlying strategy on which our research is based. According to our account, biases such as the base rate neglect and the conjunction fallacy are, in some cases, the result of processes that do not fulfil the judgement task's goals but are effective in a different context. Such context has been identified here as the learning of predictive relationships between events and category learning may be considered as a particular case (Shanks, 1995). Thus, an adequate characterisation of those processes that induce biases requires the previous understanding of the processes involved in the learning of predictive relationships. In turn, this requires the identification of the environmental variables which are crucial to detect predictive relationships (see also López, Cobos, Caño & Shanks, 1998 for further details). Consequently, we come to the conclusion that to understand the processes that induce biases in probability judgements, the judgement task must be analysed within the framework of predictive relationship learning rather than only within the framework of the normative theory the reasoner violate (Bayes's theorem and conjunction theorem). Those processes that induce biases can only be identified from a previous analysis of the learning task for which they are designed. According to this, our explanation of the biases obtained in the judgement phase is completely determined by the analysis of the learning tasks participants had to solve previously. For instance, the direction of the predictions (S-D), as well as the relative validity of cues, are crucial features of the learning task to understand biases in the judgement phase.

To some extent, our research program falls into an *ecological approach*, which seems to be a present-day and promising view (it can be more explicit or implicitly appreciated in e. g. Anderson, 1991; Brase, Cosmides & Tooby, 1998; Fiedler, 1996; Gigerenzer & Goldstein, 1996). What is essential in this approach is that the analysis of the basic tasks that humans have to solve in their normal environment to survive is taken as a heuristic to understand the processes involved in laboratory tasks and to analyse such tasks.

Curiously, within the heuristics and biases approach, it was first thought that the processes that induce biases in probability judgements could be related to categorisation processes and to the way in which knowledge about categories is represented in normal life (Kahneman & Tversky, 1973). However, the possibility of taking category learning as a framework was not taken any further to augment our understanding of such bias induction processes. Instead, normative theories, whose principles were violated by participants, have been considered the basis for the description of the processes responsible for the biases. This is probably one of the main reasons why the understanding of biases has advanced so slowly for such a long time, as Gigerenzer has pointed out (Gigerenzer, 1996).

ACKNOWLEDGEMENTS

This work is part of a research project supported by Junta de Andalucía (HUM0105).

REFERENCES

AGNOLI, F., & KRANTZ, D. H. (1989): «Suppressing natural heuristics by forma instructions: The case of the conjunction fallacy». *Cognitive Psychology, 21,* 515-50.

ALLAN, L. G. (1980): «A note on measurement of contingency between two binary variables in judgement tasks». *Bulletin of the Psychomic Society, 15,* 147-149.

— (1993): «Human contingency judgments: rule based or associative?» *Psychological Bulletin, 114,* 435-448.

ANDERSON, J. R. (1991): «Is human Cognition adaptive?» *Behavioral and Brain Sciences, 14,* 471-517.

BAKER, A. G., MERCIER, P., VALLÈ-TOURANGEAU, F., FRANK, R., & PAN, M. (1993): «Selective associations and causality judgments: the presence of a strong causal factor may reduce judgments of a weaker one». *Journal of Experimental Psychology: Learning, Memory, and Cognition, 19,* 414-432.

BENEDICT, J. O., & AYRES, J. B. (1972): «Factors affecting conditioning in the truly random control procedure in the rat». *Journal of Comparative and Physiological Psychology, 78,* 323- 330.

BRASE, G. L., COSMIDES, L., & TOOBY, J. (1998): «Individuation, counting, and statistical inference: The role of frequency and whole-object representations in judgment under uncertainty». *Journal of Experimental Psychology: General, 127,* 3-21.

CHAPMAN, G. B., & ROBBINS, S. J. (1990): «Cue interaction in human contingency judgment». *Memory and Cognition, 18,* 537-545.

CHENG, P. W. (1997): «From covariation to causation: A causal power theory». *Psychological Review, 104,* 367-405.

CHENG, P. W., & HOLYOAK, K. J. (1995): «Complex adaptive systems as intuitive statisticians: causality, contingency, and prediction». In J. A. Meyer, & H. Roitblat (Eds.), *Comparative approaches to cognition,* Cambridge, MA: The MIT Press.

COBOS, P. L. (1996): *Una aproximación conexionista al estudio de los errores de estimación de probabilidades en tareas de categorización probabilÌstica.* Unpublished doctoral dissertation.

COBOS, P. L., & ALMARAZ, J. (1995): «Representación de conceptos y categorización: Un modelo conexionista». In M. Carretero, J. Almaraz, & P. Fernández (Eds.), *Razonamiento y Comprensión,* pp. 133-52. Trotta, Madrid.

COBOS, P. L., LÓPEZ, F. J., RANDO, M. A., FERNÁNDEZ, P. & ALMARAZ, J. (1993): «Conectionism and probability judgement: Suggestions on biases». *In Proceedings of the 15th annual conference of the Cognitive Science Society* (pp. 342-346). Hillsdale, N.J.: Erlbaum.

COHEN, L. J. (1981): «Can human irrationality be experimentally demonstrated». *Behavioral and Brain Sciences, 4,* 317-370.

DICKINSON, A. (1980): *Contemprorary animal learning theory.* Cambridge: Cambridge University Press.

DICKINSON, A., & SHANKS, D. R. (1985): «Animal conditioning and human causality judgment». In L. G. Nilsson and T. Archer (Ed.), *Perspectives on Learning and Memory,*pp. 167-191. Erlbaum, Hillsdale, NJ.

DICKINSON, A., SHANKS, D. R., & EVENDEN, J. L. (1984): «Judgment of act-outcome contingency: the role of selective attribution». *Quarterly Journal of Experimental Psychology, 36A,* 29-50.

DOUGHERTY, M. R. P., GETTYS, C. F., & OGDEN, E. E. (1999): «MINERVA-DM: A memory processes model for judgments of likelihood». *Psychological Review, 106,* 180-209.

DURLACH, P. J. (1983): «Effect of signalling intertrial unconditional stimuli in autoshaping». *Journal of Experimental Psychology: Animal Behavior Processes, 9,* 374-389.

ESTES, W. K., CAMPBELL, J. A., HATSOPOULOS, N. & HURWITZ, J. B. (1989): «Base-rate effects in category learning: A comparison of parallel network and memory storage-retrieval models». *Journal of Experimental Psychology: Learning, Memory and Cognition, 15,* 556-571.

FIEDLER, K. (1988): «The dependence of the conjunction fallacy on subtle linguistic factors». *Psychological Research, 50,* 123-129

— (1996): «Explaning and simulating judgment biases as an aggregation phenomenon in probabilistic multiple-cue environments». *Psychological Review, 103,* 193-214.

GIGERENZER, G. (1996): «On narrow norms and vague heuristics: A reply to Kahneman and Tversky (1996)». *Psychological Review, 103,* 592-596.

GIGERENZER, G., & GOLDSTEIN, D. G. (1996): «Reasoning tha fast and frugal way: Models of bounded rationality». *Psychological Review, 103,* 650-69.

GIGERENZER, G., & MURRAY, D. J. (1987): *Cognition as intuitive statistics.* Hillsdale, New Jersey: Lawrence Erlbaum Associates.

GLUCK, M. A. & BOWER, G. H. (1988): «From conditioning to category learning: An adaptive network model». *Journal of Experimental Psychology: General, 117,* 227-247.

HAMMOND, L. J., & PAYNTER, W. E. (1983): «Probabilistic contingency theories of animal conditioning». *Learning and Motivation, 14,* 527-550.

HINTON, G. E. (1990): «Mapping part-whole hierarchies into connectionist networks». *Artificial Intelligence, 46,* 47-76.

JOHNSON-LAIRD, P. N. (1983): *Mental models.* Cambridge University Press, Cambridge, UK.

JOHNSON-LAIRD, P. N., & BYRNE, R. M. J. (1991): *Deduction.* Earlbaum, Hillsdale, NJ.

JOHNSON-LAIRD, P. N., LEGRENZI, P., GIROTTO, V., SONINO-LEGRENZI, M., & CAVERNI, J. P. (1999): «Naive Probability: A mental model theory of extensional reasoning». *Psychological Review. 106,* 62–88

KAHNEMAN, D., & TVERSKY, A. (1973): «On the psychology of prediction». *Psychological Review, 80,* 237-251.

KAMIN, L. J. (1968): «Attention-like» processes in classical conditioning. In *Miami symposium on the prediction of behavior: Aversive stimulation.* (ed. M.R. Jones), pp. 9-33. University of Miami Press, Miami.

KOEHLER, J. J. (1996): «The base rate fallacy reconsidered: Descriptive, normative, and methodological challenges». *Behavioral and Brain Sciences* 19 (1): 1-53.

KRUSCHKE, J. K. (1992): «ALCOVE: An exemplar-based connectionist model of category learning». *Psychological Review, 99,* 22-44.

— (1996): «Base rates in category learning». *Journal of Experimental Psychology: Learning, Memory and Cognition, 22,* 3-26

LÓPEZ, F. J., ALMARAZ, J., FERNÁNDEZ, P., & SHANKS, D. R. (1998): «Adquisición progresiva del conocimiento sobre relaciones predictivas: Curvas de aprendizaje en juicios de contingencia». *Psicothema, 11,* 337-49.

LÓPEZ, F. J., COBOS, P. L., CAÑO, A., & SHANKS, D. R. (1998): «The rational analysis of human causal and probability judgement». In M. Oaksford & N. Chater (Eds.), *Rational models of cognition,* pp. 314-52. Oxford University Press, New York.

MATUTE, H. (1996): «Illusion of control: Detecting response-outcome independence in analytic but not in naturalistic conditions». *Psychological Science, 7,* 289-93.

MCCLELLAND, J. L. (1998): «Connectionist models and Bayesian inference». En M. Oaksford & N. Chater (Eds.), *Rational models of cognition,* pp. 21-53. OUP, New York.

MCCLELLAND, J. L., & RUMELHART, D. E. (1985): «Distributed memory and the representation of general and specific information». *Journal of Experimental Psychology: General, 114,* 159-88.

MYERS, J. L., LOHMEIER, J. H., & WELL, A. D. (1994): «Modelling probabilistic categorisation data: Exemplar memory and connectionist nets». *Psychological Science, 5,* 83-89.

NOSOFSKY, R. M., KRUSCHKE, J. K., & MCKINLEY, S. (1992): «Combining exemplar-based category representations and connetionist learning rules». *Journal of Experimental Psychology: Learning, Memory and Cognition, 18,* 211-233.

PEARCE, J. M. (1994): «Similarity and discrimination: A selective review and a connectionist model». *Psychological Review, 101,* 587-607.

POLITZER, G., & NOVECK, I. A. (1991): «Are conjunction rule violations the result of conversational rule violations». *Journal of Psycholinguistic Research, 20,* 83-103.

PRICE, P. C., & YATES, J. F. (1995): «Associative and rule-based accounts of cue interaction in contingency judgment». *Journal of Experimental Psychology: Learning, Memory and Cognition, 21,* 1639-1655.

RATCLIFF, R., & MCKOON, G. (1996): «Bias effects in implicit memory tasks». *Journal of Experimental Psychology: General, 125,* 403-21.

RESCORLA, R. A. (1966): «Predictability and number of pairings in pavlovian fear conditioning». *Psychonomic Science, 4,* 383-384.

— (1968): «Probability of shock in the presence and absence of the CS in fear conditioning». *Journal of Comparative and Physiological Psychology, 66,* 1-5. [Versión en castellano de Aguado, L. (1983), *Lecturas de aprendizaje animal* (pp. 179-192). Madrid: Debate].

RESCORLA, R. A., & WAGNER, A. R. (1972): «A theory of Pavlovian conditioning: variations in the effectiveness of reinforcement and nonreinforcement». En A. H. Black, & W. K. Prokasy (Eds.), *Classical conditioning II: current research and theory,* (pp. 64-99). Nueva York: Appleton-Century-Crofts.

SHANKS, D. R. (1990): «Connectionism and the learning of probabilistic concepts». *Quarterly Journal of Experimental Psychology, 42A,* 209-237.

— (1991): «Categorisation by a connectionist network». *Journal of Experimental Psychology: Learning, Memory and Cognition, 17,* 433-443.

— (1993): «Human instrumental learning: a critical review of data and theory». *British Journal of Psychology, 84,* 319-354.

— (1995): *The psychology of associative learning.* Cambridge: Cambridge University Press.

SHANKS, D. R., & LÓPEZ, F. J. (1996): «Causal order does not affect cue selection in human associative learning». *Memory and Cognition, 24*, 511-522.

SLOMAN, S. A. (1996): «The empirical case for two systems of reasoning». *Psychological Bulletin, 119*, 3-22.

SUTTON, R. S., & BARTO, A. G. (1981): «Toward a modern theory of adaptive networks: Expectation and prediction». *Psychological Review, 88*, 135-170.

TOLMAN, E. C., & BRUNSWICK, E. (1935): «The organism and the causal texture of the environment». *Psychological Review, 42*, 43-77.

TVERSKY, A., & KAHNEMAN, D. (1983): «Extensional versus intuitive reasoning: The conjunction fallacy in probability learning». *Psychological Review, 90*, 293-315.

VAN HAMME, L. J., & WASSERMAN, E. A. (1993): «Cue competition in causal judgments: The role of manner of information presentation». *Bulletin of the Psychonomic Society, 31*, 457-60.

WAGNER, A. R., LOGAN, F. A., HABERLANDT, K., & PRICE, T. (1968): «Stimulus selection in animal discrimination learning». *Journal of Experimental Psychology, 76*, 171-180.

WASSERMAN, E. A. (1990): «Detecting response-outcome relations: toward an understanding of the causal texture of the environment». In G. H. Bower (Ed.), *The Psychology of Learning and Motivation*, vol. 26, pp. 27-82. Academic Press, San Diego, CA.

WASSERMAN, E. A., ELEK, S. M., CHATLOSH, D. L., & BAKER, A. G. (1993): «Rating causal relations: Role of probability in judgments of response-outcome contingency». *Journal of Experimental Psychology: Learning, Memory, and Cognition, 19*, 174-88.

WIDROW, B., & HOFF, M. E. (1960): «Adaptive switching circuits». *1960 IRE WESCON Convention Record (Pt. 4)*, pp. 96-104.

WOLFORD, G., & TAYLOR, H. A. (1990): «The conjunction fallacy?» *Memory & Cognition, 18*, 47-53.

11

EYE MOVEMENTS DURING SYLLOGISTIC REASONING

ORLANDO ESPINO
CARLOS SANTAMARÍA
ENRIQUE MESEGUER
MANUEL CARREIRAS

En este capítulo pretedemos examinar la influencia de dos factores que generan dificultad en el proceso de razonamiento silogístico. Uno de ellos es la figura del silogismo y el otro es el número de modelos. De acuerdo a la teoría de modelos mentales (Johnson-Laird & Byrne, 1991) estos son los principales factores de dificultad. Para esta teoría los silogismos de un modelo son más fáciles que los de múltiples modelos y los silogismos de la figura 1 (A-B/B-C) son más fáciles que los de la figura 2 (B-A/C-B). Para comprobar estas predicciones hemos usados una técnica de movimientos oculares. Esta técnica, novedosa en este campo, se basa en la concepción de que los movimientos de nuestros ojos (fijaciones, movimientos hacia adelante o hacia atrás, etc.) nos puede informar acerca de los procesos cognitivos que está llevando a cabo la mente.

Los resultados del experimento que aquí se presenta confirman las principales predicciones de la teoría de modelos mentales (Johnson-Laird & Byrne, 1991). En cuanto a la figura los participantes cometen más errores, usan más tiempo para procesar las premisas y realizan más movimientos sacádicos en los silogismos de la figura 2 (B-A/C-B) que en los silogismos de la figura 1 (A-B/B-C). Aparte de la teoría de modelos (Johnson-Laird & Byrne, 1991) ninguna de las teorías actuales de razonamiento puede explicar estas diferencias (Ford, 1995; Polk y Newell, 1995; Yule & Stenning, 1992). También hemos encontrado que en los problemas de un modelo los participantes dan más respuestas correctas, emplean menos tiempo en procesar las premisas y realizan menos movimientos sacádicos (hacia adelante y hacia atrás) que cuando los problemas son de múltiples modelos. Por último, hemos encontrado que las respuestas erróneas que los participantes cometen en los problemas de múltiples modelos se corresponden con algunos de los modelos iniciales de dicho problemas. A excepción de la teoría de modelos, ninguna de las teorías actuales de reglas de inferencia (Braine, 1978; Rips, 1994) pueden explicar este patrón de errores.

INTRODUCTION

Syllogisms are arguments from two premises to a conclusion. Both premises and conclusion are statements of one of four types or moods: «all the A are B», «Some of the A are B», «None of the A are B» and «Some of the A are not B». Each statement in the premises contains two terms: one of them, the middle term (B), occurs in both premises, while the other two (A and C) are the end terms. The arrangement of the middle and end terms in each of the premises gives rise to the figure of the syllogism :

Figure 1	Figure 2	Figure 3	Figure 4
A-B	B-A	A-B	B-A
B-C	C-B	C-B	B-C

The mood and the figure of the syllogism can result in some syllogisms being more difficult than others and can produce responses biases (Bucciarelli & Johnson-Laird, in press; Dickstein, 1978; Espino, 1995; García-Madruga, 1989; Johnson-Laird & Bara, 1984). The main theories of reasoning offer alternative explanations about these phenomena (Ford, 1995; Johnson-Laird & Byrne, 1991; Stenning & Yule, 1997; Rips, 1994). From all these theories, the model theory (Johnson-Laird & Byrne, 1991) has explained these phenomena more thoroughly. The fundamental idea underlying the mental model theory is that people interpret assertions by constructing models of the corresponding situations. In syllogistic reasoning the mental model theory proposes that reasoning consists of four main stages: a) The initial interpretations of the premises, b) the combination of these interpretations into a single model, c) the formulation of a conclusion, and d) the search for alternative models that might refute the conclusion.

The initial interpretation of a premise represents a set of entities by a small arbitrary number of mental tokens. For example, for the premise «all of the A are B», the model theory postulates the following initial model:

[a] b
[a] b
...

where each line represents a separate entity in the same model, and the ellipsis represents an implicit entity with no initial explicit properties. Square brackets indicate that the a's are exhaustively represented. New tokens of A's can be added to the model.

In the second stage, forming an integrated model combines the separate models of the two premises. This composite model is obtained by temporally matching the middle terms in the premises. In figure 1 (a-b/b-c), the composite model of both premises could be obtained directly, because the middle terms (b) are adjacent. However, in figure 2 (b-a/c-b) the order of the two models should be reversed to make the middle terms adjacent (c-b/b-a). The model theory is the only account of syllogistic reasoning that makes the explicit prediction that the processing of syllogisms in the second figure should be harder (more time and more errors) than the processing of syllogisms in the first figure. This is due to the additional computation needed to reverse the order of the two models (Espino, Santamaría & García-Madruga, submitted, have confirmed these predictions for reading times).

In the third stage, the conclusion is formulated by describing the relation between the tokens representing the two end terms. For the model theory (Johnson-Laird & Bara, 1984), the position of the end-terms in the conclusion is determined by their position in the composite model: the first information into working memory is the first information out of it (first in, first out; Broadbent, 1958). In figure 1 syllogisms, «a» is the first end-term in the composite model, so it would become the first end-term in the conclusion. In figure 2 syllogisms, «c» is the first end-term in the composite model and it would appear as the first end-term in the conclusion. For the model theory, this principle can explain the figural effect.

Finally, the reasoners attempt to search for alternative models that could falsify the initial conclusion. If such a model can be constructed, they return to stage 2, but if not, they conclude that the initial conclusion is valid. The most important point of this phase is the number of models that subjects should construct in order to falsify the conclusion. For example, in the syllogism: «all of the A are B /all of the B are C», the initial mental representation would be:

[[a] b] c
[[a] b] c
...

which supports the initial conclusion: «all of the A are C», and there is no way of fleshing out the model to refute this conclution. Moreover, in the syllogism «all of the B are A /None of the B are C», the procedure is more complicated. In this cases, the reasoner build the following sort of initial model:

[a [b]]
[a [b]]
[c]
[c]
...

which supports the conclusions: «none of the A are C» or «none of the C are A». This is the most common error for this problem. The model theory predicts that the conclusions that are supported by one of the possible models of the premises will be the most common error. The following model refutes the former conclusion:

    [a [b]]
    [a [b]]
    a [c]
    [c]
    ...

and the two models together support the conclusions: «some of the A are not C» or «some of the C are A». But, this second conclusion is refuted by the model:

    [a [b]]
    [a [b]]
    a [c]
    a [c]
    ...

in this moments some reasoners could be infer wrongly that there is no valid conclusion. Moreover, all three models support a conclusion that cannot be refuted: «some of the A are not C». The model theory predicts that the problems that require just one model are easier than those that require more than one model.

In the present paper an experiment was conducted to test some of the main predictions of the model theory in syllogistic reasoning (Johnson-Laird & Byrne, 1991): one-model syllogisms are harder than multiple-model syllogisms and figure 2 syllogisms are harder than figure 1 syllogisms. Moreover we aim to examine whether the erroneous conclusions in multiple-model problems correspond with a single model interpretation of them. To confirm these predictions we used an eye-movement technique. This technique, which is novel in the reasoning field, is based on the assumption that the direction of our eyes can tell us something about the processing that is being conducted by our mind. Variations in eye fixation reflect variations in the difficulty of the problem being looked at, and so the eye movements and fixation measures can be considered as providing a direct on-line indication of the processing. We predicted that the participants would make more forward and backward movements and would take more time to process multiple-model problems than one-model problems. In the multiple-model problems, the participants need to construct and manipulate several models to generate the valid conclusion while in the one-model problems the people can generate the valid conclusion with the initial representation of premises. If the people only need to construct and manipulate one model in order to solve a problem then they will use less time to process the problem than if they need to construct and manipulate more models (Bucciarelli & Johnson-Laird, in press). If the multiple-models problems require more re-analyses of the premises to generate the valid conclusion then these problems should present more forward and backward movements, than the one-model problems.

Moreover, we predicted that the participants would make more forward and backward movements and would use more time to process the figure 2 syllogisms than figure 1 syllogisms. In the case of figure 1, no additional operation is required to integrate the premises into a composite model whereas of figure 2 the order of premises must be reversed in order to obtain the composite model. If the participants have to reverse the order of the premises then they need more time to process the syllogism than when they don't need to reverse the order. Moreover, to reverse the order of premises require more forward and backward movements than when reversing the order of premises is not necessary.

METHOD

Participants. 32 students at Universidad de La Laguna, who received course credit for their participation.

Design. It was a within-participants 2x2 design. The first factor was the type of problem (one model versus multiple models) and the second factor was the figure of the syllogism (figure 1 and figure 2). The dependent variables were the proportion of correct responses, the reading times of the premises, the forward and backward movements, and the direction of responses (A-C or C-A).

Materials. Each participant received a total of 8 experimental problems. Four of them were of figure 1 and four were of figure 2. Four problems were one-model syllogisms (two of each figure) and four were multiple-model syllogisms (two of each figure). Eight additional problems were used as filler problems (EA3, AE3, AO3, IE3, IA4, AI4, AO4, AA4). The content of the problems referred to jobs and nationalities, and was counterbalanced across the experimental problems. The experimental syllogisms used were: AA1, IA1, EA1, IE1, AA2, AI2, EI2, AE2. According to the analysis made by Johnson-Laird and Byrne (1991), the syllogisms AA1, IA1, AA2, AI2, were considered one-model problems, while EA1, IE1, EI2, AE2 were taken as multiple model problems.

Syllogisms were presented one by one in random order to each participant. Each syllogism was on one line and the participants had to press a key and give the conclusion. The subjects self-administered the exposure time of the syllogisms. A SRI Dual-Punkinje Generation 5.5 eye-tracker monitored the readers' eye movements. The tracker has an angular resolution of 10° arc. The tracker monitored only the right eye's gaze direction. A PC displayed items on a VDU 70 cm. from the readers' eyes. The VDU displayed four characters per degree of visual angle. The tracker monitored the reader's gaze direction every millisecond and the software sampled the tracker's output in order to establish the sequence of eye fixations and their start and finish times.

Procedure. Participants were tested individually in a quiet room. Their task was to consider a series of problems, and, for each of them, to draw a conclusion that had to be true given that the premises were true. When the participants finished each problem, they pressed a key that erased it from the screen. They then verbally gave the conclusion. An experimenter recorded the conclusions produced.

RESULTS AND DISCUSSION

We analyzed the results of the experiments in four main sections. First, we evaluated the predictions of the model theory concerning the correct responses in relation to the number of models and figure (figure 1 and figure 2). We also analyzed the type of erroneous conclusions in multiple-model problems. Second, we analyzed the same predictions for total processing time. Third, the same predictions were tested with the forward and backward movements. Fourth, we analyzed the direction of the responses (A-C or C-A) for each figure.

   1. *Analysis of correct responses.* Table 11.1 presents the percentages of correct responses for each syllogism depending on figure and number of models. An analysis of variance showed reliable effects for the number of models [$F(1,31)= 167,40$, mse=0.06, $p<0.0001$]. As the model theory predicts, the one-model syllogism yielded more correct conclusions (68.5%) than the multiple-model syllogisms (11.5%). The effect of the figure types was also reliable [$F(1,31)=16.49$, mse=0.05, $p<0.0001$]. There were more correct conclusions in figure 1 problem (47%) than in figure 2 problem (33%). This result supports the prediction of the model theory that the figure affects the accuracy of conclusions. For this theory, the difference is due to the additional processing required in figure 2 with respect to figure 1 in order to obtain the composite model. We found a reliable interaction between the factors [$F(1,31)=7.75$, mse = 0.06, $p=0.01$] in the sense that there were more correct responses in figure 1 than in figure 2 for the one-model problems. This effect is due to the particular difficulty of the problem AA2.

TABLE 11.1
Percentages of correct responses to each syllogism according to the problem type (one-model and multiple models) and figure type (figure 1 and figure 2)

	One-model		Multiple-model	
Figure 1	AA	88	EA1	0
	IA	75	IE1	25
Figure 2	AA	31	EI2	16
	AI	75	AE2	3

   The majority of the wrong responses given by the participants in this experiment were those predicted by the model theory for the multiple model problems. These conclusions were those consistent with at least one but not all of the models. Table 11.2 presents the models for the multiple-model problems and the predicted responses. Although the predicted conclusions are always a minority of the possible responses, the participants gave more predicted (68%) than unpredicted (12.5%) conclusions (Wilcoxon test, z=4.20, $p<0.0001$).

TABLE 11.2

Mental models for the four multiple model problems used in the experiments, invalid conclusions predicted by the model theory (with their percentages of occurrence), and correct conclusions (in capitals). NVC means «No valid conclusion»

No A are B
All B are C

```
[a] -b      [a] -b  c    [a] -b  c
[a] -b      [a] -b       [a] -b  c
   [b] c       [b] c        [b] c
   [b] c       [b] c        [b] c
```

No A are C	56.3%
No C are A	25.0%
Some A are C	0.0%
Nvc	0.0%
SOME C ARE NOT A	0.0%

None B are A
Some C are B

```
c [b] -a      c    [a]      c      a
c             c [b] -a      c [b] -a
   [b] -a        [b] -a        [b] -a
   [a]           [a]        c  [a]
   [a]
```

No C are A	25.0%
No A are C	40.6%
Nvc	0.0%
SOME C ARE NOT A	12.5%

Some A are B
No B are C

```
a [b] -c      a    [c]      a      c
a             a [b] -c      a [b] -c
   [b] -c        [b] -c        [b] -c
   [c]           [c]        a  [c]
   [c]
```

No A are C	21.9%
No C are A	21.9%
Nvc	0.0%
SOME A ARE NOT C	21.9%

All B are A
No C are B

```
[c] -b      [c] -b  a    [c] -b  a
[c] -b      [c] -b       [c] -b  a
   [b] a       [b] a        [b] a
   [b] a     c [b] a        [b] a
```

No C are A	56.3%
No A are C	25.0%
Some C are A	0.0%
Nvc	0.0%
SOME A ARE NOT C	0.0%

---

2. *Analysis of total processing time of the premises.* Table 3 presents the processing time of the premises for each of the syllogisms depending on the figure and number of models. An analysis of variance showed reliable effects for the problem type[$F(1,27)= 16.58$, mse=2540556, $p<0.0001$]. One-model syllogisms were processed more quickly (13.1 sec.) than the multiple-model syllogisms (15.9 sec.). This result supports one of the main proposals of the model theory: that one-model problems are easier than multiple model problems. The type of figure was reliable [$F(1,27)= 4.60$, mse=913416, $p<0.05$]. The participants processed the premises more quickly in figure 1 (13.9 sec.) than in figure 2 (15.1 sec.). This result conforms to the model theory hypothesis, that the figure 2 syllogisms need additional processing to obtain the composite model. The interaction was not reliable [$F(1,27)= 1.56$, mse= 1148191, $p=0.22$].

TABLE 11.3

Processing time of the premises (in seconds) for each of the syllogisms depending on problem type (one-model problem and multiple-model problem) and figure type (figure 1 and figure 2)

		One-model		Multiple-model	
Figure 1	AA	10.5	EA1	13.4	
	IA	14.3	IE1	17.5	
Figure 2	AA	11.9	EI2	17.8	
	AI	15.7	AE2	15.0	

3.1. Forward movements. Table 11.4 presents the sum of the additional forward movements form each region to the following ones for each syllogism depending on the figure and number of models. An analysis of variance showed reliable effects for the number of models [$F_{(28,1)} = 13.45$, mse=25.13, $p<0.001$]. As the model theory predicts, participants made less forward movements in the one-model problems (mean=18.42) than in the case of multiple-model problems (mean = 22.01). The figure was also reliable [$F_{(28,1)}= 7.31$, mse=12.51, $p<0.025$] in the sense that the participants made less forward movements in figure 1 syllogisms (mean = 19.24) than in figure 2 syllogisms (mean = 21.20). The small amount of forward movements in syllogisms of figure 1 can indicate that the participants do not need additional processing for the composite model. Again, the interaction was not reliable [$F_{(28,1)}= 0.08$, mse = 11.34, $p=0.785$].

TABLE 11.4

Means of forward and backward movement for each of the syllogisms according to problem type (one-model problem and multiple-model problem) and figure type (figure 1 and figure 2)

		One-model		Multiple-model		
		Forward	Backward		Forward	Backward
Figure 1	AA	15.03	11.41	EA	17.78	13.96
	IA	19.87	14.56	IE	24.61	20.12
Figure 2	AA	16.40	12.21	EI	24.75	19.81
	AI	22.34	16.28	AE	21.35	16.51

3.2. Backward movements. Table 11.4 presents the sum of the additional backward movements from each region to the following ones for each syllogism depending on the figure and the number of models. An analysis of variance showed reliable effects for the problem type [$F_{(28,1)} = 14.77$, mse= 23.94 $p<0.001$]. In one-model problems participants made less backward movements (mean = 13.64) than in the multiple-model problems (mean = 17.49). The effect for the figure types did not reach statistical significance [$F_{(28,1)}= 3.35$, mse= 10.04, $p=0.07$]. In the figure 1 syllogisms there were less backward movements (mean = 14.97) than in figure 2 syllogisms (mean = 16.16), but the difference was not statistically significant. However, this result shows the tendency predicted by the model theory. The interaction was not reliable [F (28,1)= 0.23, mse = 7.74, p=0.63].

4. *Direction of responses.* In figure 1 the participants produced more A-C (68%) than C-A (24%) conclusions (Wilcoxon test, z=3,58, p<0.0005). In figure 2 we found that the participants produced the same amount of A-C responses (47%) than C-A responses (47%; Wilcoxon test, z=0.08, p=0.90). This result conformed to the usual patterns found for figure 1, but not for figure 2.

GENERAL DISCUSSION

The results of this experiment, in which we used a new technique (eye-movement), confirm that both the number of models and the syllogism figure affects the overall difficulty of syllogism. As the model theory predicts, the one-model problems are easier than the multiple-model problems. We found that reasoners obtained more correct responses, used less time to process the premises, and made less forward and backward movements in the one-model problems than in the multiple-model problems.

Another prediction confirmed in our experiment was that the majority of the erroneous conclusions corresponded to those based on a single model of multiple-model problems. Current formal rule theories (Rips, 1994) offer no account of these systematic errors. For formal rule theories, errors are haphazard and they would occur when the inference calls for the use of more complex rules, or when it calls for a greater number of steps.

We also found that the participants committed more errors, used more time to process the premises, and made more forward and backward movements in the figure 2 syllogisms than in figure 1 syllogisms. For the model theory these differences are due to the additional processing required in figure 2 with respect to figure 1. This additional processing is necessary to obtain the composite model in figure 2 syllogisms. Apart from the model theory no current theory of syllogistic reasoning can explain this difference.

By using moving-window experiments, Carreiras and Santamaría (1997) found that an additional processing time was required in multiple-model problems in the particular segment where the participant needed more than one model. The same result has been recently found (Espino *et al.*, submitted) for categorical syllogisms where both the number of models and the figure affected the processing time of the second premise. The eye-movement technique permits the detection of these effects without the need to segment the problems. The clear advantage of this methodology is that it allow the problems to be presented in a way that is similar to the usual paper and pencil experiments.

REFERENCES

BROADBENT, D. E. (1958): *Perception and communication*. London: Pergamon.
BUCCIARELLI, M., & JOHNSON-LAIRD, P. N. (in press): «Strategies in syllogistic reasoning». *Cognitive Science*.

CARREIRAS, M., & SANTAMARÍA, C. (1997): «Reasoning about relations: spatial and nonspatial problems». *Thinking and reasoning, 3* (3), 161-240.

DICKSTEIN, L. S. (1978): «The effects of figure on syllogistic reasoning». *Memory and Cognition*, 6, 76-83.

ESPINO, O. (1995): «Factores estructurales y semánticos en el razonamiento silogístico [structural and semantic factors in syllogistic reasoning]». Ph.d thesis, Universidad de La Laguna, Tenerife, Spain.

ESPINO, O., SANTAMARÍA, C., & GARCÍA MADRUGA, J. A. (in press): «Figure and difficulty in syllogistic reasoning». Submitted.

FORD, M. (1995): «Two modes of mental representation and problem solution in syllogistic reasoning». *Cognition*, 54, 1-71.

GARCÍA-MADRUGA, J. A. (1989): «Inferencia y comprensión en el razonamiento silogístico [Inference and comprehension in syllogistic reasoning]». *Cognitiva, 2*, 323-350

JOHNSON-LAIRD, P. N., & BARA, B. (1984): «Syllogistic inference». *Cognition, 16*, 1-61.

JOHNSON-LAIRD, P. N. & BYRNE, R. M. J. (1991): *Deduction*. Hillsdale, NJ: Lawrence Erlbaum Associates.

POLK, T. A., and NEWELL, A. (1995): «Deduction as verbal reasoning». *Psychological Review, 102*, 533-566.

RIPS, L. J. (1994): *The psychology of proof*. Cambridge, MA: MIT Press.

WETHERICK, N. E., & GILHOOLY, K. J. (1990): «Syllogistic reasoning: Effects of premise order». In Gilhooly, K.J., Keane, M.T.G., Logie, R.H., and Erdos, G. (Eds.) *Lines of Thinking, Vol. I.* New York: John Wiley.

YULE, P., & STENNING K. (1992): «The figural effect and ghaphical algorithm for syllogistic reasoning». *Proceedings of the Fourtheenth Annual Conferences of the Cognitive Sciences Society*, Bloomingthon, Indiana. Hillsdale, NJ: LEA:

— (1997): «Image language in human reasoning: a syllogistic illustration». *Cognitive Psychology, 34*, 109-159.

12

SPATIAL AND TEMPORAL CONTENT AND WORKING MEMORY USAGE IN LINEAR SYLLOGISTIC REASONING

André Vandierendonck
Gino De Vooght
Vicky Dierckx

En la investigación presentada en este Capítulo se compara el rendimiento en los silogismos lineales basados en relaciones espaciales y temporales. De acuerdo con las teorías de reglas de inferencia, el rendimiento no debería diferenciarse en función del contenido del problema porque el razonamiento está basado en reglas formales. Por el contrario, la teoría de los modelos mentales propone que el razonamiento se ajusta a un procedimiento de tres pasos en el que se empieza por la construcción de un modelo inicial, seguido de la formulación de una conclusión tentativa y de la búsqueda de contraejemplos en combinación con la suma o el cambio de los modelos que se construyeron inicialmente. Dado que los modelos se construyen en función de las relaciones expresadas en las premisas, el proceso de razonamiento puede depender del contenido del problema.

En la primera parte de este trabajo se presentan algunos resultados obtenidos en estudios anteriores. Estos estudios estaban basados en problemas con relaciones bidimensionales semejantes a los estudiados por Byrne y Johnson-Laird (1989). Los resultados muestran que la dificultad de los problemas de las tareas de razonamiento espacial y temporal se ajustan a las predicciones de la teoría de los Modelos Mentales. Sin embargo, la dificultad de los problemas de razonamiento temporal también concuerda con el orden predicho por la perspectiva de la competencia lógica.

En la segunda parte se describen una serie de estudios sobre tareas duales. El objetivo principal de esta investigación se centró en identificar cuáles eran los componentes del sistema de la memoria de traba-

*jo que se encontraban implicados en el razonamiento relacional. Los re-
sultados indicaron que tanto los problemas temporales como los espaciales necesitaban los recursos visoespaciales de la memoria de trabajo, además del ejecutivo central que presumiblemente controla el
razonamiento. Sin embargo, la precisión y la latencia de respuesta también dependían de los recursos fonológicos.*

*Otra serie de estudios intentó aclarar esta cuestión despojando a
las premisas del contenido verbal y comparando las relaciones temporales y espaciales implícitas entre objetos y actividades. Los resultados
de estos estudios confirmaron que en los problemas espaciales se construyen representaciones visoespaciales estáticas, aunque los resultados también sugieren la construcción de representaciones visoespaciales cinéticas para aquellos problemas que conllevan actividades
organizadas temporalmente.*

*En la discusión final se revisan varios de los componentes cogni-
tivos que han desempeñado algún papel en el razonamiento relacional.
Se considera que la importancia de la dependencia de los recursos visoespaciales de la memoria de trabajo y las diferencias encontradas en
las variaciones de la tarea constituyen la base para enfatizar la importancia de las elecciones estratégicas y el papel que desempeñan las restricciones de la memoria de trabajo en estas elecciones.*

INTRODUCTION

The time notion is important. Without it, our social organization would collap-
se: almost everything we do everyday is based on a time schedule, a calendar
or a clock. Daily, people produce reasonings based on temporal relations. For
example, if I can manage to be at the doctor's office after my committee meeting
but before dinner time, then I can prepare my talk before the committee
meeting.

It is a major question for cognitive psychology to explain how people
perform this and other kinds of relational reasoning. The French philosopher
Guyau (1890[1988]) already observed that temporal representations used in
modern society are essentially spatial. The time of the day is shown by the
arms of the clock that follow a specified spatial path. The days of the week
are often displayed in tabular form on calendars. On a larger scale, time is
usually depicted as a left-right (sometimes a bottom-up) axis with earlier events
to the left of (below) later ones.

No doubt, spatial representations are a rather general tool for representing
structure and relations (see e.g., Gattis, 1999), and the question may be raised
whether people indeed map temporal relations onto spatial ones in each task
they perform, and more specifically in reasoning about temporal relations.
An alternative could be that relations are mentally represented in a model or
an abstract format. The latter view is endorsed by the rule theory of reasoning
(see e.g., Braine, 1978; Rips, 1983, 1994). According to this theory, content
forms no part of the fundamental reasoning mechanism, and therefore one

should not expect reasoning about temporal relations to be any different from reasoning about spatial relations, or about anything that can be expressed in an order relation. In fact, the theory assumes that the available rules operate on an abstract representation of the relations. Consequently, differences in reasoning difficulty on the basis of relational content find their cause outside the reasoning process per se. The difference may, for instance, be due to a preparatory stage in which the content relations are mapped on the appropriate relational format.

The theory of mental models (see e.g., Johnson-Laird, 1983, in press; Johnson-Laird & Byrne, 1991), on the contrary, proposes that reasoning is a semantically based inference process, relying on the construction and comparison of mentally represented models of the information given in the premises. As these models are temporary constructions, they are held in working memory in a format the working memory system is capable of handling. This view implies that working memory capacity limits the number of models held. When many models have to be maintained in memory in order to obtain a solution of the reasoning problem, the system may become overloaded. This results in slower processing and an increased probability of errors due to the loss of information or to the reasoner's decision not to elaborate the problem representation. Because the working memory system is assumed to be a flexible multicomponental system (see e.g., Baddeley, 1986, 1997; Baddeley & Hitch, 1974), models may be represented in different formats. Typically, the phonological subsystem would hold verbally coded models, whereas the visual-spatial system would be used for spatially coded relations. It may be expected, then, that a problem represented verbally would favor different mental operations than a problem represented spatially and this could lead to differences in reasoning performance with respect to speed of reasoning and to accuracy.

SPATIAL VERSUS TEMPORAL RELATIONS

Whether reasoning is based on spatial rather than verbal representations may depend on a lot of factors, the most important one is probably the reasoning task itself. In the present paper, only linear syllogisms and related tasks are considered. A linear syllogism typically consists of a series of premises in which the terms can be linked together in a linear series. If, for example, Spain is on average warmer than Belgium and Belgium is on average warmer than Finland, then it may be inferred that Spain is on average warmer than Finland. Because the premises are consistent with only one state of affairs, the inferred one, this is called a one-model problem. In contrast, it may be the case that no valid inference can be drawn as in:

Spain is larger than Belgium
Spain is larger than Finland.

These premises are consistent with more than one possible world or model, namely «Belgium is larger than Finland» and «Finland is larger than Belgium», and «Finland and Belgium are of equal size», and is therefore referred to as a multi-model problem.

Over the years there has been a vivid debate as to whether such reasoning tasks are solved by means of spatial representations, as was proposed by the spatial array theory (e.g., De Soto, London, & Handel, 1965; Huttenlocher, 1968; Potts, 1974), or whether the linguistic representation is crucial (e.g., Clark, 1969, 1971, 1972). According to a review by Evans et al. (1993), there is some merit to both viewpoints, but the evidence is by and large consistent with the spatial array view and more generally with the mental model theory.

Byrne and Johnson-Laird (1989; Johnson-Laird & Byrne, 1991) used two-dimensional spatial problems, such as:

> The house is to the left of the church
> The school is to the right of the church
> The birch is in front of the house
> The pine is in front of the school
> Which relationship holds between the birch and the pine?

and showed that more errors occurred in two-model problems than in one-model problems and that whether or not a transitive inference was required did not affect error performance.

Schaeken, Johnson-Laird, and d'Ydewalle (1996) and Vandierendonck and De Vooght (1994, 1996) used similar problems with temporal relations, for example:

> John went fishing before he went to the movies
> John took dinner before he went to the movies
> While John was fishing, Lisa mowed the lawn
> While John took dinner, Lisa watched the television
> Which relation holds between the mowing of the lawn and the television watching?

Schaeken et al. (1996) found that performance was completely in line with mental models predictions, which indicates that the reasoners must have constructed models of the relationship.

Vandierendonck and De Vooght (1994, 1996) directly compared performance on spatial and temporal problems. The premises were presented one at a time in the center of a computer screen. The order of the premises was maximally connected; this means that as much as possible one of the terms in the premise was a repetition of the same term in the immediately preceding premise. Four problem variations were used, namely (i) one-model problems which did not require a transitive inference, (ii) one- model problems based on a transitive inference, as in the spatial example above, (iii) two-model problems without transitive inference, and (iv) two-model which did not yield a valid conclusion as in the temporal example above.

According to the mental model theory, performance parameters depend on the number of models maintained in working memory. Since problem variants (i) and (ii) require only one problem, they are expected to be easier than the other two variants which require two models. The mental model theory also expects that problem variant (iv) will be more difficult than the other variants because in order to obtain a correct answer the two models are strictly necessary and the inconsistency of the two models must be recognized. The logical competence view, in contrast, assumes that performance parameters are related to the amount and the complexity of the operations needed to reach the conclusion. Because problem variant (ii) requires a transitive inference and variants (i) and (iii) do not, it is expected that the former variant will be more difficult. In addition, since problem variant (iv) requires the recognition that no correct conclusion is possible, it should be the most difficult variant.

In summary, the two predictions can be expressed in the following two rank orders:

MM: i=ii<iii<iv
LC: i=iii<ii<iv

Performance of the reasoners in the experiment, was consistent with the mental model theory predictions, as well in the number of correct solutions (accuracy) as in the solution latencies. Interestingly, however, even though overall the mental model theory was more consistent with the data than the logical competence theory, there were differences as a function of problem content. In the spatial content domain, performance accuracy correlated highly with the rank order predicted by the mental model theory (r =.95) but not with the rank order predicted by the logical competence theory (.61). Similarly, the solution times were more in agreement with the mental models difficulty order (r =.83) than with the logical competence order (r =.33). In the temporal domain, on the contrary, a different pattern of results was observed: accuracy data as well as solution times were in agreement with both predicted rank orders (respectively r =.85 and. 82 for the mental models prediction and r =.86 and.82 for the logical competence prediction).

The main reason for this difference is that in the temporal content domain problem variants (ii) and (iii) are about equally difficult, while in the spatial domain variant (ii) is easier than variant (iii). A discussion of all the factors that may contribute to this effect is beyond the scope of the present paper. We restrict the discussion to variations in the task setting. A closer look at the materials used in these studies immediately suggests a number of possible explanations. The spatial problems are two-dimensional while time represents only one dimension, so that the use of simultaneous activities plays the role of the second dimension. Furthermore, the temporal reasoning problems are in general linguistically more complex than the spatial problems: on average, the words are longer, the sentences are grammatically more complex and contain more words. Also the terms in the premises are linguistically different: in the spatial premises the terms refer to concrete objects and hence are highly imaginable, whereas the temporal terms refer to activities to be performed by a person. In addition, the temporal context may induce different representations or even different strategies.

RELATIONAL CONTENT AND WORKING MEMORY

Because the mental model theory is concerned with models constructed and maintained in working memory, it may be argued that it first should be clear whether there are any differences between spatial and temporal problems in the load and the usage of working memory resources. This can best be explored by means of a dual-task methodology, in which reasoners have to solve reasoning problems while being engaged in a second task that competes for a part of the working memory resources. If the secondary task is known to load a particular component of the working memory system, then the reasoning task should be impaired only if reasoning calls on the same component.

Vandierendonck and De Vooght (1997) used this methodology with secondary tasks that loaded either the phonological component (articulatory suppression), the visual-spatial component (matrix tapping) or the central executive (the RIR task, shadowing a random sequence of bleeps; see Vandierendonck, De Vooght, & Van der Goten, 1998b). The participants were given (one-dimensional) four-term series problems with the premise presented in a maximally connected order one at a time in the center of the screen. In each of the four dual-task conditions, the participants first solved a practice problem and then were given five problem variants in a random order. The problem variants were (i) a one-model problem with verification of a given premise, (ii) a one-model problem with verification of a transitive inference, (iii) a two-model problem with verification of a given premise, (iv) a two-model problem with verification of a transitive inference, and (v) a two-model problem with as correct answer that there is no valid conclusion.

First, it was shown that in comparison to the single-task control condition reasoning accuracy was impaired in each of the three dual-task conditions. The simplest explanation is that this is caused by non-specific task interference. In order to further clarify these observation, in another study, half of the participants were presented the premises at a fast rate (3 instead of 7 seconds per premise). The rationale here was that if the processing time per premise was shortened, it may become more difficult to integrate the information of successive premises so that the reasoner must try to memorize the raw premises and has to do the reasoning afterwards with the remembered materials. At the same time, the other half of the participants had a self-paced premise presentation procedure. It may be expected that with such a presentation schedule, the participants select the most optimal strategy and hence the time taken to process each premise could give indications about the kind of processing going on. More specifically, in combination with the dual-task methodology, this procedure might yield data showing that particular working memory components are more involved than other ones.

Again, accuracy was impaired by each of the secondary tasks, and as was expected, performance was poorer under fast premise presentation, but this factor did not interact with any of the factors in the design. This suggests that participants do not follow a different strategy under fast premise presentation than under self-paced presentation. There were no differences as a function of the relational content and the latter factor did not interact with the other factors in the design.

Premise processing times in the self-paced conditions were affected by the presence of secondary tasks. In comparison to the single-task control condition, premise time was almost 2 seconds slower in the condition with a central-executive secondary task. With the visual-spatial task, processing time was more than 1 second slower, while the articulatory suppression task had no effect whatsoever on the premise processing duration. Interestingly, the relational content did not affect premise time and did not interact with the dual-task factor.

DISENTANGLING THE CONTRIBUTING FACTORS

Thus it seems that the same resources are used in temporal and in spatial linear syllogisms. The question still remains why spatial reasoning is more consistent with the mental model predictions than temporal reasoning. Given that the same resources are used in both kinds of problems, it may be that these resources are used differently. Spatial relations can easily be represented by a static image containing all the objects and their positions relative to each other. Although this is also possible for temporal reasoning, it could be that the representation of activities more easily evokes a kinematic image, an image that changes over time. While inferences from a static image can be made on the basis of this single image, inferences from a kinematic image probably require processing over different states of the image stream and this may cause differences with respect to the probability of errors and to the time course of the inference.

As pointed out before, spatial and temporal premises differ in a large number of respects. In order to find out whether the relationship as such or the concreteness of the terms contribute to the observed effect, a procedure was developed in which all other (linguistic) differences were stripped from the premises. Instead of presenting full sentences, only two terms were presented, for example «school-church» or «washing-mowing». These terms were either presented simultaneously in a left-right (spatial) position or they were presented sequentially at the same central position of the screen. The simultaneous presentation format is implicitly spatial, while the sequential format is implicitly temporal in that one term appears before another term. With this dissociation it becomes possible to make all combinations of terms (objects or activities) and relations (spatial or temporal).

A first experiment compared reasoning performance and premise processing times in a dual-task situation where the terms were objects presented either in a spatial format (simultaneously) or in a temporal format (sequentially). The same problem variants as before were used.

Reasoning accuracy did not differ as a function of presentation format, but was again impaired by any task that competed for the working memory resources. Premise processing times were not different across the two presentation formats but they were longer in the conditions with the visual-spatial and the executive interference tasks, irrespective of the presentation format, and hence the kind of relation.

The second experiment was similar to the first one, except that the terms were activities instead of objects. With respect to reasoning accuracy, no overall effects of presentation mode were observed. It appeared, however, that the visual-spatial secondary task did not impair reasoning accuracy, while the articulatory and the executive interference tasks resulted in poorer reasoning performance. Closer inspection of the data revealed, however, that the secondary central-executive task had a significant disruptive effect on performance in the simultaneous condition only.

Premise processing times, however, were longer when the secondary task was a visual-spatial or an executive task. Interestingly, with a simultaneous presentation of the terms, this difference was large, as in the previous experiments. With a sequential presentation mode, on the contrary, the difference was rather small.

Taking the findings of the two experiments together, they seem to suggest that when the terms are objects, the premise information is encoded visual-spatially. Based on results presented by Vandierendonck, De Vooght, Desimpelaere, and Dierckx (in press), the premise information is probably integrated into a static visual-spatial representation in which only one model is fleshed out and the other models are left implicit by placing a tag or a marker indicating how the models can be made explicit. Also when the terms are activities, the reasoners try to make visual-spatial encodings. This is supported by the observation of lengthened premise reading times under conditions of visual-spatial interference. However, it is possible that the representation achieved is not a static one. If it can be assumed that the bulk of the effort during premise presentation and processing is in integrating the information, then it may be assumed that the central executive load and the visual-spatial load is smaller when a kinematic image is constructed, but probably this is only possible with support from long-term memory resources. If there is indeed long-term memory support, it can be predicted that inferences could be reached with less intervention from the central executive, and with a smaller load on the visual-spatial system. The latter prediction is consistent with the accuracy data obtained: with activities in a sequential presentation format, the central executive task did not significantly impair performance, and the effect of the visual-spatial task tended also to be smaller.

It is clear that this is a speculative interpretation, but it has testable implications. Focused research efforts are now needed to clarify this issue and to find out if indeed problems with activities are translated into dynamic representations changing over time. This is an important point, because the findings collected so far could also be interpreted by assuming that reasoners divert to a mixed spatial/verbal strategy when confronted with activities. By spreading the load over the two slave systems of working memory, it is possible to avoid strong visual-spatial interference. However, by doing this, one would expect that the load on the central executive becomes larger because the executive must intervene to co-ordinate the contents of the two slaves. But exactly the latter expectation is not borne out in the findings.

DISCUSSION

In this paper findings were presented that emanated from a line of research which seems to be promising. Thus far it has produced some interesting clarifications with respect to reasoning in simple linear syllogisms about spatial and temporal relations. In essence, the research has shown that, for these tasks at least, the mental model theory outperforms the logical competence view. We elaborate on this point with respect to three issues, namely the matter of relational content, the usage of working memory resources and the involvement of strategies.

The basic motivation for the present research was in the exploration of the similarities and differences between temporal and spatial reasoning. Starting with the 5-term problems introduced by Byrne and Johnson-Laird (1989), it was found that the rank order of difficulty predicted by the mental model theory was found both in temporal and in spatial reasoning problems. However, it appeared that also the predicted rank order based on the logical competence view highly correlated with problem difficulty of the temporal problems. It may be tempting to interpret this finding as evidence in favor of the logical competence view. Yet, the finding is at variance with this view because it assumes that reasoning is performed independent of content and the basic reasoning mechanism postulated works on the basis of general rules that can applied to any content. Hence, content differences are at odds with such a viewpoint.

Even though the data suggest that at least part of the time problem difficulty corresponds to the rank order predicted by the logical competence view, reasoning by means of mental models might still be the basis for the effect observed. For example, if it were the case that temporal problem statements are encoded by means of dynamic (kinematic) representations, a transitive inference would be based on sequential processing by playing the sequence and while it plays checking whether A precedes B. As a consequence, this inference would take more time and would be more prone to errors than the same inference obtained from a static spatial representation. This hypothesis can explain the basic finding, but thus far there is no clear-cut and convincing evidence for its correctness.

The present paper has also discussed several studies that used the dual-task methodology to study the resources involved in linear reasoning. The dominant finding was that visual-spatial and central-executive secondary tasks impaired premise processing. By far the simplest explanation for this finding is that the secondary tasks and the reasoning task competed for the same working memory resource, so that accuracy but also model construction suffered from this interference. Because the logical competence view assumes that reasoning is performed either on linguistic or on abstract codes, it is difficult for this theoretical viewpoint to explain why visual-spatial resources would be required in a linear reasoning task. For the mental model theory, it is straight forward to assume that models may be constructed in a visual-spatial medium.

A few times we mentioned that strategic decisions on the part of the reasoner may play a role. While in the studies of Vandierendonck, De Vooght, Dierckx, and Desimpelaere (1998a) and Vandierendonck *et al.* (in press), in which only spatial linear syllogisms were used, no effects of strategy were found, it is clear that strategies are important in all kinds of reasoning processes (see for example the book by Schaeken, De Vooght, Vandierendonck, & d'Ydewalle, 1999). In an unpublished study performed in our laboratory, subjects were instructed to use a verbal strategy to solve linear reasoning problems. Two strategies were explained, one based on repetition of the premise information and one based on recoding of the premise information. After a short training period with both strategies, subjects shifted rather quickly to another strategy when a problem was presented that required a high working memory load for one of the strategies. This shows that reasoners have at least tacit knowledge of the cognitive load imposed by a particular strategy, even if it is a rather new one.

In view of the heavy reliance of model construction on working memory resources, this result indicates that the strategies used by the reasoners must be taken into account. Again, the concept of a reasoning strategy, is one that fits in nicely with the mental model theory. Unless, it can be shown that there are rule based procedures for proving or inferring a conclusion from a series of premises and that these procedures or inferring a conclusion from a series of premises and that these procedures differ with respect to the cognitive load imposed by the procedure, the logical competence view is not expected to foster our understanding of strategy usage. At least in the domain of linear syllogisms, theories based on logical competence do not seem to offer possibilities for strategical variation.

REFERENCES

BADDELEY, A. (1986): *Working memory*. Oxford: Oxford University Press.
— (1997): *Human memory. Theory and practice.* (2nd ed.). Hove: Psychology Press.
BADDELEY, A. D., & HITCH, G. (1974): «Working memory». In G. H. Bower (Ed.), *The psychology of learning and motivation* (Vol. 8, pp. 47-89). New York: Academic Press.
BRAINE, M. D. S. (1978): «On the relation between the natural logic of reasoning and standard logic». *Psychological Review*, 85, 1-21.
BYRNE, R. M. J., & JOHNSON-LAIRD, P. N. (1989): «Spatial reasoning. Journal of Memory and Language», 28, 564-575.
CLARK, H. H. (1969): «Linguistic processes in deductive reasoning». *Journal of Experimental Psychology,* 76, 387-404.
— (1971): «More about "Adjectives, comparatives, and syllogisms"». *Psychological Review,* 78, 505-514.
— (1972): «On the evidence concerning J. Huttenlocher and E.T. Higgins' theory of reasoning: A second reply». *Psychological Review*, 5, 428-432.
DE SOTO, C. B.; LONDON, M., & HANDEL, S. (1965): «Social reasoning and spatial paralogic». *Journal of Personality and Social Psychology,* 4, 513-521.
EVANS, J. S. B. T., NEWSTEAD, S. E., & BYRNE, R. M. J. (1993): *Human reasoning. The psychology of deduction.* Hillsdale, NJ: Lawrence Erlbaum Associates.
GATTIS, M. (1999): «Spatial strategies in reasoning». In W. Schaeken, G. De Vooght, A. Vandierendonck, & G. d'Ydewalle (Eds.), *Deductive reasoning and strategies.* New York: Lawrence Erlbaum Associates.

GUYAU, J.-M. (1890[1988]): «La genese de l'idee de temps. [The origin of the idea of time]». In J. A. Michon, V. Pouthas, & J. L. Jackson (Eds.), *Guyau and the idea of time* (pp. 37-90 [p. 93-148]). Amsterdam: North Holland.

HUTTENLOCHER, J. (1968): «Constructing spatial images: A strategy in reasoning». *Psychological Review, 75*, 550-560.

JOHNSON-LAIRD, P. N. (1983): *Mental models*. Cambridge: Cambridge University Press.

— (in press): «Deductive reasoning». *Annual Review of Psychology*.

JOHNSON-LAIRD, P. N., & BYRNE, R. M. J. (1991): *Deduction*. London: Lawrence Erlbaum Associates.

POTTS, G. R. (1974): «Storing and retrieving information about ordered relationships». *Journal of Experimental Psychology, 103*, 431-439.

RIPS, L. J. (1983): «Cognitive processes in propositional reasoning». *Psychological Review, 90*, 38-71.

— (1994): «Deduction and its cognitive basis». In R. J. Sternberg (Ed.), *Thinking and problem solving* (pp. 150-178). New York: Academic Press.

SCHAEKEN, W., DE VOOGHT, G., VANDIERENDONCK, A., & D'YDEWALLE, G. (1999): *Deductive reasoning and strategies*. New York: Lawrence Erlbaum Associates.

SCHAEKEN, W., JOHNSON-LAIRD, P. N., & D'YDEWALLE, G. (1996): «Mental models and temporal reasoning». *Cognition, 60*, 205-234.

VANDIERENDONCK, A., & DE VOOGHT, G. (1994): «The time-spatialization hypothesis and reasoning about time and space». In M. Richelle, V. De Keyser, G. d'Ydewalle, & A. Vandierendonck (Eds.), *Temporal reasoning and behavioral variability* (pp. 99-125). Liege: Interuniversity Pole of Attraction, Temporal Reasoning and Behaviorial Variability, Issue 3.

— (1996): «Evidence for mental model based rea-soning: a comparison of reasoning with time and space concepts». *Thinking and Reasoning, 2*, 249-272.

— (1997): «Working memory constraints on linear reasoning with spatial and temporal contents». *Quarterly Journal of Experimental Psychology, 50A*, 803-820.

VANDIERENDONCK, A., DE VOOGHT, G., DESIMPELAERE, C., & DIERCKX, V. (1999): «Model construction and elaboration in spatial linear syllogisms». In W. Schaeken, G. De Vooght, A. Vandierendonck, & G. d'Ydewalle (Eds.), *Deductive reasoning and strategies*. New York: Lawrence Erlbaum Associates.

VANDIERENDONCK, A., DE VOOGHT, G., DIERCKX, V., & DESIMPELAERE, C. (1998a): *Mental model construction in spatial reasoning: One, two or more models?* Manuscript submitted for publication.

VANDIERENDONCK, A., DE VOOGHT, G., & VAN DER GOTEN, K. (1998b): «Interfering with the central executive by means of a random interval repetition task». *Quarterly Journal of Experimental Psychology, 51A*, 197-218.

AUTHOR NOTE

The paper presents research results of the Belgian programme on Interuniversity Poles of Attraction initiated by the Belgian State, Prime Minister's Office, Science Policy Programming, Grants nr. P3/31 and nr. P4/19 from the Department of Science Policy to the first Author. The scientific responsibility is assumed by its authors.

Correspondence about the paper can be directed to: Andre Vandierendonck, Department of Experimental Psychology, University of Gent, Henri Dunantlaan 2, B-9000 Gent, Belgium. E-mail: Andre.Vandierendonck@rug.ac.be.

PART III

PROPOSITIONAL AND CONDITIONAL
REASONING

13

TRUTH AND FALSITY IN PROPOSITIONAL REASONING: THE NEGATION HEURISTIC

Carlos Santamaría
Orlando Espino

En este capítulo presentamos una hipótesis sobre un procedimiento heurístico que las personas podrían utilizar para razonar sobre lo falso. Desde el punto de vista de los modelos mentales, las personas razonan a partir de una representación de algunas de las situaciones en que un determinado enunciado es verdadero, pero los modelos mentales no representan lo falso. Este supuesto conduce a la predicción de que las personas tendrán mayor dificultad en aquellos problemas cuya resolución dependa de que el sujeto tenga en cuenta lo que es falso, como sucede por ejemplo en la tarea de selección de Wason.

Sin embargo, hay situaciones en que se pide directamente a las personas que piensen en lo falso. En tales situaciones se podría hacer uso de un procedimiento heurístico basado en la siguiente suposición: «lo contrario de lo que es verdadero, es falso». Lo que se propone es que las personas parten de su representación de lo verdadero para llegar a los casos falsos, lo que conlleva que existan algunos casos falsos que vengan a la mente antes que otros (los casos contrarios a aquellos que aparecen en el modelo mental), e incluso que algunos casos verdaderos se tomen por falsos por tener una polaridad contraria al modelo mental. El procedimiento heurístico citado podría recibir el nombre de «heurístico de negación» pues consiste en cambiar la polaridad de los modelos mentales para obtener los casos falsos.

Como otros heurísticos, éste da lugar a una respuesta correcta en la mayor parte de los casos, pero no garantiza que se llegue a ella. Por ejemplo, en el condicional, el modelo inicial representa el caso en que tanto el antecedente como el consecuente son verdaderos, de forma que el heurístico de negación llevaría a la conclusión de que el caso en que tanto el antecedente como el consecuente son falsos sería falso. Sin embargo, el condicional (entendido como implicación material) sólo es falso cuando el antecedente es verdadero y el consecuente es falso. Así, *el resultado de la aplicación del heurístico de la negación llevaría en este caso a una respuesta errónea.*

Presentamos dos experimentos para comprobar las predicciones en tareas de tablas de verdad con conjunciones y condicionales. También se manipuló la presencia de negaciones en los enunciados. En el primer experimento, con un diseño intergrupo en el que unos participantes eran preguntados por los casos verdaderos y otros por los falsos, encontramos que, con los dos tipos de regla, el primer caso falso que los participantes producían era aquel en que los dos constituyentes eran falsos, lo que es una de las respuestas correctas en la conjunción, pero es una respuesta errónea en el condicional. Dado que este resultado no concuerda con los hallazgos de otros investigadores en tareas similares hicimos un segundo experimento en el que contrabalanceamos el orden de presentación de las tareas, lo que redujo el efecto en los participantes que hicieron la tarea de falsación después de haber obtenido los casos verdaderos, pero los resultados del primer experimento se replicaron para la condición de orden contrario.

INTRODUCTION

A property of mental models is that they only represent what is true. According to this theory (Johnson-Laird & Byrne, 1991), when faced with an expression like: *there is a square and there is a circle*, people build a model that matches the true case:

However, models do not represent the cases in which the statement is false, which for the previous sentence are:

where the symbol «¬» stands for negation. This property entails a clear advantage in terms of cognitive economy because the false cases are usually numerous and sometimes infinite.

A consequence of this property is that people are not used to representing false entities. However, in some situations people have to deal with what is false. A straightforward procedure to cope with this problem could be to represent the true entities (mental model/s) and then deny them (this procedure was proposed by Barres & Johnson-Laird, 1997). This heuristic strategy is commonly useful because the opposite of what is true is false, and vice versa. However, the negation of a true model could also be true, as happens in the material conditional. For example, the sentence: *If there is a square, then there is a circle,* yields the models:

■   ●

        …

where «...» represents an ellipsis with no explicit content. But the negation of the explicit model produces a negative model that is also true for the conditional:

As a consequence of the use of the *negation heuristic,* some reasoners could consider that the former conditional is false when *there is not a square and there is not a circle*. A complementary phenomenon should be expected for conjunction, where the negation of the mental model results in a false case, but there are other false situations that the reasoner could not consider when using the heuristic. For example, the negation of: *there is a square and there is a circle*:

is false, but:

■   ¬●

and

¬■   ●

are false as well in the same domain.

In this chapter we will test the predictions of the negation heuristic in truth table construction tasks where participants are asked to produce either the true or the false cases for conjunctive and conditional statements. According to the model theory (Johnson-Laird & Byrne, 1991), in a verification task most people will produce as their first option the constituents of the explicit models, which for conjunctions and conditionals correspond to the true cases (TT). This response is the only correct response for conjunctions, and one of the correct responses for conditionals. For the falsification task we predict that the most common response will be that with the opposite polarity of the explicit model: the case in which both constituents are false (FF). In this case, this response is not correct for conditionals, and one of the correct responses for conjunctions.

There are a number of experiments that use the truth table task with affirmative and negative constituents (Evans, 1972; Evans, Clibbens & Rood, 1996; Evans, Legrenzi & Girotto, in press; Johnson-Laird & Tagart; 1969; Oaksford & Stenning, 1992; Ormerod, Manktelow & Jones, 1993). Most of them are devoted to the phenomenon of *matching bias* (see Evans, 1998, for a review). The *matching bias* is «a tendency to see cases as relevant in logical reasoning tasks when the lexical content of a case matches that of a propositional rule [...] which applies to that case» (Evans, 1998, p. 45). For example, in an affirmative rule like: *If there is a square, then there is a circle* the matching cases are «square» and «circle», and the same applies to a negative rule like: *If there is not a square, then there is not a circle*. That is to say, the matching cases are those mentioned in the rule irrespective of their polarity.

In truth-table tasks matching bias can explain some errors that occur when the participants are asked to produce the false cases, especially with conditional rules. For example, Evans *et al.* (in press, Experiment 1) found a 49.2% of matching in their falsification task with the conditional rule. Our proposal of a negation heuristic could explain only 15.5% of responses from the same data. However, the most frequent case produced by the participants in this experiment is the correct falsifying instance (the case in which the antecedent is true and the consequent is false: TF) with a 57.7% of occurrence overall. This suggests that the participants have fleshed-out the implicit models in this task. As the verification and falsification tasks were intermixed in the experiment (and, consequently they received instructions to verify and falsify right from the start), some participants could have used the full models and reached the correct answer. In our first experiment we will use a between-participants design to test this hypothesis.

EXPERIMENT 1

Method

Participants. 60 students of the University of La Laguna.
Materials and procedure. Participants were randomly assigned into two groups of 30 members. They were given written instructions to produce cases that either verified or falsified (depending on the experimental condition) the given rules, which referred to geometric shapes supposedly drawn on imaginary pages. They could produce up to three cases. Each participant received 8 problems in random order: 4 conditionals and 4 conjunctions. The four problems for each connective were obtained by applying explicit negations to the constituents of the propositions. For example:

Conjunctions

    — There is a square and there is a circle on the page.
    — There is a square and there is not a circle on the page.
    — There is not a square and there is a circle on the page.
    — There is not a square and there is not a circle on the page.

Conditionals

    — If there is a square, then there is a circle on the page.
    — If there is a square, then there is not a circle on the page.
    — If there is not a square, then there is a circle on the page.
    — If there is not a square, then there is not a circle on the page.

All the materials were presented to the participants in their native language of Spanish. There was no time limit to complete the task.

Results and discussion

In this chapter we only present the data of the first case produced by the participants. The percentages of cases in the verification and falsification tasks are presented in Table 13.1. 6.8% of unclassifiable responses were excluded. For conjunctions, it could be observed that the most frequent verification instance was TT, which in this case is the only correct response (as compared to the next most frequent, Wilcoxon, z=4.82; p<.0001; all the hypotheses are considered one-tailed). The most frequent falsification instance was FF, which is one of the three correct responses (as compared to the next most frequent, Wilcoxon, z=2.40; p<.01). It should be noted that the percentages for the other correct responses (TF and FT) were very small. These data confirm our predictions for conjunctions: the majority of the participants produced the cases from the initial model in the verification task and the opposite cases in the falsification task.

TABLE 13.1

The percentages of cases in the verification and falsification task for conjunctions and conditionals in Experiment 1 (only the first case produced by the participants in each trial are included)

	Verification Task				Falsification Task			
	TT	**TF**	**FT**	**FF**	**TT**	**TF**	**FT**	**FF**
Conjunctions								
p & q	90.0	0.0	0.0	6.7	0.0	3.3	26.7	56.7
p & ¬q	80.0	3.3	3.3	0.0	0.0	10.0	3.3	80.0
¬p & q	80.0	3.3	0.0	6.7	3.3	3.3	20.0	66.7
¬p & ¬q	83.3	3.3	3.3	3.3	0.0	0.0	0.0	100.0
Overall	83.3	2.5	1.6	4.2	0.8	4.1	12.5	75.8
Conditionals								
If p then q	86.7	3.3	0.0	3.3	0.0	23.3	13.3	46.7
If p then ¬q	80.0	0.0	0.0	10.0	0.0	46.7	10.0	40.0
If ¬p then q	83.3	0.0	6.7	3.3	0.0	13.3	30.0	53.3
If ¬p then ¬q	76.7	6.7	3.3	10.0	0.0	26.7	10.0	60.0
Overall	81.6	4.9	2.5	6.6	0.0	27.5	15.8	50.0

Note: TT= first constituent true and second constituent true. TF= first constituent true and second constituent false. FT= first constituent false and second constituent true. FF= first constituent false and second constituent false.

For conditionals we found a similar pattern for the verification task, where TT, which in this case is one of the three correct answers, was the most frequent (as compared to the next most frequent, Wilcoxon, z=4.35; p<.0001). For the falsification task, where FF is an incorrect response, the difference was not so pronounced, but still reliable (as compared to the next most frequent, which in this case is the correct response, Wilcoxon, z=1.79; p<.05).

The results confirm our predictions both for verification and falsification tasks in conjunctions and conditionals. The weaker strength of the results for the conditionals in the falsification task, suggests that some participants could have fleshed-out the models and avoided the bias. It should also be noted that the percentages of responses predicted by the *matching bias* in this experiment are clearly smaller than those predicted by our hypotheses. The percentages of responses predicted by matching bias and initial-models/negation heuristic are, respectively, in the conjunction-verification task:(24%/83%), conjunction-falsification task: (32%/76%), conditional-verification task: (26%/82%), conditional-falsification task: (34%/50%).

EXPERIMENT 2

The results of Experiment 1 confirmed our predictions that participants use the explicit model in the verification of the rules and the negation heuristic to falsify them. However, our results are quite different to those found in the previous literature, particularly for the falsification task. This we attribute to the differences in the procedure because we used a between participants design, so that when searching for the false instances participants do not think of the true cases. To confirm this hypothesis we carried out in this second experiment a counter-balanced design, where half of the participants completed the falsification task after the verification task and the other half worked in the opposite way. We predicted that the order would affect the responses; in particular, that the participants would perform better in the falsification tasks with the conditional forms (more TF and less FF) when they had already solved the verification problems perhaps because they used full models.

Method

Participants. 58 students of the University of La Laguna.
Materials and procedure. The rules were the same as used in the previous experiment. The only difference for the response format was that the space to respond was divided in two parts to avoid the unclassifiable responses that had occurred in Experiment 1 (i.e. for Experiment 2 the participants had to draw a shape in each part of an imaginary page delineated on the paper). The participants were randomly assigned into two groups of 29 members. One of the groups completed the verification task before the falsification task, and the other group vice-versa. Each group received the instructions for the second task after completing the first task, so that the second task or its instructions could not affect the first task. The order of the problems within each block (falsification and verification) was randomised.

Results and Discussion

The percentages of the first case produced by the participants in each rule and experimental condition, for the verification and falsification tasks, are presented in Table 13.2. Order 1 refers to the condition in which the verification task was presented first, and Order 2 was the opposite order. For Order 1, the conjunction results are similar to those of Experiment 1. The most frequent verification case was TT (as compared to the next most frequent, Wilcoxon, $z=5.16$; $p<.0001$). It seems that participants took advantage of the new response format and this shifted the total percentages by eliminating the unclassifiable responses. The same result was found for Order 2 (when comparing TT to the next most frequent response, Wilcoxon, $z=5.30$; $p<.0001$). As in Experiment 1, the most frequent falsification instance for conjunctions was FF, (as compared to the next most frequent, Wilcoxon, $z=3.34$; $p<.0005$, for Order 1, and Wilcoxon, $z=3.86$; $p<.0001$, for Order 2).

The patterns for the conditionals in the verification tasks are quite similar. TT was clearly the most frequent response in both orders (as compared to the next most frequent, Wilcoxon, $z=5.23$; $p<.0001$, for Order 1, and Wilcoxon, $z=5.30$; $p<.0001$, for Order 2). However, for the falsification tasks the pattern of Experiment 1 was only replicated when the falsification task was presented first (FF was more frequent that TF; Wilcoxon, $z=2.10$; $p<.02$), while for Order 1 the difference was not reliable (Wilcoxon, $z<1$); in fact the tendency went in the opposite direction. This interactive result confirms our hypothesis that attributes the low effects of the negation heuristic in previous research to the perceived relevance of the false cases after the participants have found the true cases.

When the verification task was presented first (Order 1), the percentages of responses predicted by matching bias and initial-models/negation heuristic were, respectively, in the conjunction-verification task: (27%/98%), conjunction-falsification task: (35%/62%), conditional-verification task: (26%/98%), and conditional-falsification task: (29%/35%). The reduction of FF as a falsification response for the conditional was clear in this condition but not as important as, for example, in the data of Evans *et al.* (in press). This difference could be mainly due to the instructions of the verification and falsification tasks that are presented apart from each other in our experiment. For Order 2 (when the falsification task was presented first), the percentages of responses predicted by matching bias and initial-models/negation heuristic were, respectively, in the conjunction-verification task: (25%/99%), conjunction-falsification task: (35%/75%), conditional-verification task: (26%/99%), and conditional-falsification task: (31%/60%).

General discussion

The results in this chapter clearly support the existence of a *negation heuristic* in reasoning about what is false. The mental model theory of propositional reasoning (Johnson-Laird & Byrne, 1991) could explain quite easily how people produce the true cases in a truth-table task: they just use the cases in their mental models. However, to produce the false cases would be a very hard task for a system based on mental models if it had to flesh the models out to detect the cases that are not present. It seems reasonable that people avoid this task

TABLE 13.2

The percentages of cases in the verification and falsification task for conjunctions and conditionals in both orders of presentation (Experiment 2; only the first case produced by the participants in each trial are included)

| | Order 1 | | | | | | | | Order 2 | | | | | | | |
| | Verification Task | | | | Falsification Task | | | | Verification Task | | | | Falsification Task | | | |
	TT	TF	FT	FF	TT	TF	FT	FF	TT	TF	FT	FF	TT	TF	FT	FF
Conjunctions																
p & q	100.0	0.0	0.0	0.0	0.0	13.8	17.2	69.0	100.0	0.0	0.0	0.0	0.0	24.1	10.3	65.5
p & ¬q	96.6	3.4	0.0	0.0	0.0	27.6	13.8	58.6	100.0	0.0	0.0	0.0	0.0	27.6	3.4	69.0
¬p & q	96.6	3.4	0.0	0.0	0.0	10.3	41.4	48.3	96.6	3.4	0.0	0.0	0.0	6.9	20.7	72.4
¬p & ¬q	96.6	0.0	0.0	3.4	0.0	20.7	6.9	72.4	100.0	0.0	0.0	0.0	0.0	6.9	0.0	93.1
Overall	97.5	1.7	0.0	0.8	0.0	18.1	19.8	62.1	99.2	0.8	0.0	0.0	0.0	16.4	8.6	75.0
Conditionals																
If p then q	100.0	0.0	0.0	0.0	0.0	24.1	51.7	24.1	100.0	0.0	0.0	0.0	3.4	10.3	31.0	55.3
If p then ¬q	96.6	0.0	0.0	3.4	3.4	44.8	17.2	34.5	96.6	3.4	0.0	0.0	0.0	37.9	0.0	62.1
If ¬p then q	96.6	0.0	3.4	0.0	0.0	34.5	27.6	37.9	100.0	0.0	0.0	0.0	0.0	13.8	24.1	62.1
If ¬p then ¬q	100.0	0.0	0.0	0.0	0.0	44.8	10.3	44.8	100.0	0.0	0.0	0.0	0.0	31.0	10.3	58.6
Overall	98.3	0.0	0.8	0.8	0.8	37.1	26.7	35.3	99.1	0.8	0.0	0.0	0.8	23.3	16.4	59.5

Note: TT= first constituent true and second constituent true. TF= first constituent true and second constituent false. FT= first constituent false and second constituent true. FF= first constituent false and second constituent false. Order 1: verification and then falsification; Order 2: the opposite.

by using a heuristic procedure. We propose that they use a negation heuristic that changes the polarity of the tokens in the mental models.

This heuristic may not be necessary when the reasoner has already fleshed the models out, or when the alternative instances are presented first in the task (see Evans, Handley & Buck, 1998; Girotto, Mazzocco & Tasso, 1997), because the order may affect the modelling process. This could explain the reduction of the effect when the verification task was presented first in our Experiment 2, and when the verification and falsification problems are intermixed (e.g. Evans *et al.*, in press). The accommodation of these results within mental-logic theories (e.g. Braine & O'Brien, 1991) is not straightforward because, in principle, the order of the application of the rules should have no effect on reasoning. Moreover, the similarity between the results obtained with conditionals and conjunction tasks are hard to explain for these theories.

An alternative account of reasoning about falsity is the proposal of *matching bias*. In principle, *matching bias* could be applied both to falsification and verification tasks: reasoners could produce the elements mentioned in the rule for both tasks. However, in this case it would predict the same pattern of responses for both kinds of tasks. *Matching bias* is more appropriate as an explanation of the results in the falsification task. However, this account cannot easily explain the differences between conjunction and conditional tasks, and the effects of the order in the conditional tasks.

Further research is needed to explore the possibilities of the negation heuristic to explain some results found with other reasoning tasks.

ACKNOWLEDGMENT

The authors would like to thank Jonathan Evans, Vittorio Girotto and Phil Johnson-Laird for helpful discussions on some data in this chapter.

REFERENCES

BARRES, P. E., & JOHNSON-LAIRD, P. N. (1997): «Why is it hard to imagine what is false?» In M.G. Shafto and P.Langley. *Proceedings of the Nineteenth Conference of the Cognitive Science Society*. Stanford, CA: Stanford University.

BRAINE, M. D. S., & O'BRIEN, D. P. (1991): «A theory of if: A lexical entry, reasoning program, and pragmatic principles». *Psychological Review*, 98 (2), 182-203.

EVANS, J. St. B. T. (1972): «Interpretation and matching biases in a reasoning task». *British Journal of Psychology*, 24, 193-199.

— (1998): «Matching bias in conditional reasoning: Do we understand it after 25 years?» *Thinking and Reasoning*, 4 (1), 45-82.

EVANS, J. St. B. T., CLIBBENS, J., & ROOD, B. (1996): «The role of implicit explicit negation in conditional reasoning bias». *Journal of Memory and Language*, 35, 392-409.

EVANS, J. St. B. T., HANDLEY & BUCK (1998): «Ordering of information in conditional reasoning». *British Journal of Psychology*, 89, 383-403.

EVANS, J. St. B. T., LEGRENZI, P., & GIROTTO, V. (in press): «The influence of linguistic form on reasoning: the case of matching bias». *Quarterly Journal of Experimental Psychology.*

GIROTTO, V., MAZZOCO, A., & TASSO, A. (1997): «The effect of premise order in conditional reasoning: A test of the mental model theory». *Cognition, 63,* 1-28.

JOHNSON-LAIRD, P. N., & BYRNE, R. (1991): *Deduction.* Hove & London: Lawrence Erlbaum Associates Ltd.

JOHNSON-LAIRD, P. N., & TAGART, J. (1969): «How implication is understood». *American Journal of Psychology,* 2, 367-373.

OAKSFORD, M., & STENNING, K. (1992): «Reasoning with conditional containing negated constituents». *Journal of Experimental Psychology: Learning, Memory and Cognition,* 18, 835-854.

ORMEROD, T. C., MANTTELOW, K. I., & JONES, G. V. (1993): «Reasoning with three types of conditional: Biases and model mental models». *Quarterly Journal of Experimental Psychology,* 46A, 653-678.

14

TIME MEASURES IN RIPS'S PROBLEMS

Juan A. García Madruga
Sergio Moreno
Nuria Carriedo
Francisco Gutiérrez

La mayor parte de los hallazgos en el campo del razonamiento deductivo están basados en estudios en los que se han utilizado medidas de precisión, así como juicios sobre la dificultad de los problemas; existe, por el contrario, poca evidencia proveniente del uso de medidas temporales. Sin embargo, el uso de medidas temporales podría ser de gran importancia para tratar de establecer el proceso de razonamiento de los sujetos y, así, ayudar a descubrir las diversas estrategias utilizadas. Además del alto coste y la mayor dificultad de las medidas temporales, podemos aducir como causa de su escaso uso en el estudio de las inferencias deductivas el que ninguno de los dos enfoques teóricos enfrentados, reglas mentales y modelos mentales, está «definido en forma completa y precisa» (Evans & Over, 1997). No obstante, entre los dos enfoques teóricos hay algunas diferencias básicas con respecto a su habilidad para predecir e interpretar los resultados temporales del proceso inferencial. En este capítulo presentamos algunos resultados hallados con los problemas de tres premisas de Rips, en los que aparece en la primera premisa una conjunción o una disyunción, seguida de dos condicionales. Aunque la teoría de los modelos mentales predice que los problemas conjuntivos (un modelo) deberán ser serán más fáciles que los problemas disyuntivos (modelos multiples), Rips no halló ninguna diferencia signicativa entre ellos en un estudio en el que utilizó una tarea de evaluación (Rips, 1990). Llevamos a cabo dos experimentos previos en los que las medidas de precisión mostraron que, al utilizar una tarea de construcción y al cambiar el orden de presentación de las premisas, los problemas conjuntivos eran significativamente más fáciles que los disyuntivos. En un nuevo experimento introdujimos un procedimiento controlado por el ordenador que permitía registrar los tiempos que los participantes utilizaban en leer las premisas y evaluar la conclusiones. Manipulamos, asimismo, el orden de las premisas: un orden fue el mismo que el de Rips, con la conjunción- disyunción como primera premisa que precedía a los condicionales, mientras que en el orden «inverso» los condicionales precedían a la conjunción o la disyunción. Cuando la la conjunción o la disyunción aparecían primero los tiempos de lectura mostraron que la construcción del modelo múltiple de la disyunción que el modelo único de la conjunción, asimismo los tiempos de lectura de las premisas siguientes tendían a disminuir. Por el contrario, cuando los dos condicionales eran presentados primero, los resultados mostraron que la interpretación del segundo condicional requería más tiempo y que las latencias de respuesta para los problemas conjuntivos era menor que para los disyuntivos. Estos resultados confirman la teoría de los modelos mentales y su explicación plantea algunas dificultades para las teorías de reglas mentales

INTRODUCTION

Thirty years ago Peter Wason published a seminal paper on the selection task: «Reasoning about a rule» (Wason, 1968), which might be considered a milestone in the new cognitive psychology of reasoning. These three decades of research have led to an outstanding increase in our empirical knowledge as to how people really reason in different deductive tasks. Moreover, there has been considerable improvement from the theoretical point of view. The earlier situation of multiple mini-theories specifically designed for each task or experimental paradigm has been superseded by two main general approaches: mental rules and mental models. Both theories permit us to explain a considerable body of evidence and to make some interesting and new predictions.

The theories of formal rules hold that the reasoning process consists of the application of a set of mental rules or inferential schemas, similar to those of logic. Based on these rules human beings are capable of deriving answers to the deductive problems they might be faced with. Thus, there is a rule for a conjunction that allows to infer A (also B), from a conjunctive statement having a structure as the following one:

A and B

In other words, mental logic theories maintain that human beings posses a *A&B, therefore A* mental rule.

There is another rule for disjunctions that from the following two assertions:

A or B
not A

allows us to draw the following valid conclusion:

Therefore: *B.*

The two main current mental rules theories include both of these rules (see, Braine, 1990, Braine, Reiser & Rumain, 1984, O'Brien, Braine &Yang, 1994; Rips, 1983, 1994). These theories maintain that the reasoning process would include three main stages: a) discovering the abstract form of the statements; b) applying of the formal rules leading to a valid conclusion; and c) re-translating the conclusion drawn into the specific problem content (see Evans, Newstead & Byrne, 1993). However, the inferential work is done in the middle phase in which reasoners have to derive a conclusion by means of the applying of the rules or inference schemas. Therefore, the main prediction of rule theories comes from the number of rules or intermediate steps required for reaching a conclusion: the longer the process of deriving a conclusion, the greater the difficulty of the problem.

From the mental model theory, the reasoning process is analysed in a clearly distinct way. According to the model theory, reasoners apply their knowledge to construct models that represent the state of affairs described in the premises, try to formulate a parsimonious conclusion that accounts for the models constructed, and finally, try to validate their conclusion by searching for alternative models or counterexamples (Johnson-Laird & Byrne, 1991). Mental model theory assumes a sort of principle of cognitive economy: given the limited nature of human cognitive resources and in order to avoid overloading the working memory, people try to represent explicitly as little information as possible. Thus, naive human reasoners make most of everyday inferences from the initial and incomplete representation or models of the premises. As can be observed in Table 14, the mental model of the conjunction includes only a model, and therefore the initial representation coincides with the explicit one. On the other hand, in the case of connectives such as disjunctions and conditionals, the initial representation is simpler than the complete one (Johnson-Laird, Byrne, & Schaeken, 1992). The main prediction of mental model theory is, hence, that the difficulty of an inferential problem

TABLE 14.1
Initial and final wholly explicit representation for the main propositional connectives (from Johnson-Laird, Byrne and Schaeken, 1992)

MODELS			
Connectives	**Initial**	**Explicit**	
p and q	p q	p q	
		Inclusive	**Exclusive**
p or q	p	p q	p ¬q
	q	p ¬q	¬p q
		¬p q	
		Conditional	**Biconditional**
if p then q	p q	p q	p q
	...	¬p q	¬p ¬q
		¬p ¬q	

will correspond to the number of models reasoners have to build to reach the conclusion: the greater the number of models the harder the inference will be.

Three main measures have been used to test reasoners' performance and evaluate the difficulty of inferences: accuracy measures, i.e. number of valid conclusions and errors, metalogical judgments of the problems' difficulty, and time measures. Most of findings on deductive reasoning research are based on accuracy measures, as well as difficulty's judgments; there is little evidence coming from the use of time measures, which would include the reading times of premises and the latencies of the responses. However, time measures could be of the highest importance to establish people's reasoning process, and therefore they may help to uncover the diverse strategies used by reasoners. Besides the higher cost and difficulty of time measures, we can adduce as a cause of the scarce time evidence in deductive inferences that neither of the two confronted approaches, mental rules and mental models, is «fully and precisely defined in itself» (Evans & Over, 1997).

Nevertheless, there are some prime differences between the two approaches concerning to their ability to predict and interpret time results of the inferential process. In this chapter we shall present some results found using Rips's three-premises problems: a conjunction or a disjunction in the first premise, followed by two conditionals. Besides to replicate Rips's study introducing some methodological changes, we have also introduced a computer-controlled procedure that enabled us to record the participant's times to read each premise and to evaluate the conclusions.

Rips's Problems

In the problems studied by Rips (1990, 1994, p. 365-369) participants were faced to some inferential arguments such as those shown in Table 14.2.

TABLE 14.2
Problems used by Rips and PSYSCOP's rules to solve them

	Arguments		Rules
One model problems	(1) p AND q IF p, r IF q, r — r	(3) NOT p AND NOT q IF NOT p, r IF NOT q, r — r	*Forward And Elimination* P AND Q P *Forward IF Elimination* IF P THEN R P R
Multiple model problems	(2) p OR q IF p, r IF q, r — r	(4) NOT p OR NOT q IF NOT p, r IF NOT q, r — r	*Forward Dilemma* P OR Q IF P THEN R IF Q THEN R R

The task of the participants was to evaluate the necessity of the given conclusion, answering «Yes» or «No». According to rules theories (see Table 14.2), solving problems (1) and (3) would call for the applying of two rules drawn from the basic set of inference schemas posed by the main theories (see Braine, 1990, Braine, Reiser & Rumain, 1984, Rips 1983, 1994). In Rip's most recent PSYSCOP theory of logical reasoning participants would need to apply the forward AND and IF Elimination rules. For problems (2) and (4), the rules theories posses a single rule that allows a valid conclusion to be reached directly. In terms of Rips's PSYSCOP theory, reasoners would need to apply the Forward Dilemma rule (Rips, 1994, p.368). As we can see, according to rules theories, problems (1) and (3) demand the application of two rules and problems (2) and (4) demand only one rule. However, as Rips maintains (1994, p.368), applying the Dilemma rule is «somehow harder», given that it calls for the coordination of three premises, whilst the rules to be applied in the case of the conjunctive arguments only call for the coordination of one or two. Thus, although the second kind of problems demands the application of fewer rules, Rips concludes that «There is no reason to think that one of these methods should be much easier than the other» (1994, p.368-369).

According to the mental model theory, meanwhile, conjunctive problems and disjunctive problems require quite different cognitive work, and difficulty predictions are therefore very different in each: problems (1) and (3) will probably be easier than problems (2) and (4). However, it is worth looking more closely at the two affirmative inferences (1) and (2).

Inferential problem (1) would be quite easy in the light of the mental models theory. Reasoners must build up their model of the first premise (the conjunction) and then the initial representation of either of the conditionals to achieve an integrated representation that would allow them to infer that «r» is necessarily true. The representation of the first premise «p AND q» would be the very simple model:

P   Q

The initial representation of the second conditional premise, «IF p, r», demands the construction of the following two models:

P   R

   ...

The first explicit model (P   R) includes a representation with two components: the antecedent and the consequent of the conditional assertion. The three dots stand for the second implicit model that expresses the existence of other possible models. Using the initial representation of the conditionals, reasoners can easily integrate the meaning of the conditional with the first conjunctive premise, and thus reach a model representation as follows:

P   Q   R

This composite model is very simple and allows people to directly infer that «r» is necessarily valid.

As to the second type of inferential problem (2), mental model theory maintains that the reasoning process would be quite similar although the result would be very different. The initial representation of first disjunctive premise, «p OR q», would require the construction of two initial models:

P

  Q

The initial representation of the second conditional premise, «IF p, r», includes the same set of models as those in inferential problem (1), that is:

P   R

  ...

These models can be combined with those for the first premise. The result is obtained simply by adding the R component to first model of disjunction, yielding the following set of models:

P   R

  Q

These models can, in turn, be combined with the models of the third premise:

Q   R

  ...

Again the result is obtained simply by adding the R component to the prior model:

P   R

  Q   R

From these models, reasoners can directly infer that «r» is necessary. The completely explicit representation of this problem would be as follows:

P   ¬Q   R

¬P   Q   R

As we have seen, the conjunctive problem (1) is a one-model problem, whereas the disjunctive problem (2) demands two models to be constructed. The same can be said for the problems (3) and (4) that contain negations. Thus, according to mental model theory conjunctive inferences should be easier than disjunctive inferences.

In Rips's study, reasoners had to evaluate whether the conclusions were «necessarily true» or «not necessarily true». Result showed no significant differences between conjunctive problems and disjunctive ones (Rips, 1990, p. 297). However, with the negated inferences, the difference was in the direction predicted by model theory, even though it was only marginally significant ($p < .10$). These results seem to confirm Rips theory and run against the model theory prediction.

More recently, we have carried out two experiments that attempt to replicate Rips's study (García Madruga, Moreno, Carriedo, Gutiérrez & Johnson-Laird, in press). Our idea was that the lack of reliable differences between conjunctive and disjunctive problems might be due to the type of task used by Rips. This task and the kind of problems used could lead to a «ceiling effect» that may have been hiding the differences between the problems. The objective of the two new experiments was to eliminate this possible «ceiling effect». Thus, in the first experiment we compared reasoners performance when facing the problems presented in Table 14.1, using both evaluation and construction tasks. There were two groups of participants in the Experiment, each group being given a different task. According to mental model theory, apart from the supplementary difficulty of putting the conclusions into words, which construction tasks require, reasoners may adopt different strategies with evaluation and construction tasks; in particular they can work backwards from the given conclusion in the evaluation task, whereas this strategy is not possible in the construction task. According to Rips's theory, the rules involved in solving these problems would be all «forward», and these rules would be almost automatically employed (see, Rips 1994, p.122). Therefore, the change from an evaluation to a construction task should not imply any relevant difference. Likewise, from the point of view of Braine's theory, the solving of these problems demands only the direct and automatic application of some of the rules of the basic set (Braine *et al.*, 1984; Braine, 1990) and, hence, nor is any relevant difference predicted with the introduction of a construction task.

The aim of the second experiment was to rule out the possible «ceiling effect» changing the order in which the premises were presented. The influence of the change of the order of premises is borne out by Girotto, Mazzoco, and Tasso (1997) on conditional inferences. They found that the classical difference in difficulty between *modus ponens* (If p then q, p, therefore q) and *modus tollens* (If p then q, not-q, therefore: not-p) tended to disappear: when the categorical premise was presented preceding the conditional sentence in *modus tollens* (not-q, if p then q, therefore: not-p) reasoners increased their correct responses, whereas the change of the order of premises did not affect to the *modus ponens*. According to mental model theory, and as these authors say, «when reasoners have to treat the categorical premise before the conditional one, they can easily represent the negated consequent from the start. When they then begin to consider the conditional, they can eliminate the model representing the antecedent and the consequent, and thus free up the working memory capacity.» (Girotto, Mazzoco, & Tasso, 1997, p.4). It occurred to us that the change of the order of premises, presenting the two conditionals preceding the conjunction or the disjunction, could also affect Rips's problems, since the integration of the semantic information of the premises in a final representation would probably be harder and therefore more error-prone. Whereas in Rips's order the meaning of the two conditional premises can be smoothly integrated in the prior conjunctive or disjunctive representation, in the opposite order reasoners have to integrate first the two conditionals and then the final conjunction or disjunction premise. In the experiment 2, reasoners had to solve the same problems but presented in an «inverse» order: they received the conjunction-disjunction as the final premise. As in the experiment 1 there were two groups of participants, each group being given a different task: evaluation or construction.

The results of the two experiments can be observed in Figures 14.1 and 14.2, respectively. The results concerning to the evaluation task clearly replicate those found by Rips in his study: disjunctive problems tend to be harder than conjunctive ones, as mental model theory predicts, but the differences are not significant. As for the construction task, results do confirm the mental model theory. Problems including as a first premise a disjunction are reliably harder to solve than those including a conjunction. As we predicted, the shift of task

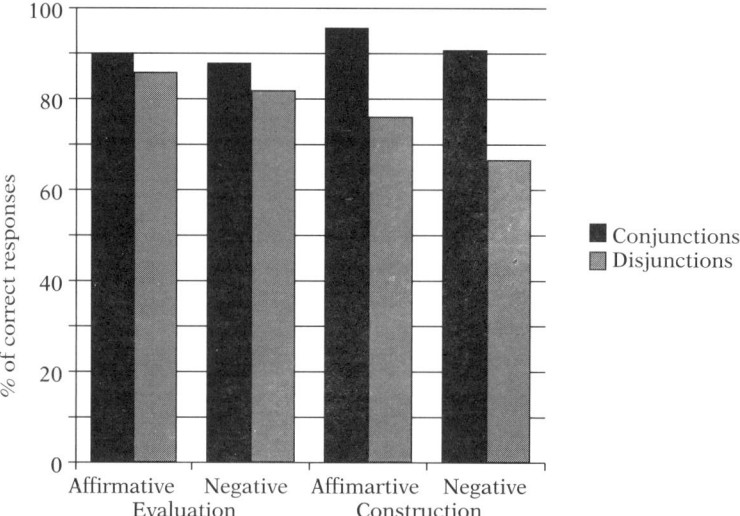

Figure 14.1. Percentages of correct responses for Rips's problems in experiment 1 (conjunction-disjunction first).

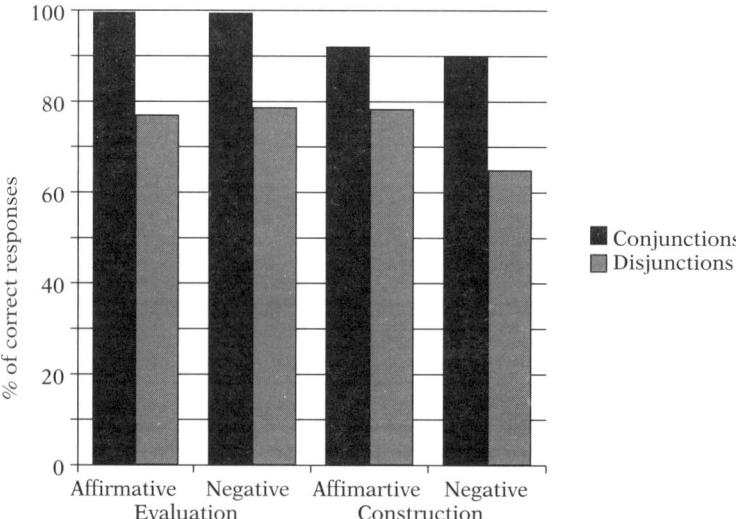

Figure 14.2. Percentages of correct responses for Rips's problems in experiment 2 (conjunction-disjunction last).

seems to have increased the difficulty of the problems, showing some differences which were hitherto obscured by the great ease and simplicity of the problems posed. The results of the Experiment 2 also bear out the predictions of mental models theory concerning to the change of the order of premises: For both, the evaluation and the construction task, one-model problems were reliably easier than multiple-model ones.

TIMING THE PROCESS AND THE RESULT OF REASONING

The aim of this experiment was to record some time measures of the reasoners' mental processes while solving Rips's problems in both orders of premises: the classical and the inverse one. In this experiment, the analysis and predictions we made with regard to the task will be quite different depending on the theory, rules theories or mental model theory. Rules theories maintain that inferential problems can be of two types: a) Simple Problems requiring only the automatic, direct applying of rules (forward ones), b) More complex problems requiring also the use of the «strategic component» and backward rules (see, O'Brien, Braine & Yang, 1994; Rips, 1994; see also, Evans & Over, 1997). As we said before Rips's problems are simple problems of the first kind. They demand only the direct application of some basic rules and need no strategic component. Nevertheless, the change in the order of the premises would probably force reasoners to re-order the premises.

Therefore, as to reading times, rules theories do not predict any difference between conjunctive problems and disjunctive ones. Neither do they predict that in the «inverse order» there is a particular difficulty in integrating the meaning of premises. As for response latencies: the change in the order of premises might increase latency of responses (people would need to re-order the premises), but this increase would affect both kinds of problems; i.e. conjunctive inferences (two rules) should be either slower or no different from disjunctive inferences (only one rule) in both groups.

In contrast, according to model theory we can analyze reasoners' task and make some explicit predictions as to the reading measures. Theory's basic principle rests upon the construction and combination of models from which the participant can then «read off» his/her conclusions. According to mental model theory, the introduction of the inverse order will probably determine the use of a different strategic pattern of problem processing and solving. Therefore in this experiment we can make the following predictions as to times measures:

- Reading conjunctions should be faster than disjunctions.
- The integration of semantic information from premises should be harder and hence more time consuming in the inverse order.
- Response latencies for conjunctive inferences should be faster than for disjunctive inferences.

In this experiment we introduced a computer-controlled procedure that enabled us to record the participant's times to read each premise and to evaluate the conclusions. Likewise, we manipulated the order of the premises. One order was the same as in Rips's original experiment, with the conjunction-disjunction premise preceding to the two conditionals; the other was the «inverse» order in which the two conditional premises preceded the conjunction or the disjunction. The task in both cases was to evaluate given conclusions. Participants were forty two students from the UNED of Madrid, assigned at random to one of the two groups (21 in each group).

Time results of this experiment can be observed in Table 14.3 and Figures 14.3 and 14.4. Response latencies confirmed the predictions of mental model theory. The overall latencies of the conjunctive problems were reliably faster than those of the disjunctive problems (means of 2.96 and 4.87 secs., respectively; p <.02, one-tail). However, in analyzing the two groups, this difference was significant only for the inverse order group that received the conjunction-disjunction premise after the two conditionals (p<.02, one-tail)

The reading times of the premises also appear to support mental model predictions. When the participants received the premises in Rips's order (see Figure 14.3), the reading times of conjunctions were significantly shorter than those of disjunctions (p <.002, one-tail). Likewise, the reading times for the first conditionals seem to be different between conjunctive and disjunctive inferences, although this difference was only marginally reliable (p =.07, one-tail). Another interesting result with the Rips's order, that can be easily observed in Figure 14.3, is the quite clear descending pattern of time measures.

When the participants received the premises in the inverse order (see Figure 14.4), as model theory predicted, the pattern of time measures is rather different. First of all, the unexpected difference between the reading times of first conditional premise for conjunctive and disjunctive problems is not reliable (p>.20, two-tail). Neither are significant the differences concerning to the second conditional premise and those between conjunction and disjunction in the third premise. The only reliable difference between conjunctive and disjunctive inferences is that already

TABLE 14.3
Mean reading times and correct response latencies (in secs.), by order condition and kind of problems in exp. 3

		Conj-disj	1st cond.	2nd cond.	Resp. Lat.	Overall processing time
Rips' order Arguments	One model problems	9.52	6.73	6.27	2.87	22.51
	Mult. model problems	11.62	7.76	7.23	3.78	26.61
Inverse order Arguments	One model problems	8.54	6.39	10.80	3.04	25.72
	Mult. model problems	8.38	8.80	11.78	6.02	28.97

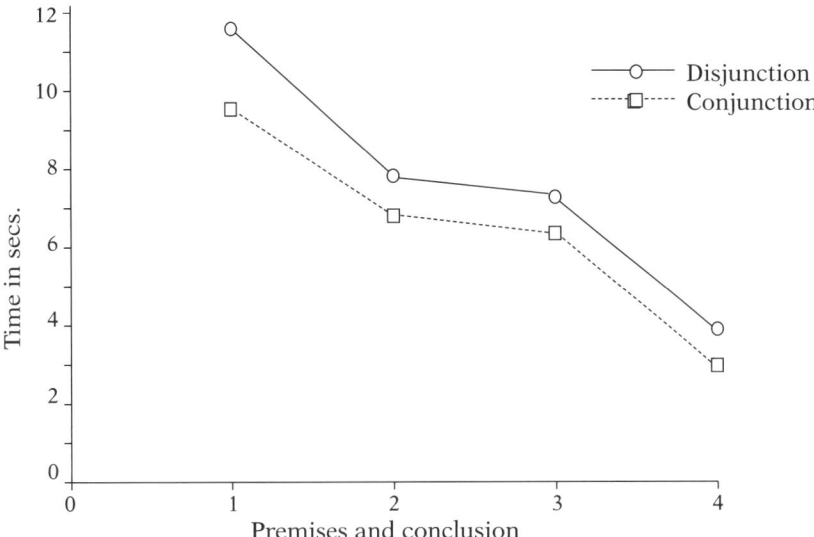

Figure 14.3. Times measures in Rips's order problems (conjunction-disjunction first).

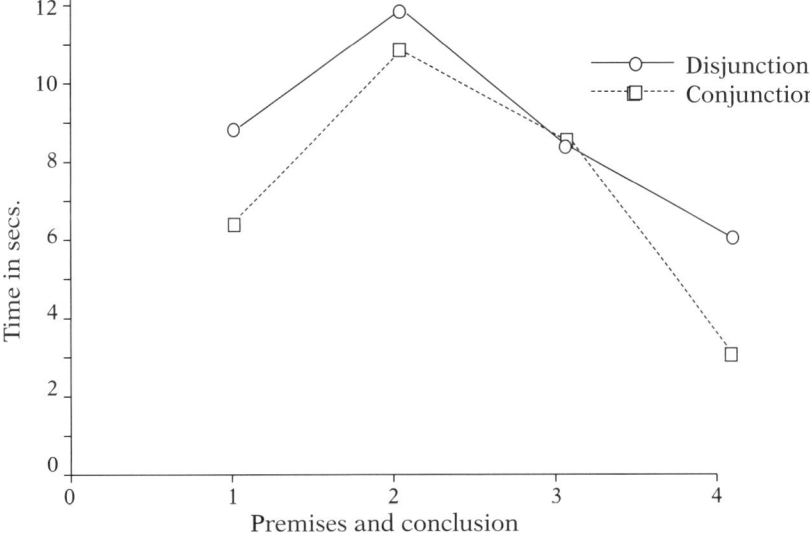

Figure 14.4. Time measures in inverse order problems (conjunction-disjunction last).

mentioned concerning to response latencies. However, the reading times of the second conditional were significant higher than those of the first conditional, both for the conjunctive problems as well as for the disjunctive ones (p <.001 and p <.01, one-tail, respectively). This is quite an interesting new outcome, since it seems to show that the integration of the meaning of the two conditionals is harder when they are not preceded by either a conjunction or disjunction.

SOME FINAL PROPOSALS

The results found may be summarized in two main points:

1. Whenever there is a difference between conjunctive and disjunctive problems these differences are the predicted by model theory, and run against rules theories. This is the case of the shorter reading times for conjunctions than for disjunctions in Rips's order problems, and in inverse order the shorter latencies for conjunctive problems than for disjunctive ones.

2. As mental model theory predicts, changing the order of premises leads to a different strategic pattern. This new pattern is illustrated by the sharp increase in reading times of the second conditional for inverse order inferences.

According to rules theories the solving of Rips's inferences demand only the direct application of certain rules. Both kinds of results found seem to refute mental rules theories. In any case, these results affecting core assumptions of mental rules theories, would be difficult to accommodate.

According to mental model theory, the process of solving deductive problems is not deterministic, but strategic. Our results seem to corroborate the model theory. Nevertheless, in the light of our results there are some open questions as to the process of reasoning, particularly some as the following ones (see also, García-Madruga, Moreno, Carriedo & Gutiérrez, 1999):

Do the reasoners construct the models for each premise while reading them off?

Are the meanings of the premises brought together while they are being read off or only after participants see the final question?

On studying multiple conditional problems, we have found that reasoners probably maintain the information from the early premises in a buffer, waiting to build their models or integrate them at the end of the problem when offered the final premise, or when they are asked to give their conclusions (García-Madruga & Johnson-Laird, 1994; Gutiérrez, García-Madruga, Carriedo & Moreno, this volume). We also suppose that the integration of new information in a given mental model representation may lead to quite different operations, consuming diverse cognitive resources. Therefore, we may propose at least two kinds of integration operations:

*   Addition that implies the simple aggregation of new information to the previous model.
*   Reconstruction that implies building a new model representation. This kind of integration would obviously consume more cognitive resources and require more time

In this way, whenever a new premise is read, reasoners have three options:

*   To maintain the information provided by the new premise in a buffer.
*   To integrate the new information by means of simply adding it to the previous model representation.
*   To integrate the new information by means of a reconstruction.

Our results can be explained using these assumptions. In Rips's order inferences, when facing with the first premise reasoners take longer to read and build the multiple model of disjunction than the single model of conjunction. As we showed earlier the integration of the other premises in the initial models is quite easy and requires only the adding of some more information to the existing models. This representation is updated with the arriving of a new premise and the integration of new semantic information. Hence, the continuous activation and use of this basic model representation could account for the lack of significant differences between the latencies for conjunctive and disjunctive problems.

As to the inverse order, the possible explanation is somehow more difficult and less trustworthy. After having built the model of the first conditional, If p then r:

P   R
    ...

reasoners must integrate the model of the second conditional, if q then r:

Q   R
    ...

This integration requires a reconstruction of the composite representation, by means of the building up of a new model, as follows:

P   R
Q   R
    ...

This operation, as our results show, appears to be more difficult and consumes more processing time. From this composite model representation, the integration of the meaning of conjunction (p and q) demands only its simplification to reach a final representation as:

P   Q   R

As to the disjunction (p or q) reasoners' task also consist in simplifying previous composite models to reach the following final representation:

P   R
Q   R

However, as response latencies show, reasoners now seem to expend more time scanning this two model final representation of disjunctive inferences than the simpler one of conjunctive inferences.

We are aware that this account of the timing data found is clearly «ad hoc», but we feel this to be the way forward. Mental model theory would probably need to be more precise about the different ways in which reasoners can integrate the meaning of premises in a final composite mental representation of the problems, as well as how these models are manipulated before giving a conclusion. In undertaking this work we must bear in mind three main points: first, we need to assume the principle of cognitive economy, i.e. reasoners will probably choose the simplest and least demanding way to reach a conclusion; second, as work on strategies have shown (see, Siegler, Adolph,

& Lemaire, 1996; see also, García-Madruga *et al.*, 1999), differences between and within subjects would be the norm, not the exception; finally, given the adaptive nature of human cognition, and as our results have shown, the introduction of minor methodological changes, for instance in the instructions reasoners receive or the experimental procedure, may lead to important modifications in the process of reasoning and its result.

REFERENCES

BRAINE, M. D. S. (1990): «The "Natural Logic" Approach to Reasoning». In W.F. Overton (Ed.), *Reasoning, Necessity and Logic: Developmental Perspectives*. (pp.135-157) Hillsdale, N.J.: Lawrence Erlbaum.

BRAINE, M. D. S., REISER, B. J., & RUMAIN, B. (1984): «Some empirical justification for a theory of natural propositional reasoning». G. H. Bower (ed.), *The psychology of learning and motivation. Vol. 1.* (pp.313-371) New York: Academic Press.

EVANS, J. St. B. T., & OVER, D. (1997): «Rationality in reasoning: The problem of deductive competence». *Cahiers de Psychologie Cognitive/Current Psychology of Cognition, 16*, 3-38.

EVANS, St. B. T., NEWSTEAD S. E., & BYRNE R. M. J. (1993): *Human Reasoning.* Hove (UK): Lawrence Erlbaum Associates, Publisher (LEA).

GARCÍA MADRUGA, J. A., & JOHNSON-LAIRD. P. N. (1994, september): «Multiple conditionals: Rules or Models?» Paper presented at the *Seventh Meeting of European Society for Cognitive Psychology*. Lisbon.

GARCÍA-MADRUGA, J. A., MORENO, S., CARRIEDO, N., & GUTIÉRREZ, F. (1999): «Task, order of premises and strategies in Rips's conjunction-disjunction and conditionals problems». In W. Schaeken, G. De Voogth, A. Vandierendonk and G. D'Ydewalle (Eds.), *Deductive Reasoning and Strategies*. Mahwah, N.J.: Lawrence Erlbaum.

GARCÍA-MADRUGA, J. A., MORENO, S., CARRIEDO, N., GUTIÉRREZ, F., & JOHNSON-LAIRD, P. N. (in press): «Are conjunctive inferences easier than disjunctive inferences? A comparison of rules and models». *Quarterly Journal of Experimental Psychology*.

GIROTTO, V., MAZZOCO, A., & TASSO, A. (1997): «The effect of premise order in conditional reasoning: a test of the mental model theory». *Cognition, 63*, 1-28.

JOHNSON-LAIRD, P. N., & BYRNE, R. M. J. (1991): *Deduction.* Hillsdale, New Jersey: LEA.

JOHNSON-LAIRD, P. N., BYRNE, R., & SCHAEKEN, W. (1992): «Propositional reasoning by model». *Psychological Review, 99*, 418-439.

— (1994): «Why Models Rather Than Rules Give a Better Account of Propositional Reasoning: A Repply to Bonatti and to O'Brien, Braine & Yang». *Psychological Review, 101*, 734-739.

O'BRIEN, D. P., BRAINE, M. D. S., & YANG, Y. (1994): «Propositional Reasoning by Mental Models? Simple to Refute in Principle and Practice». *Psychological Review, 101*, 711-724.

RIPS, L. J. (1983): «Cognitive processes in propositional reasoning». *Psychological Review, 90*, 38-71.

— (1990): «Paralogical reasoning: Evans, Johnson-Laird, and Byrne on liar and truth-teller puzzles». *Cognition, 36*, 291-314.

— (1994): *The Psychology of Proof. Deductive reasoning in Human Reasoning.* Cambridge, Mass.: MIT Press.

SIEGLER, R. S., ADOLPH, K. E., & LEMAIRE, P. (1996): «Strategy Choices Across the Life-span». In L.M. Reder (Ed.), *Implicit Memory and Metacognition*. (pp.79-121) Mahwah, N.J.: Lawrence Erlbaum Associates, Publisher (LEA).

15

IS THERE AN INNATE MODULE
FOR DEONTIC REASONING?

Monica Bucciarelli
Philip N. Johnson-Laird

Los niños de 3 años pueden realizar una tarea de razonamiento (la versión reducida de la Tarea de Selección de Wason) en la cual tienen que seleccionar la evidencia relevante que les permita detectar las violaciones a una regla condicional. Este fenómeno es considerado por muchos psicólogos como una evidencia de un módulo innato para razonar sobre obligaciones y permisos. El presente capítulo cuestiona esta interpretación y quizá el fenómeno en sí mismo. En nuestro primer experimento, observamos que los niños realizaban de forma más precisa la construcción de un caso de obediencia, que de un caso de desobediencia, y sin embargo, no hubo diferencias significativas entre la construcción de un ejemplo de verdad y un ejemplo de mentira, lo cual suponía una dificultad intermedia. Esta interacción es difícil de explicar en términos de un módulo innato para el razonamiento deóntico. En el segundo experimento se examinó la ejecución de los niños en la tarea de selección completa. Tampoco se encontró ninguna ventaja en el razonamiento de los niños sobre obligaciones deónticas en comparación con el razonamiento sobre generalizaciones fácticas. Los niños a menudo cometían errores al seleccionar dos tarjetas de la misma categoría. Por lo tanto, los resultados sugieren una reconsideración de la tarea de selección reducida, en la cual los participantes tenían que elegir una sola categoría. Los resultados son interpretados en términos de la Teoría de los Modelos Mentales. Uno de los principios fundamentales de la Teoría de los Modelos Mentales es que la falsificación es el núcleo de nuestra capacidad para razonar. Los humanos somos racionales en principio, pero falibles en la práctica: cometemos errores porque se sobrestiman las posibilidades. Desde nuestro punto de vista, la capacidad para comprender las premisas, junto con la capacidad para buscar contraejemplos, da cuenta de los orígenes de la capacidad para razonar, tanto deóntica como fácticamente. Los contextos deónticos pueden hacer que los contraejemplos sean más salientes desde la perspectiva de uno de los protagonistas o del otro: el actor que impone la obligación, y el receptor sobre el que la obligación es impuesta. Del mismo modo, los contextos fácticos pueden hacer salientes a los contraejemplos cuando otros individuos son responsables de las afirmaciones que pueden chocar con las propias creencias de los individuos. La capacidad para construir modelos mentales y para buscar contraejemplos podría depender de qué es innato y qué adquirido, particularmente como resultado de las interacciones sociales. Una posibilidad saliente es que los niños aprendan a partir de otros individuos que hay modelos alternativos de la realidad aparte del suyo propio. Una vez que han captado la posibilidad de modelos alternativos, el siguiente paso en el dominio fáctico es comprobar cuál de los modelos es correcto. Y esta capacidad probablemente subyace a la búsqueda de contraejemplos en el razonamiento deductivo.

What is the origin of our ability to reason? The answer to this question is likely to depend on how we reason. If we rely on rules of inference akin to those of a logical calculus, it may be that the mechanism is innate. Likewise, if we rely on specialized modules for reasoning about life-and-death matters, then these modules could have evolved to meet the exigencies in the lives of our evolutionary ancestors. But, if reasoning depends on the ability to envisage situations and to test putative conclusions against them, then its origin could result from an interaction between innate and acquired components. It could depend in part on an innate component underlying the ability to conceive truth, falsity, permissibility, and other cognate matters. But, the ability to search for counterexamples could be acquired in part from interactions with other people.

Our aim in the present paper is to make progress in delineating the roots of reasoning, and we will do so by examining children's performance in two experiments. The first experiment tested their understanding of factual and deontic assertions, and the second experiment used Wason's (1966) selection task, which called for them to select the evidence relevant to the truth or falsity of factual assertions and to obedience or disobedience of deontic obligations.

In the classical version of the selection task (Wason, 1966), the participants select whichever of four cards should be turned over in order to find out whether a conditional assertion is true or false. They are invited to consider four cards laid out on a table with A, B, 2 and 3 uppermost, and they are told that the cards have a number on one side and a letter on the other side. The conditional to be tested is:

If there is an 'A' on one side of a card, then there is a '2' on the other side.

The participants tend to select either the A card alone, or the A and the 2 card. Surprisingly, they fail to select the 3 card, yet if it had an A on its other side, the conditional would be false. Because the selection task is sensitive to Bayesian considerations, some authors have argued that it does not call for deduction, and that the selection of A and 2 is rational (see Chater & Oaksford, 1999). The claim is premature. On the one hand, deductions can yield probabilistic conclusions, and such deductions can be accounted for by the model theory (Johnson-Laird, Legrenzi, Girotto, Legrenzi, & Caverni, 1999). On the other hand, Keith Stanovich (personal communication) has discovered that individuals who are more intelligent, as revealed by their performance on the SAT test, tend to be more likely to make the logically correct selections.

In contrast to the classical task, when the conditional lays down a deontic obligation, and the task is to choose potential violations, both adults and children tend to make the correct selections (see e.g. Johnson-Laird, Legrenzi, & Legrenzi, 1972; Griggs and Cox, 1983). A variety of deontic rules yield correct selections. They include abstract principles (Cheng & Holyoak, 1985), e.g.:

If one is to take action A, then one must first satisfy precondition P.

They include legal requirements (Griggs & Cox, 1983), e.g.:

If a person is drinking beer then that person must be over 19 years of age.

And they include everyday permissions (Manktelow & Over, 1991), as when a mother says to her son:

If you tidy your room then you may go out to play.

In all these cases, the participants tended to select those cards that were potential violations of the conditional principles.

There was also an effect of point of view. The preceding conditional, for example, is likely to elicit a biconditional interpretation:

If, and only if, you tidy your room then you may go out to play.

Strictly speaking, it is necessary to select all four cards in order to test for potential violations. But individuals may be reluctant to do so, because the selection task invites parsimony. Perhaps in consequence, as Manktelow and Over (1995) showed, there is a marked effect of the point of the view that the participants take towards the potential violations. The mother's concern is that her child does not cheat, and those participants told to take her point of view tended to select the cards:

Did not tidy   Went out to play

Her son's concern is that his mother does not renege on the deal, and those participants with his point of view tended to select the cards:

Tidied   Did not go out to play

Individuals who have a neutral point of view do indeed tend to select all four cards (Politzer & Nguyen-Xuan, 1992).

The nature of these phenomena is highly controversial. Cheng and Holyoak (1985) claimed that a deontic conditional maps onto a 'pragmatic reasoning schema' such as:

If the action (such as going out to play) is to be taken, then the precondition (such as tidying up the room) must be satisfied.

Cosmides (1989) proposed that there is an innate module for 'checking for cheaters'. But, Manktelow and Over (1995) argued against both these positions in favor of the theory of mental models. However, these authors also suggested that this theory underestimates the importance of probabilities, preferences, and pragmatic factors.

One important variant of the selection task is the 'reduced array' selection task (RAST) in which the participants make their selections only from two cards (Wason, 1968). With a conditional rule of the form:

If p then q

they have to choose which cards to select from a reduced array consisting of the q card and the not-q card. A striking discovery was that even children can get this version of the selection task right if it is framed deontically (see Girotto, Light, & Colbourn, 1988). Indeed, it was these investigators who first demonstrated the effects of point of view when they tested children (Light, Girotto, & Legrenzi, 1990). Recently, Cummins (1996) has reported that children as young as three years of age appear to be able to cope with the reduced array selection task. She replicated Girotto *et al's* results (1988) with 9- to 10-year old children, but she also showed that three- and four-year olds were more likely to adopt a violation-detection strategy when testing a deontic rule than when testing an indicative rule. Thus, she concluded that by the age of three, a distinction between reasoning about factual and deontic matters is already evident in children's reasoning strategies.

What accounts for the prodigious performance of children on the reduced array selection task? Evolutionary psychologists, such as Cosmides (1989), claim that the mind is divided into separate 'modules' specialized for different tasks. These modules evolved, they say, as adaptations to deal with the exigencies in the lives of our evolutionary forbears. Thus, there is supposedly a causal relationship between the adaptive problems that our ancestors repeatedly encountered during their evolution and the modules of the mind. For example, Cosmides proposed an innate module for reasoning about cheating, because social exchanges were important to the hunter-gatherers of the Pleistocene era. She corroborated this prediction in the study to which we referred earlier: when she used a selection task with contents concerning potential cheaters, most participants made the correct response.

Cummins (1996) goes further. She agrees that there are domain-specific reasoning strategies, and that they emerge early in development. But, in her view, the greatest selective pressure faced during the evolution of the mammalian reasoning system was the need to reason about dominance hierarchies and social interactions, not just potential cheating. And the ability to cope with such problems called for deontic reasoning. As a consequence, she argues that human beings, like their non-human ancestors, are equipped with an innate module for deontic reasoning.

Whatever the truth about innate modules for reasoning, the evolutionary theory is ambitious. It is also highly speculative, going well beyond the results of the psychological experiments deemed to support it. Indeed, there is a feasible alternative explanation for their results, and it is to such an account that we now turn.

THE MENTAL MODEL THEORY OF THE SELECTION TASK

Readers can find a more detailed account of the theory elsewhere in this book (see e.g. the chapter by Johnson-Laird), and so we will merely sketch the theory here. The theory postulates that individuals reason by envisaging the situations described by premises, i.e. they construct mental models of them, where each such model corresponds to a possibility (see e.g. Johnson-Laird & Byrne, 1991). They infer that a conclusion is necessarily true if it holds in all the models of the premises, that it is probably true if it holds in most of the models of the premises (granted that they are each equiprobable), and that it is possibly true if it holds in at least some model of the premises. The theory accordingly offers a unified account of deductive, modal, and probabilistic reasoning.

A central tenet of the model theory is the so-called 'principle of truth':

Individuals normally represent what is true, but not what is false, in order to keep the processing load on memory as light as possible. The model theory accordingly postulates that people normally represent a conditional of the form:

If there's an A then there's a 2

by constructing the following two mental models, each shown on a separate line:

A   2
    ...

The first model represents the possibility in which there is an A and a 2. The second model, the ellipsis, is a place holder with no explicit content. It corresponds to the possibilities in which the antecedent of the conditional (There's an A) is false. Reasoners make a mental footnote about the falsity of A in this case, but independent evidence shows that they soon forget these footnotes. The explicit model governs their performance of the abstract selection task. Hence, they tend to consider only the A and the 2 cards, and they fail to consider the 3 card.

The model theory predicts that any manipulation that overrules the principle of truth should improve performance in the selection task, i.e., any manipulation that emphasizes what would falsify a factual rule (the case of A and not 2 falsifies, 'If there's an A then 2') or violate a deontic rule. This prediction contrasts with those based on an innate module for deontic reasoning or on pragmatic reasoning schemas. In fact, such effects do occur, even in tasks that are neither deontic nor concern checking for cheaters (e.g. Wason & Green, 1984). Likewise, instructions to check for violations improved performance in the abstract task (Platt & Griggs, 1983; Griggs, 1995; Dominowski, 1995). Green (1995) showed that instructions to envisage counterexamples also improved performance (see also Green & Larking, 1995). In work that brings together the model theory and Bayesian considerations, Green, Over, and Pyne (1997) showed that reasoners' assessments of how likely they were to encounter a counterexample (in four stacks of cards) predicted their selections (see also Green, 1997). Sperber, Cara, and Girotto (1995) used a more indirect procedure to render counterexamples more relevant, and thereby improved performance. Love and Kessler (1995) used a context that suggested the possibility of counterexamples, and Liberman and Klar (1996) demonstrated that apparent effects of 'checking for cheaters' are better explained in terms of the participants' grasp of appropriate counterexamples and of the relevance of looking for them. Hence, poor performance on the selection task is probably attributable to a failure to consider what would be a counterexample to the conditional. A corollary of the preceding account is that deontic contexts improve performance on the selection task because they are more likely to induce reasoners to think about counterexamples.

AN EXPERIMENT ON THE COMPREHENSION OF FACTUAL AND DEONTIC CONDITIONALS

If the model theory is correct, then reasoning depends on the ability to understand the premises. Perhaps surprisingly, no other current theory of reasoning seems to be committed to this view. Reasoners cannot carry out the selection task, for example, if they do not understand the meaning of conditionals, whether factual or deontic. Our first experiment accordingly examined children's grasp of the meaning of conditionals. Their task was to construct examples and counterexamples of factual and deontic conditionals. Such a task, of course, transcends the mere ability to grasp the meaning, or truth conditions, of assertions. Yet, if children are unable to carry it out, the prospects for their performance in the selection task are surely dim. Granted the principle of truth, the model theory predicts that they should be more accurate in constructing true instances of conditionals than in constructing false instances of conditionals.

In the first experiment, we tested 72 Italian children in three different age groups (24 children in each group of 3 years, 4 years, and 5 years). Each child listened to the experimenter, who enacted two stories with puppets. After one story, the child carried out two construction tasks concerning a factual generalization in the story, and after the other story the child carried out two construction tasks concerning a deontic obligation in the story. We counterbalanced the order of the two stories; we also counterbalanced the content of the stories, making a factual and a deontic version of each of them.

Both stories were about two sorts of animals and their possible locations. Both versions of each story ended with a critical assertion made by a character in the story, e.g. Michele. For example, in the factual version of a story, Michele asserts:

Therefore, all the hens are in the house.

The child's first task is to answer the question:

Where are the hens if Michele is telling the truth?

The child has to put the animals in the appropriate place. The child's second task is to answer the question:

Where are the hens if Michele is lying?

In the deontic version of the story, Michele asserts:

Therefore, I made a rule. The rule is: all of the hens must stay in the house.

And in this case the questions put to the child are:

Where are the hens if they obey Michele?

and:

Where are the hens if they disobey Michele?

TABLE 15.1
The percentages of correct constructions in Experiment 1

Type of question	Type of story		Overall
	Factual	Deontic	
Truth/Obey	65	89	76
Lie/disobey	68	42	54
Overall	67	65	65

There was no significant difference in the accuracy with which the children answered the factual questions and the deontic questions (Wilcoxon test: $z = -.31$, $p > .7$). They were more accurate in answering questions about compliance than in answering questions about non-compliance (Wilcoxon test, $z = -3.21$, $p < .0002$). This corroborated a prediction of the mental model theory: it is easier to envisage what satisfies a description than what violates it. But, all three age groups showed the same reliable interaction: they answered questions about obeying more accurately than questions about disobeying (Wilcoxon test, $z = -4.57$, $p < .001$), whereas they did not differ in answering questions about truth and lies (Wilcoxon test, $z = -.29$, $p > .77$).

There was a reliable improvement in performance over the three age groups: three-year olds were correct on a mean of 2.2 questions (out of four), the four-year olds were correct on a mean of 2.5 questions, and the five-year olds were correct on a mean of 3.25 questions (Jonckheere trend test for independent groups, $z = 3.55$, $p < .0002$). The chance probability of responding correctly to the pair of questions following a story is .25. In the three-year old group, 6 children constructed both factual cases correctly and 4 children constructed both deontic cases correctly — a performance that is not significantly better than chance (Binomial tests with an *a priori* probability of .25 yield p >.5 for at least 6 cases and p >.88 for at least 4 cases). In the four-year old group, 8 children (p >.23) constructed both factual cases correctly and 7 children (p >.39) constructed both deontic cases correctly. In the five-year old group, 16 children (p <.00005) constructed both factual cases correctly and 15 children (p <.0005) constructed both deontic cases correctly; only the five-year old group produced pairs of correct constructions to both sorts of task significantly more often than one would expect by chance. Thus, the meanings of the metalinguistic terms ('truth' and 'lies') and the deontic terms ('obey' and 'disobey') are probably not mastered in full by many children until the age of five. Of course, our task calls for more than merely grasping the contribution of these terms to the truth conditions of sentences, and so skeptics could argue that children learn the meanings of these terms slightly earlier. Nevertheless, if they are from the population that we sampled and they have to reason on the basis of metalinguistic and deontic terms, they are unlikely to be successful until the age of five.

AN EXPERIMENT ON THE SELECTION TASK

In a second experiment, we examined the performance of children and adults in the full selection task. The participants had to carry out one factual and one deontic selection task. We tested three different age groups of Italian children (three-year olds, four-year olds and five-year olds) and one group of Italian adults (over the age of 21 years), with 24 participants in each group. Adults were invited to do exactly the same task as the children, with the same content. The experimenter acted out with puppets two stories similar to those of the previous study. The factual story culminated in the assertion, e.g.:

Therefore, all the hens are in the house

and the corresponding deontic story culminated in the assertion:

Therefore, all the hens must be in the house.

The four cards depicted a hen, a pig, the house, the yard. The participants were told that by turning a card with an animal on it they would discover its location, and that by turning a card with a location on it they would discover the animals in that location. After the factual story, the participants carried out two selection tasks, one framed as a test of whether the protagonist was telling the truth, and the other framed as a test of whether the protagonist was lying. After the deontic story, the participants carried out two selection tasks, one framed as a test of whether the animals obeyed the assertion, and the other framed as a test of whether they disobeyed the assertion. The order of the two selection tasks was fixed, but the order and contents of the two sorts of stories were counterbalanced.

We scored each participant's selections according to their correctness: +1 for each correct card, and –1 for each incorrect card, where the correct cards are p and not-q, given a rule of the form, if p then q. Table 15.2 summarizes the experimental results.

There was a reliable improvement in performance with age (Jonckheere trend test for independent groups, z = 4.38, p <<.00005). There was no overall advantage for deontic tasks over factual tasks (Wilcoxon test: z =.009, p >.46). But, the participants were marginally more accurate in testing for non-compliance than in testing for compliance (Wilcoxon test: z = 1.59, p =.056). On the assumption that a participant will always choose at least one card and never choose all four cards, then only the five year-olds and adults were more accurate in the tasks than one would expect by chance.

TABLE 15.2
The mean of correct responses in Experiment 2

Type of question	Type of story		Overall
	Factual	Deontic	
Truth/Obey	0.20	0.36	0.28
Lie/disobey	1.08	0.40	0.74
Overall	0.68	0.76	0.51

The children showed no overall advantage for the deontic tasks, but, as the model theory predicted, they did tend to be more accurate when asked to test for violations than to test for compliance. (There was no such effect for the adults). This pattern of results might also reflect the existence of an innate deontic module for testing for cheaters, because an individual who lies or disobeys is trying to cheat other people. But, this interpretation is overshadowed by a general characteristic of the children's performance. Their selections were driven by the main categories in the experiment, that is, they tended to select pairs of cards that corresponded either to the two sets of animals or to the two locations (see Figure 15.1).

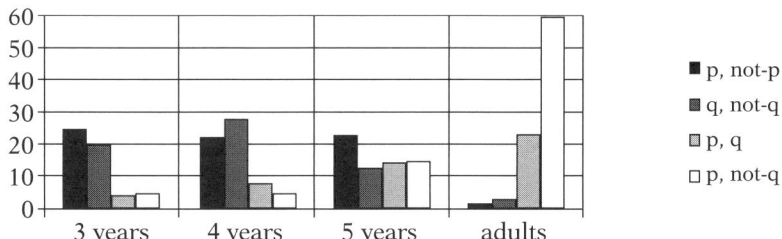

Figure 15.1. The main patterns of selections made by the four groups of participants in Experiment 2 (pooled over the different tasks).

Nearly two-thirds of the children made at least one selection of this sort. Such a pattern of performance obviously cannot be detected by a reduced array selection task, because the children then merely choose between the two locations. Hence, one implication of the present results is that children may perform the reduced array selection task correctly without a genuine insight into what they are doing. They could select the potentially falsifying instance without grasping that it is the one case that could refute the generalization.

Why did framing a selection task as a test of non-compliance yield a better performance than framing it as a test of compliance? The model theory argues that any manipulation emphasizing falsity should improve performance in the selection task. Another possible explanation is that the contrasting frames lead the reasoner to assume different perspectives on the task (Tom Ormerod, personal communication). This explanation is consistent with the effects of point of view, which we discussed in the introduction (see Manktelow & Over, 1991; & Politzer & Nguyen-Xuan,1992). In our opinion, the effects of point of view should be just as likely to occur with biconditionals that are not deontic (see the prediction in Johnson-Laird & Byrne, 1996). Two recent unpublished studies have corroborated this prediction (one carried out by Ken Manktelow and his colleagues, and the other independently carried out by Steve Sloman and his colleagues). Likewise, in our tasks, the 'obey' condition could focus the reasoner on the animals' point of view, and thus lead them to select the pair of cards, p and q. In contrast, the 'disobey' condition could focus the reasoners on the owner's point of view, and thus lead them to select the cards, p and not-q. Indeed, the children were more likely to select p and q in the complying conditions.

GENERAL DISCUSSION

Our first experiment showed that children were more accurate in constructing cases complying with an assertion than in constructing cases that did not comply with an assertion. The model theory predicted this result on the basis of its principle of truth: individuals normally represent what is true, not what is false. The results also showed a robust interaction: the participants were more accurate in constructing a case of obeying than a case of disobeying, whereas they did not differ reliably in constructing an instance of the truth than an instance of a lie. Why was the interaction so robust? One answer is that it arises from an idiosyncratic feature of the task, and that the construction of external instances is not a genuine measure of semantic competence. Yet, performance did improve with age, and so the task has some validity as a measure of competence. Another possibility is that the acquisition of the meaning of deontic and metalinguistic concepts is not a simple matter, and that it depends on complicated interactions between innate factors and social experience. We can certainly conclude that the interaction is difficult, if not impossible, to explain in terms of an innate module for deontic reasoning.

Our second experiment examined children's performance in the full Wason selection task. Once again, performance improved with age. And, once again, we failed to find any advantage for children in reasoning about deontic obligations as opposed to factual generalizations. A common error that the children made was to select two cards from the same category, either both the animals or both the locations. Because more than half the children made such an error, the results call for a re-appraisal of the reduced selection task in which the participants make a choice only within one category. Unless performance is clearly above chance, many participants may make the right response for the wrong reason, or indeed for no reason at all. For the other patterns of response, we suggested an interpretation in terms of the participants' point of view. However, such an interpretation holds just for the 5 year olds. An explanation in terms of point of view, however, does not in itself account for the mental processes underlying the choice of cards. Following the mental model theory, we suggest that a specific perspective focuses reasoners on the construction of examples or counterexamples relevant to a biconditional interpretation.

How might the ability to reason depend, in part, on social interactions? One salient possibility is that individuals learn from such interactions that there are alternative models of reality apart from their own. Once they have grasped the possibility of alternative models, the next step in the factual domain is to test which model is correct. And this ability is likely to underlie the search for counterexamples in deductive reasoning.

This account leads to the prediction that reasoners should be more likely to search for counterexamples to other people's conclusions than to their own. One phenomenon that is consistent with this prediction is an observation in our experiment on the full selection task. The context was one in which the participants had to test the beliefs or deontic views of a protagonist in the story. The results showed that the children did not differ in their ability to test factual beliefs or deontic obligations.

In our view, two main abilities account for the origins of the ability to reason (both deontically and factually): the ability to understand the premises, and the ability to search for counterexamples. Deontic contexts can make counterexamples salient from the point of view of one or other of the protagonist: the actor who imposes the obligation and the receiver on whom it is imposed. Factual contexts can make counterexamples salient when other individuals are responsible for the assertions. These assertions often clash with the reasoner's own beliefs.

A major tenet of the mental model theory is that falsification is at the core of our ability to reason. Humans are rational in principle, but fallible in practice: they err because they overlook possibilities. The ability to construct mental models and to search for counterexamples could depend both on what is innate and on what is acquired, particularly, as a result of social interactions. Various findings are consistent with this account Scholnick and Wing (1992), for example, found that young children's logical capacities in conversation are considerably greater than those reported in test situations. Such a Vygotskian argument that «the origin of logic is collaborative» is echoed in the findings by Dunn (1995). In a series of longitudinal studies she found out the significance of early emotion understanding for a range of developmental outcomes.

REFERENCES

CHATER, N., & OAKSFORD, M. (1999): «Ten years of rational analysis of cognition». *Trends in Cognitive Science, 3*, 57-65.

CHENG, P. W., & HOLYOAK, K. J. (1985): «Pragmatic reasoning schemas». *Cognitive Psychology, 17*, 391-416.

COSMIDES, L. (1989): «The logic of social exchange: has natural selection shaped how humans reason? Studies with the Wason selection task». *Cognition, 31*, 187-276.

CUMMINS, D. D. (1996): «Evidence of deontic reasoning in 3- and 4-year-old children». *Memory and Cognition, 24(6)*, 823-829.

DOMINOWSKI, R. L. (1995): «Content effects in Wason's selection task». In S. E. Newstead and J. St. B. T. Evans (Eds.), *Perspectives on Thinking and Reasoning: Essays in Honour of Peter Wason*, pp. 41-65. Hillsdale, NJ: Erlbaum.

DUNN, J. (1995): «Children as psychologists: The later correlates of individual differences in understanding of emotions and other minds». *Cognition and Emotion, 9*, 187-201.

GIROTTO, V., LIGHT, P., & COLBOURN, C. J. (1988): «Pragmatic schemas and conditional reasoning in children». *Quarterly Journal of Experimental Psychology, 40A*, 469-482.

GREEN, D. W. (1995): «Externalization, counter-examples and the abstract selection task». *Quarterly Journal of Experimental Psychology, 48A*, 424-446.

— (1997): «Hypothetical thinking in the selection task: amplifying a model-based approach». *Current Psychology of Cognition, 16*, 93-102.

GREEN, D. W., & LARKING, R. (1995): «The locus of facilitation in the abstract selection task». *Thinking and Reasoning, 1*,183-199.

GREEN, D. W., OVER, D., & PYNE, R. (1997): «Probability and choice in the selection task». *Thinking and Reasoning, 3*, 209-235.

GRIGGS, R. A. (1983): «The role of problem content in the selection task and in the THOG problem». In J. St. B. T. Evans (Ed.), *Thinking and reasoning: Psychological approaches*. London: Routledge & Kegan Paul.

— (1995): «The effects of rule clarification, decision justification, and selection instruction on Wason's abstract selection task». In S. E. Newstead and J. St. B. T. Evans (Eds.), *Perspectives on Thinking and Reasoning: Essays in Honour of Peter Wason*, pp. 17-39. Hillsdale, NJ: Erlbaum.

GRIGGS, R. A., & COX, J. R. (1983): «The elusive thematic materials effect in Wason's selection task». *Current Psychological Research and Reviews, 3*, 3-10.

JOHNSON-LAIRD, P. N., & BYRNE, R. M. J. (1991): *Deduction*. Hillsdale, NJ: Lawrence Erlbaum Associates.

JOHNSON-LAIRD, P. N., & BYRNE, R. M. J. (1996): «A model point of view: A comment on Holyoak and Cheng». *Thinking and Reasoning, 1*, 339-350.

JOHNSON-LAIRD, P. N., LEGRENZI, P., & LEGRENZI, M. S. (1972): «Reasoning and a sense of reality». *British Journal of Psychology, 63*, 395-400.

JOHNSON-LAIRD, P. N., LEGRENZI, P., GIROTTO, V., LEGRENZI, M., & CAVERNI, J-P. (1999): «Naive probability: a mental model theory of extensional reasoning». *Psychological Review*, in press.

LIBERMAN, N., & KLAR, Y. (1996): «Hypothesis testing in Wason's selection task: social exchange cheating detection or task understanding». *Cognition, 58*, 127-156.

LIGHT, P. H., GIROTTO, V., & LEGRENZI, P. (1990): «Children's reasoning on conditional promises and permissions». *Cognitive Development, 5*, 369-383.

LOVE, R., & KESSLER, C. (1995): «Focussing in Wason's selection task: Content and instruction effects». *Thinking and Reasoning, 1*,153-182.

MANKTELOW, K. I., & OVER, D. E. (1991): «Social roles and utilities in reasoning with deontic conditionals». *Cognition, 39*, 85-105.

— (1995): «Deontic reasoning». In S. E. Newstead and J. St. B. T. Evans (Eds.), *Perspectives on Thinking and Reasoning: Essays in Honour of Peter Wason*, pp. 91-114. Hillsdale, NJ: Erlbaum

PLATT, R. D., & GRIGGS, R. A. (1993): «Facilitation in the abstract selection task: The effects of attentional and instructional factors». *Quarterly Journal of Experimental Psychology, 46A*, 591-613.

POLITZER, G., & NGUYEN-XUAN, A. (1992): «Reasoning about conditional promises and warnings: Darwinian algorithms, mental models, relevance judgements or pragmatic schemas?» *Quarterly Journal of Experimental Psychology, 44*, 401-412.

SCHOLNICK, E. K., & WING, C. S. (1992): «Speaking deductively: Using conversation to trace the origins of conditional thought in children». *Merrill-Palmer Quarterly, 38*, 1-20.

SPERBER, D., CARA, F., & GIROTTO, V. (1995): «Relevance theory explains the selection task». *Cognition, 52*, 3-39.

WASON, P. (1966): «Reasoning». In B. M. Foss (Ed.), *New horizons in psychology* (pp. 135-151). Harmondsworth, UK: Penguin.

— (1968): «Reasoning about a rule». *Quarterly Journal of Experimental Psychology, 20*, 273-281.

WASON, P., & GREEN, D. W. (1984): «Reasoning and mental representation». *Quarterly Journal of Experimental Psychology, 36A*, 597-610.

16

THE EFFECTS OF RULE CLARIFICATION AND ATTENTIONAL FACTORS ON WASON´S ABSTRACT SELECTION TASK

ANTONIO CORRAL

Se han propuesto muchas explicaciones para dar cuenta de la dificultad que entraña la tarea de selección de Wason, especialmente en su versión abstracta (si «A» entonces «7»). Los sujetos tienen dificultades para acceder a las representaciones alternativas necesarias para resolver la tarea. Nuestro objetivo es facilitar el acceso a las representaciones implícitas. Con este fin manipulamos (1) el efecto de la clarificación de la regla (si «A» entonces «7» no supone si «7» entonces «A») con el objetivo bloquear la interpretación bicondicional y (2) el efecto de forzar a los participantes a pensar sobre la relevancia de la tarjeta «no q» ó sobre la irrelevancia de la tarjeta «q». El experimento 1 se diseñó para analizar el efecto de los factores atencionales (factor 2). Quienes recibieron la ayuda 2 aumentaron su porcentaje de selecciones de «no q» cuando eran centrados en esta tarjeta, y disminuyeron el porcentaje de elección de la tarjeta «q» cuando eran focalizados en esta tarjeta; aunque no aumentó el porcentaje de selección de las tarjetas «p» y «no q». Sin embargo en el experimento 2, los participantes que recibieron ambas ayudas (1 y 2, en este caso focalización en «no q») aumentaron el porcentaje de selecciones «p» y «no q» hasta llegar al 64.81%. La mejora no se produjo con la ayuda 1, esto es, el bloqueo del bicondicional.

INTRODUCTION

Various explanations (Garnham & Oakhill, 1994) have been proposed to account for the difficulty presented by Peter Wason's selection task, particularly in relation to the standard abstract form of the task (if «A» then «7», for example.).

Among the first explanations is *confirmatory bias*: we tend to confirm the hypothesis rather than rejecting it. This strategy in this task leads to a deficient performance. Later, Evans (Evans, Clibbens & Rood , 1996) suggested the *matching bias* model: the card with the letter A and the number 7 would be more likely to be chosen because it is explicitly named in the rule that must be tested. Other researchers (Cheng & Holyoak, 1985) suggest the so-called *pragmatic reasoning schemas*: in a great variety of deductive reasoning tasks that include the check hypothesis, people tend to use rules of inference according to the particular context. On the other hand, taking into account the effect of content in this task, Cosmides (1989) bases her explanations on *social contracts*: in social exchanges, if anyone obtains a benefit it is supposed that the other person will pay a cost for it. People will reason well in versions of the selection task in which the rule can be interpreted as a social contract. Another explanatory line related to the *formal rules theory* (Gebauer & Laming, 1997) states that logically incorrect answers are caused by incorrect comprehension of the rule that must be tested. Perhaps the most promising explanation is the *mental model theory*. According to this theory reasoners code the information established explicitly in the models, but leave other implicit possibilities.

Consider, as an example, the abstract version of the task:

There are four cards in front of you, with numbers and letters printed on them. When there is a letter on one side of the card, then there is always a number on the other side. You should check the following rule: If there is an «A» on one side of the card, then there is a «7» on the other side of the card. To test the rule, you must turn over cards. Please turn over only as many cards as you really must in order to be able to decide if the rule is true or false.

According to Johnson-Laird and Byrne (1991): «1: The subjects consider only those cards that are explicitly represented in their models of the rule, and 2: They then select those cards for which the hidden value could have a bearing on the truth or falsity of the rule». Thus, in the abstract version of Wason's four-card task (if «A» then «7»), subjects create an explicit pattern in which there is an «A» on one side and a «7» on the other (A/7), but not necessarily either of the other possibilities (B/2; B/7) or an explicit representation of the non-permitted combination (A/2)... unless such explicit representation is provided by some experimental manipulation».

This study tries to explore this possibility. We considered, first, that if the participants are forced to think about the «not-q» card, they may realize that it is relevant. The opposite must occur with the «q» card. Second, we considered that clarification of the rule can avoid subjects making a bi-conditional interpretation. We did not know whether either of these aids in isolation would be sufficient to achieve an explicit representation of the other combinations of cards, or whether both aids are necessary to enable the fleshing out of all the possible combinations.

General Hypotheses

The hypotheses were the following: First, the group that focuses on card «not q» («2») will increase its choice, and the group that focuses on card «q» («7») will decrease its choice (Study 1); second, reasoners who benefit from the two aids (1. Focus on «not-q» and 2. Clarification) will achieve a higher percentage of «not-q» («2») choices and a lower percentage of «q» («7») choices in comparison to the benefit obtained from only one aid or neither. These reasoners would also obtain a higher percentage of the combination: p, not-q («A», «2») than the other groups (Study 2).

According to these hypotheses, the manipulation was focused on two aspects: First, forcing some subjects, after seeing the four cards, to think only of card «2» (not-q), and others only of card «7» (q), with the aim of focusing their attention on these cards, thus helping them to understand the importance of card «2» (not-q) and the lack of importance of card «7» (q), respectively; and second, the effects of rule clarification (If «A» then «7» does not entail if «7» then «A»), with the aim of inhibiting bi-conditional interpretation.

EXPERIMENT 1

Ninety-two (92) second-year psychology students from the UAM participated voluntarily in this experiment. Three groups were formed, comprising, respectively, 30, 31 and 31 subjects: Group (1) (standard procedure) were faced with an abstract version of the task; Group (2) (Focus on «not-q», card «2») had to examine first the advisability of turning over (or not) card «not-q» («2»), and then that of all four cards, and Group (3) (focus on «q», card «7») had to examine first the advisability (or not) of turning over card «q» («7») and then that of turning over all four cards.

The instructions for each group were as follows: Group (1) were faced with an abstract version of the task:

A B 7 2

«If there is an A written on one side then there is a 7 written on the other side of the card». Your task consists in indicating which card or cards it is necessary to turn over to find out whether this rule is true».

Group (2) had to examine first the advisability of turning over (or not) card «not-q» («2») and then that of turning over all four cards:

A B 7 2

«Some people say it is essential to look at the other side of card 2 to prove the truth of the rule. However, others maintain that it is not essential to do so. What do you think? Is it necessary to turn over card 2 (yes or no) to find out whether the rule is true? Remember that only card 2 is considered in this case, so that we are not considering the possibility of turning over the rest of the cards».

Once this stage had been completed, subjects were given the following instructions: «Now you must make a decision about all the cards, and indicate which card or cards it is necessary to turn over to find out whether the rule is true«.

Group (3) had to examine first the advisability of turning over card «q» («7»), and then that of turning over all four cards. That is, the same as group (2) but with card «7» fulfilling the function of card «2».

Results

The average number of selections of card «not-q» increased when subjects focused on «2» (not-q), and the average number of selections of «7» (q) decreased when they focused on «7» (Table 16.1), but neither of the two approaches improved the average number of selections of «A» and «2» (p and not-q) (Table 16.2).

TABLE 16.1
Percentage of choice of each card according to the three conditions. The percentages of 34 experiments, summarized by Oaksford & Chater (1994), are also presented. Difference between standard and the others: * p<0.05 ** p=0.06

	Oaksford & Chater	Standard	Focus «not-q» («2»)	Focus «q» («7»)
Card «p»	89	86.66	74.19	77.41
Card «not-q»	25	30	51.61*	22.58
Card «q»	62	63.51	64.51	45.16**
Card «no p»	16	26.66	41.93	29.03

We can observe a change in the pattern of selections of the different combinations of cards in Group 3 (focus on «q»). The category «Others» improves significantly. The focus on card «q» appears to produce a superior fleshing out of the other possible combinations.

TABLE 16.2
Percentage of the different combinations of selected cards in the three experimental conditions. Differences between standard and the others: * p<0.05

	Standard	Focus «not-q» («2»)	Focus «q» («7»)
«p»	26.66	9.67	22.58
«p», «q»	30	19.35	25.80
«p», «no q»	0	6.45	0
All	16.66	29.03	6.45
«p», «q», «no q»	6.66	6.45	6.45
Others	20	29.03	41.93*

EXPERIMENT 2

The aim of this experiment was to explore the effects of rule clarification on task performance.

115 students from the Mathematics Faculty of the UCM, the Engineering and Computer Science Faculty of the UNED and the University of A Coruña participated voluntarily in this experiment.

Two groups were formed: Group I was made up of 61 participants and Group II comprised 54 participants: Group I (1, standard presentation; 2, focus on «not-q»; and 3, standard presentation) and Group II (1, standard presentation and explanation of the rule to block the bi-conditional interpretation; 2, focus on «not-q»; and 3, standard presentation with the explanation of the rule for blocking bi-conditional interpretation). The first and third pieces of paper were the same in the two groups.

Group I was first given an abstract version of the task; secondly, they had to examine the advisability of turning over card «not-q», card «2»; finally, they were again given the abstract version of the task. Three pieces of paper were presented:

(1st) Standard
A B 7 2
«If there is an A written on one side of the card, then there is a 7 written on the other side» You have to indicate which card or cards it is necessary to turn over to find out whether the rule is true.

(2nd) Focus on «not-q»
«Some people say it is essential to look at the other side of card 2 to prove the truth of the rule. However, others maintain that it is not essential to do so. What do you think? Is it necessary to turn over card 2 (yes or no) to find out whether the rule is true?

Remember that only card 2 is considered in this case, so that we are not considering the possibility of turning over the rest of the cards».

(3rd) Standard
«Now, on the basis of what you have just done, you must make a decision about all the cards, and indicate which card or cards it is necessary to turn over to find out whether the rule is true».

Group II were given, first, an abstract version of the task and the explanation of the rule to block the bi-conditional interpretation. They then had to examine the advisability of turning over card «not-q» («2») and, finally, they were given the abstract version with the explanation of the rule to block the bi-conditional interpretation. Three pieces of paper were presented:

(1st) Standard and explanation of the rule with the aim of blocking the bi-conditional interpretation
A B 7 2
«If there is an A written on one side of the card then there is a 7 written on the other side.

Remember that the rule only says that if a card has an «A» on side then it has a «7» on the other; it does not say the contrary, that is, if a card has a «7» on one side then it has an «A» on the other».

(2nd) Focus on «not-q»
The same as the second piece of paper of Group I.

(3rd) Standard with explanation of the rule
«Now, on the basis of what you have just done, you must make a decision about all the cards, and indicate which card or cards it is necessary to turn over to find out whether the rule is true».

Remember the rule only says that if a card has an «A» on one side then it has a «7» on the other; it does not say the contrary, that is, if a card has a «7» on one side then it has an «A» on the other».

Results

Participants that received both aids (1, Focus on «not-q» and 2, Clarification) increased the average number of selections «2» (not-q) to 72.22% and decreased the average number of selections «7» (q) to 7.40% (Table 3). Nevertheless, participants that received one aid (bi-conditional blockade or focus «not-q») performed more poorly.

TABLE 16.3
Percentage of selections for each of the four cards according to the different conditions

	Standard (n=61)	Biconditional Blockade (n=54)	Focus «not-q» («2») (n=61)	Biconditional blockade and Focus «not-q» («2») (n=54)
Card «p»	86.88	96.29	91.80	96.29
Card «not-q»	39.34	37.03	59.01*	72.22*
Card «q»	36.06	9.25	40.98	7.40*
Card «no p»	13.11	3.70	24.59	3.70

Standard: Answers given by Group I to the 1st piece of paper.
Biconditional blockade: Answers given by Group II to the 1st piece of paper.
Focus on «not-q»: Answers given by Group I to the 3rd piece of paper.
Biconditional blockade and Focus on «not-q»: Answers given by Group II to the 3rd piece of paper.
Differences between the standard and the others: * $p<0.01$.

Participants that received both aids (1, Focus on «not-q» and 2, Clarification) increased the average number of selections «A» and «2» (p and not-q) to 64.81%. Nevertheless, this improvement was less with only aid 1, blocking the biconditional (Table 16.4).

TABLE 16.4
Percentage of selections for each of the four cards according to the different experimental conditions

	Standard (n=61)	Biconditional Blockade (n=54)	Focus «not-q» («2») (n=61)	Biconditional blockade and Focus «not-q» («2») (n=54)
«p»	27.86	53.70	24.59	24.07
«p», «q	26.22	7.40	14.75	3.70
«p», «no q»	19.67	31.48	26.22	64.81*
All	3.27	1.85	19.67	1.85
«p», «q», «no q»	3.27	0	4.91	0
Others	19.67	5.55	9.83	5.55

Standard: Answers given by Group I to the 1st piece of paper.
Biconditional blockade: Answers given by Group II to the 1st piece of paper.
Focus on «not-q»: Answers given by Group I to the 3rd piece of paper.
Biconditional blockade and Focus on «not-q»: Answers given by Group II to the 3rd piece of paper.
Differences between the standard and the others: * $p<0.01$.

When participants received both aids (1, Focus on «not-q» and 2, Clarification) the selection of the combinations of the cards was reduced to two categories: «p» (24.07%) and «p» and «not-q» (64.81%). The other categories tended to disappear.

CONCLUSIONS

The data from Experiment 2 support Grigg's conclusions (1995): «the degree of facilitation [rule clarification] may vary not only with the type of explanation but also with the presence or absence of other factors». In this case, the focus on «not-q» appears to have some importance.

The inhibition of the bi-conditional interpretation would have facilitating effects, but these are not clearer than when it is combined with the focus on «not-q». Bi-conditional blocking does not in itself imply understanding of the importance of «not-q», though it does imply understanding of the unimportance of «q». The focus on «not-q» is only useful in helping reasoners to be «more coherent» with their trend of bi-conditional interpretation of the conditional rule, and thus to select the «not-q» card.

We have presented two aspects that contribute to explaining the pattern of answers observed in this task: (i) the trend to carrying out a bi-conditional interpretation, perhaps due to the coherence of this interpretation with a natural language context, which is more ambiguous than formal language, and (ii) the cognitive difficulty for considering the «not-q» card. We have achieved through these two manipulations (focusing and clarification), that is, without changing the content of the card and the formulation of the rule, that a very high percentage of subjects select the combinations (p, not-q).

There remains one doubt. The sample of participants from science courses obtained higher scores in the standard task than those achieved by the psychology students of Experiment 1. It would therefore be advisable to repeat Experiment 2 with non-science students.

It would also be interesting to design a new experiment for observing how the combination of bi-conditional blocking with focus on «q» may affect performance.

REFERENCES

CHENG, P. W., & HOLYOAK, K. J. (1985): «Pragmatic reasoning schemas», *Cognitive Psychology*, *17*, 391-416

COSMIDES, L. (1989): «The logic of social exchange has natural selection shaped how humans reason. Studies with the Wason selection task», *Cognition, 31*, 187-276.

EVANS, J.; CLIBBENS, & ROOD (1996): «The role of implicit and explicit negation in conditional reasoning bias». *Journal and Memory and Language, 35*, 392-409.

GARNHAM, A., & OAKHILL, J. (1994): *Thinking and Reasoning*. Oxford: Blackwell Publishers.

GEBAUER, G., & LAMING, D. (1997): «Rational choices in Wason´s selection task». *Psichological Research 60*, 284-293

GRIGGS, R. A. (1995): «The effects of rule clarification, decision justification, and selection instruction on Wason´s abstract selection task». En S. E. Newstead y J. Evans, *Perspectives on thinking and reasoning*. Hove: LEA

JOHNSON-LAIRD, P., & BYRNE, R. (1991): *Deduction*. Hove: LEA

OAKSFORD, M., & CHATER, N. (1994): «A rational analysis of the selection task as optimal data selection». *Psychological Review, 101*, 608-631

17

CONDITIONAL REASONING:
THE IMPORTANCE OF INDIVIDUAL DIFFERENCES

M.ª Dolores Valiña
Gloria Seoane
M.ª José Ferraces
Montserrat Martín

Uno de los temas que demanda mayor investigación en Psicología del Razonamiento es el estudio de las diferencias individuales. Uno de los objetivos de este trabajo es profundizar en el estudio de las diferencias individuales en la ejecución de la Tarea de Selección de Wason (Wason, 1966, 1968), con distintos contenidos e instrucciones experimentales.

Para ello se estudió la relación entre el rendimiento en diferentes tests psicométricos que evalúan distintas habilidades cognitivas (de comprensión verbal y razonamiento) y la ejecución con la tarea de las cuatro tarjetas. También se analizó si sujetos con puntuaciones extremas en la versión española de la Batería de Comprensión Lectora de Morton Gernsbacher, diferían en su ejecución con la tarea de selección.

Otro de los objetivos del trabajo era estudiar la influencia del contenido de la regla y de las instrucciones experimentales incluídas en la tarea sobre la ejecución. En este sentido, se trataba de averiguar si el contenido, las instrucciones, o ambos factores, influían de forma diferencial sobre la ejecución de los sujetos con puntuaciones extremas en varias pruebas psicométricas.

El experimento se realizó en dos fases. En la primera fase los sujetos realizaban las tareas psicométricas propuestas. En la segunda fase, cada sujeto era asignado aleatoriamente a uno de los dos grupos experimentales (instrucciones de verificación/falsación versus instrucciones de infracción). Todos los sujetos realizaban tres versiones diferentes de la tarea de selección (abstracta, temática-permiso y temática-obligación).

Los resultados obtenidos indicaron que las habilidades de razonamiento verbal eran mejor predictor de la ejecución con el problema de las cuatro tarjetas que las habilidades de comprensión. En concreto, los sujetos que habían obtenido las puntuaciones más altas en el test DAT-VR eran los que registraban los índices lógicos más elevados en la tarea de Wason. Esta relación no fue observada en las pruebas de comprensión.

Además, la ejecución lógica estaba modulada por el contenido de la regla y las instrucciones experimentales. En concreto, se registraron efectos principales significativos de ambos factores. Los índices lógicos más elevados se observaron en la versión temática que expresaba una obligación. Igualmente se registró la mejor ejecución en el grupo de sujetos que recibieron intrucciones de infracción de la regla. El efecto interactivo registrado entre ambos factores indicaba que en la versión temática que expresaba una obligación, los sujetos que recibieron instrucciones de violación de la regla eran los que registraban los índices lógicos más elevados.

Los resultados de este trabajo no son consistentes con las teorías formales de razonamiento y pueden ser explicados desde la Teoría de Modelos Mentales (Johnson-Laird, 1983; Johnson-Laird & Byrne, 1991) y desde la Teoría del Doble Proceso Heurístico-Analítico de Evans (1984, 1989).

INTRODUCTION

The study of thinking and reasoning is a topic of central interest for economists, anthropologists, logicians, pedagogues and of course for psychologists. A central problem in the experimental investigation in Psychology is to describe how people think and reason deductively and inductively.

There are three fundamental theoretical approaches to deductive reasoning in the Cognitive Psychology: mental logic, mental models and pragmatic schemas (see Evans, Newstead & Byrne, 1993, for a detailed review).

There are several proponents of a universal mental logic (Inhelder & Piaget, 1958) or natural logic (Braine, 1990; Braine & O'Brien, 1991; Rips, 1983, 1994). Other authors propose that reasoning is based on the construction and the evaluation of mental models (Johnson-Laird, 1983; Johnson-Laird & Byrne, 1991). A third approach asserts that reasoning is not based on general inference rules and assumes that people have domain-specific reasoning mechanisms such as pragmatic reasoning schemas inductively acquired (Cheng & Holyoak, 1985, 1989; Cheng, Holyoak, Nisbett & Oliver, 1986) or innate procedures for identify potential deviations from social contracts (Cosmides 1985, 1989).

Psychometrics studies thinking from a different perspective. The central interest for the researchers in Psychometrics is not the understanding of underlying cognitive processes and mental representations but the study of the individual differences in these mental processes.

However, despite the differences between these two approaches to the study of human reasoning the categorical syllogisms and linear syllogisms were included on early intelligence tests (Burt, 1919, 1921; Thurstone, 1938; Guilford, 1959). Moreover, in the past decades there is a novel and comparatively neglected field: the study of qualitative and quantitative differences in reasoning. Roberts (1993, p. 575) suggested that:

«The problem of individual differences is as follows: if a theory of reasoning is being proposed that is intended to describe the processes used by all people for all reasoning tasks, then what is the status of this theory if it is subsequently found that not all people are using the same processes?».

Galotti, Baron and Sabini (1986) examined the correlates of reasoning ability on a syllogistic reasoning task. They found evidence for the use of both models and rules of reasoning. In a previous work Sternberg and Weil (1980) found individual differences in reasoning strategies (a mental model strategy, a deduction rule strategy and a mixture of both) in the resolution of experimental tasks that involve linear syllogisms.

Alternatively, Sternberg and Gastel (1989) investigated information processing during the solution of inductive reasoning problems (analogies, classifications and series completions) and also administered five psychometric tests to each subject. They show correlations between experimental tasks and psychometric tests. These correlations address two principal questions. First, are scores on the experimental tasks related to scores on the psychometric tests? Second, do the correlations with the reasoning tests differ from those with verbal/perceptual factor? It was found that the correlations of the experimental task with the reasoning tasks are higher than those with verbal/perceptual tasks. Thus, *«the experimental tasks do appear to tap abilities related to those tapped by the psychometric tests»* (p. 8).

Despite the importance of conditional reasoning in daily life, the study of qualitative individual differences has not become a central focus on cognitive or psychometric studies. There is nearly no previous experimental research about this issue.

Valiña and de Vega (1986) studied the relation between attentional resources allocation in cognitive tasks and the scores obtained in different psychometric tests. The authors observed a significant relation between attentional capacity and the scores in a verbal reasoning test (DAT-VR). In a later study, Valiña, Seoane, Ferraces and Martín (1995) found that the mentioned test was a good predictor for performance on a reasoning task: Wason's Selection Task. The possible relation between two comprehension tasks (PMA-V and Gernsbacher's Battery Comprehension) and subjects' performance on the four card problem was also analyzed in this work. None of both tasks seemed to be related to selection task performance.

In the present experiment we also explore the relation among different measures in psychometric ability tests (verbal comprehension and reasoning) and the performance on this experimental conditional reasoning task.

THE EXPERIMENTAL TASK

The Wason selection task is one paradigm widely used for studying conditional reasoning. The original problem was elaborated by Wason (1966, 1968). He presented a conditional rule *«every card that has a vowel on one side has an even number on the other»* and four cards: E, K, 4 and 7. The subjects' task is to decide which cards should be turned over to test the conditional rule.

Frequently, the subjects only selected the E card (p) or the E and 4 cards (p and q). The correct response is the selection of the E and 7 cards (p and *not-q*), but only 5-10% of the subjects chose these cards. The subjects selected a case for which the rule is true, but it is a negative instance which provides a violating case and can prove the truth or the falsity of the rule.

We have researched the role of knowledge using different experimental paradigms (see for example Valiña, Seoane, Ferraces & Martín, 1997, 1999). Nevertheless, in this study we selected the Wason Selection Task basically because it has long been of interest to experimental psychologists (see Evans, Newstead & Byrne, 1993; Newstead & Evans, 1995, for recent revisions) and moreover because it is one of the most widely used paradigms for studying the importance of factors related to the role of knowledge in reasoning (Wason & Shapiro, 1971; Johnson-Laird, Legrenzi & Legrenzi, 1972; Pollard & Evans, 1987; Girotto, Gilly, Blaye & Light, 1989; Valiña, Seoane, Ferraces & Martín, 1995,1998; Santamaría, García-Madruga & Carretero, 1996, among others).

We specially examined the following issues in this paper: (1) the relation among different measures in psychometric ability tests (verbal comprehension and reasoning), the computerised measure of comprehension skills and the subjects' performance in the experimental task of conditional reasoning, (2) whether or not good and poor comprehenders systematically differ in their performance in Wason's selection task (Wason, 1966, 1968) and (3) the differential influence of rule content and instructions on the subjects´ performance in the selection task.

METHOD

Participants

One hundred and fifty-four undergraduates (20 males, 134 females; mean age 21 years), studying Psychology at the University of Santiago de Compostela (Spain) participated in this study. The students took part as partial fulfillment of a course requirement. They had not participated in similar experiment and none had any prior training in formal logic.

Data from 18 participants were not used because they failed to follow the experimental instructions or they had not completed all the task.

Materials and apparatus

1. Psychometric tests

The participants completed three Spanish versions of three psychometric ability tests: PMA-V, PMA-R and DAT-VR.

PMA-V: The aim of this task is to evaluate the capacity to understand ideas expressed in words. This task includes fifty multiple-choice problems. Participants have four minutes to select one of the words proposed as possible synonymous with each item.

PMA-R: The purpose in this case is to assess subjects' capacity to solve logic problems and to foresee and plan. Subjects have six minutes to complete thirty problems which consist of finding out the logic sequence for a series of letters and choose which would be the next appropriate letter.

DAT-VR: This test is applied in order to evaluate subjects' ability to understand concepts expressed through words and employ them to generalize and think in a constructive way. The task consists of fifty incomplete sentences. There are two words missing in each sentence, the first one and the last one. Participants have fifteen minutes to complete the sentences in the way they are meaningful by choosing the correct pair of words from among five alternatives.

2.   Gernsbacher's Battery Comprehension

The Spanish version of the Battery was presented on a DX-486 computer using a computer program elaborated by Manuel de Vega, of the University of La Laguna (Spain). The aim of this program is to find out the participants' comprehension skills. The program presented 4 narrative texts with times of exposition on the screen of 3,5 seconds for each sentence. The subjects read sentences that were presented sentence-by-sentence on the computer monitor. After the last sentence of each story disappeared, a test of five alternative-questions about each experimental text appeared. The presentation times of each question about the story were of 20 seconds. The participants' task was to select as rapidly and as accurately as possible the correct alternative that occurred in the text they had just finished reading. Finally, the program presented the next text 15 seconds after the final response of the subject.

The program registered both the correct responses and the reaction times of the participants to the questions about the stories.

3.   Selection task

Each subject received three rules, with the following types of content: abstract, thematic-permission and thematic-obligation. Half of the subjects received true-false instructions and the other half violation instructions. The test booklets were used in previous investigations (Martín, 1996; Valiña, Seoane, Ferraces & Martín, 1996, 1998). The information for each of the three tasks was as follows:

*a)   **Abstract selection task**. «If a Wasit card has an A on one side, then it must have a 3 on the other».

The four cards presented to the subjects were: «A», «K», «3» and «7».

*b)   **Thematic-permission**. In this rule a law was expressed; therefore it is similar to a permission. The rule was: «If a person is more than 18 years old, then he has the right to vote».

The four cards said: «20 years old», «16 years old», «you have the right to vote» and «you do not have the right to vote».

c) ***Thematic-obligation***. The rule expressed a traffic regulation: «If a person rides a motorbike, then they must wear a helmet».

The four cards that were represented were: «motorbike», «car», «helmet» and «cap».

The instructions were used previously (Chrotowski & Griggs, 1985; Yachanin, 1986; Valiña et al, 1995, 1996, 1998).

In the **true-false version**, the instructions were:

«Your task consists of selecting cards and only those that must be turned over to decide if the rule is true or false (select those cards which you consider necessary to turn over to check if the person carrying out the experiment has lied or not in relation to the composition of the rule)».

For the **violation version**, the instructions were:

«Your task consists of selecting only those cards that must be turned over in order to decide if the rule is being violated or not».

Two different versions were made for each of the types of booklets. In one of these the thematic versions were at the beginning, followed by the abstract rule and in the other the abstract version was included at the beginning. Additionally, the order of presentation of the two thematic versions was counterbalanced.

Procedure

Participants met in groups of up to 12 with two experimenters over 2 days. On the 1st day they received in the laboratory both the psychometric tests with conventional instructions and the Spanish version of the Gernsbacher's Battery Comprehension. Subjects were tested with each interacting on a separate microcomputer in the same laboratory.

On the 2nd day of the experiment, participants were assigned at random to each of the two experimental groups: (1) true-false instructions and (2) violation instructions. Subjects were tested in groups of 12. Each subject received a booklet with instructions on the first page, followed by three selection tasks (an abstract task and two thematic ones). The instructions were read to the subjects and questions were solicited to ensure that they understood the instructions. Finally, they were instructed to work at their own rhythm, without time limit.

RESULTS

We performed ANOVAs 2 x 3 (instructions x content) to test the differential influence of rule content and instruction on subjects' performance in the selection task (Wason, 1966, 1968). These analyses were carried out with the data from the 136 subjects, once those who had not completed the task had been eliminated.

The logical and matching indices were calculated for each of the three tasks. Both indices vary between +2 and –2, according to Pollard and Evans (1987)[1]. The logical index was computed for each attempted solution to each problem by adding a score of one for each correct *p* or *not-q* selection made and subtracting one for each incorrect *not-p* or *q* selection made. The matching index was computed by adding a score of one for each *p* or *q* selection made and subtracting one for each *not-p* or *not-q* selection. Now we are going to present the main results obtained with both indices.

a)   Logical Index

Subjects obtained higher logical indices in the thematic-obligation version (*M*=.765), followed by the abstract rule (*M*=.449). The lowest logical indices were registered in the thematic version which expressed a permission (*M*=.154). These differences were significant ($F_{(1.82; 244.52)} = 21.61$; $p < .0001$; $\varepsilon = .912$).

Similarly, the logical indices were higher in those subjects who received violation instructions (*M* =.87) compared with those who received true-false instructions (*M* =.31). These differences were statistically significant ($F_{(1, 134)} = 6.59$; $p < .011$).

Figure 17.1 shows the interaction between instructions and content. When the subjects reasoned with the abstract task, no differences were registered between the two types of experimental instructions. However, in the thematic versions of the task, the subjects presented higher logical indices with the violation instructions (*M*=.233) than with the true-false instructions (*M*=.063).

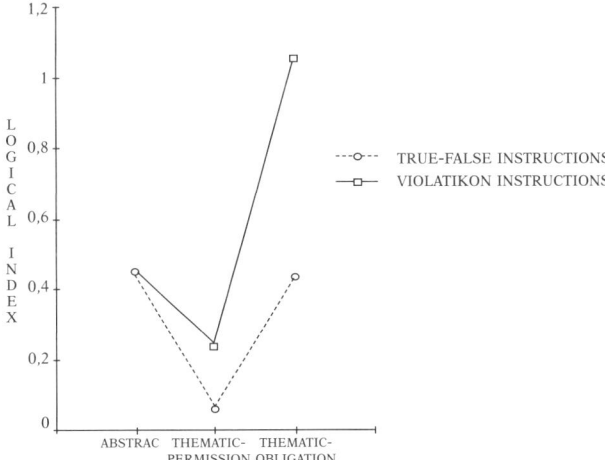

Figure 17.1. Interactive effects between instructions and content in the logical index.

---

[1]   Unfortunately, we had not heard of the Antecedent Matching Index, the Consequent Matching Index nor the more recent version of the Directionality Index (see Evans, Legrenzi & Girotto, 1999, pp. 206-207). Posterior analyses of these data will, undoubtedly, provide us with very relevant information.

This difference in the logical indices between the two groups of instructions was greater in the thematic task which expressed an obligation, (M= 1.05 for the violation instructions group and M=.429 for the checking instructions group). Moreover, this interaction between instructions and content was statistically significant ($F_{(1.82; 244.52)}$ = 6.32; p <.003; ε =.912).

b) Matching index

A significant main effect of the content was found ($F_{(2, 268)}$ = 25.64; p <.0001). Specifically, the highest matching indices were obtained with abstract content (M = 1.11), followed by the thematic-obligation (M =.897) and the thematic-permission (M =.375). The abstract content differs significantly from the other groups ($F_{(1,134)}$ = 24.42; p <.0001) and similarly the thematic-permission version differs significantly from the thematic-obligation content ($F_{(1, 134)}$ = 26.97; p <.0001) by orthogonal tests.

Participants obtained higher matching indices with instructions for checking the rule (M = 1.042) compared to those who received violation instructions (M =.58). This effect of the instructions was also significant ($F_{(1, 134)}$ = 11.31; p <.001).

Finally, analyses with groups of subjects who had extreme scores in three psychometric ability tests: PMA-V, PMA-R and DAT-VR and the Gernsbacher´s Battery Comprehension, were performed. Thus, ANOVAs group (good vs. poor verbal comprehenders / good vs. poor reasoners) x instructions (violation vs. true-false) x content (abstract, thematic-permission and thematic-obligation), with repeated measures on the last factor were performed with both indices.

In terms of differential analyses, there were no differences in the logical and matching indices between good and poor verbal comprehenders (PMA-V & Gernsbacher's Battery Comprehension) or subjects with high and low scores in the PMA-R. Nevertheless there were significant differences between good and poor reasoners (DAT-VR).

The logical index was considerably better (M = 1.131) in the higher reasoning-verbal group vs. the group with low scores in the DAT-VR (M =.386). The differences were significant ($F_{(1, 70)}$ = 8.52; p <.005).

There were no differences in the matching index of good reasoners in function of the experimental instructions. However, the subjects with low scores in the DAT-VR obtained higher matching indices with instructions for checking the rule (M= 1.23) than the subjects who received violation instructions (M=.27). In Figure 17.2, the significant interaction between group and instructions is shown ($F_{(1,70)}$= 5.02; p <.028).

c) Correlations between the experimental task
   and the psychometric tests scores

We performed another analyses in order to provide a test of the relation among different measures in verbal and comprehension psychometric tests, the computerised measures of comprehension skills and subjects' performance

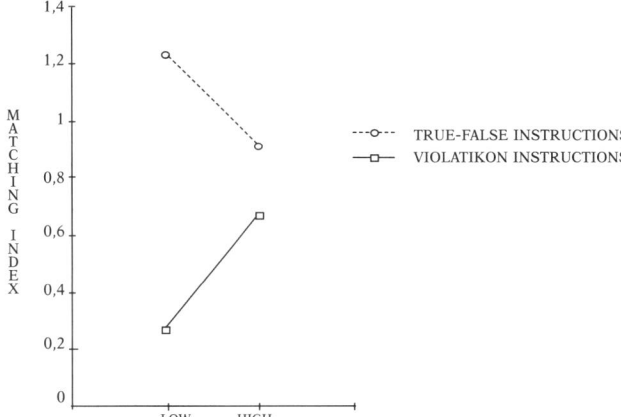

Figure 17.2. Interactive effects between group and instructions in the matching index.

in the experimental task with the logical index. The analyses were carried out (a) with the data from the total of 136 subjects and (b) with de data from the two experimental groups (true-false instructions and violation instructions).

The results showed for the total sample (N = 136) that: (a) the scores of the DAT-VR were related with the performance in Wason's selection task with the abstract content (r =.317; p <.0001) and with the thematic-permission rule (r =.266 ; p <.002) in terms of the logical index and (b) there was a significant relation between the scores in the DAT-VR psychometric test and the computerised measures of Gernsbacher's Battery Comprehension (r =.166; p <.05). (See Table 17.1).

With the **true-false instructions** (N = 63) there was found a significant relation between scores in the DAT-VR and the logical index (r =.352; p <.005)

TABLE 17.1
Correlation matrix for the total sample (N=136)

	PMAV	**PMAR**	**DATVR**	**GEBAT**	**ALI**	**T1LI**	**T2LI**
PMAV							
PMAR	.298***						
DATVR	.322***	.452***					
GEBAT	.047	.138	.166*				
ALI	.087	.157	.317***	.165			
T1LI	.102	.078	.266**	.013	.363***		
T2LI	.009	.076	.073	−.002	.318***	.099	

*** 0.001 level of significance (two-tailed)
** 0.01 level of significance (two-tailed)
* 0.05 level of significance (two-tailed)

PMAV- PMA Verbal Reasoning factor; PMAR- PMA Abstract Reasoning factor; DATVR- DAT Verbal Reasoning factor; GEBAT- Gernsbarcher's Battery; ALI- Abstract, Logical Index; T1LI- Thematic-permission, Logical Index; T2LI- Thematic-obligation, Logical Index.

with the abstract content. There was also a significant relation between measures in the Gernsbacher's Battery Comprehension and the logical index for this abstract content ($r = .286$; $p < .023$). (See Table 17.2).

TABLE 17.2
Correlation for the true-false instructions group (N=63)

	PMAV	PMAR	DATVR	GEBAT	ALI	T1LI	T2LI
PMAV							
PMAR	.270*						
DATVR	.297*	.488***					
GEBAT	.117	.132	.144				
ALI	.210	.232	.352**	.286*			
T1LI	.074	−.047	.013	.067	.427***		
T2LI	−.031	.182	−.096	.111	.203	−.141	

*** 0.001 level of significance (two-tailed)
** 0.01 level of significance (two-tailed)
* 0.05 level of significance (two-tailed)

PMAV- PMA Verbal Reasoning factor; PMAR- PMA Abstract Reasoning factor; DATVR- DAT Verbal Reasoning factor; GEBAT- Gernsbarcher's Battery; ALI- Abstract, Logical Index; T1LI- Thematic-permission, Logical Index; T2LI- Thematic-obligation, Logical Index.

With the **violation instructions** (N = 73) there was a significant relation between measures in the DAT-VR and the logical index for the abstract content ($r = .294$; $p < .012$) and the thematic-permission content ($r = .432$; $p < .0001$). (See Table 17.3).

TABLE 17.3
Correlation for the violation instructions group (N=73)

	PMAV	PMAR	DATVR	GEBAT	ALI	T1LI	T2LI
PMAV							
PMAR	.324**						
DATVR	.353**	.427***					
GEBAT	−.003	.145	.190				
ALI	−.012	.091	.294*	.075			
T1LI	.130	.176	.432***	−.019	.313**		
T2LI	.057	−.007	.109	−.053	.433***	.207	

*** 0.001 level of significance (two-tailed)
** 0.01 level of significance (two-tailed)
* 0.05 level of significance (two-tailed)

PMAV- PMA Verbal Reasoning factor; PMAR- PMA Abstract Reasoning factor; DATVR- DAT Verbal Reasoning factor; GEBAT- Gernsbarcher's Battery; ALI- Abstract, Logical Index; T1LI- Thematic-permission, Logical Index; T2LI- Thematic-obligation, Logical Index.

GENERAL DISCUSSION AND CONCLUSIONS

Interesting results were obtained in this experiment:

- Effect of the problem content was obtained in both, the logical and matching indices. The best performance was registered with the thematic-obligation rule. The lowest logical index was obtained with the thematic-permission version. Moreover, the highest matching index was observed with the abstract rule and the lowest with the thematic-permission content. To sum up, the logical indices in the three types of content were, from high to low: (a) Thematic-obligation, (b) Abstract, (c) Thematic-permission. Also, the matching indices were, from high to low: (a) Abstract, (b) Thematic-obligation, (c) Thematic-permission. The results of the present study confirm the results obtained, with both indices, in a previous work (Valiña *et al.*, 1998).
- Effects of the experimental instructions were also registered in the logical and matching indices. Participants who received the violation instructions obtained the highest logical indices. However, subjects who reasoned with the true-false instructions registered the highest matching indices.
- In the logical index, the interaction observed between instructions and content showed that in the thematic-obligation task, higher indices were obtained in those subjects who reasoned with the violation instructions.
- Significant differences were not registered in the selection task performance between the subjects with high and low scores in PMA-V and Gernsbacher´s Battery Comprehension.
- The DAT-VR test was a good predictor for the performance with the four card problem. The logical index was considerably better in the higher reasoning verbal-group. Moreover, in the lowest reasoning verbal-group, the matching indices were higher with the instructions for checking the rule.

The results obtained in this work support the influence of the thematic factors on subjects´ ability when they performed the Wason selection task. However, this facilitating effect of the thematic content does not seem to be as simple as pointed out in previous works. In fact, only when the subjects were presented with the thematic rules which expressed an obligation, they registered logical indices superior to abstract ones; nevertheless, when they reasoned with the thematic rules which expressed a permission, the logical indices registered were inferior to the formal version of the task.

It is difficult to explain this result from formal theories which defend that subjects´ reasoning is based on syntactic rules. Neither does the Theory of Pragmatic Schemas (Cheng & Holyoak, 1985, 1989; Cheng *et al.*, 1986; Holyoak & Cheng, 1995), allow us to explain the differences in the performance between the two thematic versions of the task. However, the Theory of Mental Models (Johnson-Laird, 1983; Johnson-Laird and Byrne, 1991), and the Heuristic-Analytic Theory of Evans (1984, 1989) can explain the empirical results of this investigation.

To be exact, if the subjects reason elaborating representations (or mental models) from the information contained in the premises and their knowledge of the world, as is defended by the Mental Models Theory; the deontic or indicative character of the conditional relation can be modulating the number of mental models necessary to generate a conclusion. Particularly, when they reason working from an indicative conditional (as is the thematic-permission version in our work), subjects tend to represent an explicit model (which satisfies the rule) and an implicit one (which contemplates the possibility that the statement does not occur). However, when they reason with a conditional deontic rule (as in the thematic-obligation version or the abstract version), they show a tendency to generate the conclusion from a unique mental model which would represent what is permissible (see for example Byrne & Johnson-Laird, 1990; Johnson-Laird & Byrne, 1992; Bell & Johnson-Laird, 1998).

In this sense, the least number of mental models necessary to generate the conclusion with conditional deontic statements, could explain the high logical indices registered in the thematic-obligation version in our work, and even in the abstract version, (which included a deontic modal verb), versus the thematic-permission, which presented an indicative conditional statement. Manktelow and Over (1991) established an explanation based on the elaboration of mental models and the importance of two factors: (1) the inclusion of deontic terms in the rule and (2) the influence of perspective to explain the best participants´ performance with the selection task.

On the other hand, the highest matching indices have been registered in the abstract version followed by the thematic content which expressed an obligation. In this sense, our results seem to show that the mere presence of thematic content does not always improve the performance and neither does it necessarily reduce or eliminate their matching answers. The Theory of Mental Models explain these high matching indices on the assumption that the subjects only represent *explicitly* in their models the card values mentioned in the rule. According to the Heuristic-Analytic Theory, the poor performance and the high matching indices registered in the abstract version of the task, are due to the attention subjects focus towards those cards mentioned in the rule.

These results, which reflect the influence of subjects´ knowledge in reasoning, are on the same line to the ones we have obtained in previous works, by using different experimental paradigms: (a) with the Wason Selection Task (Valiña *et al.*, 1995, 1996, 1998), (b) using conditional statements included in texts (Valiña *et al.*, 1997), or (c) with decontextualized conditional statements (Valiña, Seoane, Gehring, Ferraces & Fernández-Rey, 1992; Valiña, Seoane, Martín, Fernández-Rey & Ferraces, 1992; Valiña *et al.*, 1999).

Another relevant aspect in this work is related to the results obtained with regard to the influence of the experimental instructions on subjects´ performance with the selection task. According to Johnson-Laird and Byrne (1991, pp. 80-81, 1992, 1993), any manipulation of the rule which tends to focus the attention towards counter-examples of the rule should be improve subjects´ attention.

In this sense, we have registered in the logical index a significant main effect of the instructions, as the performance in those subjects who received the violation instructions were better than the performance observed in those subjects who had to reason with the true-false instructions. Apart from this, the logical indices were much higher in those participants who received the violation instructions when they reasoned with the thematic-obligation content. In the matching index, the main effect of the type of instructions showed that the subjects who received true-false instructions obtained the highest indices.

According to Yachanin and Tweney (1982), the facilitation effect of the violation instructions is related to the nature of the task. With the true-false instructions, the truth status of the rule is assessed. This version requires participants to assess the truth status of an hypothesis (reason *about* a rule). In the violation version, the rule is given as true and subjects have to select the card or cards that definitely need to be turned over to determine whether or not the rule has been violated (reason *from* a rule). Consequently, as Tweney and Doherty (1983) claimed, the cognitive load is greater and therefore will increase the difficulty of the task with the true-false instructions.

As Platt and Griggs (1993) claimed, the violation instructions can guide the subjects towards the selection of the cards which break the rule (or in terms of the Theory of Mental Models, to include the card *not-q* in the explicit model). Along these lines, the true-false instructions of the rule could be increasing the tendency of the subjects to elicit verification strategies and, therefore, in our case, to develop the observed matching strategy. Platt and Griggs (1995) obtained similar results and they interpreted them in terms of the Theory of Mental Models and the Theory of Heuristic-Analytic. According to the Heuristic-Analytic Theory, the violation instructions «*may produce their effects via the attentional mechanisms involved in the task. They put more emphasis on the not-q card and make the subject more likely to encode it as relevant*» (Platt & Griggs, 1995, p. 57). In terms of the Theory of Mental Models, the violation instructions lead subjects to flesh-out more easily the explicit representation of «*p and not-q*».

Apart from analyzing the influence of the content and the experimental instructions in the Wason selection task, another of the objectives which we wish to achieve in this work was to study the possible existence of differentiating strategies in the selection task performance between the extreme groups of each one of the psychometric test used, or as Roberts (1993) claims, the possible existence of individual qualitative differences.

From different perspectives, it has been previously accounted for the importance of studying individual differences in reasoning and the possible difficulty for explaining these individual differences from different universal reasoning theories (see for example Legrenzi, Girotto & Johnson-Laird, 1993; Evans, Newstead, Allen & Pollard, 1994; Roberts, 1993; Torrens, Thompson & Cramer, 1999).

The purpose of this work was to examine individual differences in a metainference task: the four card problem. The main theoretical explanations on selection task performance are the Theory of Mental Models and the Heuristic-Analytic Theory (but see Evans, Legrenzi & Girotto, 1999, for a recent review).

The Mental Models Theory (Johnson-Laird and Byrne, 1991, p. 79), have argued that: *The subjects consider only those cards that are explicitly represented in their models of the rule.*

(1)   They then select from those cards for which the hidden value could have a bearing on the truth or falsity of the rule.

According to this theory, any manipulation that leads to the fleshing out of the models of the conditional with explicit representation of the card corresponding to the negated consequent, will tend to yield insight into the task (Johnson-Laird, 1995 Johnson-Laird & Byrne, 1995).

From Evans´ Dual Process Theory (1984, 1989, 1995, 1996), people reason analytically about problem information that is preconsciously selected as *relevant* at a prior heuristic stage. He has argued that in the selection task analytic reasoning does not alter the choices made and serves only to rationalise or confirm them. Recently, the author reported that *«responses reflect only heuristic judgements of relevance and the analytic reasoning processes do not come in to play»* (Evans, Legrenzi, & Girotto 1999, p. 189).

In an investigation of individual differences in reasoning (Stanovich & West, 1998), they recorded an improved performance in different thematic and deontic versions, compared to abstract and indicative versions. However, they found that the small number of participants who performed correctly the indicative versions of the task, had a significantly high «g» factor level of general intelligence than those who failed. By contrast, there was no relationship between intelligence and success on deontic versions of the task.

These results could be interpreted within the dual process framework (Evans & Over, 1996, 1997). As Evans (1998) suggested, abstract and indicative selection tasks could require rationality$_2$ and the application of conscious hypothetical reasoning. This explicit thinking system could be related to «g» (general intelligence factor). On the other hand, performance on deontic selection tasks could require rationality$_1$ and depends upon the use of the implicit and preconscious system which is independent of «g».

In this experiment no differences were registered, in the logical and matching indices, between the groups with the extreme scores in the tests PMA-V, PMA-R and Gernsbacher´s Battery Comprehension. Nevertheless, significant differences were found between the good and the poor reasoners, keeping in mind that DAT-VR scores, registering superior logical indices in the group with the high scores. In the matching index, no differences were registered with regard to the instructions in the group of subjects who obtained the highest scores in the DAT-VR, nevertheless we registered significant differences in the group with low scores. Specifically, the matching indices in the group with low scores were higher with the true-false instructions.

Our results confirm the importance of the experimental instructions similar to the idea claimed by Tweney and Doherty (1983) and Platt and Griggs (1995). So, the true-false instructions require greater attentional capacity. This is reflected empirically in both a lower performance in the subjects with low scores in the DAT-VR as the higher matching indices in the condition of the true-false instructions. Our work shows empirical evidence of the differential attentional capacity in the performance with the selection task both in the abstract content and in different types of thematic content, in line with previous investigations (Hunt *et al.*, 1979; Hunt, 1980; Valiña & De Vega, 1986).

Moreover, if we establish a comparative analysis among the results obtained in this investigation with an earlier work which we carried out in the field of individual differences in reasoning, we can observe that the test DAT-VR seems to be a good predictor for the performance on the experimental tasks not only in conditional reasoning (see Seoane, Valiña, Ferraces & Martín, 1997; Valiña *et al.*, 1995), but also in disjunctive reasoning (Martín, Seoane, Valiña & Ferraces, 1998). A result which we consider interesting to mention in order to compare the mentioned previous study with this one, is that the comprehension test did not appeared as a good predictor for subjects´ performance with the Wason selection task; however in the work by Martín & cols. (1998), in which another different metainference task was used (the THOG problem), not only the verbal reasoning tests were seem as good predictors, but also the comprehension tests were good predictors in subjects´ performance with the mentioned task.

We consider that the results of this experiment could be explained by the Mental Models Theory and the Heuristic-Analytic Theory. For the Theory of Mental Models, the selection task performance is explained by a «*focussing effect*» in which people are assumed to concentrate on cases explicitly represented in mental models. For the Heuristic-Analytic Theory (Evans, 1984, 1989), subjects reason analytically about problem information that is preconsciously selected as *relevant* at a prior heuristic stage. Nevertheless, we are assisting the approximation of both theories. In fact, Evans (1993), argued that the Mental Models Theory is similar to the Heuristic-Analytic account if we equate relevance with focussing effects which arise from selective attention to that which is explicitly represented in a model.

Finally, the results obtained in this investigation support those theories which defend that subjects seem to consider that the task is more like a decision making than a reasoning task (Evans, Over & Manktelow, 1993). Also, the subjects improve their task performance, when different factors related to the knowledge (including the deontic terms, instructions or scenarios) allow them to *focus their attention* towards the card *not-q*, in terms of Johnson-Laird, or to consider its *relevance* in terms of Evans.

As we mentioned before, different tentatives of approximation between both the Mental Models Theory and the Dual Process Theory have taken place (Evans, 1991), however in the following years, we should assist not only to «*a greater integration of theoretical accounts*» (Evans *et al.*, 1993, p. 282), but also to a deepening in the differential analysis of reasoning. Actually a number of issues were left unresolved. We claimed that the study of individual differences on processing capacity and their influence on reasoning requires further investigation not only with other experimental reasoning tasks but also from different perspectives, as the developmental perspective (see for example Barrouillet & Lecas, 1998) and the psychometric perspective. The latter will allow us to analise the way in which the differences obtained with the psychometric instruments are related to individual differences obtained in experimental reasoning tasks. Finally, we claim that an effort on behalf of the researchers would also be necessary towards the experimental research design related to daily life reasoning, which will allow the study of the importance of subjects´ knowledge in human reasoning.

ACKNOWLEDGMENTS

We specially thank Manuel de Vega for providing us with his Spanish computerised version of Gernsbacher's Battery Comprehension. We are also grateful to Juan Antonio García-Madruga for his valuable comments of a draft of this paper.

REFERENCES

BARROUILLET, P., & LECAS, J.-F. (1998): «How can mental models theory account for content effects in conditional reasoning? A developmental perspective». *Cognition*, *67*, 209-253.

BELL, V. A., & JOHNSON-LAIRD, P. N. (1998): «A model theory of modal reasoning». *Cognitive Science*, *22*(1), 25-51.

BRAINE, M. D. S. (1990): «The "natural logic" approach to reasoning». In W.F. Overton (Ed.), *Reasoning, neccesity and logic: Developmental perspectives*. Hillsdale, NJ: Erlbaum.

BRAINE, M. D. S., & O'BRIEN, D. P. (1991): «A theory of If: A lexical entry, reasoning program, and pragmatic principles». *Psychological Review*, *98*, 182-203.

BURT, C. (1919): «The development of reasoning in school children». *Journal of Experimental Pedagogy*, *5*, 68-77, 121-127.

— (1921): *Mental and scholastic tests*. London: Kinf.

BYRNE, R. M. J., & JOHNSON-LAIRD, P. N. (1990): «Models and deductive reasoning». In K.J. Gilhooly, M.T.G. Keane, R.H. Logie and G. Erdos (Eds.), *Lines of thinking. Volume 1* (pp. 139-151). England: John Wiley & Sons Ltd.

CHENG, P. W., & HOLYOAK, K. J. (1985): «Pragmatic reasoning schemas». *Cognitive Psychology*, *17*, 391-416.

— (1989): «On the natural selection of reasoning theories». *Cognition, 33*, 285-313.

CHENG, P. W.; HOLYOAK, K. J., NISBETT, R. E., & OLIVER, L. M. (1986): «Pragmatic versus syntactic approaches to training deductive reasoning». *Cognitive Psychology, 18*, 293-328.

CHROSTOWSKI, J. J., & GRIGGS, R. A. (1985): «The effects of problem content, instructions and verbalization procedures on Wason's selection task». *Current Psychological Research and Reviews*, *4*, 99-107.

COSMIDES, L. (1985): *Deduction or darwinian algorithms?: An explanation of the «elusive» content effect on the Wason selection task*. Doctoral Dissertation, Harvard University. University Microfilms 86-02206.

— (1989): «The logic of social exchange: Has natural selection shaped how humans reason? Studies with the Wason selection task». *Cognition, 31*, 187-276.

Evans, J. St. B. T. (1984): «Heuristic and analitic processes in reasoning». *British Journal of Psychology*, *75*, 451-468.

— (1989): *Bias in human reasoning: Causes and consequences*. Hove, UK: Lawrence Erlbaum Associates Ltd.

— (1991): «Theories of human reasoning: The fragmented state of the art». *Theory and Psychology*, *1*, 83-105.

— (1993): «The mental models theory of conditional reasoning: critical appraisal and revision». *Cognition*, *48*, 1-20.

— (1995): «Relevance and reasoning». In S.E. Newstead and J.St.B.T. Evans (Eds.), *Perspectives on thinking and reasoning. Essays in honour of Peter Wason* (pp. 147-171). Hove, UK: Lawrence Erlbaum Associates Ltd.

— (1996): «Deciding before you think: Relevance and reasoning in the selection task». *British Journal of Psychology*, *87*, 223-240.

Evans, J. St. B. T., Legrenzi, P., & Girotto, V. (1999): «The influence of linguistic form on reasoning: The case of matching bias». *The Quarterly Journal of Experimental Psychology*, *52A*(1), 185-216.

Evans, J. St. B. T., Newstead, S. E., Allen, J. L., & Pollard, P. (1994): «Debiasing by instruction: The case of belief bias». *The European Journal of Experimental Psychology*, *6*(3), 263-285.

Evans, J. St. B. T., Newstead, S. E., & Byrne, R. M. J. (1993): *Human reasoning: The Psychology of deduction*. Hove, UK: Lawrence Erlbaum Associates Ltd.

Evans, J. St. B.T., & Over, D. E. (1996): *Rationality and reasoning*. Hove, UK: Psychology Press.

— (1997): *Rationality in reasoning: The problem of deductive competence. CPC, 16* (1-2), 3-38.

Evans, J. St. B. T., Over, D. E., & Manktelow, K. I. (1993): «Reasoning, decision making, and rationality». *Cognition*, *49*, 165-187.

Galotti, K. M., Baron, J., & Sabini, J. (1986): «Individual differences in syllogistic reasoning: Deduction rules or mental models?», *Journal of Experimental Psychology: General*, *115*,16-25.

Girotto, V., Gilly, M.; Blaye, A., & Light, P. (1989): «Children´s performance in the selection task: Plausibility and familiarity». *British Journal of Psychology*, *80*, 79-85.

Guilford, J. P. (1959): «Three faces of intellect». *American Psychologist*, *14*, 469-479.

Holyoak, K. J., & Cheng, P. W. (1995): «Pragmatic reasoning about human voluntary action: Evidence from Wason´s selection task». In S.E. Newstead and J.St.B.T. Evans (Eds.), *Perspectives on thinking and reasoning. Essays in honour of Peter Wason* (pp. 67-89). Hove, UK: Lawrence Erlbaum Associates Ltd.

Hunt, E., Lansman, M., & Wright, J. (1979): «Some remarks on doing two things at one». *Technical report Department of Psychology*. University of Washington, Seattle.

Hunt, E. (1980): «Intelligence as an information-processing concept». *British Journal of Psychology*, *71*, 449-474.

Inhelder, B., & Piaget, J. (1958): *The growth of logical thinking*. New York: Basic Books.

Johnson-Laird, P. N. (1983): *Mental models. Towards a cognitive science of language, inference and consciousness*. Cambridge, England: Cambridge University Press.

— (1995): «Inference and mental models». In S.E. Newstead and J.St.B.T. Evans (Eds.), *Perspectives on thinking and reasoning. Essays in honour of Peter Wason* (pp.115-146). Hove, UK: Lawrence Erlbaum Associates Ltd.

JOHNSON-LAIRD, P. N., & BYRNE, R. M. J. (1991): *Deduction*. Hove, U.K.: Lawrence Erlbaum Associates
— (1992): «Modal reasoning, models, and Manktelow and Over». *Cognition, 43*, 173-182.
— (1993): «Précis of "deduction", and authors´ response: Mental models or formal rules?». *Behavioral and Brain Sciences, 16*, 323-333, 368-376.
— (1995): «A model point of view». *Thinking and Reasoning, 1*(4), 339-350,
JOHNSON-LAIRD, P. N., LEGRENZI, P., & LEGRENZI, S. (1972): «Reasoning and a sense of reality». *British Journal of Psychology, 63*, 336-400.
LEGRENZI, P., GIROTTO, V., & JOHNSON-LAIRD, P. N. (1993): «Focussing in reasoning and decision making». *Cognition, 49*, 37-66.
MANKTELOW, K. I., & OVER, D. E. (1991): «Social roles and utilities in reasoning with deontic conditionals». *Cognition, 39*, 85-105.
MARTÍN, M. (1996): *Una exploración del razonamiento cotidiano: Importancia del conocimiento en inferencia condicional*. Unpublished doctoral dissertation. University of Santiago de Compostela, Spain.
MARTÍN, M., SEONE, G., VALIÑA, M.ª D., & FERRACES, M.ª J. (1998, July): «La importancia de las diferencias individuales en razonamiento disyuntivo». *Proceedings of the II Congreso Iberoamericano de Psicología*. Madrid.
NEWSTEAD, S. E., & EVANS, J. St. B. T. (1995): *Perspectives on thinking and reasoning. Essays in honour of Peter Wason*. Hove, UK: Lawrence Erlbaum Associates Ltd.
PLATT, R. D., & GRIGGS, R. A. (1993): «Facilitation in the abstract selection task: The effects of attentional and instructional factors». *The Quarterly Journal of Experimental Psychology, 46A*, 591-613.
— (1995): «Facilitation and matching bias in the abstract selection task». *Thinking and Reasoning, 1*(1), 55-70.
POLLARD, P., & EVANS, J. St. B. T. (1987): «On the relationship between content and context effects in reasoning». *American Journal of Psychology, 100*(1), 41-60.
RIPS, L. J. (1983): «Cognitive processes in propositional reasoning». *Psychological Review, 90*, 38-71.
— (1994): *The psychology of proof: Deductive reasoning in human thinking*. Cambridge, MA: MIT Press.
ROBERTS, M. J. (1993): «Human Reasoning: Deduction Rules or Mental Models, or Both?». *The Quarterly Journal of Experimental Psychology, 46A*(4), 569-589.
SANTAMARÍA, C., GARCÍA-MADRUGA, J. A., & CARRETERO, M. (1996): «Universal connectives in the selection task». *The Quarterly Journal of Experimental Psychology, 49A*(3), 814-827.
SEOANE, G., VALIÑA, M.ª D., FERRACES, M.ª J., & MARTÍN, M. (1997, July): «Comparing measures of individual differences in performance of conditional reasoning». *Proceedings of the 10th European Meeting of the Psychometric Society*. Santiago de Compostela, Spain.
STANOVICH, K. E., & WEST, R. F. (1998): «Cognitive ability and variation in selection task performance». *Thinking and Reasoning, 4*(3), 193-230.
STERNBERG, R. J., & GASTEL, J. (1989): «If dancers ate their shoes: Inductive reasoning, with factual and counterfactual premises». *Memory & Cognition, 17*(1), 1-10.
STERNBERG, R. J., & WEIL, E. M. (1980): «An aptitude x strategy interaction in linear syllogistic reasoning». *Journal of Educational Psychology, 72*(2), 226-239.
THURSTONE, L. L. (1938): «Prymary mental abilities». *Psychometric Monographs, 1*. (Adpt. in Tea, 1972).
TORRENS, D., THOMPSON, V. A., & CRAMER, K. M. (1999): «Individual differences and the belief bias effect: Mental models, logical necessity, and abstract reasoning». *Thinking and Reasoning, 5*(1), 1-28.

TWENEY, R. D., & DOHERTY, M. E. (1983): «Rationality and the psychology of inference». *Synthese, 57*, 139-161.

VALIÑA, M.ª D., SEOANE, G., FERRACES, M.ª J., & MARTÍN, M. (1995): «Tarea de selección de Wason: Un estudio de las diferencias individuales». *Psicothema, 7*(3), 641-653.

— (1996, August): «Wason's selection task: Content effect, instruction effect or both?». *Proceedings of The Third International Conference on Thinking.* British Psychological Society. Cognitive Psychology Section. University College London.

— (1997, August): «Pragmatic factors in conditional reasoning with narrative texts». In M.G. Shafto and P. Langley (Eds.), *Proceedings of the Nineteenth Annual Conference of the Cognitive Science Society.* Stanford, California: LEA.

— (1998): «La tarea de selección de Wason: ¿efecto del contenido, efecto de las instrucciones o ambos?». *Estudios de Psicología, 60*, 15-34.

— (1999): «The importance of pragmatic aspects in conditional reasoning». *The Spanish Journal of Psychology, 2*(1), 20-31.

VALIÑA, M.ª D., SEOANE, G., GEHRING, S., FERRACES, M.ª J., & FERNÁNDEZ-REY, J. (1992, September): *Conditional reasoning: Scenario or context effects?* Paper presented at The Fifth Conference of the European Society for Cognitive Psychology. Paris.

VALIÑA, M.ª D., SEOANE, G., MARTÍN, M., FERNÁNDEZ-REY, J., & FERRACES, M.ª J. (1992, September): *The role of content and context in pragmatic reasoning.* Paper presented at The Fifth Conference of the European Society for Cognitive Psychology. Paris.

VALIÑA, M.ª D., & DE VEGA, M. (1986): «Estudio de las diferencias individuales en gastos atencionales, a partir de una tarea de papel y lápiz». *Estudios de Psicología, 26*, 29-40.

WASON, P. C. (1966): «Reasoning». In B.M. Foss (Ed.), *New horizons in Psychology* (pp. 135-151). Harmondsworth: Penguin.

— (1968): «Reasoning about a rule». *The Quarterly Journal of Experimental Psychology, 20*, 273-281.

WASON, P. C., & SHAPIRO, D. (1971): «Natural and contrived experience in a reasoning problem». *The Quarterly Journal of Experimental Psychology, 23*, 63-71.

YACHANIN, S. A. (1986): «Facilitation in Wason's selection task: Content and instructions». *Current Psychological Research and Reviews, 5*, 20-29.

YACHANIN, S. A., & TWENEY, R. D. (1982): «The effect of thematic content on cognitive strategies in the four card selection task». *Bulletin of the Psychonomic Society, 19*, 87-90.

18

CONDITIONAL SYLLOGISMS AND CONTRAST CLASSES

WALTER SCHAEKEN
WALTER SCHROYENS

En este capítulo presentamos dos experimentos en los cuales se investiga el efecto de la magnitud de la clase de contraste en silogismos condicionales. Se contrastaron los efectos de la negación sistemática de los constituyentes de las cuatro inferencias fundamentales de los condicionales: Modus Ponens (i.e., inferencias de la forma: Si p entonces q; p ∴ q); Modus Tollens (Si p entonces q; no-q ∴ no-p); Afirmación del Consecuente (Si p entonces q; p ∴ no-q); y Negación del Antecedente (Si p entonces q; no-p ∴ no-q). La premisa categórica puede afirmar o negar explícitamente una parte del enunciado «Si entonces» (ver ejemplos anteriores) o puede afirmar o negar implícitamente una parte (e.g., Si p entonces q; z). Las reglas se referían a conjuntos de dos, tres, cinco, o nueve elementos.

En el experimento 1 se observó un efecto significativo de la negación explícita en los problemas de Modus Tollens y Negación del Antecedente: Las inferencias se realizaban más frecuentemente cuando del condicional se deriva una conclusión negativa (e.g., Si p entonces no q; q ∴ no-p) que cuando del condicional se deriva una consecuencia afirmativa (e.g., Si no p entonces q; no-q ∴ p). Además, observamos un efecto similar, aunque menor, en los problemas de Afirmación del Consecuente. Asimismo, observamos un efecto significativo de la premisa categórica (afirmativa o negativa), especialmente en los problemas de Afirmación del Consecuente. Finalmente, observamos un efecto de la magnitud de la clase de contraste. Los resultados se discuten en función del sesgo de conclusión negativa, del sesgo de premisa afirmativa, y de la dificultad de la doble negación, y cómo estos resultados pueden integrarse en las recientes teorías de razonamiento deductivo, i.e., la teoría de los modelos mentales, y las teorías basadas en reglas.

*En el experimento 2, se observó que la afirmación y la negación
implícita conducían a menos inferencias condicionales que la negación
explícita. Además, el efecto de la afirmación implícita es mayor que el
efecto de la negación implícita. En tercer lugar, se observó que la
utilización de materiales binarios eliminaba la diferencia en el efecto
tamaño de la clase de contraste entre afirmación y negación implícita.
Los resultados se discuten en el marco de la teoría de los modelos
mentales del razonamiento, y se propone una versión revisada que
considere el sesgo de emparejamiento en la tarea de selección.*

Reasoning with conditional assertions is an important part of deduction.
For philosophers, logicians, and psychologists it is a popular research object
(for a recent review, see Evans, Newstead, & Byrne, 1993). The research shows
that reasoning with sentences with for instance *and*, *or*, or *if then* is in some
cases very easy, but in other cases reasoners make many errors against formal
logic. Psychologists have manipulated three important aspects of reasoning with
conditional assertions. First, one manipulated the task that is presented to the
participants. This could be the famous Wason selection task (Wason, 1966), a
truth table construction task (see, e.g., Johnson-Laird & Tagard, 1969), or a
conditional syllogisms task (see, e.g., Evans, 1972). In this chapter we will
focus on the latter. Second, one manipulated the content of the different rules
presented to the participants (see, e.g., Johnson-Laird, Legrenzi, & Legrenzi,
1972). We will concentrate on rules with abstract material. Finally, one
manipulated the presence or absence of negatives in the conditional assertions.
We will present research in which this kind of manipulation, which is called
the negations paradigm, was used.

In this paper, we want to investigate the role of a potential important
factor on conditional reasoning, which is seldom studied in the psychology
of reasoning, that is, the ease of constructing and eventually negating the
contrast class. Consequently, this research is also concerned with the influence
of negations. Indeed, a negated constituent often identifies a contrast class.
Oaksford and Stenning (1992) give the example of a nosy roommate, who asks
«Did you enjoy your walk» in an oblique attempt to discover what you did
while you were out of the room. You may evasively reply «I did not go for a
walk», thereby ruling out one member of the contrast class of activities you
could have engaged in. Oaksford and Stenning (1992) were one of the first
to manipulate the effect of the contrast class. We will investigate the role of
contrast class in conditional syllogism. We will report two experiments in
which the contrast classes were manipulated. The first study concerns explicit
negation and deals primarily with the inferential clause (the clause about
which one has to form a conclusion, e.g., the consequent in the case of a
Modus Ponens problem) and the second study concerns implicit negation
and deals primarily with the referred clause (the clause which the categorical
premise refers to).

CONDITIONAL SYLLOGISMS

There are four sorts of conditional syllogisms. There is *Modus Ponens* (MP), which is any inference of the form «*if p then q; p; therefore, q*». There is *Modus Tollens* (MT), which is any inference of the form «*if p then q; not-q; therefore, not-p*». There is *Affirmation of the Consequent* (AC), which is any inference of the form «if p then q; q; therefore, p» and there is *Denial of the Antecedent* (DA), which is any inference of the form «*if p then q: not-p; therefore, not-q*». MP and MT are valid deductions, that is, their conclusions must be true given that their premises are true. AC and DA are fallacious. Unless the 'if-then' premise is interpreted as a bi-conditional (*if and only if p then q*), one has to conclude for AC and DA that nothing follows necessarily.

Two main theories try to explain conditional reasoning. On the one hand there are syntactic rule-based theories (see, e.g., Braine & O'Brien 1991; Rips 1994). These theories postulate a collection of rules (which resemble the rules found in formal logic). Rule theories predict that the longer the derivation of the proof of a conclusion, the harder the inference should be. There is no rule for MT, it is only indirectly that one can solve the problem. Hence, the valid inference MT requires more reasoning steps; consequently the rule theories predict that it is a more difficult inference. Additionally, they propose that rules differ in their accessibility or ease of use.

On the other hand, the mental model theory assumes that reasoning is a semantic process in which individuals build models of the situations under description (see Johnson-Laird, 1983; Johnson-Laird, Byrne, & Schaeken, 1992, 1994). According to the model theory, reasoning consists in three main stages. First, the premises are understood: A mental model is constructed on the basis of their meaning and of relevant general knowledge. Second, reasoners formulate a conclusion on the basis of this model. Third, a search is made for alternative models of the premises in which the putative conclusion is false. If there is no such model, then the conclusion is valid. If there is such a model, then it is necessary to return to the second stage to determine whether there is any conclusion that holds over all the models so far constructed. The theory's essential processing assumption is that the more models that have to be constructed the harder the inferential task will be. In recent accounts, it is often assumed that the search for counterexamples is not mandatory (see e.g., Evans, in press; Handley, Dennis, Evans, & Capon, in press; Ormerod, in press; Schaeken, De Vooght, Vandierendonck, & d'Ydewalle, in press). In many situations, reasoners are satisfied when they have build one model and formulated a putative conclusion.

Let us give an example of the original theory. Consider the following conditional:

If there is an A, then there is a 2.

The initial model of this assertion is:

[A]   2

   ...

Reasoners realise that both elements may be present, but also that the assertion is consistent with other possibilities. The three dots signify an *implicit* model and the square brackets represent that the antecedent is exhaustively represented in the explicit model, and so it cannot occur in the implicit model. The categorical premise «*there is an A*» picks out the situation represented in the first model and eliminates the second model. The remaining model:

[A]   2

yields the MP conclusion «*there is a 2*».

In order to draw the valid deduction MT, reasoners have to flesh out the models. In the case of a conditional interpretation, the models are:

A   2
¬A   2
¬A   ¬2

The categorical premise calls for the elimination of the models containing a '2'. As a result, only one model is left behind:

¬A   ¬2

which yields the MT conclusion «*there is not an A*».

IMPLICIT AND EXPLICIT NEGATION

Recently, there has been a growing interest in the effects of negatives on conditional reasoning. One can make a distinction between two sorts of negation. On the one hand, there is explicit negation, in which an explicit negative is introduced in the categorical premise. An example is the following MT problem:

If there is not an A, then there is a 2. There is not a 2.

The 'not a 2' of the categorical premise denies explicitly the '2' in the consequent of the if-then assertion, or in other words, it denies the content of the referred clause. On the other hand, there is implicit negation, in which the categorical premise negates one part of the if-then assertion, without the presence of an explicit negative. Consider the following example of a MT problem:

If there is not an A, then there is a 2. There is a 3.

The '3' of the categorical premise denies implicitly the '2' in the referred clause.

Independently of implicit or explicit negation, one can manipulate the presence of negatives in the conditional assertion (e.g., the negated antecedent in the example above). In the two studies reported in this paper, we will use explicit and implicit negation with conditional syllogisms.

THE EFFECT OF EXPLICIT NEGATION

It has been known for a long time that the presence of explicit negatives influences reasoning with conditional syllogisms. However, the explanation for this phenomenon isn't clear at all. Evans (1993) evaluates the different proposals and summarises them in two biases. The first bias is called a *affirmative premise bias*. Inferences from an affirmative categorical premise should be made more often than those from a negative categorical premise. The basis for this bias is the theory of Johnson-Laird and Byrne (1991) about the Wason selection task, which states that that a negation is likely to call to mind the affirmative alternative. Hence, conditionals with negated consequents, such as:

If there is an A, then there is not a 2.

would yield the initial models:

[A]   ¬2
       2

Consequently, affirmative premises would be represented in the initial models of both affirmative conditionals and negated conditionals without the need for fleshing out. However, Evans (1993; Evans, Clibbens, & Rood, 1995) did find only tenuous evidence for this bias. We will not follow the proposal of Johnson-Laird and Byrne (1991) in this chapter.

Evans (1993) reports a second bias, that is, *negative conclusion bias*. According to this bias, reasoners favour negative conclusions over affirmative conclusions. Evans *et al.* (1995) found clear evidence for the negative conclusion bias. However, because the bias was largely restricted to the denial inferences, they favoured an explanation in terms of the difficulty of double negation. Reasoners have difficulty in seeing that a double negative equals an affirmative.

The two major theories can incorporate this finding in their theories. Most rule-based theories propose a rule for double negation. Consequently, the MT problem with a negated antecedent requires an extra-step in comparison with the MT problem with an affirmative antecedent. The model theory can incorporate the double negation effect, at least when it does not presuppose that a negation calls to mind the affirmative alternative. Making the MT and DA inference requires fleshing out the implicit model. A negated antecedent in the former and a negated consequent in the latter forces reasoners to make a double negation if they flesh out the initial models. If a double negation is difficult, reasoners will have more difficulty with these problems, than with problems which do not require this double negation.

WHAT INFLUENCES THE DIFFICULTY
OF DOUBLE NEGATION?

Oaksford and Stenning (1992) say that a negation is not always used to deny a presupposition, but that a negated constituent often identifies a contrast class. Could it be that one of the main sources of the difficulty of the double negation is the difficulty of the construction and negation of the contrast class? Consider an example of the sorts of problems used by Evans et al. (1995):

If the letter is not an A, then the number is 4. The number is not 4.

This MT problem is a difficult one: Reasoners have to negate the 'not-A' in order to come up with the valid inference 'A'. However, reasoners only know that each problem concerns an imaginary letter-number pair. Hence, 'not-A' can mean any letter except the 'A': «B or C or D or … or Y or Z». One can imagine that the construction of such a large contrast class is difficult. The negation of such an expanded disjunction is also difficult.

Hence, it could be that if reasoners would have a clearer idea of what 'not-A' means, they would perform better on problems like the one above. We will present an experiment in which the set-size of the contrast class is stringently tested.

EXPERIMENT 1: THE EFFECT OF CONTRAST CLASSES ON EXPLICIT NEGATION

We set up an experiment in which we presented explicitly binary conditionals (hence, the conditional referred to a set of two elements), conditionals which referred to a set of three elements, a set of five elements, and a set of nine elements. The rules in the experiment were about cards with a letter on one side and a number on the other side.

In the binary condition, the participants were informed that the letters could be an 'A' or a 'B' and that the number could be a '1' or a '2'. Consequently, if they were told that the letter was not an 'A', they could know that the letter was a 'B'. In the case of conditionals referring to a set of three elements, we made it explicitly to the participants that the letters could be 'A', 'B' or 'C' and that the numbers could be '1', '2', or '3'. In the case of conditionals referring to a set of five and nine elements, the possible letters were respectively 'A', 'E', 'I', 'O', or 'U' and 'A', 'B', 'C', 'D', 'E', 'F', 'G', 'H', or 'I'. The possible numbers were respectively '1', '3', '5', '7', or '9', and '1', '2', '3', '4', '5', '6', '7', '8', or '9'.

The 120 participants acted as their own controls and carried out instances of all four sorts of inference (MP, MT, AC, DA) from conditionals with systematically negated constituent propositions. They had to draw their own conclusions in their own words. There were four versions of each sort of inference as a result of the presence or absence of negative constituents of the conditional (if p then q, if not p then q, if p then not q, and if not p then not q). Each participant carried out 16 inferences presented in a different random order. The manipulation of the contrast class was between participants.

Table 18.1 presents the percentages of responses for the sixteen different inferences for the different contrast classes. All statistic in the present and the following experiment are done by means of non-parametric statistics (see

Siegel & Castellan, 1988). Overall, collapsing over the four sorts of conditional and the four sorts of contrast classes, MP occurred reliably more often than MT (97% vs. 70%; p <.0005) and AC occurred reliably more often than DA (80% vs. 75%; p <.0005).

TABLE 18.1

The percentages of conditional conclusions corresponding to the four sorts of inferences with the four sorts of conditionals and the four sorts of set-sizes in Experiment 1

	MP				AC				DA				MT			
	2	3	5	9	2	3	5	9	2	3	5	9	2	3	5	9
if p then q	100	100	100	100	79	82	69	82	79	71	55	64	79	77	83	75
if p then not-q	100	100	100	86	76	50	59	46	69	38	24	11	90	85	86	86
if not-p then q	97	97	93	89	90	94	93	92	79	65	59	68	72	62	52	46
if not-p then not-q	97	94	97	100	76	82	72	71	72	50	41	39	59	47	69	50

In order to get good evidence for the two biases, we follow Evans et al. (1995) by abstracting two indices. The *Negative Conclusion Index (NCI)* is the number of conditional inferences drawn on arguments with negative conclusions minus the number of inferences drawn on arguments with affirmative conclusions. The *Affirmative Premise Index (API)* is the number of conditional inferences drawn on arguments with an affirmative categorical premise minus the number of inferences drawn on arguments with a negative categorical premise.

Overall, the NCI and the API were significant (p <.00005 and p <.0001 respectively). The NCI was significant for all the conditions separately (set-size 2: p <.01; set-size 3: p <.00005; set-size 5: p <.0005; set-size 9: p <.0005), while the API was only significant for the set-sizes 3 and 9 (set-size 3: p <.01; set-size 9: p <.05).

There was no evidence for a significant NCI on MP. There was, however, a significant NCI for the other three inferences (AC: p <.00005; DA: p <.00005; MT: p <.00005;). The NCI was significant for each of the conditions separately for DA (set-size 2: p <.05; set-size 3: p <.01; set-size 5: p <.005; set-size 9: p <.001) and MT (set-size 2: p <.01; set-size 3: p <.005; set-size 5: p <.05; set-size 9: p <.001). For AC, the NCI was significant for the set-sizes 3, 5 and 9 (respectively p <.001, p <.001, and p <.05).

There was no evidence for a significant API on MP and MT. There was a significant effect on DA in general (p <.005), but if one looks to the conditions separately, there was only a significant effect for set-size 9 (p <.05). The API was significant for AC in general (p <.00005), and it was also significant for each of the four conditions separately (set-size 2: p <.05; set-size 3: p <.005; set-size 5: p <.05; set-size 9: p <.005).

Finally, we want to have a closer look at the effects of the contrast-classes on the two biases. Overall, there is a clear effect of the contrast-classes on NCI. Indeed,

NCI is significantly smaller in the binary condition than in the other conditions (set-size 3: p <.05; set-size 5: p <.05; set-size 9: p <.005). For API, there is only one significant effect in general: API is smaller for set-size 2 than for set-size 9 (p <.05).

In view of these findings, we analysed the effect of contrast-classes for each of the four inferences. NCI is smaller with set-size 2 than with set-size 3 for AC and DA (for AC: p <.05; for DA: p <.06) and with set-size 5 (for AC: p <.05; for DA: p <.05). For DA, NCI is also smaller for set-size 2 than for set-size 9 (p <.005). The only other significant effect is on DA: NCI is significantly smaller for set-size 3 than for set-size 9 (p <.05). There is no significant effect of the contrast-class on the API when one considers MP and MT. There are some effects when one considers DA and AC. For AC, API is smaller with set-size 2 than with set-size 3 (p <.05) and with set-size 9 (p <.05). For DA, API is smaller for set-size 2 than for set-size 9 (p <.05) and it is smaller for set-size 3 than for set-size 9 (p <.05).

We can conclude four important points from this experiment. First, MP is easier than MT. This is in accordance with the predictions of both the rule-based theories and the mental model theory. Furthermore, reasoners made more AC inferences than DA inferences. This is in accordance with the predictions of the mental model theory and also with some of the rule-based theories (e.g., Rips, 1994; pace Braine & O'Brien, 1991).

Second, the NCI is significant for AC, DA, and MT. This can be interpreted as evidence in favor of negative conclusion bias. Indeed, according to the double negation hypothesis, there should be an effect on DA and MT, but not on AC. The negative conclusion bias hypothesis predicts an effect on all inferences, except MP (see Evans *et al.*, 1995). This would lead us to the conclusion that we found evidence for the negative conclusion bias hypothesis. However, some data in our experiment contradict this conclusion. Indeed, the NCI for AC was significantly smaller than the NCI for DA and for MT. Therefore, we want to argue that the double negation effect and the negative conclusion bias are not mutually exclusive. The first has to do with the processing of the information, while the latter is a response bias. Hence, it is perfectly possible that both factors affect the results. Indeed, the significant NCI on AC can be interpreted as the working of the negative conclusion bias, while the significant NCI on DA and MT can be interpreted as a result of both the difficulty of double negation and negative conclusions bias.

Third, we observed a significant API. If one wants to explain this effect, one must consider the following points. First, the API is only clearly significant for AC. Second, the double negation hypothesis and the affirmative premise bias hypothesis sometimes make contradictory predictions. Consider, for example, the following MT problem:

If not-p, then q; Not-q.

According to the affirmative premise bias hypothesis, this inference should be rather easy. Indeed, according to this hypothesis, the valid inference 'p' would be represented in the initial models. The double negation hypothesis, however, makes the opposite prediction. According to this hypothesis, this MT problem should be rather difficult, because it leads to a double negation. The data clearly support the double negation hypothesis: This is a difficult inference (overall, it is only solved correctly in 58% of the cases).

Therefore, there must be another explanation for the significant API. A plausible explanation is to interpret the significant API as evidence for a *negative categorical premise bias*. It could be argued that a negative categorical premise triggers a negative conclusion (for a similar explanation in categorical syllogisms, see, e.g., Begg & Denny, 1969; Woodworth & Sells, 1935). If the conclusion the reasoner infers is affirmative, then there could be a suppression of this answer because of the conflict with the atmosphere of the problem. Consider the following AC problem:

If p then not-q; Not-q.

The negative categorical premise triggers a negative conclusion. This conflicts with the inferred conclusion 'p', which might lead to a suppression of the inference 'p'.

There is some additional evidence for this explanation. First, there is a tendency for MP to be more difficult with «if not-p then q» than with the other rules (93% vs 97%). The conflict between the negative categorical premise and the affirmative conclusion might cause this small difference. Likewise, it can explain why «if p then not-q» is more difficult than «if not-p then not-q» for DA (25% vs 44%). For both inferences, one has to solve a double negation, but for the first rule there is a contradiction between the atmosphere of the categorical premise and the conclusion. In the experiments of Evans *et al.* (1995) the same trend can be found. As we said already, the proposal of a negative categorical premise bias is only speculative.

Fourth, we observed an effect of the size of the contrast class: The NCI and API were smaller for the binary condition than for the other conditions. In the condition with set-size 2, one knows precisely what is meant by a negated clause: 'not-A' means 'B' and 'not 1' means '2'. In all the other conditions, one cannot come up with such a clear affirmative alternative. The only thing one can come up with is a disjunction of 2 (set-size 3), 4 (set-size 5), or 8 elements (set-size 9). For instance, in the latter condition, 'not 1' means '2 or 3 or 4 or 5 or 6 or 7 or 8 or 9'. Hence, we are more inclined to argue that some reasoners use the affirmative alternative if it is just one element. As soon as it is a disjunction of two or more elements, reasoners work with the negated element.

EXPERIMENT 2: THE EFFECT OF CONTRAST CLASSES ON IMPLICIT NEGATION

In the previous study, we observed an effect of contrast classes on explicit negation. Is there an effect of contrast classes on implicit negation as well? Before we will discuss this issue, we will review some recent evidence concerning conditional syllogisms and implicit negation. In order to clarify in advance some of the terminology used, we will give some examples. Consider the following DA-problem:

If there is an A, then there is a 3. There is an E.

This is an example of implicit negation: The categorical premise negates the antecedent, but it does this in an implicit way (in the antecedent and the categorical premise are two different items mentioned). You can also construct problems with implicit affirmation. Consider the following MP-problem:

If there is not an A, then there is a 3. There is an E.

The categorical premise affirms the antecedent in an implicit way.

Evans and Handley (in press), and Schroyens *et al.* (1998a, 1998b) independently established that using implicit affirmation and denial introduces matching bias (see above). Indeed, a) fewer MP inferences are made when the antecedent is negative than when it is affirmative, b) fewer AC inferences are made when the consequent is negative than when it is affirmative, c) fewer DA inferences are made when the antecedent is affirmative than when it is negative, and d) fewer MT inferences are made when the consequent is affirmative than when it is negative.

A plausible account for this effect is in terms of the perceived relevancy of the categorical premise with respect to the referred clause. When the topic of the categorical premise does not match the topic of the referred proposition (which is the case for implicit affirmation and denial), people consider the premises irrelevant one to another and conclude that nothing can be inferred.

Schroyens et al. (1998a, 1998b) observed that the inhibitory effect of implicit affirmation is larger than the inhibitory effect of implicit denial: The decrease in the percentages of conditional inferences when using implicit affirmation problems is larger than the decrease when using implicit denial problems. On the basis of this and other evidence, Schroyens *et al.* (1998a) make a theoretical distinction between implicit affirmation and denial. They suggest that the greater difficulty implicit affirmation is due to uncertainty or failure to recognise that the contrast class of a negative is affirmed by one of its instances. Consider the following MP-problem:

If there is no A, then there is a 2. There is a B.

People who construct the contrast class of 'A' would interpret the information in the categorical premise as relevant: 'B' is an element of the class of not-A's. However, reasoners could doubt whether the one element 'B' is sufficient for the antecedent condition to be satisfied ('B or C or D or ... Z') and, hence, could be uncertain whether the '2' follows necessarily. Reasoners do not need to traverse this hurdle in the case of an implicit denial. Indeed, consider the following example:

If there is an A, then there is a 2. There is a B.

Reasoners would have no particular difficulty in considering that the letter 'B' denies that there is an 'A' on the front (a B is not an A).

In order to test the idea that uncertainty contributes to the larger effect of implicit affirmation we decided to manipulate the scope of the contrast class. We hypothesise that reasoners consider a case-wise affirmation of a negative to be incomplete because the affirmed case (i.e., the categorical premise) is only one element out of the many elements in the contrast class. However, when the set size of the class of elements is binary, the contrast class of a negated element is actually a singleton. We therefore expect that such problems would not show a differential effect of implicit affirmation and denial. Hence, the effect of implicit affirmation should interact with the scope of the contrast class. This interaction would not be observed on the denial problems: The scope of contrast classes would not affect the ease by which reasoners consider that the presence of one element denies the presence of the another element (e.g., 'A is no B').

It is important to emphasise that in this experiment we are mainly concerned with the effect of negation in the referred clause, that is, the clause in the conditional assertion that is linked with the categorical premise. We will not discuss in detail the effect of negation in the inferential clause.

We tested 96 participants in Experiment 2, which had the same method and procedure as the Experiment 1, except that we used implicit negation and affirmation in the categorical premise. Table 18.2 presents the percentages of responses for the sixteen different inferences for the different contrast classes.

TABLE 18.2
The percentages of conditional conclusions corresponding to the four sorts of inferences with the four sorts of conditionals and the four sorts of set-sizes in Experiment 2

	MP				AC				DA				MT			
	2	3	5	9	2	3	5	9	2	3	5	9	2	3	5	9
if p then q	100	100	100	100	65	76	95	70	52	64	48	44	70	80	57	56
if p then not-q	100	100	95	100	78	16	29	7	57	16	5	7	96	92	91	89
if not-p then q	87	60	62	56	91	92	100	89	70	80	91	74	57	36	19	41
if not-p then not-q	83	56	29	48	70	48	38	33	57	52	68	56	70	52	71	44

First, the implicit problems resulted in fewer conditional inferences then the explicit problems (82% vs. 58%; $p < .000001$) and the effect of implicit affirmation was larger than the effect of implicit denial (43% vs. 27%; $p < .005$).

The effect of implicit affirmation and denial did not differ when the conditionals were constructed with binary set-sizes (10% vs.14%). This finding corroborates our hypothesis that the multiplicity of elements in the contrast class induces people to doubt whether one of these elements (the categorical premise) suffices to confirm the entire contrast class. Since there is no such multiplicity within a binary context, people would not have such doubt.

Second, within the non-binary groups the effect of implicit affirmation was larger than the effect of implicit denial (53% vs. 31%; $p < .01$). The binary versus non-binary set sizes affected the effect of an implicit versus explicit type of referencing more for the affirmation problems (10% vs. 53%; $p < .000005$) than for the denial problems (14% vs. 31%; $p < .05$). Contrary to expectations, however, binary set sizes also reduced the effect size of implicit denial. This seems mainly due to results of the group of participants who received the problems with a non-binary set size of 5 elements. Indeed, the percentages of implicit versus explicit denial inferences observed in this group differed reliably from those observed in the binary group (14% vs. 48%; p <.005), whereas it did not for the other non-binary groups (14% vs. 24%). Also, the group given set sizes of 5 elements did not show a larger effect of implicit affirmation versus implicit denial (58% vs. 48%).

The effects of a negation in the inferential clause were very similar to the ones obtained in Experiment 1. Therefore, we will not discuss them further.

In sum, the overall pattern of results parallels the effects observed by Schroyens *et al.* (1998a, 1998b) and Evans and Handley (in press). First, implicit referencing leads to fewer conditional inferences. Second, the effect of implicit affirmation is larger than the effect of implicit denial. Our hypothesis about the effect of contrast class was confirmed: When the categorical premise exhausts the contrast class (a binary set size), the effect of implicit affirmation and denial are the same. One might expect that the absolute scope of non-binary set sizes would also affect the uncertainty of implicit affirmation. However, the result indicate that increasing set sizes do not further increase the effect of implicit affirmation.

GENERAL DISCUSSION

The present chapter explored the role of the magnitude of the contrast class on conditional syllogisms. We presented two different experiments, which both led to interesting results.

In Experiment 1, we observed a reliable effect of explicit negatives on DA, and MT in all conditions: Participants more often endorsed a conclusion that was negative rather than affirmative. We observed a similar effect of explicit negatives on AC, when the values were not binary. An effect of the magnitude of the contrast class on DA inferences was observed as well: Inferences that yield an affirmative conclusion (or that require a double negation) are more difficult with a larger contrast class. We observed the same pattern on MT, but the difference was only significant when one compares the condition with set-size 2 with the condition with set-size 9. We observed some interesting results on AC, which led us to the claim that the double negation hypothesis and the negative conclusion bias hypothesis are not mutually exclusive. Finally, we asked the question whether the affirmative premise bias is not better reformulated into a negative categorical premise bias.

In Experiment 2, we observed three main findings. First, when conditional inference problems are set up with implicit affirmation and denial, people make less conditional inferences than when they are set up with explicit affirmation and denial. Second, like previous studies, we observed that the effect of implicit affirmation is larger than the effect of implicit denial. Third, we observed that using binary materials eliminates the difference in effect size between implicit affirmation and denial. These observations confirm our hypothesis: Given that mismatching cases are considered relevant one to another (e.g., the categorical premise 'B' is relevant for the conditional assertion 'if not-A, then 2'), reasoners still need to perceive that the truth of an instance is sufficient to affirm the contrast class in the case of implicit affirmation. In other words, we want to emphasise that we did not argue that a binary context eliminates matching bias. Indeed, we argued that a binary context eliminates the discrepancy between implicit affirmation and denial. Perceiving the multiplicity of elements in the contrast class (which is different from representing each of these multiple elements as such) seems to be sufficient for reasoners to doubt that a contrast class is be affirmed by a single instance in the class.

In sum, the present study shows the value of a very simple manipulation, that is, the manipulation of the magnitude of the contrast class. Indeed, this manipulation did lead to significant changes in the inferences made by the reasoners and consequently to new theoretical hypotheses with respect to conditional syllogisms. Both explicit and implicit negation were strongly influenced by the manipulation of the magnitude of the contrast class. This observation lead to crucial theoretical developments with respect to the effects of explicit and implicit negation. Nevertheless, because these are the first studies using this paradigm with conditional syllogisms, it is clear that more research is necessary. Especially the relatively new research on implicit negation needs further investigation.

ACKNOWLEDGEMENTS

Walter Schaeken and Walter Schroyens are supported by the Fund for Scientific Research Flanders. We would like to thank Kristien Dieussaert and Nikola Verschueren for their many helpful comments and suggestions concerning the research reported in the manuscript.

REFERENCES

BEGG, I., & DENNY, J. P. (1969): «Empirical reconciliation of atmosphere and conversion interpretations of syllogistic reasoning errors». *Journal of Experimental Psychology, 81,* 351-354.

BRAINE, M. D. S., & O'BRIEN, D. P. (1991): «A theory of If: A lexical entry, reasoning program, and pragmatic principles». *Psychological Review, 98,* 182-203.

EVANS, J. St. B. T. (1972): «Reasoning with negatives». *British Journal of Psychology, 63,* 213-219.

— (1993): «The mental model theory of conditional reasoning: Critical appraisal and revision». *Cognition, 48,* 1-20.

— (1999): «What could and could not be a strategy in reasoning». In W. Schaeken, G. De Vooght, A. Vandierendonck, & G. d'Ydewalle (Eds.), *Deductive reasoning and strategies.* Mahwah, NJ: Erlbaum.

EVANS, J. St. B. T., CLIBBENS, J., & ROOD, B. (1995): «Bias in conditional inference: Implications for mental models and mental logic». *Quarterly Journal of Experimental Psychology, 48A,* 644-670.

EVANS, J. St. B. T., & HANDLEY, S. (in press): «The role of negation in conditional inference». *Quarterly Journal of Experimental Psychology*.

EVANS, J. St. B. T., NEWSTEAD, S. E., & BYRNE, R. M. J. (1993): *Human reasoning: The psychology of deduction*. Hillsdale, NJ: Erlbaum.

HANDLEY, S.; DENNIS, I., EVANS, J. St. B. T., & CAPON, I. (1999): «Individual differences and the search for counter-examples in syllogistic reasoning». In W. Schaeken, G. De Vooght, A. Vandierendonck, & G. d'Ydewalle (Eds.), *Deductive reasoning and strategies*. Mahwah, NJ: Erlbaum.

JOHNSON-LAIRD, P. N. (1983): *Mental models: Towards a cognitive science of language, inference, and consciousness*. Cambridge: Cambridge University Press.

JOHNSON-LAIRD, P. N., & BYRNE, R. M. J. (1991): *Deduction*. Hillsdale, NJ: Erlbaum.

JOHNSON-LAIRD, P. N., BYRNE, R. M. J., & SCHAEKEN, W. (1992): «Propositional reasoning by model». *Psychological Review, 99*, 418-439.

— (1994): «A defence of the model theory of propositional reasoning: A reply to Bonatti, and to O'Brien, Braine, and Yang». *Psychological Review, 101*, 734-739.

JOHNSON-LAIRD, P. N., LEGRENZI, P., & LEGRENZI, M. S. (1972): «Reasoning and a sense of reality». *British Journal of Psychology, 63*, 395-400.

JOHNSON-LAIRD, P. N., & TAGART, J. (1969): «How implication is understood». *American Journal of Psychology, 2*, 367-373.

OAKSFORD, M., & STENNING, K. (1992): «Reasoning with conditionals containing negated constituents». *Journal of Experimental Psychology: Learning, Memory, and Cognition, 18*, 835-854.

ORMEROD, T. C. (1999): «Mechanisms and strategies for rephrasing». In W. Schaeken, G. De Vooght, A. Vandierendonck, & G. d'Ydewalle (Eds.), *Deductive reasoning and strategies*. Mahwah, NJ: Erlbaum.

RIPS, L. J. (1994): *The psychology of proof*. Cambridge, MA: Routledge.

SCHAEKEN, W., DE VOOGHT, G.; VANDIERENDONCK, A., & D'YDEWALLE, G. (1999): «Strategies and tactics in deductive reasoning». In W. Schaeken, G. De Vooght, A. Vandierendonck, & G. d'Ydewalle (Eds.), *Deductive reasoning and strategies*. Mahwah, NJ: Erlbaum.

SCHROYENS, W., SCHAEKEN, W., VERSCHUEREN, N., & D'YDEWALLE, G. (1998a): «Implicit versus explicit affirmation and denial in conditional reasoning with negations». Manuscript submitted for publication.

— (1998b): «Conditional reasoning with negations: Matching bias and implicit versus explicit or denial». Manuscript submitted for publication.

SIEGEL, S., & CASTELLAN, N. J. (1988): *Nonparametric statistics for the behavioral sciences*. New York: McGraw-Hill.

WASON, P. C. (1966): «Reasoning». In B. M. Foss (Ed.), *New horizons in psychology*. Harmondsworth: Penguin.

WOODWORTH, R. S., & SELLS, S. B. (1938): «An atmosphere effect in syllogistic reasoning». *Journal of Experimental Psychology, 18*, 451-460.

19

REASONING WITH MULTIPLE CONDITIONALS. WHEN DO REASONERS CONSTRUCT MENTAL MODELS?

Francisco Gutiérrez
Juan A. García-Madruga
Nuria Carriedo
Sergio Moreno

Se han propuesto dos principales teorías para explicar la competencia humana de razonamiento deductivo: la teoría de los modelos mentales y la teoría de la lógica mental. Ambas teorías difieren en cuanto a la naturaleza del conocimiento que se postula como base de las inferencias y en cuanto al tipo de proceso que subyace a la ejecución en las distintas tareas de razonamiento. Los problemas deductivos con múltiples condicionales (de la forma Si e entonces a, Si a entonces b, Si b entonces c, Si c entonces d; ¿Cuál es la relación, si existe, entre a y d?) permiten contrastar estas dos propuestas dado que las predicciones que se realizan desde ambas sobre la ejecución son prácticamente opuestas. La teoría de los modelos mentales relaciona la dificultad de los problemas con el número de modelos que es necesario construir a fin de resolverlos, mientras que la teoría de la lógica mental, por su parte, explica esta dificultad en función del número y complejidad de los esquemas de inferencia que deben aplicarse para derivar la conclusión.

En un estudio anterior García-Madruga y Johnson-Laird (1994) contrastaron este tipo de predicciones a partir de problemas multicondicionales como el descrito y utilizando medidas temporales (latencias de respuestas y tiempos de lectura de las premisas) además de la usual medida de precisión (porcentaje de respuestas correctas). Los resultados obtenidos apoyaban claramente la teoría de los modelos mentales, si bien se encontraron algunos resultados no previstos; concretamente, se observó un claro «efecto techo» en las medidas de precisión —no hubo diferencias para los distintos problemas— y, por otro lado, respecto a los problemas de «dos modelos» se encontró un tiempo de lectura sorprendentemente alto en la tercera premisa; lo que

—en principio, y comparando entre sí los problemas de múltiples modelos—, resultaba extraño. Con el fin de comprobar la consistencia de este tipo de resultados, decidimos llevar a cabo un nuevo experimento con el mismo método y las mismas predicciones. En esta ocasión los resultados con las medidas de precisión confirmaron claramente las predicciones de la teoría de los modelos mentales: los problemas que requerían construir un solo modelo para responder correctamente fueron significativamente más fáciles que los que requerían dos y tres modelos. Sin embargo, las medidas temporales de nuevo mostraron un patrón complejo y difícil de interpretar.

En lo que sigue, describimos de manera resumida estos dos trabajos y discutimos sus resultados, no sólo en cuanto sustentan la teoría de los modelos mentales sino también en relación con algunas primeras ideas que sugieren en torno a los detalles del proceso subyacente; concretamente en referencia a las posibles operaciones por las que se construyen los modelos y se combina la información de las premisas. Como se sabe, esto atañe a la primera fase de «comprensión» que la teoría postula dentro de un proceso general eminentemente semántico. En particular, avanzamos la idea de que posiblemente, en ciertas condiciones más demandantes, el razonador haga uso de un «buffer» de memoria a fin de mantener temporalmente cierta información antes de integrarla en la representación ya construida; lo que sería más probable en la medida en que estas operaciones de integración consuman mayores recursos cognitivos. Por otra parte, esto implica que no necesariamente los modelos se construyen y completan a medida que se recoge la información de las premisas. En la discusión, pues, ofrecemos algunas reflexiones y sugerencias en torno a estas ideas, las cuales tratamos de relacionar con las asunciones de la teoría de los modelos mentales acerca de las limitaciones de procesamiento de la cognición humana y el funcionamiento «estratégico» que ello puede suponer.

INTRODUCTION

At present there are two main competing theories to explain people's competence in deductive reasoning. On the one hand, mental models theory (see, Johnson-Laird, 1983; Johnson-Laird & Byrne,1991, 1993; Johnson-Laird, Byrne & Schaeken,1992) maintains that people reason by representing the state of affairs described in the premises. This is conceived as a semantic process that implies the construction and manipulation of alternative mental models of assertions, and their evaluation in order to check their consistency. On the other hand, mental logic theorists (see e.g. Braine & O'Brien, 1991, 1998; Rips, 1993, 1994), defend a more deterministic process based on the application of formal rules of inference. Table 19.1 presents in summarized fashion the general representation and processes postulated by the two theories. As this table shows, the mental models theory of deductive reasoning differs from the mental rule theories with respect to the nature of *knowledge on which general competence is based* (knowledge of specific formal rules of inference vs. general knowledge about the world and language) and with respect to the *general process that underlies performance* (application of rules vs. construction and evaluation of alternative mental models based on comprehension). Perhaps more important, however, are the *different predictions* that these kinds of knowledge and processes imply in the explanation of performance in particular problems. We shall present two studies with multiconditional problems that support mental models predictions. From the results obtained in these studies we shall reflect on how to extend the theory in order to describe details of processing, taking into account assumptions concerning the strategic nature of human cognition.

TABLE 19.1

General representation and process described by mental rules and mental models theories of deductive reasoning

From Mental Rules theories	From Mental Models theory
1.—Uncovering the logical form of premises.	1.—Comprehension: Reasoners have to understand the premises by using their knowledge of language and general knowledge. The result of this stage is the construction of a mental model of the state of affairs described in the premises.
2.—Accessing the repertory of rules to construct a mental derivation of the conclusion.	2.—Description: Reasoners try to formulate a parsimonious but informative conclusion from the models they have built up.
3.—Translating the content-free conclusion in the content of premises.	3.—Validation: Reasoners search for counterexamples or alternative models of the premises in which their putative conclusion is false. If there is no such alternative model, then the conclusion is valid.

(Based on García-Madruga and Johnson-Laird, 1994)

Strategic [1] processing in Mental Models theory

Among the most important assumptions of mental models theory are those concerning the *processing limitations* of the human cognitive system and the *strategic functioning* that these limitations imply. Mental models theory postulates

---

[1]   Recently, Johnson-Laird, Savary and Bucciarelli (1999) have made an important distinction between strategies and tactics. Whereas strategies are conceived as the deliberate operations that reasoners make in order to solve problems, tactics are defined as the underlying steps in the application of strategies, which are seldom available to consciousness. From this point of view, tactics would be the cognitive level at which the construction and manipulation of mental models take place, and the reasoner may use them in different and more or less demanding strategies (see also García-Madruga, Moreno, Carriedo, Gutiérrez and Johnson-Laird, in press). Bearing in mind this proposal, it is convenient to mention that in the present paper we shall speak only at the tactical level.

that, in order to minimize the load on the limited resources of working memory, reasoners tend to represent in an explicit form the minimum amount of information required by task demands and objectives. Part of the information remains only in *implicit models* as representations that allow —if necessary— for subsequent specification of content. In general, explicit models represent only those instances explicitly asserted in the premises, whereas implicit ones represent possible alternative instances not asserted in the premises. This can be described as a basic *principle of cognitive economy* by which reasoners «*try to work with just a single representative sample from the set of possible models, until they are forced to consider alternatives*» (Johnson-Laird & Byrne, 1991, p. 36).

The valid inferences in conditional arguments illustrate well both types of representation (see Table 19.2). According to mental models theory, the '*modus ponens*' (MP) inferences can be solved directly by the initial representation of the conditional statement. As Table 19.2 shows, this initial representation includes two models (the two lines):

[p] q
...

The first is an explicit model and the second —shown by the three dots— is an implicit one. Because the first model explicitly ties the existence of antecedent «p» —that is asserted in the second premise— to the existence of consequent «q», this information allows reasoners to make '*modus ponens*' inferences without specifying the content of the implicit model. In contrast, '*modus tollens*' (MT) inferences require a *complete fleshing out* of the implicit representation, since the initial explicit model does not include information about the categorical premise (¬q). The full and combined representation of the two premises contains two further explicit models about negated consequents (see table), which permit the solution of inferences: the third model supports the correct conclusion that the antecedent cannot occur in the absence of the consequent.

TABLE 19.2
Valid Inferences in conditional arguments and mental model representation

	Argument	Representation	
Modus Ponens (MP)	If p then q p therefore, q	[p] q ...	*explicit model* *implicit model*
Modus Tollens (MT)	If p then q no q therefore, no p	p q ¬p q ¬p ¬q	*explicit model* « «

Difficulty of problems: number of models or number of rules?

According to this type of assumption, mental models theory predicts the difficulty of deductive problems as a function of the *number of explicit models* to be constructed in order to solve them: *the more models that have to be constructed, the harder the inferential task will be.* Thus, mental models theory appropriately explains the greater difficulty of MT compared to MP; as we have pointed out, MT involves more models to be explicitly represented before the conclusion can be obtained.

However, there is an alternative explanation of human performance in deductive problems. As we have stated before, some psychologists suppose that people reason by applying formal rules of inference that they know (mental rules), and that the difficulty of problems depends particularly on the length of the derivation process. That is, difficulty is related to the *number of rules or inferential steps* to be applied in order to reach the conclusion, although other factors —such as the complexity of rules— that may affect performance are also recognized (see Braine, 1990; Rips, 1994). According to this interpretation, MT is harder than MP because it requires accessing and applying more rules than MP. Therefore, a general prediction of mental rules theories can be formulated as follows: *the more mental rules that have to be applied and inferential steps that have to be made for solving a deductive problem, the harder the inferential task will be.*

Multiple conditional problems as a test of both theories

Multiple conditional problems are based on arguments with various conditional sentences as premises that can form a chain of transitive relations. The following is a canonical example:

> if e then a
> If a then b
> If b then c
> What follows between a and c?

This kind of problems can be used to evaluate the relative plausibility of mental models and formal rules theories, since they lead to *different predictions* based on the different representations and processes that each theory proposes (see Table 19.3).

According to mental rules theories, multiconditional problems can be solved by applying two basic schemas of inference: the *'modus ponens'* rule, which allows direct 'modus ponens' inferences and the *schema for conditional proof*, that allows a conditional of the form, *if a then d*, to be derived whenever a hypothesis, *a*, yields a conclusion, *d*. (see Braine, 1978; Braine & O'Brien, 1991; Rips, 1983). Thus, for the example presented above, given that the first conditional premise is irrelevant, the mental derivation would follow an inferential chain as follows:

> a   [by Hypothesis-H]
> b   [Modus Ponens of the second proposition-MP2]
> c   [Modus Ponens of the third proposition-MP3]
> If a then c   [Conditional Proof-CP]

Thus, as we can see, the process postulated by rules theories requires the application of several rules.

According to mental models theory, the comprehension of the first conditional premise, 'if e then a', yields a semantic representation:

[e]   a
    ...

where the second conditional premise, 'if a then b', can be directly added to the first model, yielding the following representation:

[[e]   a]b
    ...

Likewise, the third conditional premise, 'if b then c', can also be added, yielding the following initial representation of the problem:

[[[e]   a]b]c
    ...

From these models an informative and valid conclusion can easily be drawn: 'if a then c'. People do not need to flesh out the implicit models.

Consider now a new multiple conditional problem:

if e then b
If a then b
If b then c
What follows between a and c?

Given that the first premise is also irrelevant, rules theories postulate exactly the same set of rules for reaching the conclusion. However, mental models theory postulates a different representation. The first conditional statement yields:

[e]   b
    ...

where the second conditional cannot be added, so that the construction of a new model is required:

[e]   b
[a]   b
    ...

Finally, the remaining premise can be added to the existing explicit models, yielding the following initial representation of the problem:

[[e]   b]c
[[a]   b]c
    ...

As we can see, mental models theory postulates that this problem demands the construction of two models, and that it will therefore be harder than the previous one.

In sum, whereas for the mental rules theories the two problems have the same degree of difficulty —they require the application of the same set of rules—, the mental models theory postulates a different degree of difficulty, that depends on the number of models to be constructed. Below we present two studies designed to test just this differential prediction using *response latency* measures in addition to *accuracy* ones. Our second main objective was to investigate the *process* of reasoning by using the *reading times of the premises*. This is a point on which formal rules theories does not make specific predictions, since the process they postulate is purely *deterministic*. In contrast, as we have seen, from the point of view of mental models theory the process is *strategic*. In this respect we wanted to know whether the first comprehension stage (understanding of premise's information) can be analyzed from the reading times of premises. We think that this measure must reflect the difficulties of model construction, viewing this process as a progressive integration of the successive information stated by the premises. So, globally speaking, we expect that the construction of multiple-model representations will imply more reading times at some moment of the process. Obviously, the principal problem here is to elucidate the specific operations —more or less demanding and time consuming— that may underlay the construction of each type of representation and if we can identify particular steps into this process associated to the successive premises. In the following studies we explore some hypothesis about these issues.

A FIRST STUDY WITH MULTICONDITIONALS

In a previous study, García Madruga and Johnson-Laird (1994) tested the different predictions of mental rules theories and mental models theory about difficulty —measured in terms of *accuracy* and *response latency*— with the problems presented in Table 19.3. As we can see, the three problems were valid and according to model theory, they require the construction of one, two and three models for their solution, respectively. Thus, it was expected that one-model problems would be easier than multiple ones and that there would be an order of progressive difficulty: one-model, two-model, three-model. However, according the mental models theory, the crucial difference should be between one-model and multiple-model problems. In contrast, from the standpoint of mental logic, the first and second problems were exactly the same —they implied the same five formal rules of derivation—, whilst problem three should be easier —only implying four lines. Thus, in line with this analysis, the predictions of model and formal rules theories are basically the opposite.

Similarly, as for the *reading times of premises*, it was predicted that the difficulties for integrating information from new premises would consume more time in multiple-model problems than in one-model problems; consequently, the fourth premise reading time of multiple-model problems should be longer than in one-model problems, assuming that this process concludes at the end of the set of premises. There were no clear predictions as to the reading times of second and third premises. Finally, as for first premise no differences was predicted, since it implies exactly the same condition for all problems.

TABLE 19.3
Application of the general representation and process to some multi-conditional problems

Problems	Formal rules of derivation	Mental model representation
1- If e then a If a then b If b then c If c then d What follows between a and d? Conclusion: *If a then d*	***5 lines:*** *1ˢᵗ premise irrelevant* a[by Hypothesis] b[MP of 2ⁿᵈ pre.] c[MP of 3ʳᵈ pre.] d[MP of 4ᵗʰ pre.] if a then d [Conditional Proof]	***1 model (1m):*** [e]a [[e]a]b [[[e]a]b]c [[[[e]a]b]c]d **[[[[e] a] b] c] d** ...
2-(*) If e then b If a then b If b then c If c then d What follows between a and d? Conclusion: *If a then d*	***5 lines:*** *1ˢᵗ premise irrelevant* a[H] b[MP2] c[MP3] d[MP4] if a then d[CP]	***2 models (2m):*** [e]b [e]b/[a]b [[e]b]c/ [[a]b]c [[[e]b]c]d/ [[[a]b]c]d **[[[e] b] c] d** **[[[a] b] c] d** ...
3-(*) If e then b If a then b If c then b If b then d What follows between a and d? Conclusion: *If a then d*	***4 lines:*** *1ˢᵗ and 3ʳᵈ premise irrelevant* a[H] b[MP2] d[MP4] if a then d[CP]	***3 models (3m):*** [e]b [e]b/ [a]b [e]b / [a]b / [c]b [[e]b]d / [[a]b]d / [[c]b]d **[[e] b] d** **[[a] b] d** **[[c] b] d** ...

(*)   The studies used, as distracters, an invalid form of multiple model problems (2 and 3) by formulating the question for two non-related items (*What follows between a and e?);* in these cases the correct answer was «Nothing follows».

Twenty Princeton University graduates were presented with two examples of each sort of problem, following two inverse orders. The premises always described conditional relations between food ingredients, and were presented as recipes for hypothetical dishes from the cuisine of an imaginary country. The following illustrates this content in a one-model problem:

If I use mayonnaise then I use lemon
If I use lemon then I use haddock

If I use haddock then I use endive
If I use endive then I use escarole
What follows between lemon and escarole?

Participants were tested individually by means of a computer program (Mac-Laboratory Reaction Time) that permits the measurement of latencies: reading time for each premise and response time (from the question until the participant indicates that he/she has drawn a conclusion). To obtain these separate measures, the premises and final question appeared successively on the computer screen, being controlled by a key that had to be pressed. Specifically, participants were asked to type a letter («c») when they had understood each premise and when they had decided upon an answer to the final question. They received previous instructions and some practice problems with feed-back about correct conclusions; this feed-back was omitted in the experimental trials.

Results and discussion

The global results are shown in Figures 19.1 and 19.2. As we can see, the results clearly confirmed the general predictions of mental models theory —particularly in relation to response latencies—, although some unexpected results were found. First, there were no significant differences in the *percentages of correct conclusions*, all scores being around 100% correct responses (100, 95 and 97 for one, two and three-model problems, respectively). We suggest that this ceiling effect might be produced by the special characteristics of the sample. The participants were all post-graduates having a research position in different Princeton University departments and they were most skillful with computer tasks. Anyhow, from the point of view of the final outcome of performance *(product)*, the *accuracy* results do not offer clear information, though the trend of the data is consistent with our hypothesis.

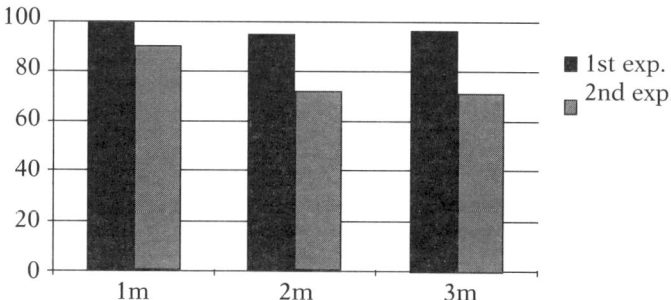

Figure 19.1. Percentages of correct conclusions in the two experiments.

However, as for the *response latencies* (see Figure 19.2), the data clearly confirmed mental models theory predictions: as expected, there was an order of difficulty: one-model problem responses were faster than two-model ones, and two-model problem responses were faster than three-model ones (6.45; 7.98

and 9.01 respectively; Page's L=255, n=19; p<0.02). Likewise, one-model problems were significantly faster than multiple-model problems (Wilcoxon's T=39, n=19, p<0.025, one-tail). These results cannot be easily explained by mental rules theories, since their predictions are practically the opposite. The clearest contrast is between one-model and multiple-model problems (problem 1 vs. 2 and 3), not between problems of four and five rules of derivation (3 vs. 1 and 2).

With regard to *reading times of premises*, the results were also consistent with the main prediction concerning the fourth premise: one-model problems (3.47) were reliably read more quickly than multiple-model problems (4.47; Wilcoxon's T=42, n=19, p<0.025, one-tail). Similarly, one-model problems were read more quickly than two-model (4.74) and three-model (4.20) problems (Wilcoxon's T=36, n=19, p<0.01 and T=44, n=19, p<0.025, respectively, one-tail). Hence, the idea that the fourth premise —the last— have a particular implication in the models construction process seems plausible. But we will return later to this point on the base of the second experiment results (see discussion).

Also expected was the absence of significant differences between problems with regard to the first premise. However, a notorious result not predicted was found: reading times were significantly longer for the third premise in two-model problems (5.68) than in one-model (4.22) and three-model (3.51) problems (Wilcoxon's T=31, n=19, p= 0.01 and Wilcoxon's T=10, n=19, p<0.001; respectively, two-tails). There were no significant differences in this premise between one-model and three-model problems.

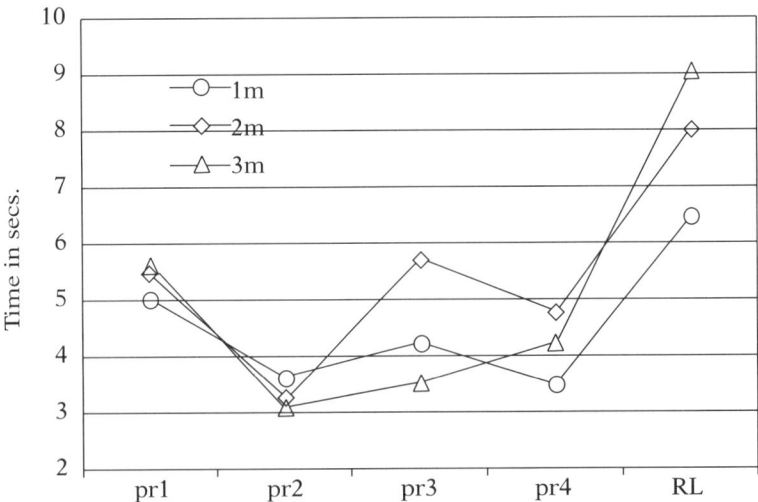

Figure 19.2. Premise reading times and response latencies (1st exp.).

This last result is difficult to explain, since the third premise does not seem to imply a particular condition, comparing the two multiple model problems. Taking into account direct representation (see Table 3), the fourth premise on three-model problems appears to be an equivalent condition: both problems require the multiple integration of the new item into previous models. In fact, the last case should perhaps be more demanding —integration of item «d» into three models for three-model problems vs. integration of «c» into two models for two-model problems— but the times consumed are not similar or significantly longer. This type of inconsistency suggests that the information is not necessarily combined and integrated into the models as soon as the premise is read. Perhaps the information of some premises is kept in a temporal buffer, which leads to a crucial question: when do reasoners construct mental models?

A REPLICATION OF THE PREVIOUS STUDY

In order to clarify some of the unexpected results found in the first experiment, we carried out another study with the same predictions. We tried to avoid the ceiling effect found and to check processing time data. So, the design and procedure were as in the previous study, as were the measures (*percentage of correct conclusions* and *response latencies* as measures of reasoning product and *premise reading times* as a measure of reasoning process). This time, however, in order to avoid the ceiling effect, the participants were 20 Spanish UNED graduate students, not particularly experienced and skillful with this kind of task. Participants solved the same three types of problem in a translated Spanish version. Consequently, this second experiment can be considered as a replication study.

Results and discussion

Results are shown in Figures 19.1 and 19.3. As we can see in Figure 19.1, data about accuracy of responses show now clearly the predicted pattern of difficulty. That is to say, the ceiling effect has disappeared favoring mental models theory predictions. One-model problems were significantly easier than multiple-model ones (90% and 72,5% of correct responses, respectively; Wilcoxon's T=3, n=20, p<0.02, one-tail). Specifically, one-model problems were easier than two-model (Wilcoxon's T = 0, n=20, p<0.01, one-tail) and three-model problems (Wilcoxon's T=2, n=20, p<0.04, one-tail). The difference between the two multiple-model problems was not significant.

On the other hand, the expected pattern of differences in response latencies (see Figure 3) was not completely achieved. Although we found the same predicted order of difficulty [one-model (7.66) < two-models (9.77) < three-models (10.58)] and that one-model problems were faster than two-model problems (Wilcoxon's T=22, n=15, p<0.025, one-tail), the difference between one-model and three-model problems was only marginally significant (Wilcoxon's T=32, n=15, p=0.055, one-tail).

As for *processing time measures*, we have found that, as in the previous study, the third premise in two-model problems takes more time to process than in the other two types, although in this case the differences between two-model problems (6.50) and one-model (5.29) and three-model (5.44) problems was not significant. However, the differences in the fourth premise were clearly confirmed: reading time was reliably faster in one-model problems (4.33) than in two-model problems (4.98; Wilcoxon's T=11, n=14, p<0.05, one-tail) and three-model problems (5.71; Wilcoxon's T=9, n=15, p<0.01, one-tail). The difference between the two multiple-model problems were not significant. Hence, the more demanding process that mental models theory attribute to construction of multiple-model problems seems clearly supported by these consistent results about reading times in fourth premise.

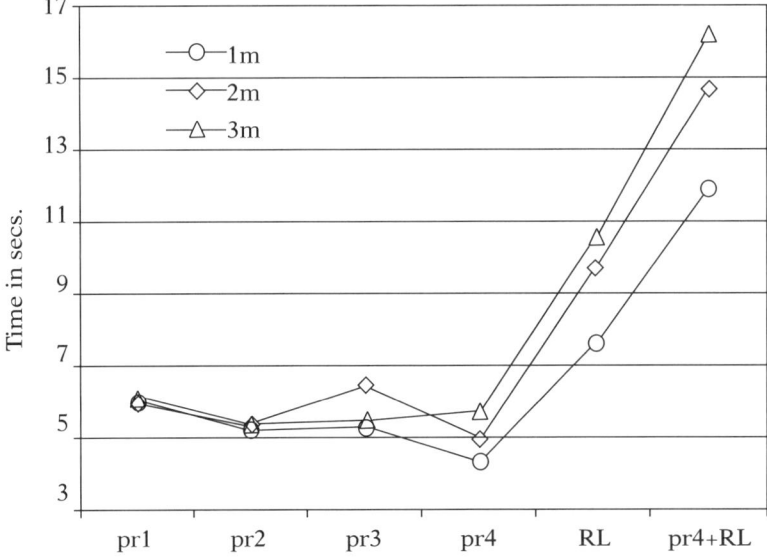

Figure 19.3. Premise reading times and response latencies (2nd exp.).

Thus, overall, the results replicate those of the previous study, but some data still requires explanation. First, the reading time of the third premise in one-model problems is once again the longest; although the differences with one-model and three-model problems does not reach a significant level (p=0.10 and p=0.055, respectively) they suggest the existence of a consistent tendency. How can we explain it? Let us consider the semantic nature of processing postulated by mental models theory to try and explain this trend. When the reasoner faces the third premise in this kind of problem, he/she has already built two models in which he/she must integrate the new item «c» (see Table 19.3). Thus, the process would imply a «double integration». Insofar as this *multiple integration* uses up more resources, it would explain the remarkable processing time compared to the simple integration required in one-model problems. However, if this is the case, why does the similar «triple integration» required by the fourth premise in three-model problems not show a comparable or even significantly longer reading time? Let us consider the following: presumably, the working memory load is greatest at the time of processing the fourth premise, and reasoners know that it is the final information before the question. Thus, a plausible strategic way of minimizing processing and economizing resources is to *suspend multiple integration* of new items, pending more information about the demands of the problem. That is, reasoners may *keep the new items in a buffer* (without integrating them into the models) until they know which specific model must be completed in order to answer the final question. This explanation is consistent with the above-mentioned principle of cognitive economy, since it indicates that reasoners tend to minimize their cognitive work.

The second issue that requires explanation is the absence of a entirely significant difference in response latency between one-model and three-model problems in this second study. However, according to the previous explanation, it is difficult to be precise about the exact moment at which each step is made in the course of model's construction. In multiple models problems, the final step may be made by reasoners only when they know the specific demands (after the question) and they have completed the construction of only the relevant model. In other words, given the structure of task it is possible that some reasoners decide to use the strategy of waiting until the question is read in order to complete the construction of the model, while others might decide not to wait, and integrate all of the information at the end of the fourth premise. Therefore, the *critical time measure for evaluating the difficulty of processing* in some cases *would probably be neither the fourth premise reading time nor the response latency, but the addition of the two*. In fact, this new measure was analyzed in the second study, and shows the most consistent differences related to the number of models (see Figure 3). That is, if we add up the reading times of the fourth premise and the response latency we obtain significant differences in the direction predicted by mental models theory: one-model problems (11.99) are solved more quickly than two-model (14.75; Wilcoxon's T=14, n=15, p<0.01, one-tail) and three-model (16.29; Wilcoxon's T=20, n=15, p<0.05, one-tail) problems.

CONCLUSIONS

Mental models theory emphasizes the role of the problem's final representation in order to make predictions about the reasoner's performance. The data reported in the two studies presented here, suggest the necessity of analyzing and extending the theory to the model's construction process —particularly the successive integration of premise information into models that are being constructed. In this regard, processing times in multiconditional problems suggest various issues related to the strategic processing assumed by mental models theory. First, the complete integration of premise information into multiple alternative models may be a particular demanding task; second, as the load on processing resources increases, the simple retention of new information in a temporal buffer would be the preferable option for reasoners, and thus, third, reasoners may wait until the final question in order to only complete the construction of the model which is necessary to make a relevant conclusion.

Furthermore, this line of thinking allows also to make a first tentative response to the central question we have posed: when do reasoners construct mental models? Do they construct the models for each premise while reading them? Are the meanings of the premises brought together while they are being read only after the final question has been encountered? In accordance with the general strategic nature of processing and the particular suggestions of multiconditional studies, we can formulate the following points:

— Reasoners integrate the incoming information into explicit models that are being built, as long as the load on working memory does not exceed a certain limit.
— The more alternative models yielded by the comprehension of premises, the more demanding the integration process will be.
— In these circumstances, the probability of using a buffer to reserve some information, increases as more processing resources are consumed without knowing which model will be relevant to the conclusion.
— The global process must be analyzed in terms of the commonly rec[ognized trade-off between the structural limits of working memory capacity and the functional possibilities of strategic processing.

Obviously, these proposals need more specific research, though we have already found some other results in the same direction (see García Madruga *et al.* this volume). In particular, we must establish and define the different operations reasoners may use at different moments of processing and the amount of resources they consume in various circumstances. In this sense we hypothesize, for example, that to integrate the new information by simple addition to the prior model representation should be less demanding than the integration that involves a complete reconstruction of the model. Such ideas will be explored in further experiments that are in preparation.

ACKNOWLEDGEMENTS

We thank Phil Johnson-Laird and Ruth Byrne who suggested the original idea for this work. The research was part of the «Comprehension and inference in conditional reasoning» project funded by the Spanish Ministry of Education and Science (PB94-0394).

REFERENCES

BRAINE, M. D. S. (1978): «On the relation between the natural logic of reasoning and the standard logic». *Psychological Review, 85,* 1-21.
— (1990): «The «Natural Logic» Approach to Reasoning. In W.F. Overton (Ed.), *Reasoning, Necessity and Logic: Developmental Perspectives.* Hillsdale, NJ: Lawrence Erlbaum Associates.
BRAINE, M. D. S., & O'BRIEN, D. P. (1991): «A theory of If: A lexical entry, reasoning program, and pragmatic principles». *Psychological Review, 98,* 182-203.

BRAINE, M. D. S., & O'BRIEN, D., eds. (1998): *Mental Logic.* Mahwah, NJ: Lawrence Erlbaum Associates.

GARCÍA-MADRUGA, J. A., & JOHNSON-LAIRD, P. N. (1994): «Multiple Conditionals: Rules or Models». Paper presented at *Seventh Meeting of European Society for Cognitive Psychology.* Lisbon, September, 1994.

GARCÍA-MADRUGA, J. A., MORENO, S., CARRIEDO, N., GUTIÉRREZ, F., & JOHNSON-LAIRD, P. N. (in press): «Are conjunctive inferences easier than disjunctive inferences? A comparison of rules and models». *Quarterly Journal of Experimental Psychology.*

JOHNSON-LAIRD, P. N. (1983): *Mental Models.* Cambridge: Cambridge University Press.

JOHNSON-LAIRD, P. N., & BYRNE, R. M. J. (1991): *Deduction.* Hove, East Sussex: LEA.

— (1993): «Models of conditionals: a defense». *Cognition, 48,*

JOHNSON-LAIRD, P. N., SAVARY, F., & BUCCIARELLI, M. (1999): «Strategies and tactics in reasoning». In N. Schaeken, G. de Vooght, A. Vandierendonek & G. D'Y dewall (Eds.), *Deductive reasoning and strategies*, Mahwah, NJ: Erlbaum.

JOHNSON-LAIRD, P. N., BYRNE, R. M. J., & SCHAEKEN, W. (1992): «Propositional reasoning by model». *Psychological Review, 99,* 418-439.

RIPS, L. J. (1983): «Cognitive processes in propositional reasoning». *Psychological Review, 90,* 38-71.

— (1994): *The Psychology of Proof. Deductive reasoning in Human Reasoning.* Cambridge, Mass.: MIT Press.

20

COUNTERFACTUAL THINKING AND CAUSAL REASONING

ALICE MCELENEY
RUTH M. J. BYRNE

Las personas comparan a menudo la realidad con lo que pudo, debería o podría haber sido. Por ejemplo, un individuo implicado en un accidente de automovil podría pensar que podía haber evitado el accidente si no hubiera ido a tanta velocidad. Este tipo de pensamiento contrafáctico sobre alternativas imaginarias a los acontecimientos y situaciones reales tiene una influencia considerable en los juicios que realizamos, en los sentimientos y en las acciones.

La investigación y la teoría previa sugieren que las consecuencias psicológicas del pensamiento contrafáctico son el resultado de sus implicaciones causales, y que el principal propósito del pensamiento contrafáctico es determinar las causas de los acontecimientos. Cuando las personas piensan sobre cómo un determinado resultado podía haber sido diferente, mentalmente deshacen aspectos de la situación fáctica, y en particular, los antecedentes que conducen al resultado. Esta simulación mental de situaciones alternativas podría ser importante en el establecimiento de relaciones causales entre acontecimientos antecedentes y resultados. Las conclusiones causales que las personas pueden extraer a partir del pensamiento contrafáctico podrían depender de qué aspectos de la situación deshacen, y estas inferencias causales podrían influir en sus juicios de acontecimientos pasados y en sus intenciones sobre futuros comportamientos.

En este capítulo, consideramos la relación entre pensamiento contrafáctico y explicación causal. La investigación previa sugiere que el pensamiento contrafáctico puede influir en los juicios de causalidad. Sin embargo, nuestra evidencia experimental muestra que las personas producen espontáneamente pensamientos contrafácticos y explicaciones en diferentes situaciones: los pensamientos contrafácticos se producen más a menudo en situaciones con antecedentes controlables y resultados negativos, sin tener en cuenta si el resultado es esperado o no; mientras que las explicaciones se producen más a menudo en situaciones con resultados inesperados y negativos, sin tener en cuenta si los antecedentes son o no controlables. Estos resultados apoyan la idea de que el pensamiento contrafáctico y las explicaciones causales sirven para propósitos distintos, pero complementarios: el pensamiento contrafáctico está relacionado con la prevención y la explicación causal con la predicción. Se discuten las implicaciones de estas conclusiones para las teorías de los procesos implicados en el pensamiento contrafáctico y en el pensamiento causal.

> *I coulda been a contender. I coulda had class and been somebody. Real class. Instead of a bum, which is what I am.*
>
> On the Waterfront

People often compare reality with what could have, should have, or might have been. In the film *On the Waterfront*, the character Terry Malloy, played by Marlon Brando, compares his real situation (being a «bum») to an imaginary *counterfactual* alternative (being a successful boxer), and he laments that if his brother hadn't held him back, this counterfactual world could have been a reality. The main feature of counterfactual thoughts that distinguishes them from other forms of imaginary thinking is that they are always evoked by some real outcome, and in general the aim of generating counterfactual scenarios is to mentally *undo* this outcome by imagining changes to preceding events. For example, a person involved in a car accident might construct a counterfactual alternative in which the accident is avoided by mutating the fact that she was speeding: «If only I hadn't been speeding, I wouldn't have crashed». Counterfactual thoughts are often expressed as conditionals, including both an antecedent and a consequent, and in English their counterfactual nature is usually suggested by the use of the subjunctive mood.

Counterfactual thinking about imaginary alternatives to real events seems to be a central characteristic of human thought. Perhaps the earliest documentation of the use of counterfactual thinking is in the works of the early Greek philosophers, who often employed counterfactuals to explain ideas about the nature of reality (see Rescher, 1995). Today, the widespread use of counterfactual thinking in many intellectual disciplines, including philosophy, science, economics, law, history and politics, attests to its versatility and sophistication as a cognitive tool (see, e.g., Tetlock & Belkin, 1996). Moreover, in addition to intentionally constructing counterfactuals in order to solve intellectual problems, people often *spontaneously* generate counterfactual alternatives to events in their everyday lives, and these thoughts can have significant cognitive and emotional consequences (e.g., Davis, Lehman, Silver, Wortman & Ellard, 1995).

The philosophical nature of counterfactual statements has been debated for centuries, but it is only in the last two decades that the psychological processes involved in counterfactual thinking have begun to be systematically investigated. One issue that has been addressed by cognitive psychologists is the question of *how* people construct counterfactual alternatives to reality. Research from this perspective has been concerned with the *content* of people's counterfactual thoughts, that is, which aspects of reality people change when they think about counterfactual alternatives. Another question that has been raised is *why* people generate counterfactual scenarios. Most research from this perspective has been concerned with the *consequences* of counterfactual thoughts, and the psychological functions they may serve.

This chapter addresses the issue of why people engage in counterfactual thinking. We are particularly interested in the role of counterfactual thoughts in everyday reasoning. Counterfactual thinking may be involved in a wide range of cognitive processes. As an example, in this chapter we will focus on the relationship between counterfactual thinking and causal reasoning. We begin by reviewing previous research on the cognitive processes that determine the consequences of counterfactual thinking. We then discuss the relationship between counterfactual thinking and causal explanation, considering in particular, the determinants of spontaneous counterfactual thoughts and causal explanations (McEleney & Byrne, 1998). Finally, we discuss the implications of the results for theories of counterfactual and causal thinking within the mental models framework.

COGNITIVE PROCESSES AND COUNTERFACTUAL CONSEQUENCES

Counterfactual thoughts can have significant psychological consequences. For example, thinking about how an unwanted outcome could have turned out better can exacerbate emotional reactions to the event (e.g., Davis *et al.*, 1995; McMullen, Markman & Gavanski, 1995), and such thoughts can also lead to biased judgements of responsibility and blame (e.g., Branscombe, Owen, Garstka & Coleman, 1996). Much research on the consequences of counterfactual thinking has been concerned with such negative implications. However, counterfactual thinking may also have useful consequences. For example, thinking about how changes in one's own behaviour could have made an outcome different increases perceived control (e.g., McMullen *et al.*, 1995), and it may inspire a sense of hope for the future (Boninger, Gleicher & Strathman, 1994). Furthermore, prompting people to generate counterfactual alternatives after failure at a task increases their intentions to perform success-facilitating behaviours in the future, and results in improvements in their subsequent performance (Roese, 1994).

What cognitive processes determine the consequences of counterfactual thoughts? The emotional consequences may result mainly from *contrast effects*, whereas the cognitive and behavioural consequences may result from *causal inference effects* (e.g., Roese & Olson, 1995, 1997; Roese, 1997). Contrast effects occur when a comparison of an outcome with a better or worse alternative makes the real outcome seem either worse or better in contrast, thereby making emotional reactions to the outcome more extreme. Causal inference effects occur because the conditional structure of a counterfactual statement suggests that there is a causal relationship between the antecedent and the consequent. For example, the counterfactual conditional, «If I had not been lazy, I would not have failed the exam» may suggest that I failed the exam *because* I was lazy. The causal conclusions people draw from counterfactual conditionals depend on which aspects of the factual situation they undo, and these inferences may influence their judgements of past events and their intentions for future behaviour.

If the cognitive and behavioural consequences of counterfactual thinking depend on the causal implications of counterfactual thoughts, then counterfactual thinking and causal reasoning may be very closely related cognitive processes. Our aim in this chapter is to further explore the relationship between counterfactual thinking and causal thinking.

COUNTERFACTUAL THINKING AND CAUSAL EXPLANATION

Philosophers have long suggested that counterfactuals are useful in determining causality. For example, Mill's (1967/1843) method of difference states that if two occurrences with different outcomes otherwise differ only in the presence or absence of a particular antecedent, this antecedent can be judged to be a cause of the outcome. Similarly, Lewis (1973, p. 557) argues that counterfactuals are our best means of understanding the concept of causality: «we think of a cause as something that makes a difference from what would have happened without it. Had it been absent, its effects...would have been absent as well». This intuition has also been discussed by legal analysts (e.g., Hart & Honore, 1985), and it is even reflected in tort law: «The defendant's conduct is not a cause of the event, if the event would have occurred without it» (Prosser, 1971, p. 239).

More recently, psychologists have provided empirical evidence that counterfactual thinking can influence people's judgements of the causal relations between events. For example, when a scenario outcome can be mentally undone by imagining that a preceding event had been different, people judge that event to be more causal of the outcome than when changing the event would not undo the outcome (e.g., Roese & Olson, 1996; Wells & Gavanski, 1989). Some theorists have argued that counterfactual thinking is central to the process of causal reasoning (e.g., Lipe, 1991; Wells & Gavanski, 1989), and others have even questioned whether counterfactual thinking and causal explanation should be considered distinct processes: «the entire counterfactual literature might be viewed as an elaborate reformulation of traditional attribution theories» (Roese, 1997, p. 22).

However, other research suggests that there are important differences between counterfactual thinking and causal attribution. For example, people tend to focus on different antecedent events when they are asked to mentally undo an outcome than when they are asked about the causes of the outcome (e.g., Mandel & Lehman, 1996; N'gbala & Branscombe, 1995). In one experiment based on a scenario about a woman whose husband was killed in a plane crash (Mandel & Lehman, 1996), most participants' counterfactual statements focused on events that were under her control (e.g., «She should have pleaded with him not to go by plane»), whereas their causal explanations focused on events that general knowledge would suggest covary with the outcome (e.g., an engine malfunction, or pilot error). The authors argue that causal and counterfactual statements differ in content because they serve different functions: causal explanations are concerned with the *prediction* of future outcomes, whereas counterfactual thoughts are concerned with the *prevention* of unwanted outcomes. Their interpretation suggests that counterfactual thinking and causal explanation are distinct phenomena that rely on different reasoning processes.

However, Roese and Olson (1997, p. 37) propose that counterfactual thinking and causal thinking *are* very closely related processes, and that differences in people's answers to counterfactual and causal questions may merely reflect conversational norms: «Asking someone how something could have been different might cue implicit expectations for personal, controllable actions, whereas asking someone about the cause of an event might implicitly suggest a wider causal search, one that embraces a variety of causal candidates.». The suggestion that participants' responses in studies of counterfactual thinking may be strongly influenced by task demands is supported by several studies that have found significant differences in participants' responses depending on the type of instructions they were given (e.g., Kasimatis & Wells, 1995; Roese & Olson, 1997; Sanna & Turley, 1996).

SPONTANEOUS COUNTERFACTUAL THOUGHTS AND EXPLANATIONS

We have recently completed a series of experiments on counterfactual and causal thinking (see McEleney & Byrne, 1998). One of our aims was to clarify whether differences in the content of counterfactual thoughts and causal explanations reflect genuine differences in their functions, or the effects of task demands. In two experiments, we compared the antecedents of spontaneous counterfactual thoughts and explanations. Unlike differences in the content of *directed* counterfactual thoughts and explanations, differences in the determinants of *spontaneous* counterfactual thoughts and explanations cannot be attributed merely to differences in the assumptions cued by different questions. Comparing the situations in which people spontaneously generate counterfactual thoughts and explanations may be a more fruitful way to determine the genuine functions of these thoughts in everyday life.

In one experiment, we constructed eight versions of a scenario about moving to a new town. The versions varied in whether the outcome was good or bad, and expected or unexpected, and in whether the four antecedent events were controllable or uncontrollable. An example of the scenario —the good, expected outcome version with uncontrollable antecedents— is as follows (the changes made to the scenario in the different versions are presented in Appendix 1):

«You're moving house to start a new job in a different city. The night before you leave, you write down your thoughts about the move in your diary:

...I've got mixed feelings about moving to a place where I know hardly anyone - my friends and social life are so important to me. But I'm sure it will be easy to settle in to the new town - I've never had any trouble making new friends...

A lot happens in your first two weeks in the new town. During your first week at work, a staff dinner is held. You have to go because your boss has asked all the staff to be there. You enjoy the evening and meet a lot of people. That weekend, your next-door neighbours invite you to a party. Most of the people who live on your road will be there. However, that evening you're extremely ill with the flu, so you can't go. The next week, you happen to bump into an old friend who lives in the town and he insists on showing you around. He takes you out the following evening and he introduces you to a lot of his friends. A few days later, a colleague tells you there's a membership vacancy at her sports club. You think joining would be a good way to meet people, but there's no way you can afford the membership fee.

Six weeks after the move, things have turned out exactly as you had expected. You've made a lot of good friends in the new town, and you feel quite happy and at home. You are very pleased, but not surprised.»

In the experiment, 248 undergraduates from the University of Dublin were randomly allocated one of the eight versions of the scenario. The participants were asked to read the scenario and to imagine themselves in the situation described. They were asked to consider what they would think if the events had really happened to them, and to write a one-page diary entry about their imagined experience. The dependent measures were the numbers of spontaneous counterfactual thoughts and explanations that participants produced in these diaries. A counterfactual was defined as «any mention of a change to a scenario event that would change the outcome», and an explanation was defined as «any statement that attempts to explain why the outcome occurred». The frequencies were recorded by the first author and by an independent rater who was unaware of the hypotheses or experimental conditions. Discrepancies were resolved by discussion. Examples of two counterfactuals are, «I could have made more of an effort to meet new people» and, «Perhaps if I'd gone to the neighbours' party, I'd have made friends». Examples of two explanations are, «Everyone is making me welcome so that it is much easier for me to make friends» and, «I do feel lonely and upset, probably because it is all so new».

The results showed that first, participants produced more counterfactuals in the bad outcome conditions than in the good outcome conditions (M = 1.22 vs M = 0.38, F (1, 240) = 52.67, p < 0.01). They also produced more explanations in the bad outcome conditions than in the good outcome conditions (M = 1.91 vs M = 1.34, F (1, 240) = 12.26. p < 0.01). Second, there was no difference in the number of counterfactuals participants produced in the unexpected conditions and the expected conditions (M = 0.83 vs M = 0.76, F (1, 240) = 0.14, p = 0.7). In contrast, they produced somewhat more explanations for unexpected outcomes than for expected outcomes, although this effect did not reach statistical significance (M = 1.79 vs M = 1.47, F (1, 240) = 2.78, p = 0.1). Finally, participants produced more counterfactuals in the controllable conditions than in the uncontrollable conditions (M = 1.1 vs M = 0.5, F (1, 240) = 26.62, p < 0.01), whereas there was no difference in the number of explanations they produced in the controllable conditions and the uncontrollable conditions (M = 1.72 vs M = 1.6, F (1, 240) = 0.02, p = 0.88). Table 20.1 presents the mean numbers of counterfactuals and explanations for each condition.

TABLE 20.1
Mean numbers of counterfactuals and explanations for each condition

	Counterfactuals	Explanations
Controllable		
Unexpected		
Bad outcome	1.75	2.19
Good outcome	0.42	1.45
Expected		
Bad outcome	1.63	1.70
Good outcome	0.57	1.20
Uncontrollable		
Unexpected		
Bad outcome	0.81	1.81
Good outcome	0.29	1.55
Expected		
Bad outcome	0.65	1.93
Good outcome	0.24	1.15
Mean	0.79	1.76

The findings support the idea that causal explanation and counterfactual thinking serve distinct but complementary functions (Mandel & Lehman, 1996). The results show that both counterfactual thoughts and explanations are evoked more by bad outcomes than by good outcomes, consistent with the suggestion that both processes are ultimately motivated by an intention to avoid future failures. However, explanations (but not counterfactuals) are also evoked somewhat more by unexpected outcomes than by expected outcomes, consistent with the idea that explanations are mainly concerned with the *prediction* of future outcomes (explanations may be evoked by unexpected outcomes because unexpected outcomes indicate that prediction has failed). Furthermore, counterfactual thoughts (but not explanations) are also evoked more by controllable antecedents than by uncontrollable antecedents, consistent with the idea that counterfactual thoughts are mainly concerned with the *prevention* of unwanted outcomes (counterfactual thoughts may be evoked more by controllable antecedents because controllable antecedents indicate that an outcome is potentially preventable). These conclusions have implications for theories of the cognitive processes involved in counterfactual and causal thinking, and we will discuss these implications in the rest of the chapter.

COUNTERFACTUAL THOUGHTS DO NOT
DETERMINE CAUSAL THOUGHTS

Previous research and theory have suggested that counterfactual thinking is central to causal reasoning. However, if, as our findings suggest, counterfactual thinking is more concerned with preventability than causality, counterfactuals may not be very useful in determining causes. People make a distinction between the *strong cause* of an outcome and the *enabling conditions* that allowed the cause to have its effect (e.g., Cheng & Novick, 1991). For example, a dropped cigarette butt might be viewed as the cause of a forest fire, whereas the presence of oxygen would be considered a mere condition that enabled the fire to occur, rather than a cause. However, an outcome can be prevented by undoing either causes or enabling conditions: if either the cigarette butt or the oxygen had been absent, the fire would not have occurred. As counterfactual statements about how an outcome could have been prevented need not make a distinction between causes and enabling conditions, they are not sufficient to determine causality, at least in the «strong» sense of the term.

Consistent with this view, participants asked to generate questions they would like to have answered in order to assess a causal hypothesis very rarely generate counterfactual questions (e.g., Lipe, 1991). Moreover, although spontaneous counterfactual thoughts are often related to judgements of preventability, they are very often unrelated to judgements of causality. For example, in a study of bereaved parents, most participants spontaneously generated counterfactuals in which changes to their own behaviour prevented their child's death, however very few participants judged that their behaviour might have caused the child's death (Davis *et al.*, 1995). Even young children make a distinction between the concepts of preventability and causality: pre-school children produce counterfactual statements significantly more often in response to questions about how an outcome could have been prevented than in response to questions about why the outcome occurred (e.g., Harris, German & Mills, 1996). Furthermore, developmental evidence indicates that children understand the causal relations between events before they have the ability to engage in counterfactual thinking about such events, which suggests that such causal understanding cannot depend on prior counterfactual thinking (e.g., Robinson & Beck, 1998).

CAUSAL THOUGHTS DETERMINE
COUNTERFACTUAL THOUGHTS

In contrast to the idea that counterfactual thoughts determine causal judgements, we argue that causal thoughts determine counterfactual thoughts. A consideration of the cognitive processes that are involved in counterfactual thinking demonstrates that people must first understand the causes of an outcome before they can construct counterfactual alternatives. In order to generate a counterfactual scenario, people change some aspects of their mental representation of the factual situation, with the aim of undoing the factual outcome. In order to achieve the goal of undoing the factual outcome, they have to undo events that were necessary for the outcome to occur, and in order to know which events were necessary, they must understand the causal structure of the situation.

People's mental models of causal relations may represent strong causes, which are both necessary and sufficient to bring about an outcome, weak causes, which are sufficient but not necessary, and allowing conditions, which are necessary but not sufficient (see Table 20.2). We suggest that people use their observations of a situation and their prior knowledge to construct a mental model of the situation which represents these causal relations. They may then use this mental model to generate counterfactual scenarios representing how the outcome could have turned out differently. Because the strong cause of an outcome and the enabling conditions that allowed the cause to have its effect are both necessary for the outcome to occur, undoing either the strong cause or an enabling condition would be sufficient to prevent the outcome from occurring. In contrast, undoing a weak cause might or might not undo the outcome.

TABLE 20.2
The major causal relations
(adapted from Johnson-Laird & Byrne, 1991, p. 72)

1. *Strong causation(a necessary and sufficient for o)*		
	a caused o	
Actual	a	o
Counterfactual	not-a	not-o
2. *Weak causation(a sufficient but not necessary for o)*		
	a caused o	
Actual	a	o
Counterfactual	not-a	not-o
	not-a	o
3. *Allowing relation(a necessary but not sufficient for o)*		
	a caused o	
Actual	a	o
Counterfactual	not-a	not-o
	a	not-o

If people must understand the causes of an outcome *before* they can construct counterfactual alternatives to it, what do they learn from counterfactual thinking? One possibility is that people learn from counterfactual thoughts despite the fact that they depend heavily on prior knowledge because they are initially unaware of such knowledge (e.g., Kahneman, 1995). People's mental models of causal relations (see Table 20.2) may initially only represent explicitly the actual situation in which the cause occurred and the effect occurred. Counterfactual possibilities, for example that the cause did not occur and the effect did not occur, may initially be implicitly understood, but not explicitly represented (e.g., Goldvarg & Johnson-Laird, 1999). Although implicit mental models may be fleshed out to be represented explicitly if necessary, in most situations people may have little reason to make their knowledge of causal relations fully explicit. Our experimental findings suggest that following controllable and unwanted outcomes, people are motivated to flesh out their initial models of causal relations to generate explicit counterfactual alternatives, and we suggest that this is because these counterfactual thoughts suggest how such outcomes can be prevented in the future.

Counterfactual conditionals can also express knowledge of relations that does not depend on *causal* models, but that does depend on models of other types of information. For example, counterfactual conditionals can express inferential relations (e.g., «If yesterday had not been Monday, today would not be Tuesday»), or deontic relations (e.g., «If the boy had finished his homework, he would have been allowed out to play»). In such cases, the advantage of stating a counterfactual conditional rather than an indicative conditional may be that a counterfactual conditional provides a more economical way of expressing the nature of the relation between antecedent and consequent. The counterfactual conditional brings to mind not only the stated counterfactual situation (the boy finishes his homework and is allowed out to play), but also the presupposed factual situation (the boy doesn't finish his homework and is not allowed out to play). In contrast, an indicative conditional (e.g., If the boy finishes his homework, he is allowed out to play») may initially bring to mind only the stated situation (he finishes his homework and is allowed out to play). Thus, counterfactual conditionals may be more informative about the relations that hold between antecedent and consequent than indicative conditionals because they bring to mind two possible situations rather than just one (e.g., Johnson-Laird & Byrne, 1991).

CONCLUSIONS

Contrary to the view that people generate counterfactual alternatives in order to determine whether there is a causal relationship between an antecedent and a consequent, we argue that a counterfactual alternative expresses a *conditional* relationship between an antecedent and a consequent, but that this conditional relationship need not be a *causal* relationship. Our experimental evidence suggests that spontaneous counterfactual thoughts are more concerned with possible prevention relations than with actual causal relations. Mental models may be essential for people to understand the causes of events. Most outcomes are produced by a complicated set of interacting causes and enabling conditions. People may generate explanations for outcomes based on initial causal models which represent explicitly how the factual situation occurred. They may also determine how such outcomes could have been prevented by fleshing out their initial models to include previously implicit counterfactual alternatives.

The adaptive benefits of humans' sophisticated *causal* reasoning abilities have long been recognized in psychology. Without causal understanding, our lives would be incomprehensible and unpredictable, and goal-directed action would be impossible. The ability to engage in *counterfactual* reasoning may also be essential for flexible and intelligent behaviour. By considering that a past outcome could have turned out differently than it did, we may realize that there is more than one possible way in which future outcomes may turn out. In particular, imagining that changes to our own controllable actions could have prevented a negative outcome from occurring may increase the likelihood that we will actually make such changes on subsequent occasions. In this chapter, we have discussed in some detail the close relationship between such counterfactual thoughts and causal understanding. We have concluded that counterfactual thinking depends on causal reasoning rather than being an important determinant of it. However, counterfactual thinking may be an important determinant of other aspects of everyday reasoning, decision-making, problem-solving and planning. Some of our on-going research aims to investigate this possibility.

REFERENCES

BONINGER, D. S., GLEICHER, F., & STRATHMAN, A. (1994): «Counterfactual thinking: From what might have been to what may be». *Journal of Personality and Social Psychology, 67,* 297-307.

BRANSCOMBE, N. R., OWEN, S., GARSTKA, T. A., & COLEMAN, J. (1996): «Rape and accident counterfactuals: Who might have done otherwise and would it have changed the outcome?» *Journal of Applied Social Psychology, 26(12),* 1042-1067.

CHENG, P. W., & NOVICK, L. R. (1991): «Causes versus enabling conditions». *Cognition, 40,* 83-120.

DAVIS, C. G., LEHMAN, D. R., WORTMAN, C. B., SILVER, R. C., & THOMPSON, S. C. (1995): «The undoing of traumatic life events». *Personality & Social Psychology Bulletin, 21,* 109-124.

GOLDVARG, Y., & JOHNSON-LAIRD, P. (1999): «Naïve causality: a mental model theory of causal meaning and reasoning». *Manuscript submitted for publication.*

HARRIS, P. L., GERMAN, T., & MILLS, P. (1996): «Children's use of counterfactual thinking in causal reasoning». *Cognition, 61,* 233-259.

HART, H. L. A., & HONORE, A. M. (1985): *Causation and the law* (2nd ed.). Oxford: Clarendon Press.

JOHNSON-LAIRD, P. N., & BYRNE, R. M. J. (1991): *Deduction.* Hove, UK: Lawrence Erlbaum Associates.

KAHNEMAN, D. (1995): «Varieties of counterfactual thinking». In N. J. Roese & J. M. Olson (Eds.), *What might have been: The social psychology of counterfactual thinking* (pp. 375-396). Mahwah, NJ: Lawrence Erlbaum Associates.

KASIMATIS, M., & WELLS, G. L. (1995): «Individual differences in counterfactual thinking». In N. J. Roese & J. M. Olson (Eds.), *What might have been: The social psychology of counterfactual thinking* (pp. 81-101). Mahwah, NJ: Lawrence Erlbaum Associates.

LEWIS, D. (1973): «Causation». *Journal of Philosophy, 70,* 556-567.

LIPE, M. G. (1991): «Counterfactual reasoning as a framework for attribution theories». *Psychological Bulletin, 108,* 3-18.

McEleney, A., & Byrne, R. M. J. (1998): «Counterfactual thinking and explanation». *Manuscript submitted for publication*.

McMullen, M. N., Markman, K. D., & Gavanski, I. (1995): «Living in neither the best nor the worst of all possible worlds: Antecedents and consequences of upward and downward counterfactual thinking». In N. J. Roese & J. M. Olson (Eds.), *What might have been: The social psychology of counterfactual thinking* (pp. 133-167). Mahwah, NJ: Lawrence Erlbaum Associates.

Mandel, D. R., & Lehman, D. R. (1996): «Counterfactual thinking and ascriptions of cause and preventability». *Journal of Personality & Social Psychology, 71(3)*, 450-463.

Mill, J. S. (1967): *A system of logic raciocentive and inductive*. London: Longmans. (Original work published 1843)

N'Gbala, A., & Branscombe, N. R. (1995): «Mental simulation and causal attribution: When simulating an event does not affect fault assignment». *Journal of Experimental Social Psychology, 31*, 139-162.

Prosser, W. L. (1971): *Handbook of the law of torts*. St. Paul, MN: West.

Rescher, N. (1995): «Thought experimentation in Presocratic philosophy». In N. Rescher (Ed.), *Essays in the history of philosophy* (pp. 27-37). Adershot, UK: Avebury.

Robinson, E. J., & Beck, S. (1998): «What is difficult about counterfactual reasoning?» In P. Mitchell & K. J. Riggs (Eds.), *Children's Reasoning and the Mind*. Hove, UK: Psychology Press.

Roese, N. J. (1994): «The functional basis of counterfactual thinking». *Journal of Personality & Social Psychology, 66(5)*, 805-818.

Roese, N. J. (1997): «Counterfactual thinking». *Psychological Bulletin, 121*, 133-148.

Roese, N. J., & Olson, J. M. (1995): «Counterfactual thinking: A critical overview». In N. J. Roese and J. M. Olson (Eds.), *What might have been: The social psychology of counterfactual thinking* (pp. 1-59). Mahwah, NJ: Lawrence Erlbaum Associates.

— (1996): «Counterfactuals, causal attributions and thehindsight bias». *Journal of Experimental Social Psychology, 32*, 197-227.

— (1997): «Counterfactual thinking: The intersection of affect and function». In M. P. Zanna (Ed.), *Advances in experimental social psychology, Vol. 29* (pp. 1-59). San Diego, CA: Academic Press.

Sanna, L. J., & Turley, K. J. (1996): «Antecedents to spontaneous counterfactual thinking: Effects of expectancy violation and outcome valence». *Personality and Social Psychology Bulletin, 22(9)*, 909-919.

Tetlock, P. E., & Belkin, A. (Eds.) (1996): *Counterfactual thought experiments in world politics: Logical, methodological, and psychological perspectives*. Princeton, NJ: Princeton University Press.

Wells, G. L., & Gavanski, I. (1989): «Mental simulation of causality». *Journal of Personality & Social Psychology, 56*, 161-169.

APPENDICES

Appendix 1: Changes made to the scenario for valence, expectancy and controllability

You're moving house to start a new job in a different city. The night before you leave, you write down your thoughts about the move in your diary :...I've got mixed feelings about moving to a place where I know hardly anyone - my friends and social life are *so* important to me.

Expected: But I'm sure it will be easy to settle in to the new town - I've never had any trouble making new friends.

Unexpected: I'm sure it will be hard to settle in to the new town - I've always had trouble making new friends.

A lot happens in your first two weeks in the new town. During your first week at work, a staff dinner is held.

Uncontrollable: You have to go because your boss has asked all the staff to be there.

Controllable: You decide to go because you want to get to know your colleagues.

You enjoy the evening and meet a lot of people.

That weekend, your next-door neighbours invite you to a party. Most of the people who live on your road will be there.

Uncontrollable: However, that evening you're extremely ill with the flu, so you can't go.

Controllable: However, that evening you decide to go to the cinema instead.

The next week,

Uncontrollable: you happen to bump into an old friend who lives in the town and he insists on showing you around. He takes you out the following evening

Controllable: you decide to ring an old friend who lives in the town and ask him to show you around. You arrange to go out with him the following evening

and he introduces you to a lot of his friends.

A few days later, a colleague tells you there's a membership vacancy at her sports club. You think joining would be a good way to meet people,

Uncontrollable: but there's no way you can afford the membership fee.

Controllable: but then you decide to spend the money on a new stereo instead.

Six weeks after the move, things have turned out

Expected: exactly as

Unexpected: nothing like

you had expected.

Good outcome: You've made a lot of good friends in the new town, and you feel quite happy and at home. You are very pleased

Bad outcome: You haven't made any real friends in the new town and you feel very lonely and isolated. You are very upset

Expected: but not surprised.

Unexpected: and very surprised.

21

COUNTERFACTUAL CONDITIONALS: REASONING LATENCIES

Ana Cristina Quelhas
Ruth M. J. Byrne

Las personas a menudo piensan de manera contrafáctica sobre lo que pudo haber sido diferente, e.g.:

Si hubiera salido antes de casa, habría llegado a tiempo a la reunión.

El pensamiento contrafáctico puede cumplir una importante función ayudándonos a pensar causalmente sobre la forma de prevenir consecuencias y para aprender de nuestros errores. Nuestro propósito en este capítulo es examinar cómo comprenden y razonan las personas con condicionales contrafácticos. Presentamos resumidamente la teoría de los modelos mentales del razonamiento con condicionales contrafácticos. La teoría propone que las personas deben mantener en la mente dos modelos explícitos de una situación: la situación contrafáctica, y la situación fáctica, mientras que necesitan mantener en la mente un solo modelo explícito de la situación fáctica. La teoría ha sido corroborada experimentalmente, por ejemplo, mediante la demostración de que las personas realizan más ciertas inferencias (aquellas que requieren el acceso a la situación contrafáctica) a partir de condicionales contrafácticos que de condicionales fácticos. Presentamos resultados experimentales adicionales que corroboran las predicciones de la teoría. Nuestros estudios examinan la cantidad de tiempo que las personas emplean para realizar inferencias a partir de condiconales contrafácticos comparados con respecto a los condicionales fácticos. Los resultados muestran que las personas realizan más inferencias negativas, como «modus tollens», a patir de contrafácticos que a partir de fácticos, y también tardan más en hacerlo. Los resultados experimentales sugieren que pensar contrafácticamente es más difícil que pensar fácticamente.

COUNTERFACTUAL CONDITIONALS

People often think about what might have been, that is, they construct counterfactual scenarios about the way a situation might have turned out differently, for example:

If Mr. Jones had left work earlier he would not have had a car accident.

(e.g., Kahneman & Tversky, 1982). The counterfactual conditional refers to a past situation which was once possible but is so no longer (Johnson-Laird & Byrne, 1991). A counterfactual seems to convey not only information about the suggested and now counterfactual state of affairs, Mr. Jones left work earlier and avoided the car accident, but also it seems to convey information about the factual state of affairs: Mr. Jones did not leave work early and he did have a car accident.

Counterfactuals are frequently conveyed using the subjunctive mood although other cues to factuality, such as shared knowledge or perception can be used instead (e.g., Johnson-Laird, 1986). They have generated considerable interest in philosophy (e.g., Stalnaker, 1968; Lewis, 1973) because their semantics seems to defy a simple truth functional account: their antecedents are always false. Interest in the psychology of counterfactuals has been sparse (e.g., Fillenbaum, 1974), and in this chapter we wish to describe some of their psychological characteristics.

MENTAL MODELS OF CONDITIONALS

One view of the psychology of counterfactual conditionals is that they can be understood within the framework of a theory of conditionals in general. The model theory proposes that a conditional is understood by constructing an initial representation or set of models of it (see Johnson-Laird & Byrne, 1991). The models correspond to the way the world would be if the assertion were true. Consider the following factual conditional:

If there was a circle on the blackboard then there was a triangle.

According to the model theory, a reasoner who fully understands the meaning of the conditional appreciates that it is consistent with three separate situations that capture the way the world would be if the conditional were true. These three situations can be represented in the following sort of diagram:

    o   Δ
    not-o   not-Δ
    not-o   Δ

where «o» represents «there is a circle», «Δ» represents «there is a triangle», and «not-o» is a propositional-like tag to represent that there is not a circle (see Johnson-Laird Byrne, 1991; Johnson-Laird, Byrne, & Schaeken, 1992). Separate models are represented on separate lines, so for example, the first model corresponds to the situation where there is a circle and there is a triangle.

The theory proposes that reasoners construct an initial representation that is more economical than the fully fleshed-out set, because of the limitations of working memory, as illustrated in the following diagram:

      o   Δ
         ...

where the three dots represent a model with no explicit content. It may be «fleshed-out» to be explicit if necessary, and it rules out a conjunctive interpretation (see Johnson-Laird & Byrne, 1991). The idea is that reasoners represent explicitly the case mentioned in the conditional, and they keep track of the possibility that there may be alternatives to it. The theory predicts that inferences that require a single model can be made more readily than inferences that require multiple models, and its predictions have been corroborated in the primary domains of deduction (e.g., Johnson-Laird & Savary, 1995; Byrne, Espino, & Santamaria, 1999).

Consider now the counterfactual conditional:

If there had been a circle on the blackboard then there would have been a triangle.

The model theory proposes that reasoners construct an economical mental representation of the counterfactual based on the information hypothesised in the premises, about the circle and the triangle, but they also keep in mind the presupposed factual situation that there is no circle and no triangle:

factual: not-o   not-Δ
counterfactual: o   Δ
            ...

They keep track of the epistemic status of their models, making a 'mental note' about whether the models correspond to actual or counterfactual situations, and they tag the models accordingly. The theory proposes that the initial mental representation of a counterfactual conditional is more explicit than the initial mental representation of a factual conditional. The counterfactual conditional brings to mind two explicit models from the outset whereas the factual conditional brings to mind just a single explicit model at the outset.

INFERENCES FROM FACTUAL AND COUNTERFACTUAL CONDITIONALS

Inferences based on an initial representation are easier than inferences that require reasoners to flesh-out models (see Johnson-Laird, Byrne, & Schaeken, 1992). The initial representation of the factual conditional contains a model corresponding to the affirmative case mentioned in the conditional (i.e., the circle and the triangle). The initial representation of the counterfactual conditional contains a model corresponding to the affirmative case mentioned in the conditional (i.e., the circle and the triangle) and also a model corresponding to the negative case presupposed by the counterfactual (i.e., no circle and no triangle). As a result, inferences that depend on access to the negative case are made more readily from the counterfactual conditional than from the factual one, whereas inferences that depend on access to the affirmative case are made equally readily from the two sorts of conditional (Byrne & Tasso, in press).

Consider for example, one of the inferences that requires access to the negative case, the modus tollens inference:

If there is a circle on the blackboard then there is a triangle.
There is not a triangle on the blackboard.
Therefore, there is not a circle.

Reasoners construct an initial model of the factual conditional:

o   Δ

    ...

and a model of the second premise:

    not-Δ

The procedures which combine models may fail at this point, because the models appear to contain nothing in common, and in fact, the most common error that reasoners make is to conclude that nothing follows (see Johnson-Laird & Byrne, 1991). The inference can be made only when the models have been fleshed out, e.g., :

            o   Δ
        not-o   not-Δ
        not-o   Δ

and the model of the second premise rules out all but the second model:

        not-o   not-Δ

and the valid conclusion can be made:

Therefore, there is not a circle on the blackboard.

The modus tollens inference is difficult because reasoners must flesh out their models and keep several alternatives in mind to make the deduction for the factual conditional. But the inference can be made more readily from the counterfactual conditional:

If there had been a circle then there would have been a triangle.
There was not a triangle.
Therefore, there was not a circle.

Reasoners first construct an initial model of the counterfactual conditional:

factual: not-o   not-Δ
counterfactual: o   Δ
                            ...

and they can readily combine these models with the model for the second premise:

        not-Δ

and there is no need to flesh them out further. Reasoners can eliminate the hypothetical models, and retain the first model only:

factual: not-o   not-Δ

which supports the valid conclusion that there was not a circle. Table 21.1, from Byrne & Tasso (in press), summarises the process of inference from a factual and a counterfactual conditional for the modus tollens inference, and for other related inferences.

TABLE 21.1
Inferences from factual and counterfactual conditionals
(from Byrne & Tasso, in press)

FACTUAL	COUNTERFACTUAL
If L then C	*If L had been then C would have been*
1. Models of first premise:	*1. Models of first premise:*
L C	factual: not-L not-C
...	counterfactual: L C
	...
MODUS TOLLENS	
2. Model of second premise: not-C	*2. Model of second premise:* not-C
3. Combined models:	*3. Combined models:*
nill	not-L not-C
4. Conclusion: Nothing follows	*4. Conclusion:* not-L
5. Fleshed-out models:	
L C	
not-L not-C	
not-L C	
6. Combined models:	
not-L not-C	
7. Conclusion: not-L	
MODUS PONENS	
2. Model of second premise: L	*2. Model of second premise:* L
3. Combined models:	*3. Combined models:*
L C	L C
4. Conclusion: C	*4. Conclusion: C*

DENIAL OF THE ANTECEDENT

2. Model of second premise: not-L	*2. Model of second premise:* not-L
3. Combined models:	*3. Combined models:*

2. Model of second premise: not-L

3. Combined models:

    nil

4. Conclude: Nothing follows

5. Fleshed-out models:

        L   C

    not-L not-C

    not-L   C

6. Combined models:

    not-L not-C

    not-L   C

7. Conclude: C may or may not

2. Model of second premise: not-L

3. Combined models:

    not-L   not-C

4. Conclude: not-C

5. Fleshed-out models:

    factual: not-L not-C

    counterfactual: L   C

                  not-L   C

6. Combined models:

    not-L   not-C

    not-L   C

7. Conclude: C may or may not

AFFIRMATION OF THE CONSEQUENT

2. Model of second premise: C

3. Combined models:

      L   C

4. Conclude: L

5. Fleshed-out models:

        L   C

    not-L not-C

    not-L   C

6. Combined models:

      L C

    not-L C

7. Conclude: L may or may not

2. Model of second premise: C

3. Combined models:

      L   C

4. Conclude: L

5. Fleshed-out models:

    factual: not-L not-C

    counterfactual: L   C

                  not-L   C

6. Combined models:

      L   C

    not-L   C

7. Conclude: L may or may not

A recent series of experiments has shown that reasoners make up to twice as many modus tollens inferences from counterfactual conditionals compared to factual conditionals (Byrne & Tasso, in press). Reasoners were given a counterfactual problem such as:

> If there had been a circle then there would have been a triangle
> There was not a triangle.
> What, if anything, follows?

They concluded that there was not a circle, and the conclusion was up to twice as frequent from a counterfactual conditional compared to a factual one (e.g., 80% versus 40%, see Byrne & Tasso, in press). The initial representation of the counterfactual conditional is more explicit than the one of the factual conditional, and as a result, modus tollens can be made directly without any need to flesh-out the set of models. A similar process occurs for the other negative inference, the denial of the antecedent inference:

> If there was a circle then there was a triangle
> There was not a circle.
> Therefore there was not a triangle.

It too is made more often from the counterfactual than from a factual conditional (Byrne & Tasso, in press).

Consider now the modus ponens inference:

If there was a circle then there was a triangle
There was a circle.
Therefore there was a triangle.

Reasoners can make the inference by accessing the affirmative instance only, and the inference is made just as readily from the factual and the counterfactual conditionals (Byrne & Tasso, in press). Likewise, reasoners who make the affirmation of the consequent inference:

If there was a circle then there was a triangle
There was a triangle.
Therefore there was a circle.

do so by accessing the affirmative instance only (a reasoner who fleshes out the models to be consistent with the conditional interpretation will resist the inference). Hence the affirmation of the consequent inference can be made as readily from the factual and the counterfactual (Byrne & Tasso, in press).

The model theory predicts that inferences that require access to the negative instance (the modus tollens inference, and the denial of the antecedent inference) should be made more readily from the counterfactual conditional than from the factual. It also predicts that inferences that require access to the affirmative instance (the modus ponens inference, and the affirmation of the consequent inference) should be made as readily from the counterfactual and the factual conditionals. These predictions have been corroborated experimentally (Byrne & Tasso, in press).

LATENCIES TO MAKE INFERENCES

Our aim in a series of experiments we have recently carried out has been to examine the relative length of time it takes reasoners to make inferences from counterfactual and factual conditionals, and we will describe some of their results here (for further details, see Quelhas & Byrne, 1999). The model theory's proposals lead us to predict that there should be a difference between factual and counterfactual conditionals, given that reasoners construct an initial set of models for factual conditionals that contains a single explicit model and they construct an initial set of models for counterfactual conditionals that contains multiple explicit models. In addition, it seems plausible to predict that the direction of the difference should be that multiple models take longer to process than single models (see Johnson-Laird & Byrne, 1991). Consider the negative inference, modus tollens. We expect that the modus tollens inference should take longer from a counterfactual conditional: the multiple models must be kept in mind throughout the process of inference and so require more processing effort. The model theory commits us to the prediction that there will be difference between the factual and the counterfactual conditional, and we suggest that the direction of the difference should be that inferences will take longer from counterfactual conditionals than factual conditionals. We will describe some of the results of one of our experiments which resolves these questions.

Counterfactual Latencies

We gave 48 Portuguese university students 12 inferential problems each. For one group of 24 participants the 12 problems were based on a factual conditional as the first premise, and the second premise and conclusion corresponded to either modus ponens, modus tollens, denial of the antecedent or affirmation of the consequent. Each participant carried out three instances of each of the four inferences. The other group were given the same set of inferences based on a counterfactual conditional.

The factual inferences were based on three factual conditionals, as follows:

1. If there was a trapezium then there was a rectangle.
2. If there was a square then there was a star.
3. If there was a circle then there was a triangle.

and the counterfactual inferences were based on the corresponding counterfactual conditionals, as follows:

1. If there had been a trapezium then there would have been a rectangle.
2. If there had been a square then there would have been a star.
3. If there had been a circle then there would have been a triangle.

The participants carried out four inferences based on each of the three conditionals for their group, either factual or counterfactual. Participants were presented with the factual or counterfactual conditional, the appropriate minor premise for one of the four inferences, and a selection of three conclusions, e.g.:

If there had been a circle then there would have been a triangle
There was not a triangle
(1) There was a circle
(2) There was not a circle
(3) There may or may not have been a circle

The set of conclusions contained the three conclusions in the fixed order shown above.

The two premises and the set of conclusions were presented all together at the same time on a computer screen using the SUPERLAB program, and the participants were instructed to read each sentence carefully and to press the key corresponding to the number of the conclusion they wished to select. In the instructions to the task they were first given an example (a disjunctive premise) to illustrate the conclusion selection task, and for each problem they were asked to «Imagine a game with geometric shapes and the following rule...», the minor premise was preceded by the information, «We know that, in fact...», and the set of three conclusions were preceded by the information,

«We can then conclude...». We gave the participants three series of the four inferences to ensure that they obtained practise with the procedure and format; we analysed the results only for the final series of four inferences, which we describe in the next section (for further details see Quelhas & Byrne, 1999).

Inference Frequencies

Our primary interest is in the length of time it takes for reasoners to make each of the inferences, that is, to select the answer which endorses the conclusion. First we will describe the frequency of such selections and then the latency to make them.

Participants made more of the modus tollens inference from the counterfactual conditional than the factual conditional (71% versus 50%), and somewhat more of the denial of the antecedent inference from the counterfactual conditional than the factual conditional (79% versus 67%), as Table 21.2 shows.

TABLE 21.2
Percentages of endorsements of conclusions to four inferences for factual and counterfactual conditionals

	MT	DA	MP	AC
Factual	50	67	79	67
Counterfactual	71	79	75	79

The first difference is reliable although the second is not ($p < 0.07$ and $p < 0.16$ respectively, for details of these chi square analyses see Quelhas & Byrne, 1999). These results are consistent with previous studies which have shown that the negative inferences tend to be made more readily from counterfactuals than factuals (Byrne & Tasso, in press).

Participants made the same amount of the modus ponens inference (75% versus 79%) from the factual and counterfactual and somewhat more of the affirmation of the consequent inference (79% versus 67%), and neither difference was reliable. There is a surprisingly low percentage of participants endorsing the modus ponens inference for the factual conditional (79%), and their difficulty in making this simple valid inference may reflect difficulties in coming to grips with the computer based presentation (for details see Quelhas & Byrne, 1999).

Inferences Latencies

Table 21.3 presents the length of time it took participants to carry out the inferential task on their third trial. The latencies are log transformed and a constant (0.640 msec) is taken from each counterfactual latency to reflect the longer reading times for these sentences. Participants took 10,129 msecs longer to understand the premises and endorse the conclusion for the modus tollens inference from the counterfactual than the factual (25,001 msec versus 14,872 msec) as Table 21.3 shows. They took 6,462 msecs longer to the carry out the task for the denial of the antecedent inference from the counterfactual than the factual (20,025 msec versus 13,563 msec). Once again, the difference is reliable in the case of the modus tollens inference but not the denial of the antecedent inference ($p < 0.02$ and $p < 0.13$ respectively, for details of these ANOVA results, see Quelhas & Byrne, 1999).

Participants also took longer to make the inferences from the counterfactual than the factual conditional for the modus ponens and affirmation of the consequent inferences but not reliably so. They took 881 msecs longer to carry out the task for the modus ponens inference from the counterfactual than the factual (13,356 msec versus 12,475 msec). Likewise, they took 6,518 ms. longer for the affirmation of the consequent inference from the counterfactual than the factual (20,831 msec versus 14,313 msecs, for further details see Quelhas & Byrne, 1999).

TABLE 21.3
Latencies (in msec) to understand the first and second premise and endorse the conclusion for factual and counterfactual conditionals

	MT	DA	MP	AC
Factual	14872	13563	12475	14313
Counterfactual	25001	20025	13356	20831
Difference	*−10129*	*−6462*	*−881*	*−6518*

Key: the endorsed conclusion given if p then q, for MP was q, for AC was p, for MT was not p and for DA was not q.

The results lend support to the model theory's prediction that there is a difference in the length of time to make an inference from a factual and a counterfactual conditional. The results show that reasoners take longer to make all inferences from counterfactual conditionals than factual conditionals, and this difference is reliable in the case of the modus tollens inference. The modus tollens inference is made more often from the counterfactual conditional than the factual, but reasoners also take longer to do so.

CONCLUSIONS

People think counterfactually about what might have been frequently in their everyday lives (e.g., Byrne, Segura, Culhane, Tasso, & Berrocal, in press). Their counterfactual thoughts are often encapsulated in counterfactual conditionals, such as:

If I had left home earlier I would have arrived at the meeting on time.

Counterfactual thoughts may serve important functions in helping us to think causally about ways to prevent outcomes and to learn from our mistakes (e.g., Kahneman & Miller, 1986). Our studies indicate that thinking counterfactually is more difficult than thinking factually. We suggest that people must keep in mind two explicit models of a counterfactual situation: the counterfactual situation and the factual situation, whereas they need keep in mind just a single explicit model of a factual situation. People take longer to understand counterfactual conditionals than factual ones, as a result. They make more of the negative inferences from counterfactual conditionals than factual conditionals, in general, because of the ready access to the negative case, but they take longer to do so, because of the overheads associated with keeping two explicit models in mind throughout the inferential process.

Counterfactual thinking may play a central role in many aspects of cognition, including creative thinking and problem solving, as well as in the search for counterexamples in deduction and so its future investigation is a promising avenue.

ACKNOWLEDGEMENT

We are grateful to Phil Johnson-Laird, Paolo Legrenzi, Teresa Garcia-Marques, Juan A. García-Madruga, Walter Schaeken, Nuria Carriedo, and Sergio Moreno for their helpful comments on the results.

REFERENCES

BYRNE, R. M. J., & TASSO, A. (in press): «Reasoning from factual, hypothetical and counterfactual conditionals». *Memory & Cognition*.

BYRNE, R. M. J., ESPINO, O., & SANTAMARIA, C. (1999): «Counterexamples and the suppression of inferences». *Journal of Memory & Language*.

BYRNE, R. M. J., SEGURA, S., CULHANE, R., TASSO, A., & BERROCAL, P. (in press): «Counterfactual thinking and the temporality effect». *Memory & Cognition*.

FILLENBAUM, S. (1974): «Information amplified: memory for counterfactual conditionals». *Journal of Experimental Psychology*, 102, 44-49.

JOHNSON-LAIRD, P. N. (1986): «Conditionals and mental models». In Traugott, E.C., ter Meulen, A., Reilly, J.S., and Ferguson, C. (1986). *On Conditionals*. Cambridge: Cambridge University Press.

JOHNSON-LAIRD, P. N., & BYRNE, R. M. J. (1991): *Deduction*. Hove and Hillsdale: Erlbaum.

JOHNSON-LAIRD, P. N., BYRNE, R. M. J., and SCHAEKEN, W. (1992): «Propositional reasoning by model». *Psychological Review*, 99, 418-439.

JOHNSON-LAIRD, P. N., & SAVARY, F. (1995): «Illusory Inferences». *Proceedings of the 17th Annual Cognitive Science Society. Hillsdale: Erlbaum*.

KAHNEMAN, D., & TVERSKY, A. (1982): «The simulation heuristic». In D. Kahneman, P. Slovic, and A. Tversky (Eds.), *Judgement under uncertainty: heuristics and biases*. (pp. 201-208). New York: Cambridge University Press.

LEWIS, D. (1973): *Counterfactuals*. Oxford, Blackwell.

QUELHAS, A. C., & BYRNE, R. M. J. (1999): *Latencies and counterfactual conditionals*. Manuscript in preparation.

STALNAKER, R. C. (1968): «A theory of conditionals». In N. Rescher (Ed.), *Studies in logical theory*. Oxford: Basil Blackwell.

22

TEMPORAL AND CAUSAL ORDER EFFECTS IN COUNTERFACTUAL THINKING

Susana Segura
Pablo Fernandez-Berrocal
Ruth M. J. Byrne

El razonamiento contrafáctico consiste en la comparación de una situación dada con otra situación alternativa imaginaria. El razonamiento sobre lo que podría haber sido toma parte en otros procesos cognitivos como el razonamiento deductivo o los juicios de causalidad. La principal consecuencia psicológica de estas cogniciones es la de ayudar a aprender, pues conlleva la simulación de cómo un resultado podría haber sido mejor.

Desde que se determinaron los primeros estudios sobre la naturaleza del razonamiento contrafáctico, los autores se han centrado en cómo los antecedentes o cómo las consecuencias de los resultados originan la producción de este tipo de razonamiento. El presente trabajo está centrado en algunas de las características de los antecedentes. En la exploración de las características de estos factores se ha mostrado que se simulan alternativas en aquellos casos en los que se razona sobre antecedentes excepcionales, sobresalientes, controlables y dinámicos. Finalmente, el razonamiento sobre alternativas se ve afectado por aspectos causales y temporales de los antecedentes. Cuando se razona sobre cómo un resultado podría haber sido diferente se tiende a deshacer mentalmente el último suceso de una serie de acontecimientos independientes. Sin embargo, se deshace mentalmente el primer suceso de una serie de acontecimientos que están relacionados de una manera causal.

Se presenta una investigación que examina los efectos causales y temporales antes mencionados. El efecto de orden temporal ha sido estudiado con series de dos acontecimientos independientes, mientras que el efecto de orden causal se ha estudiado con series causales de cuatro acontecimientos. Se les ofreció a los participantes historias en las que se describían series que estaban compuestas por dos o cuatro sucesos que podían provocar un resultado. Los sucesos estaban relacionados causalmente o temporalmente. Se encontró que las personas tendían a deshacer mentalmente el primer suceso en una serie causal, independientemente de si estaba compuesta por dos o por cuatro sucesos. Sin embargo, tendían a deshacer el primer suceso en una serie temporal que estaba compuesta por dos sucesos y a deshacer mentalmente tanto el primero como el último cuando la serie temporal estaba compuesta por cuatro sucesos. Los resultados se discuten en términos de los modelos mentales que se deben tener en cuenta cuando se contemplan los distintos eventos (Johnson-Laird & Byrne, 1991).

Counterfactual thinking is the capacity to imagine alternatives to reality and it requires a mental simulation of alternative events (e.g., Kahneman & Tversky, 1982; Kahneman & Miller, 1986). «What might have been» thoughts play a role in many cognitive processes such as causal judgments (e.g., Roese & Olson, 1997), deductive reasoning (e.g., Johnson-Laird & Byrne, 1991) and creativity (e.g., Hofstadter, 1985), as well as emotional processes such as feelings of regret (e.g., Gilovich & Medvec, 1994), and guilt (e.g., Miller & Gunasegaram, 1990). Counterfactual thinking serves important functions such as helping people to learn, e.g., to learn from mistakes when they imagine how things might have been better, and helping people to feel better, e.g., when they imagine how things could have been worse (e.g., Roese, 1994; Roese & Olson, 1995).

When people think counterfactually, they tend to focus on particular sorts of events to mentally undo in their construction of alternatives. For example, they tend to focus on actions rather than failures to act (Kahneman & Tversky, 1982; Gilovich & Medvec, 1994; Byrne & McEleney, 1997), exceptions rather than routines (Kahneman & Miller, 1986), and controllable rather than uncontrollable events (Girotto, Legrenzi & Rizzo, 1991). The focus of their counterfactual thoughts also tends to be influenced by the order in which the information is presented to them (Wells, Taylor & Turtle, 1987; Miller & Gunasegaram, 1990). Our aim in this chapter is to examine more closely the effect on counterfactual thinking of the order in which information is presented.

CAUSAL AND TEMPORAL ORDER EFFECTS

The order in which information is presented influences counterfactual thinking in several different ways. People tend to undo the first event in a *causal* sequence of events (Wells, Taylor & Turtle, 1987). Wells, Taylor, & Turtle (1987) constructed a scenario in which a character identified as William attempted to get to a shop across town to take advantage of a sale on a limited number of stereo systems. His progress was impeded by four minor misfortunes: a speeding ticket, a flat tire, a traffic jam, and a group of senior citizens crossing the street. William arrived at the shop 35 minutes after the sale started only to find that the last stereo system had been sold just a few minutes before. The scenario outlined a causal chain in which each event causally affected subsequent events and yet the removal of each event was sufficient to undo the outcome. When people read the scenario, regardless of which event was presented in which order, they tended to focus on the first event. Most people tended to consider that William could have got the stereo if only the first event, e.g., getting the speeding ticket, had not caused him to be delayed.

Counterfactual thinking about sequences of independent events is also influenced by the order in which the information is presented, but in a different way from sequences of causally related events. People tend to undo the last event when the events are presented in an independent *temporal* sequence (Miller & Gunasegaram, 1990). Consider the following example:

> Imagine two individuals (Jones and Cooper) who are offered the following very attractive proposition. Each individual is asked to toss a coin. If the two coins come up the same (both heads or both tails) each individual wins £1,000. However, if the two coins do not come up the same, neither individual wins anything. Jones goes first and tosses a head; Cooper goes next and tosses a tail. Thus, the outcome is that neither individual wins anything.

Most people judge that the outcome could most readily have been different if Cooper had tossed a head, rather than if Jones had tossed a tail. They also tend to judge that Cooper would experience more guilt, and would be blamed more by Jones (e.g., Miller & Gunasegaram, 1990; Byrne, Segura, Culhane, Tasso, & Berrocal, in press).

Why do people focus on the first event when they think counterfactually about causal sequences and on the last event when they think counterfactually about temporal sequences? One possibility is that the number of events in the sequence plays a role in the two conflicting findings. The causal order effect has been observed primarily for sequences of four events (e.g., Wells, Taylor, & Turtle, 1987). The temporal order effect has been demonstrated primarily for sequences of two events (e.g., Miller & Gunasegaram, 1990; Byrne, Segura, Culhane, Tasso, & Berrocal, in press; Spellman, 1997), although it also occurs in naturalistic situations, e.g., football leagues of ten games (Sherman & McConnell, 1996). Our aim was to examine causal and temporal order effects for scenarios with different numbers of events.

A COMPARISON OF CAUSAL AND TEMPORAL SEQUENCES

People tend to mentally undo the first event in a causal sequence of events and this *causal order effect* has been demonstrated primarily for sequences of four events (Wells, Taylor, & Turtle, 1987). Our first aim was to establish whether a causal order effect would occur for causal sequences of less than four events, such as two events, and so we compared a causal four event sequence with a two event sequence.

People tend to mentally undo the most recent event in an independent sequence of events and this *temporal order effect* has been demonstrated primarily for sequences of two events (Miller & Gunesageram, 1990; Spellman, 1997; Byrne, Segura, Culhane, Tasso, & Berrocal, in press). Our second aim was to establish whether a temporal order effect would occur for sequences of more than two events, and so we compared a temporal two event sequence with a four event sequence.

We constructed a scenario about a secretary, Patricia, who must complete a number of tasks. We devised four versions of the scenario, two causal sequences, one with two events and the other with four events, and two temporal sequences, one with two events and the other with four events. The scenario for the causal four event condition was as follows:

> Patricia is a secretary at the department of law and she wants to visit her favourite shop, which is in the last day of a sale. However, she must finish some tasks at work before she leaves. First she sent a letter, but then the vice dean saw her and asked her to send a fax. When she finished this, she ran into the head of the department who asked her to make a photocopy. Finally, when she finished, she had to make a phone call because the dean came to tell her to do so.

The scenario for the temporal four event condition was similar but that the causes for the events were omitted, as follows:

> Patricia is a secretary at the department of law and she wants to visit her favourite shop, which is in the last day of a sale. However, she must finish some tasks at work before she leaves. First she sent a letter. After that, she sent a fax. Later, she made a photocopy. Finally, she made a phone call.

The order of presentation of the four events was counterbalanced. The scenarios for the causal and temporal two event condition contained the first two events only. In all versions of the story, participants were asked to imagine a situation in which things had been different. The participants were 288 students from the Department of Psychology at the University of Malaga, Spain, who took part in the experiment voluntarily. They had not participated in such a study previously and the task was carried out during their regular class time. They were assigned at random to one of four conditions: the causal two event condition, causal four event condition, temporal two event condition, or temporal four event condition (n = 72 in each condition).

The results showed a causal order effect for the two event sequence and for the four event sequence. For the causal two event sequence, participants' counterfactual thoughts focused on the first event (56%) more than the last (second) event (37%, n = 72, z = 1.705, p = 0.02), as Table 22.1 shows. Likewise, for the causal-four event sequence, participants' counterfactual thoughts focused on the first event (54%) more than the last (fourth) event (19%, n = 72, z = 3.810, p < 0.01). They focused more on the first event than the second event (5%, n = 72, z = 7.029, p < 0.01) or the third event (14%, n = 72, z = 4.707 p < 0.01).

Unexpectedly, we did not observe a temporal order effect for either of the temporal sequences. For the temporal two event sequence, the reverse of the temporal order effect was observed: participants' counterfactual thoughts focused on the first event (60%) more than the last (second) event (27%, n = 72, z = –3.210, p < 0.01), as Table 22.1 shows. For the temporal four event sequence, no order effect was observed: participants' counterfactual thoughts focused equally on the first event (32%) and the last (fourth) event (30%, n = 72, z = –0.216, p < 0.21). They focused more on the first event than the second event (18%, n = 72, z = 1.492, p < 0.068) or the third event (14%, n = 72, z = 2.109, p < 0.02).

TABLE 22.1
The percentages of counterfactual thoughts about each of the events for the causal and temporal scenarios for two and four event sequences

	Two events	Four events
Causal		
First event	56	54
Second event	37	5
Third event	—	14
Fourth event	—	19
n	72	72
Temporal		
First event	60	32
Second event	27	18
Third event	—	14
Fourth event	—	30
n	72	72

The causal order effect was observed for the two event sequence and for the four event sequence. The temporal order effect was not observed for either sequence: the reverse of the temporal order effect was observed for the two event sequence and no effect was observed for the four event sequence.

The results indicate clearly that the causal order effect is not contingent on the number of events in the sequence: it is observed for both two event and four event sequences. The results for the temporal order effect are less clear cut. One possible explanation for the results for the temporal sequences is that the scenarios we devised differ from those in which the causal and temporal order effects have been observed previously. In our scenarios, we did not explicitly include a negative outcome, such as failing to get to the sale on time. In asking our participants to consider how things might have been different, their counterfactual thoughts were not constrained by undoing a particular consequent and subsequently undoing the antecedent events which led to that outcome. This difference in the materials may have contributed to the failure to observe the standard temporal order effect.

MENTAL MODELS OF TEMPORAL AND CAUSAL SEQUENCES

We have suggested that people construct counterfactual alternatives by revising their mental models of the factual situation (Byrne *et al*, in press). The model theory of conditional reasoning extends readily to capture the meaning of counterfactual conditionals (Johnson-Laird & Byrne, 1991) and its predictions for counterfactuals have been experimentally corroborated (Byrne & Tasso, in press). We have suggested that the theory can extend equally readily to counterfactual thinking (e.g., Byrne, 1997), and we have sketched an outline of a model theory of the temporal order effect (Byrne *et al*, in press).

Mental Models and Temporal Order

We have proposed that people construct the following sort of representation of the coin-toss scenario:

    jones - heads   cooper - tails

(Byrne et al, in press). When they must think of ways in which the outcome could have been different they may flesh out the counterfactual possibilities to be fully explicit:

factual:	jones - heads	cooper - tails	*lose*
counterfactual:	jones - heads	cooper - heads	*win*
	jones - tails	cooper - tails	*win*
	jones - tails	cooper - heads	*lose*

The temporal order effect indicates that people flesh-out their counterfactual models for just one of the options:

factual:	jones - heads	cooper - tails	*lose*
counterfactual:	jones - heads	cooper - heads	*win*

...

Early events are presupposed more than later events (Miller & Gunasegaram, 1990), and we suggest that the presupposition of earlier events arises from the sorts of cognitive processes that construct and revise mental models (Byrne *et al*, in press). The earlier event is presupposed because it *initializes* the model, that is, it provides the cornerstone or anchor for the model's foundation. The game is now 'about' heads once the first player has tossed heads and this interpretation influences the interpretation of the subsequent play. The first event is not as readily available for change in the counterfactual models because of its crucial role in integrating subsequent information into the model (Byrne *et al*, in press).

Mental Models and Causal Order

The presupposition of the first event can be cancelled, for example, by providing an available counterfactual alternative to it (see Byrne *et al*, in press). We gave people a technical hitch scenario of the following sort:

> Imagine two individuals (Jones and Brady) who take part in a television game show, on which they are offered the following very attractive proposition. Each individual is given a shuffled deck of cards, and each one picks a card from their own deck. If the two cards they pick are of the same color (i.e. both from black suits or both from red suits) each individual wins £1,000. However, if the two cards are not the same color, neither individual wins anything.
>
> Jones goes first and picks a black card from his deck. At this point, the game-show host has to stop the game because of a technical difficulty. After a few minutes, the technical problem is solved and the game can be restarted. Jones goes first again, and this time the card that he draws is a red card. Brady goes next and the card that he draws is a black card. Thus, the outcome is that neither individual wins anything.

The pre-hitch alternative (Jones picks black) provides a readily available counterfactual alternative to the first (post-hitch) player's choice (Jones picks red), and so the first player's choice is not presupposed in the usual way. The temporal order effect is eliminated in this technical hitch scenario. We have suggested that the causal order effect can be understood in a similar way (Byrne *et al*, in press). A causal relation between events in the sequence eliminates the temporal order effect. Causal relations may be understood by explicitly keeping in mind not only the factual situation in which the cause occurred and the outcome did too, but also the counterfactual situation in which the cause did not occur (e.g., Johnson-Laird & Byrne, 1991, p. 71-72). Causes may be mentally represented with a readily available counterfactual alternative, and this undermines the immutability of the otherwise presupposed first event in a sequence.

CONCLUSIONS

Counterfactual thinking about what might have been is pervasive in everyday thinking. When people construct counterfactual alternatives they tend to focus on regular aspects of factual reality, such as space, time, cause, and intentionality. The counterfactual alternatives that people construct are also influenced by the order in which the factual information is presented to them. In this chapter we have examined two serial position effects in counterfactual thinking: the causal order effect and the temporal order effect. The causal order effect, the tendency to undo the first event in a causal sequence, has hitherto been demonstrated only for sequences of four events, whereas the temporal order effect, the tendency to undo the most recent event in an independent sequence, has been demonstrated primarily for sequences of two events. We compared two events and four events for causal sequences and temporal sequences. Our results provide the first demonstration that the causal order effect is observed in two event as well as in four event sequences. We found no temporal order effect for either the two event or four event sequences, perhaps we suggest, because of an anomaly in our materials. The mental model theory can provide a framework within which to understand these two order effects in counterfactual thinking. The temporal order effect may arise because the first event provides the context in a model against which subsequent events are interpreted. This presuppositional role of the first event can be cancelled by the provision of an explicit counterfactual alternative to the first event. The causal order effect may arise because the representation of causes ensures that an explicit counterfactual alternative is readily available to the first event. The number of events in a sequence of events has been an unexplored factor in counterfactual thinking, and the effects of mental load in general on counterfactual thinking may be a promising area of research (Kahneman, 1995).

ACKNOWLEDGEMENTS

We thank Phil Johnson-Laird, Rachel McCloy, Ronan Culhane, and Alessandra Tasso for helpful discussions of the temporal order effect.

REFERENCES

BYRNE, R. M. J. (1997): «Cognitive processes in counterfactual thinking about what might have been». In D. L. Medin (Ed.), *The Psychology of Learning and Motivation, Advances in Research and Theory* (Vol 37, pp. 105-154). San Diego, CA: Academic Press.

BYRNE, R. M. J., & MCELENEY, A. (1997): «Cognitive processes in regret for actions and inactions». In M. Shafto & P. Langley (Eds.), *Proceedings of the Nineteenth Annual Conference of the Cognitive Science Society* (pp. 73-78). Mahwah, NJ: Lawrence Erlbaum Associates.

BYRNE, R. M. J., ESPINO, O., & SANTAMARIA, C. (in press): «Counterexamples and the suppression of inferences». *Journal of Memory and Language.*

BYRNE, R. M. J., & HANDLEY, S. J. (1997): «Reasoning strategies for suppositional deductions». *Cognition.* 62, 1-49.

BYRNE, R. M. J., SEGURA, S., CULHANE, R., TASSO, A., & BERROCAL, P. (in press): «The temporality effect in counterfactual thinking about what might have been». *Memory & Cognition.*

BYRNE, R. M. J., & TASSO, A. (in press): «Deductions from factual, possible and counterfactual conditionals». *Memory & Cognition.*

GILOVICH, T., & MEDVEC, V. H. (1994): «The temporal pattern to the experience of regret». *Journal of Personality and Social Psychology, 67,* 357-365.

GIROTTO, V., LEGRENZI, P., & RIZZO, A. (1991): «Event controllability in counterfactual thinking». *Acta Psychologica*, 78, 111-133.

HOFSTADTER, D. R. (1985): *Metamagical Themas: Questing for the Essence of Mind and Pattern.* London: Penguin.

JOHNSON-LAIRD, P. N., & BYRNE, R. M. J. (1991): *Deduction.* Hove, England: Lawrence Erlbaum Associates.

KAHNEMAN, D. (1995): «Varieties of counterfactual thinking». In Roese, N.J. & Olson, J.M. (1995). *What Might Have Been: The Social Psychology of Counterfactual Thinking.* Mahwah, New Jersey: Erlbaum. p. 375-396.

KAHNEMAN, D., & TVERSKY, A. (1982): «The simulation heuristic». In D. Kahneman, P. Slovic & A. Tversky, (Eds.), *Judgment under uncertainty: Heuristics and biases* (pp. 201-208). New York: Cambridge University Press.

KAHNEMAN, D., & MILLER, D. T. (1986): «Norm Theory: Comparing reality to its alternatives». *Psychological Review, 93,* 136-153.

MILLER, D. T., & GUNASEGARAM, S. (1990): «Temporal order and the perceived mutability of events: implications for blame assignment». *Journal of Personality and Social Psychology, 59,* 1111-1118.

ROESE, N. J. (1994): «The functional basis of counterfatual thinking». *Journal of Personality and Social Psychology, 66,* 805-818.

ROESE, N. J., & OLSON, J. M. (1995): «Functions of counterfactual thinking». In Roese, N. J. & Olson, J. M (Eds.), *What might have been* (pp. 169-197). Hillsdale, NJ: Lawrence Erlbaum Associates.

— (1997): «Counterfactual thinking: The intersection of affect and function». In M. P. Zanna (Ed.), *Advances in experimental social psychology* (Vol. 29, pp. 1-59.). San Diego, CA: Academic Press.

SEGURA, S., FERNANDEZ-BERROCAL, P., & BYRNE, R. M. J. (1998): «Razonamiento contrafactual: la posición serial y el número de antecedentes en los pensamientos sobre lo que podría haber sido». *I jornadas de psicología del pensamiento.* Santiago de compostela: Universidad de Santiago de Compostela.

SHERMAN, S. J., & McCONNELL, A. R. (1996): «The role of counterfactual thinking in reasoning». *Applied Cognitive Psychology, 10,* 113-124.

SPELLMAN, B. A. (1997): «Crediting causality». *Journal of Experimental Psychology, 126, 4,* 323-348.

WELLS, G. L., TAYLOR, B. R., & TURTLE, J. W. (1987): «The undoing of scenarios». *Journal of Personality and Social Psychology, 53,* 421-430.

AUTHOR INDEX

SUBJECT INDEX